Italian Magic:
Secret Lives of Women

Karyn Crisis

Book Cover Photo: Davide Tiso
Interior Photos: Davide Tiso
Copyright: Golden Bough Books, 2020.

ISBN: 978-0-578-77334-6

Thank you:

Davide Tiso, Antonietta Ghetta, Fabio Toti, Martina Bernasconi, Emanuela Tocci, Peppe Tavarone, Mario Polia, Mauro Spadoni, Irene Masci, Roberto Toderico, Gianfranco Mele, Daniela Scaglioso, Gabriella Lorusso, Mino Minarelli, Carlo Napolitano, Daniela of La Tana delle Volpi bnb in Triora, Ottorino, Christian Dellavedova, Claudia Civardi, Irene Barbina, Gabriele Zorzi, Aplini sisters, Piazza Roma Rooms in Benevento, Zio Bacco, Massimiliano Palmesano, Dario Palmesano, Alfred Parolino, Adele Hugo, Carlo Tinto, Doriana Fraschiroli, Alpini sisters, Silvia Pigna, Caroline Vitelli, Rosanna Scocca, Domenico Garofano, Filomena Foschini, Alecia Caine, Vittoria Montalbano, & Doriana Fraschiroli.

Italian Magic:
Secret Lives of Women

BIRTH
La Nascita
"Fa la luna; partorisce," si suava dire.
"Do as the Moon does: give birth",
they used to say. 1

DIVINITY ON EARTH

Every single person who has ever lived on the planet earth has literally entered into their lives through the bodies of women, completely dependent on the inner biological world of their mothers, inside of whom they developed into themselves for 3+3+3=9 months.

We have all lived inside the body of a woman, we've passed through the doorway of her birth canal or through her belly and onto this earthly plane, and before that, religions like to say that we were all spirits waiting to be born. Some people even go as far as to say that before we are born we are "a twinkle in god's eye", but of this there is no evidence: there is only evidence that this miraculous manifestation takes place through the spectacular biology of women's bodies. When people talk of using magic to create a "threshold between worlds" and "lifting the veil", they are referring to a psychic practice of interacting with the spirit/energy world while still embodied on earth's physical world. In other words, passing in and out of this threshold, conceptually, without having to die.

This actual threshold between life and death, this doorway between the world of spirits and the physical world of matter, exists in the bodies of women, and their magic is their womb and its systems (placenta, umbilical cord, and fluids) and the feminine energy of reception. Together these feminine elements ARE the literal doorway, the magical threshold between energy and physical matter made manifest. This is DIVINITY on earth.

While the christian church has claimed that a male god is the single parent of everyone and is responsible for creating all our lives, we have no evidence of this occurring whatsoever: a male entity whom no one has ever seen, who is not embodied in physical form, giving birth to physically formed people after having created all of them without having a womb. This concept of a masculine divine figurehead of childbirth makes no sense; there is no parallel example for this occurring in nature where this concept would make symbolic sense: it is a synthetically created concept.

Likewise pagan myths claim male gods birth their children through their foreheads and peni or from stones they touch, birthing them to earth often armed with a complete set of war weapons, though this is impossible. For women however, BIRTH is not merely a concept nor spiritual myth as it is with male gods in every religion and in male-centric spiritual practices...it is a life force fact.

BIRTH La Nascita

Many pagan practices, which are based on the original feminine cosmogony but usurped into a masculine expressed cosmogony, claim sperm is more important that the womb because it is the seed. However, sperm, like plant seeds, are dime-a-dozen and, without some nurturing fluid such as water or soil or amniotic and vaginal fluid, nothing can be created with the seeds. These regenerative fluids are all associated with the female body and life force, and with good cause, considering menstrual blood is scientifically proven to have regenerative stem cells, so again, the spiritual myths of divine feminine regeneration power matches the nature. And, nothing from the male body can nurture nor feed the body of the child, after birth, whereas the mother's body can produce complete food as nourishment for her babies.

The nurturing element in the earliest spiritual expression of the universe has therefore been depicted as divinely feminine, and its counterpart is honored as the feminine womb and fertility of human women, as female animals, and as nature. Horned animals were originally symbols of the divine feminine and not the gods (due to their horned skulls being the same shape as the uterus and fallopian tubes) just as the sun was also a symbol of the goddess (and not the god): all was agreed to come from the divine feminine, which was not a person but the ever-flowing life force.

MOTHERHOOD

It is women's bodies that have literally been the doorway of life and death as our entire human history has evidenced, therefore...

Motherhood is the ultimate expression of divinity on earth. Since life itself has been the miracle honored in spiritual practices, the spiritual symbol of the universe (with its life and death power, its phases of life and the eternal flow of energy) was originally celebrated as a divinely feminine power expressing itself in the above, below, and in-between. Motherhood was the original spiritual symbol of the universe, a dual motherhood really: motherhood of the universe and motherhood embodied on earth. The reason for this is natural: the miracle of life was observed taking place through the bodies of women. Motherhood is the lineage that Christianity has remodeled in the masculine father-son form. And yet, the masculine concept of motherhood is synthetic; it doesn't exist in nature.

Therefore, motherhood is also the ultimate threat to all big religions and paganisms which espouse male gods and the generators of life...because in order to convince people to turn away from the Great Mother and instead believe in a male god as The Great Father of all, they would have to be convinced to deny nature and therefore deny the sacred feminine; to deny the miracles of the womb, the umbilical cord, the placenta; the breast milk and vaginal fluid and menstrual blood. In fact, the only way to convince people to deny nature is to make people believe that nature is in some way evil; something to be feared and even hated. And, since from the earliest times women were viewed as being deeply connected to nature's regenerative power and abundance, people would also have be to be convinced to fear women and their life force power, so as to turn away and embrace a synthetic mother figure remodeled into a man.

Italian Magic: Secret Lives of Women

Conceptually it could be said that the tradition of mothers "passing down" something to their children, giving them an inheritance such as magic traditions or heirlooms, has a biological truth. Female embryos develop their ovaries in their 7th week in utero, after which immature egg cells develop and then begin their first round of cell division at around 12-14 weeks, which is a preparation stage. The developing eggs remain suspended in this state until puberty or whenever specific sex hormones arrive and continue their development, followed by ovulation, and then perhaps fertilization by sperm. So as the female embryo is developing, her ovaries are preparing to create her future lineage, and she will hold that cellular material, like an inheritance, until it's time for those cells to begin development that makes them receptive to sperm.

In the case of men, sperm are created every day. The complete process of spermatogenesis (division of diploid sperm cells, maturation of sperm cells in testicles, movement of sperm into epididymis) or sperm replenishment takes 64 days. [2]

SPIRITUAL HERITAGE

Perhaps the most significant time period that can be mentioned here, in the form of a very compressed offering of information, is one whose archaeological evidence looks drastically different from what came after it, most notably in the structural form of temples, tombs and statuary, including how they were decorated as well as the shapes used. This is important to mention, although briefly, because the spiritual beliefs and veneration rituals rooted in this historical foundation look a lot like feminine traditions that have carried on in rural Italy since ancient times and which were already being practiced when the Romans began documenting the world around them, and have continued, in part, into our contemporary times.

Two localities of this time period are in Turkey, which was home to the emergence of an important Goddess for Italy, Cibele (also written Kybele, Cybele), and two are the Italian islands of Malta and Sardinia. If there was page space to go deeper we'd also need to include the Italian regions of Puglia and Liguria, and the island of Sicily.

+ **Göbekli Tepe**: structures in the southeastern Anatolia region of Turkey, with centuries of building activity from approximately 20,000 and 9,370 years Before Present (BP). Structures from the 10th millennium BCE and from the 9th millennium BCE have also been unearthed, with structures that predate pottery, metallurgy, and the invention of writing and the wheel.

+ **Catalhöyük**: large neolithic and chalcolithic proto-city settlement in southern Anatolia, from the time period of approximately 7500BC- 5700BC.

+ **Megalithic Temples of Malta**: 7 megalithic prehistoric freestanding temples on the island of Malta, Italy, dating from 3600 BC- 2500 BC. Once considered the oldest in the world, and while certainly older that Stonehenge and the pyramids of Egypt, new research shows that Gobekli Tepe may have older temples. Note that dates vary, with some temple-building dates being stated

BIRTH La Nascita

as 5200 BC and from 4000 BC - 700 BC.

+   **Tombe dei Giganti**: Tombs of the Giants of Sardinia: megalithic tombs found across the island of Sardinia, approximately 320 have been found so far. From the early bronze age, approximately 2000 BC.

WHAT THEY HAVE IN COMMON

+ Göbekli Tepe:

-   FEMALE FIGURINES- Female figurine dated to around 12000 - 6000 BC found near a hilltop sanctuary on the highest point of a mountain ridge buried in a ritualistic way. She looks strikingly similar to the seated mother figurine depicted giving birth of Catalhöyük.

-   FEMALE SYMBOLS OF DIVINITY- in this case, animal carvings long associated with feminine regeneration and of the Goddess' energy: serpents, frogs, fish...all carved on Tau shaped columns. The Tau is the symbol of the Taurus constellation which these structures are aligned to. In the Early Bronze Age Taurus marked the location of the sun during the spring equinox, thus was the constellation of life after death (renewal, regeneration).

-   BULL SKULLS WITH HORNS (bucrania) - Goddess symbol expressing the regeneration of the uterus in women as a parallel to universal life force power.

-   CIRCULAR STRUCTURES- circular structures as opposed to square temples. One even has a long tunnel that brings to mind the placenta and umbilical cord of mothers.

-   RED OCHRE PAINT

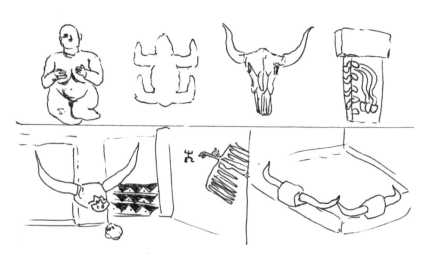

Top row l-r: female figurine from Göbekli Tepe, Frog from Catalhöyük, bull skull; Tau shaped column with serpents from Göbekli Tepe. Bottom row l-r, rooms from Catalhöyük.

Italian Magic: Secret Lives of Women

+ **Catalhöyük:**

- FEMALE FIGURINES- Goddess figurine venerating divine motherhood called "Great Mother". Seated perhaps on a throne, flanked by 2 animals, giving birth. Later, the Goddess Cybele was also depicted in this way.

- FEMALE FIGURINES- Great quantities of female figurines found primarily in areas believed to be shrines by Mellaart, the original excavator, Although a male deity existed as well, *"statues of a female deity far outnumber those of the male deity, who moreover, does not appear to be represented at all after Level 7"*. 3 To date, 18 levels have been identified. 4

- FEMALE FIGURINES- Female figurines have been found within bins used for storage of cereals, such as wheat and barley, and the figurines are presumed to be of a deity protecting the grain. 5

- BULL SKULLS WITH HORNS (bucrania) - used in tomb areas to depict life of the soul continuing on after death of the physical body, combine with vulture goddess imagery and comb-like wings design.

- RED OCHRE PAINT- on figurines, in spiral designs on stones, on animal reliefs.

Left: seated Goddess figurine from Catalhöyük. R, seated Goddess Cibele.

+ **Megalithic Temples of Malta**:

- FEMALE FIGURINES- Small Goddess figurines representing feminine energy, also large standing figurines as guardians. Noted for their full bodied shapes.

- FEMALE FIGURINES- very precise carvings of spirals, animals (such as horned animals and pigs) and repetitions of the same animals and designs.

- BULL SKULLS WITH HORNS (bucrania) -horned bull and sow carvings inside temples

- CIRCULAR STRUCTURES- circular temples, some employing sound technology, some look like bodies similar to the Goddess statues with enlarged breasts and bellies. Tau shaped pillars.

- RED OCHRE PAINT

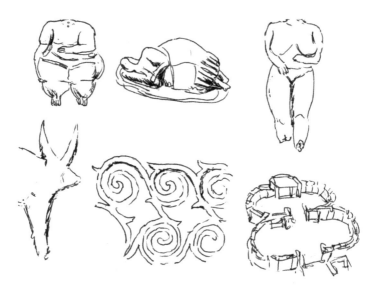

Top row l-r: figurines from Malta
Bottom row l-r: bull wall relief from Malta, spiral cravings from Malta, female body shape temple from Malta.

+**Tombe dei Giganti**: Tombs of the Giants of Sardinia:

- FEMALE FIGURINES- The tombs themselves are shaped like giant uteri with fallopian tubes. The burial place for the dead bodies is in the actual uterine cavity representative: the threshold, the doorway to life and death.

- BULL SKULLS WITH HORNS (bucrania) - These tombs, being uterus-shaped, naturally also resemble the bucranium. Many Tombs of Giants are also oriented towards the Taurus constellation. [6]

- CIRCULAR STRUCTURES- (semicircular) structure fallopian tubes of uterus.

- CIRCULAR STRUCTURES- A feature found in some of the Nuraghic megalithic towers in Sardinia (8,000 are known so far) is a bucranium-shaped keyhole that light pours in on specific dates connected to the solstice and equinox passage of light.

- CIRCULAR STRUCTURES- There are also sacred wells, *"similar to the nuraghi's architectural structure but they have been built underground. The wells[...] represented the female sexual organs as if they were the entrance and the exit towards the afterworld. The fact that the wells were full of water (the water reminds the amniotic fluid) let us think that the wells wanted to represent the womb of the mother earth. The descent (or the climb) of the staircase represents the passage from the light to the darkness and vice-versa. The water represents the birth."* [7]

The sacred well of Santa Cristina, for example features a *"staircase, the sun's light is reflected in the well during the autumn equinox (between the 22nd and the 23rd of September) and also during the spring equinox (between the 20th and the 21st of March). Among the most convincing theories there is the idea that the nuraghi were places of mother cult. Their structure could represent a mother's womb with an opening that gives light, a light which could represent the man's fertilizing force. This is one of the possibilities that explain the orientation of many nuraghi with the entrance located on the South/South-East."* [8]

- FEMALE FIGURINES - Spectacular white alabaster Cross with Divine Feminine attributes, Sardinia's "White Lady" (referring not to white skin but to the white light of solstices and equinoxes, representative of death's connection to regeneration (life after death). A rare specimen of evidence of the Divine Feminine not eradicated by patriarchal history end 5th millennium B.C. (5th millennium was span of years from 5000 B.C. to 4001 B.C.)

- RED OCHRE PAINT

+ Note: Nicknames for one of the Tombe dei Giganti is "Domus di Jana", house of fairies/ witches.

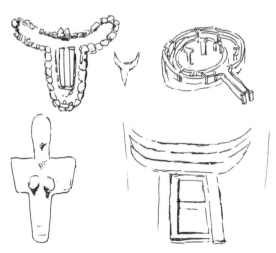

Top row l-r: Uterine Tombe dei Giganti, uterine/bull carving Domus de Janas, both Sardinia, placenta-shape

BIRTH La Nascita

structure of Göbekli Tepe. Bottom row: White alabaster cross lady from Sardinia, Domus bull/uterine portal interior of a Domus de Janas, Sardinia.

+ Notes: BULL

Although the bull has been seized by patriarchal view, starting with paganisms such as the cult of Mitra (which ritualized killing of a bull so as to synthetically emulate menstrual blood's regenerative energy) which had temples on mainland Italy, it makes no natural nor biological sense in a universal cosmic way to attribute the depth of meaning of the bull's psychic representation to that of men. In spiritual pre-pagan history the bull represents the regenerative life force that takes place after death and the assurance of rebirth, attributes that were also associated with the regenerative life force of birth, active in the earthly female. The animal's skull and horns have a natural parallel, symbolically, in the female reproductive organs. The fact that a bull is a masculine animal was not part of the symbolic equation originally. Bull's blood used in Mitra rituals for regeneration cannot naturally come from a male bull, thus the ritual slaughter is synthesized.

None of the developmental phases of human life take place within the male body. No birth (and therefore regeneration) occurs in the body of a male bull, nor in any male horned animal. Horned animals were originally honored as parallel symbols of the divine feminine embodied on earth, due to their horns and skulls having such a close shape to the uterus and fallopian tubes as well as to the moon, symbol of the Goddess. Horned animals did not symbolize a male god nor a penis, or more accurately a double male penis as paganisms and even Italian folklore try to say. Horns come in pairs. Which human male has a double penis? The earliest spiritual symbolic language was not so convoluted as to be overly conceptual in a patriarchal leaning: nature already pointed to the spiritual: to understand a concept about the spiritual, one could look to nature. There is no perfect "balance" between gender aspects in nature, but everyone, no matter which gender, including all non-binary genders, come to life through a mother.

Spiritual structures and figurines (before masculine-centric paganisms) expressed honor to and asked for protection from the Divine life force embodied in female form as an energetic symbol. Therefore womb-like symbols as a psychic language referred to energy passing through doorways that were critical to life: vaginal fluid, menstrual blood, and breast milk were identified as being key factors for the creation and sustenance of human lives. Since life came through the female body, it made sense to believe it returned there after death, which is why the Goddess for birth and death were the same: The Great Goddess Mother who is the doorway.

The male body offers no nutrients, no biological functions, and no brain activity communication towards a fetus: these things happen within the female body during pregnancy and then after birth. The female body is most comparable parallel of a self-sustaining universal life force. This is why everything was expressed as coming from the Mother, not because masculinity doesn't figure in, but because it plays a much smaller role.

Italian Magic: Secret Lives of Women

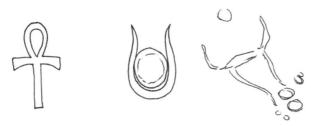

Left: symbol of Goddess Isis/Iside
Middle: Symbol of Goddess Isis/Iside
Right: Taurus constellation at Göbekli Tepe

+ **Notes**: GODDESS ISIS is one of the female representations of both sun-and-moon regenerative power, the renewal of spring's light and fertility as the east and "Easter" and is also connected to the Tau and Taurus. She also is a prominent Goddess among rural people in some areas of Italy, hidden behind the Madonna.

+ **Notes**: EGALITARIAN SOCIETIES. While the female form was used as a veneration tool and expression of the Divine Feminine, and women on earth were honored as having similarities to/ aspects of, this divinity, this was not used to elevate women over men in the societies of Catalhöyük and Gobekli Tepe. Evidence shows genders were equal; women didn't use this parallel to god-force to overpower others. There were no weapons. The Goddess figure wasn't a source of societal control and yet she was still honored over and above male gods. And, women didn't have a lower class value than men, as they have had after the establishment of masculine-centric cosmogony.

+ **Notes**: FIGURINE STYLES: the Goddess figurines mentioned here in brief are dramatically different from what is seen in Greek and Roman statuary, for example, where the female body is carved in an anatomically perfect, unified way: thin. The Roman statues of women seem to be modeled after the masculine ones in most cases, with just breasts added and a soft belly, but since they were used to advertise divinities or humanity in a form of beauty, there is little deviation from the slim body shapes offered.

   The female divinity figurines of pre-masculinized paganisms show a fullness in one body part and a drooping in another, with emphasis on the feminine-specific body parts that offer nurture to birth and life: vulva, breasts, and mouths, and showing states of life-force flux, transition and movement. These were visual choices: they were created at the same time that incredible megalithic technology was used to create the structures mentioned, and the same craftsmanship that carved repeatedly identical spirals and repeatedly identical animals on the outsides and insides of the many temples.

+ **Notes**: GRAIN GODDESSES and RURAL ITALY:

Cibele, Cybele, Kybele. While known for other things, Cibele was also a Goddess connected to grains and regeneration of the harvest, a Goddess who granted abundance. An Anatolian mother-goddess introduced to mainland Greece and Greek colonies including

Magna Graecia sometime in the 6th C BC (600 BC- 501 BC). ₉ The Greeks called her Mātēr or Mētēr ("Mother"), or from the early 5th century Kubelē. ₁₀ Romans knew Cybele as Magna Mater ("Great Mother"), among other names. Rome officially adopted her cult during the Second Punic War. ₁₁

+Demeter/Ceres, Persephone/Prosperpina and Ecate/Hekate and Cibele are also Goddesses associated with wheat and other grains used in rural Italian traditions of mothers, and they are Goddesses of abundance as well. They all assist earthly women during transitions from girlhood to womanhood, from unmarried life to married life, and they all are associated with boundaries of the spirit world. As chthonic goddesses of life and death, they all were involved in transmitting knowledge of the universe to earthly women in rural Italy. They are also Goddesses associated with having no male counterpart who were chaste, which doesn't mean virgins, but refers to not having one constant sexual partner as in marriage: they belonged to no man, and yet, could give to men as they wished, in the traditions of sex as medicine.

Demeter with wheat and poppy. Ciblele and Ecate/Hecate were also associated with wheat and flowers.

> *"The early Cult of the Goddess reflects matrifocal, matrilineal, endogmatic social order of peaceful and supportive communities, which for millenia has been at the base of Western civilization, resisting in the Old Continental Europe until 3500 BC, and in the Mediterranean islands until 1450 BC. It was a Domestic Cult, run in small shrines and homes by priestesses who ritually forged objects of worship in connection with seasonal regeneration rituals. From the excavation data in Macedonia it is known that in every Neolithic house there were altars for the worship of the Goddess and some houses were used as a neighborhood sanctuary."* ₁₂

As you'll find in this book, the Italian rural household is essentially the same set-up, with daily sacred magic operated from the home by women, and magical supplies consisting of cereals and grains and plants: the same ones connected to these ancient Goddesses of regeneration. The reality is that the inheritance from the Goddesses is medico-magical knowledge used in daily rural life, it's not reserved for ceremonies in temples. This is where the fantasies touch earth.

Italian Magic: Secret Lives of Women

BEFORE

What came BEFORE this time period is equally spectacular, such as this bas relief in Dordogne, France called "The Venus of Laussel" or "lady with horn" casually. It is painted with red ochre and was carved into a rock shelter. It is approximately 25,000 years old. She has large breasts and vulva. There is a "Y" on her thigh and her faceless head is turned toward the crescent moon. Presented is a sketch of the bas-relief. The original limestone is in a museum in France.

According to Riane Eisler, in her right hand the figure holds a crescent moon notched with 13 markings: the number of lunar cycles in a year. Her other hand, as if to instruct us of the relationship between the cycles of the moon and women's menstrual cycles, points to her vagina. 13

Figurines of goddesses embodied after this time period (but before the masculinization of the universe in spiritual myths and temples and statuary) also emphasized these parts of the female body. Women were also the time-keepers due to the fact that their own bodies tell passage of time and light and life.

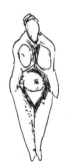

Female figurines l-r: from Balzi Rossi, Italy; from Grotta delle Veneri, Italy; from Sicily, early 4th mill. B.C.

BIRTH La Nascita

In Old Europe's early agricultural period (8,000-9,000 years ago) Neolithic art of the Goddess portrayed her as:

> *"birth-giver, fertility-giver and death-wielder and can all be traced back to 25,000 B.C. when the first sculptures used symbols (vulvas, triangles, breasts, chevrons [...] to an even earlier time. This Goddess centered art, with its striking absence of images of warfare and male domination, reflects a social order in which women as heads of clans or queen-priestesses played a central part. In Old Europe and Anatolia, [...] a balanced, non-patriarchal and non-matriarchal social system is reflected in the religion, mythologies and folklore...and is supported by the continuity of the elements of a matrilineal system in [...] ancient Greece, Etruria, Rome, and other [ancient] countries of Europe.* 14

There existed in prehistoric times a world in which women and men lived in just and peaceful societies oriented towards the model of partnership. 15 Catalhöyük was a place were true gender equality flourished, The fact that a golden-age of women had once existed put paid to the entrenched belief that women are, and always have been, inferior.16 At the same time, *one of the most powerful representations ever made of female divinity was created during this time,* 17 and it wasn't a disruption to the society. There was equality at the same time motherhood was honored and a Divine Feminine universe was celebrated. This wasn't an isolated event, as the 'Seated Mother Goddess of Catalhöyük' figurine bears resemblance to other Stone Age art going back 19,000 years – such as the famous 'Venus of Willendorf'. 18 This shared belief that everything comes from the mother: on the earth and in the universe, is inclusive and based on nature; whereas paganism only offers binary gender symbols with an emphasis on masculine pro-creation.

WHAT CAME AFTER

In a nutshell, or a **noce** shell, what came after were male warring tribes armed with weapons, repeatedly invading peaceful communities of Old Europe in 4 waves that took place from 4300 BC- 2800 BC. 19 These invasions would break up and rearrange community life, which until then had been based on women sharing their knowledge of midwifery, caretaking of children, food production and time keeping, and domestic ritual celebration of a divinely feminine universe.

The world's viewpoint on society and its relationship to the universe was forever altered towards a markedly different patriarchal view, one which eradicated the divine feminine altogether in some male-centric religions and cults. In other cults she was demoted to vengeful wife-goddess who still found her fertility having to take a backseat to male gods who somehow claimed to birth their own children from wombless bodies. And in the christian story a woman named Mary was used for her womb to forcibly bear a child, having been raped by god. Of course this story can be viewed in a positive, supernatural way, embracing at least that a woman was able to birth a physically manifested part of god as Christ, and that act of creation is one only women can perform. However more often this

20

Italian Magic: Secret Lives of Women

story is used even in contemporary church environments to encourage women to obey their husbands as power heads of the family, just like god, and to diminish the female goddess force of her womb.

The invaders would break apart feminine inheritance traditions as women were isolated and became property. The spiritual stories would be rewritten into male-centric ones of a masculine god-ruled universe. The shapes of temples would change from natural shapes and structures of caves and round domestic homes into artificially squared structures. Female roles since the earliest times (as midwives, medicine women, as farmers and harvesters) would gradually be taken over by men, and the by-products (food, knowledge) hoarded. Men would go to great lengths to deter people from trusting women ever again. For a socio-economic look at masculine competition with midwives and healers, read "Italy's Witches And Medicine Women Vol 1."

This altered view through the lens of masculine directives is what most societal operating systems are based upon since the turn away from the inclusive feminine universe. Supply and demand previously cared for by the spirit world's guidance in the form of handed-down knowledge used to improve life turned into supply and demand controlled by patriarchal warring tribes. Whether controlling food production, creating fake famines used to increase prices of necessities (and yet blaming witches), supporting poverty economics including human beings as property, a divide was created among genders. Poverty and nobility became opposing forces.

> *With the advent of new patriarchal ideologies, adopted by the ruling classes of the Indo-European invaders, the religion of the Goddess became clandestine in some regions in others it was assimilated by the official religions.* [20]

Of course, this is a very compressed version of events, events that find the Lineage cures and shamanic traditions of rural Italy surviving as "outsider, clandestine" rituals from the earliest days and continuing underfoot from the rest of society's developments. The rural magic is simply natural and not developed on top of other magical traditions the likes of which appeared in the middle ages to quench a thirst for contemporary power, in response to societal desires of wealth revenge, love and status.

L: Goddess Iside/Isis   M: A Madonna   R: rural Italian Mother

BIRTH La Nascita

What does all this have to do with rural Italy?

What you'll find in these pages is a small collection of Mother Magic rituals that are part of an even vaster lifestyle of daily sacred traditions from Italy's agricultural communities where women were the sole-centric operators of magic.

The inheritance and initiatic transmission of this oral knowledge between women is alluded to in the so-called Myth of the Descent of Demeter-Persefone; Mother and Daughter. This myth has been invaded with masculine hierarchy and violence and altered from its original and true meaning which is why we must rename name it a "so-called" myth and reclaim the original story. The original story is of the Lineage traditions.

In rural Italy these Lineages are orally transmitted knowledge passed down from mother to daughter or daughter-in-law, or from father-to-son less commonly. This knowledge is magical and curative, provided by the world of Feminine Divinity so very long ago. These rituals and knowledge are used to bring health and energy into balance when it's been affected negatively.

In this tradition, the elder healer passes down the knowledge and rituals if guided to. This in an intimate, one-on-one procedure. No certificates or hierarchy are needed nor awaited for approval. No external person creates suffering as a rite of passage in order for the initiate "to deserve" to inherit these traditions, as the Myth of the Descent would have us believe. The original story instead reflects the most ancient co-creative partnerships on earth: the Divine Feminine as provider of abundance who hands down knowledge to mothers who then transfer it to their daughters, in-keeping with oral tradition. While there are masculine lineage traditions also, men in rural communities more often offer passive apotropaic protection.

For women and female identified people, roles as central mother figures within families and as mothers for communities (biological mothers as well as spiritual mother figures) arose just as naturally as the spiritual practices that supported these roles. These practices were pervasive in daily domestic life, both a result of necessity and divine intervention as women were left to care for themselves and their babies alone. Naturally needing to know how to survive birth and grow food, keep time, teach, and cure health imbalances, mothers were bestowed with knowledge from the spirit world for how to use whatever natural resources were around them or within them to activate channeled healing and restore balance. The same grains honored as being gifted from the Divine Feminine (lentils, beans, millet, wheat) and that were used in the domestic Goddess temples of most ancient times are the same ones honored as humble proteins in rural Italy. The threads of connection to matrilinear culture are pervasive in rural daily sacred traditions...but they are not so easy to find because:

1. Rural people haven't documented their lives. Busy living in the flow of nature and working the land, creating food from its bounty, and caring for life in their families and community without modern conveniences (including reading and writing often) they instead keep their traditions alive through their daily expression and usage, living fully

Italian Magic: Secret Lives of Women

in the present moment. Any pertinent knowledge is passed down to others orally. This is an insider world, which is why knowledge and traditions become lost to time. They are not entirely lost however, but they do pass out of this earthly world along with the consciousness of the keepers of this knowledge. It is the consciousness who is the keeper, the consciousness which remains living after the death of the physical body. We come to know these keepers as "ancestors," while the creators of the knowledge they keep are known as Goddesses, Madonnas, and female Saints.

2. Feminine spiritual groups out of contemporary step have also not documented themselves. For this reason, channeling and mediumship (the skills of communicating with conscious people living as spirits without physical bodies) are vital to remain connected or to reclaim an active and open line of communication to receive this knowledge from living consciousness. Anthropologists who have written about these insider traditions are not insiders themselves, so their documentation is lacking connection to the parts of these rituals that are difficult or even impossible to explain by words and "facts" alone because they are based on experiences of psychic and mediumistic phenomena which are always challenging to describe with words.

3. Roman temple culture is dominant in historical records due to all conquerors and ruling powers enjoying favorable documentation, historically. That, and the glorification of opulence, nobility, wealth, architecture and success, even if many of these were built on top of simpler ideas. Roman temple culture is synthesized from many traditions from many lands,all of which have usurped previous rituals venerating a divinely Feminine universe and which have rewritten that source of life into a masculine one, having thus created an entirely new spiritual perspective of the universe which found itself being expressed even in feminine spiritual cults venerating Goddesses. Whether in ancient Italy or in Catalhoyuk and other sites that pre-date the pyramids where a divine feminine cosmogony was celebrated, you'll find common connections in rural Italian life and rural daily sacred transformational magic. The "real" old ways, the ones older than middle period masculinized magic, are from the feminine traditions whose rituals are pervasive throughout Italian rural culture, but the main obstacle to finding them is in the languaging. When historians talk about spiritual culture of the elite and of nobility, it's with an elevated language and respect. When historians talk about rural culture, they use accusations of superstition and poverty, etc.

Rural traditions live on in fractionated usage among most Italian families. Far and wide, these traditions have been inherited: food magic, cures for **il malocchio** the evil eye, spells, fertility practices and more, all of what may be called "superstitions" now but were divination tools and cures relied upon then and more have been mostly inherited by women to do the work they've done since the dawn of time: care for life.

All the traditions and rituals found in this book come from rural Italy and the lines of connection that begin with the first traditions, the shamanic ones, handed down to mothers and female identified caregivers at the dawn of time. These traditions were once part of a holistic daily sacred way of life inseparable from the palpable cycles of nature and with ritual meeting every moment, to bless, honor, heal, balance, request, invoke, protect, and have been pervasive throughout the entire continent of Italy and her islands, under the radar of the documentarians but acknowledged in the awareness of locals. These traditions and rituals can also be found in similar ways in indigenous cultures around the world.

This system has at its core spirit world intervention. It doesn't look like a system you'll want to see because it is not a "system" like other contemporary systems of spiritual practice: there are no lists of exercises you can use to become a better healer or more precise channeler. There are no instructions on how to meditate nor directions on how to do many of the works themselves in terms of intricacies experienced. There are no teachers to study under long-term with some exceptions of specific medico-magical cures of Sicily and other body-contact cures in some areas of Campania or Emilia-Romagna, for example, but these are an exception rather than a rule.

Instead, the core is a devotion to the Divine Feminine. And the Divine Feminine is the provider of abundance. This devotion is a life-long agreement that is ultimately decided by the Divine Feminine, while the human person finds themselves "elected" to these duties, which often means placing aside personal goals and hopes and dreams to be available to the service of others.

The "secrets", these simple instructions are inherited in secret and they are never altered by the user. There are no directions on how to prepare for this practice nor is there a manual to explain the philosophy behind the "system," (which is based upon the ancient principles of the universe, including the Natural Laws of Energy like the "Law of Attraction" and what can also be called The Abundance principles. These principles are the ones that continually find themselves renewed for each generation with a cultural or languaging upgrade. They are high concepts. In contrast, in the lower realms of contemporary magic meaning, the commercialization and masculinzation of magic that, like food and animas and housing, were hoarded and then sold back to people as: grimoires, cults, and products where you have to pass a human initiation based on hierarchy and human judgment all to learn someone else's magical theories and mediation exercises to prepare your senses. Middle period magic, which is commonly thought of as "witchcraft" that is separate from shamanism and not developed in the world of spirit before being passed to the human world is conceptualized. The rural channeled magic can only be granted by the world of spirit helpers and not by human will alone.

You will see the roots of conceptual magic here in the rural world in all its forms. Here, astral travel, magic, psychic perception and mediumistic methods, what we'd call "banishing" and "binding" and "cord cutting" of negative spirits and illness find their foundations among usage of bodily fluids, amulet preparations, protective magic and an adherence to nature's flow. In the rural world, for example, the growing moon has specific influences over the growth of plants and other expressions of nature, thus the growing moon's magical usage is based on this. In conceptual magic, the concept of the growth of light is used, but disconnected from nature's cycles beyond that of the "growing light" itself, which can be seen with the naked eye.

The feminine focus of this book's collection is not meant to overshadow the fact

Italian Magic: Secret Lives of Women

that people of all genders are equal in their abilities to heal and use magic: rather this is simply a snapshot of a way of life, whose totality dissolved starting in the 1950s-1980s in what Italians call the "deculturalization" of rural life, where communities who had lived fully within their own communities and economic conditions (caring for the land and animals and planting/harvesting/growing/processing their own food and acting as their own healers and midwives without doctors nor hospitals), came to a close as economics changed and people had to seek work in cities, whereafter some villages remain with only 5 inhabitants from the same family, or none at all.

---

*The "Myth of the Descent" tells a story of Demeter's daughter Persephone being kidnapped and taken to the underworld where Hades is in charge. He makes her strip completely naked, basically forces her to be his wife and in return gives her the secrets of the universe. Prior to the creation of this myth, women were associated as keepers of the underworld and naturally knowing all the secrets of the universe. So this pagan myth was simply a societal effort, through the re-writing of the preceding divine feminine spiritual stories, to conquer the feminine power and sublimate her to the male, just as Christianity did with Mary who was forcible impregnated.

Italian Magic: Secret Lives of Women

Museo di Triora Etnografico e della Stregoneria, Liguria.

MIDWIVES
Le Levatrici

Midwifery is an insider system of care created by women for women that was born out of need while being on the threshold of life and death. It's truly a tradition of most ancient times. In rural Italy, babies were born within communities and outside of hospitals well into the 1950s and even in some areas until the 1980s when the deculturalization of entire agricultural communities responded to economic troubles and sought work in cities.

To give some definition to these agricultural communities, consider: people who plant their own crops, harvest them, thresh their own wheat, care for their own animals and who transform milk, eggs, grains and plants into food. Where the arrangements of houses have special meanings and daily sacred magic is an inseparable part of daily life. Where babies were born in homes with midwives and the dead were cared for in their homes before the community performs ritual send-offs. Where women do love magic, fertility magic, cure illness, curse, learn from divine feminine interventions, practice astral flight... all within insular worlds where people know the cycles of the moon and its affect on nature and make decisions based on its movement, and whose lives were completely dependent on the cycles of nature. Where women were the sole proprietors of magic, offering a "double maternity", [21] magically caring for needs in the family and also out in the larger community. Where the rural medicine women (and sometimes men) were relied upon for birth, death, and in-between, having no hospitals and only a rare visit from an outside male doctor. All this occurred outside of Roman temple culture and outside of any contemporary Wiccan style system created by the patriarchy. The rural world is one like the prehistoric places mentioned: where motherhood was revered for being connected to universal secrets and truths and "Mother of god" is referred to more often than god himself.

Museo della Nostra Terra di
Ocre di Leonessa, Lazio.

MIDWIVES: Le Levatrici

As midwifery is an insider world, it's rare to find anything in writing by Italian women themselves outside of anthropological commentary by men which focus on the writers' perspectives and certainly don't give an holistic look at a lifestyle that includes also magic, cures, psychic illnesses, curses and other conditions to rural life.

Midwives operated successfully outside of the male medical establishment because they existed before the male medical establishment. This is also why in Italy and elsewhere they were attacked by the church and male-only medical establishments who wanted to divert customers away from rural women and towards masculine doctors.*

Interestingly, midwives worked alongside medical doctors in some areas of Italy in time periods where the medical establishment had a presence, but during these blended operations the midwives found their duties limited in the same way the goddess's roles were limited in paganisms (if she even had a role) and feminine divinity was eradicated in Christianity. These roles were limited, both in daily life and in spiritual roles, as the powers-that-be continued to separate women from magic, divinity, and their own life force power. Societal restrictions and spiritual restrictions ran parallel and were established in spiritual and religious myths.

Midwives were also keepers of magic and rituals, used to help both mothers and children during and after the birthing process and also to support labor, restore the body, and to protect from the evil eye. These rituals, magic, and traditions were part of a larger holistic way of life where women were the sole proprietors of daily sacred magic for their families and the greater rural community.

For sure, there are many more versions of the word "midwife" throughout Italy and her islands in various dialects than are listed in this chapter. The few here give an idea of similarities and differences among them. The names also refer to roles of women who have slightly different duties from one to the other, depending on the time period in which they were used and in which village, province, and region they were/are used.

NAMES FOR MIDWIVES

La Levatrice, This is a general term for midwife found in the unified Italian language. However, it's considered an old fashioned word and is no longer frequently used. If you visit Italy and ask local people about this, you will likely be met with confused looks unless you are talking to people in their 70s, 80s and 90s or who are still connected to the traditions. You can, however, use this word to research in the Italian language. Any research you do about Italy should be done in the Italian language anyway. Most interestingly, **levatrici** (midwives) are often associated with **lavatrici** (laundry washers) who are considered to be witches. Even in Sicily, **majare** is a dialect name that refers to female witches (like **janare** does in Campania) which is also a similar dialect name to the women who do laundry and who are midwives.

---

*to read about this period in Italy's history and the impact it had on women, see "Italy's Witches and Medicine Women Vol 1" by Karyn Crisis

Italian Magic: Secret Lives of Women

Obstetrix, This is Latin, meaning **colei che sta davanti** or "she who is in front of her". The word generated with the female role as the **obstetrici** and refers to the procedure of the midwife who "caught" the baby as it came out of the mother, during a standing or seated birth.

Le Ostetriche, a general Italian word used in the past in the region of Campania, especially in Salento, but not limited to.

LOMBARDY
VALLE D'AOSTA
FRIULI VENEZIA GIULIA
PIEMONTE
EMILIA ROMAGNA
LIGURIA
MARCHE
TUSCANY
ABRUZZO
MOLISE
UMBRIA
PUGLIA
LAZIO
CAMPANIA
SARDINIA
SICILY
CALABRIA

Regions featured in this book, also where the following names for midwives are used. Of course, there are other villages, regions and provinces where these names are used as below or in their own dialects.

Sa Levadora, Sardinian word for **levatrice** / midwife.

La maestra di parto sarda, Sardinian for delivery woman.

Sa mastra e 'partu, a Sardinian phrase meaning "a woman, in general, elderly who had acquired with experience the techniques to help women in labor, " midwife. [22]

MIDWIVES: Le Levatrici

La Cummare refers to midwives in dialects of the central part of Italy, but this word exists in other dialects of various parts of Italy and even throughout the island of Sardinia, spelled slightly differently.

La Commare is used in Naples.

La Comare is the term used for midwife in the region of Umbria but this term also generally refers to other duties such as a "godmother" would have and as a woman trusted by the entire family in an "inner circle" kind of way.

La comare is also found in Cividale del Friuli in the region of Friuli-Venezia Giulia and on the island of Sardinia too (and surely other places) as an honorable title given between women who make a special friendship dedication to each other that also has an accompanying ritual that is like an oath-bond among women, denoting a spiritual commitment. This is a term found, these days, hidden away in rural domestic magic areas, and more rarely in some modern magical groups where regional traditions are kept alive in part.

La Comare was also sometimes a Lineage healer and called as such in Avellino.

There is also a term for men: **Le Compare**, such as used in Ozieri, Sardinia.

La Comare is one of the roles for those needing assistance "within" the family group. Or, as you may have read in "Italy's Witches and Medicine Women Vol 1" it is a role for those learning together under a "mother" who teaches magic. Covens come from this concept, but there are no covens in Italian tradition, only people called **comare**, a name that designates a special friend who keeps inner-world secrets together and share spiritual traditions for a lifetime. **La comare** and **le compare** also act as stand-in parents, likened to godparents (or magical doubles) for specific community events, such as baptism.

A Cummari is used in Calabria.

La Mammana is the Sicilian word for midwife.

Le Ricoglitrice, from the general region of Campania means, literally **patrollers** or **getter** but was used in 1593 in the region of Campania and Salento as a term for a midwife who had other tasks as in "**raccoglitrice del bambino**" a kind of nurse. [23]

La comare levatrice was sometimes used altogether. [24]

Le donne che assiste/aiute. There are differences between midwives and **women/who assist/help**, and this is where historical changes made things complicated. During the time period where male doctors had begun delivering babies, some midwives were given a sort of certification allowing them to take part alongside them and had even been given some duties by the priest to baptize, when he wasn't available. However, this certification restricted midwives, and these restrictions more often than not put the mothers in labor at risk for death. Often the "wwa", the midwife and the doctor worked together in areas where they were available, which still excludes rural and remote areas. As for the midwife,

Italian Magic: Secret Lives of Women

"she only has her own hands to assist-and can also make injections (bicarbonate and permanganate solutions) to accelerate the release of the fetal appendages and examine them but has the hands tied in case of complications." [25]

While "wwa" were the remnants of rural midwives who use to operate the entire procedure of birth (with the complex knowledge, sympathetic magic, homeopathic recovery remedies and more) in this time period they were also limited when difficulties arose.

In rural areas where doctors didn't visit, women were well trained in sympathetic magic and other curative methods to deal with birth complications. These traditions were often handed down mother-to-daughter, and it was not uncommon in rural Italy for familial midwives to have helped birth 45-50 babies each in their respective villages.

La signora della nascita, general term in unified Italian meaning "the woman of birth".

The role of a midwife did become an official one under municipality, which offered official duties recognized by the church, whereas all the "homegrown" midwives and their various names not under municipal governance, still could give baptism for example, but undercover, as they were not officially recognized by church nor municipality as a real job. This gave them more freedoms, but over time found them targeted and vulnerable by vampire witch stories and unfairly blamed for infant deaths. As the masculinzation of womens' traditions grew and they became businesses with hierarchies, women were shut out or used as scapegoats when things went wrong.

Beyond the medical factors of delivering babies, midwives and women who assist were inevitably involved in deaths and the delicate threshold of the in-between. In fact, it is believed that the first 40 days after giving birth the new mother is near death, close to "an open grave", which acknowledges the delicate balance her body, mind, and spirit must endure with blood and nutrition losses during birth.

Midwives **levatrici** were also often **lavatrici:** the clothing and fabric washers, regularly engaged with the conduit of water and part of the tradition of receiving knowledge of a magical nature at these water sources. They were responsible for the duties of "making the baby" and caring for its wrappings and first days on earth. In contrast to medical doctors who assist during the actual birth and then depart, womens' intimate relationship with their bodies, its fluids, and its possibilities was extensive.

Waters as fountains, wells, rivers and lakes have long been associated with not only purification, but as places where spirits visit and give advice, or even scare people, and therefore are associated with the supernatural and the magical. By approximation, having spent so much time at these sources, midwives and washer women were therefore considered synonymous with witches: connected to this watery veiled doorway and the possibilities on the others side of it and the mysterious knowledge that uneducated women held. In fact, it was said of midwives they "made a thousand sorceries". [26]

MIDWIVES: Le Levatrici

There seem to be little benefits to the world of pregnancy and birth injected by male doctors, only complications. After all, men have no understanding personally of the female body, nor do men have any internal experience of pregnancy nor the birthing process. Men attempted to take over feminine medicine by creating hierarchy, and in many of cases this hierarchy caused death. Naturally, it makes little sense to have men become doctors for women and their bodies, and often results in a dehumanized way of approaching care for mothers and babies:

In the book "Figure Femminili, Protettrici Della Nascita: la baba, la femme-quiaide, la levatrice nella cultura europea" by Antonella Caforio, there's a tremendous cultural reveal as to the masculine attitudes towards birth and feminine medicine:

> *"The doctor who takes care of the parties since the fifties tells us: 'I do not like dressing the brat, or giving it a bath, I give it to Margherita, every village has its femme qui-aide, it's here for this",* [27] referring to the baby just born.

which is an attitude extended from the Roman and Greek era:

> *"[...] in fact, for the family women were a burden, while for those who collected it [meaning, for those who had female children instead of male] it was a good investment to start them off to prostitution or slavery."* [28]

which also goes on to explain that it was not illegal to abandon children during this time period. [29]

"Additionally, midwives *"were regarded with some distrust as people who, not controlled by men, could procure abortions or maliciously introduce a bastard into the family by helping the woman pretend pregnancy".* [30]

alongside the common masculine belief of the time that:

> *"a sterile wife is much appreciated by friends and relatives".* [31]

One example of a moon crescent birthing chair. This one is from Jacon Rueff's
"De conceptu et geratione hominis," 1554 edition.

Italian Magic: Secret Lives of Women

"The Greek woman and the Roman woman gave birth on chairs, generally, on a chair with a half-moon opening in the bottom; the midwife could thus intervene manually, during the expulsion phase, to favor the dilatation of the cervix, to cut the umbilical cord." [32]

This is a sketch of a funerary relief of a Midwife named Scribona Attica, from tomb Isola Sacra necropolis, Ostia, Italy, ca. 150-200, painted terracotta, Ancient Roman, High Empires, Antonine, 1380192 (mid 2nd century).

In the funerary relief sketch above both a midwife and woman who assists the birthing procedure are depicted. This object has ancient origins considering...

"that the Greek physician Paolo D'Egina (7th century AD) mentions in his treatises "an obstetric chair"; but it is certain that even in Roman times it was already known." [33]

In addition to seated births, other rural Italian traditions include giving birth in front of the hearth, and giving birth in bed on top of a wooden board placed under layers of sheets that were removed and replaced while the mother remained resting for **40** days before being allowed to leave house.

"These Umbrian peasant uses...with respect to the uses adopted by the majority of the mothers who give birth to lying down, rather...show the continuity of ancient customs, since in the ancient world (but the same thing happens among the cultures of interest ethnological) the woman preferred to give birth squatting in support. "In Rocchetta di Spoleto to refer to the function of the popular **levatri***, they said that she* **raccojeva** *the child, in the sense that she welcomed him in her hands at the time of birth. The same expression was used in Perugia."* [34]

MIDWIVES: Le Levatrici

Phases of the moon

ANCIENT DIVINATION TRADITIONS
For Determining the Sex OF Unborn Children

Waning Moon = Female Child   Waxing Moon = Male Child

Since there were no scientific methods to know the sex of the child [in rural and remote areas], they used methods that were used by ancestors. [35]

> *"For the health and for the life of the child and the child it was that the child took all the moons, i.e. that the period of pregnancy covered 9 lunar cycles."* [36]

This passage is from a lecture about birth in Sardinia, and it refers not to the months needed for a healthy baby and mother, but the moons; the time-keeping is based on lunar cycles. This tradition of using the moon's passage of time is not limited to Sardinia at all; it is found all over Italy, in the rural communities hidden from more modern accoutrements like doctors and hospitals, until the 1950's - 1980s.

The system of using the moon phase as an indicator of sex of the coming child is complex. While there are variances in meanings from region to region, the system remains the same. Illustrated here are the more tangible methods.

In some villages these moon phases and their links to gender are static and never changing. In others, the moon phase is used along with the birth of a child to determine the pattern of sex of the coming children. This is similar to the way people determine a "yes and no" reading to their own pendulum.

Italian Magic: Secret Lives of Women

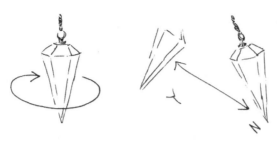

Various ways a pendulum can indicate an answer. Left: turning counter-clockwise, Right: Moving back and forth in a straight line. Other movements: pendulums can shake, jump, and move clockwise, for example.

When using a pendulum, a weighted object hanging from a thread or chain that can move in one direction or another in response to questions, a determination needs to be made of what its movements mean.

Since a question by a person towards a pendulum will be answered in the form of movement (circle left, circle right, bounce up and down, stillness, horizontal move left/right/up/down) these movements need to be understood against a fixed meaning so it can be used the same way for each question in the moment and into the future.

To "set" or "program" a pendulum to the energy of the user, often a question is asked to the pendulum regarding a fact that is known to be true by the user, and the motion that the pendulum takes is from thereafter is always attached to that answer. For example, a pendulum user may initiate use of their pendulum by holding the pendulum, weighted side down, and say "My name is _____", stating their name. They then observe whether the pendulum moves in response to their name in a counter-clockwise arc, a clockwise arc, or perhaps bounces or even remains still. This movement from hereafter is considered to be a "yes" movement. An opposing movement would then be considered a "no" answer. So, when any question is asked after this point to which the pendulum responds in that same motion as it responded to the user's name, it is known to be a positive response.

MOON PHASE DIVINATION

With moon phase and patterns, here is one example, a tradition reported by Lina Premoli from Sardinia:

> *"The moon influenced the sex of the unborn. If the first child born to the change of a moon phase was male, all the unborn children during that lunar phase would have been male. It was then said it was the moon of the males. On the other hand, if a female was born first, it was said that it was the moon of females and during that phase only females would be born."* 37

MIDWIVES: Le Levatrici

And in another area on the mainland:

"In the Marches, it was believed that if a male were born in the crescent moon, a male would be born in the next birth; if a male were born in the waning moon, a female would be born in the next birth; the birth of a female in the waning moon instead, announced the arrival of a female. [38]

"If the sex of the child coincided with the respective moon, it would also coincide with the next birth. If instead the male was born in the descending moon and the female in the growing moon, by a sort of compensation law, in the next birth the relationship between moon and sex would have returned ...male-increasing moon, female-waning moon." [39]

However, at Fogliano, it was believed that the females were born above all to the crescent moon (white moon, good moon) while the males were born in the waning moon (black moon, bad moon). In Cerreto and Valnerina it was believed the contrary: the crescent moon coincided with the birth of a male, the waning with that of a female. [40]

While the version of this system is a bit different per area, the divination system is the same: divining the sex of the coming child by moon phase.

DIVINATIONS USING A SYMPATHETIC NOTION:

In these traditions we see the same sympathetic view of nature connected to human life made part of systems for determining various outcomes. Body shape developments were used to "read" the sex of the coming child, such as: the shape of mother's spit, her belly shape and how it grows, her buttocks shape as the development of the fetus continues, and breast development and shape. Candle flames are consulted as well as, and hen bones are also tossed and "read".

Shapes are consistent from divination to divination. For example, if spit with a "hat shape" denotes male gender in one village or region, then this same shape made with oil in water during a remedy against **il malocchio** the evil eye will also denote a male gendered sender of negative energy, and onward. The shapes are part of a symbolic language and though this language varies just a bit depending on location, the same shapes will consistently denote the same answer per divinations of that area.

Italian Magic: Secret Lives of Women

DIVINATION BY BODY SHAPE DEVELOPMENT

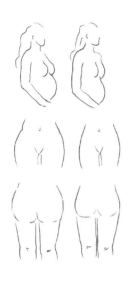

In Meggiano, in the province of Perugia in the region of Umbria: with the enlargement of the mother's belly: if it tends towards a high position, it predicts a female...but it was determined to be a male child if the belly was lower. 41

In Ruscio, in the Frazione of Monteleone di Spoleto in the region of Umbria, in addition to the shape of the belly, the shape of the buttocks is considered: if the abdomen was big while the posterior remained of the same dimensions before conception, they derived the prediction of the birth of a male, but the enlargement of the buttocks announced the birth of a daughter. 42

In Avendita, also in Umbria, another diagnostic method considered the shape of the breast of the future mother: if the breasts were turgid and growing, they announced the birth of a female. If the size of the chest remained rather small, then a male. 43

This method was also used in other villages of Umbria such as: Casale di Serravalle, Torre di Cammoro, Cerreto, Collesolio, S. Anatolia di Narco, Meggiano, Avendita, Fogliano, Castelluccio.

Similarly, in some areas of Abruzzo the underdeveloped breasts and the reduced shape and tip taken by the belly announced the birth of a male. 44

In Caligari, Sardinia, if the pregnant woman had a rosy, relaxed face or a pointed belly, the birth of a male was presaged, while the presence of dark spots on the face or a large abdomen on the hips made one think of a female. 45

DIVINATION BY SPIT SHAPE PIZZUTA

Left: female indication
M., R.: male indication

Observation of the future mother's venom, in some parts of Valnerina, the **pizzuta** *revealed that the woman was waiting for a male; the roundish shape predicated female.* 46

In Savelli and Rocchetta, on the contrary, the round shape with a "hat" predicted a male rather than female. 47

MIDWIVES: Le Levatrici

DIVINATION by CANDLE FLAME:

In Ascolano, in Vallegrascia [region of Marche], the way candles burned revealed how the birth would be: the flame that burned steadily, without wavering, predicted an easy birth. 48

DIVINATION by COIN TOSS *I*

If a woman wanted to know the sex of the unborn child she had to put a coin against her chest, slipping it under her dress. If the coin had fallen on the head, a male would have been born; instead at the cross [reverse side of the coin] a female would have arrived. 49

DIVINATIONS BY HEN BONE WISHBONE:
la consultazione dell'osso sternale

 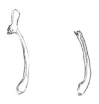

Top:
L: neutral
M: Male
R: Female

Bottom:
L: Female
R: male

DIVINATION by PULLING:

This method has different interpretations based on the region or village it is used in. In some areas, two people each take an end of the wishbone with the characteristic Y shape: when the bone broke, the longest piece with the sternal spur (called **lu cacchiu**) *predicted the birth of a male, the shortest predicted the birth of a female. However, in other areas it was the opposite.* 50

DIVINATION by TOSSING:

In Umbria, and also Ascoli area in Montegallo, the hen bone wishbone is called **forcella**, *the fork. It is thrown into the air. After falling, if it landed with the ends of the fork turned upwards, a*

Italian Magic: Secret Lives of Women

male would be born; if it fell with the ends down, it announced a female."[51]

In the Marche region, the prominent part of the bone falling up refers to a male; in other parts, the "scoop" [ends of the fork turned upwards] is interpreted as a jug for water or as an apron, both associated with the female sex".[52]

In some areas of Sardinia there were predictions about sex by throwing the sternal bone of a bird in the air. If the bone fell into the convex part it was male, on the contrary female.[53]

In addition to using divination methods to determine the sex of the unborn child, people also sought star-advisors after babies were born to understand the potentials or challenges that may face the baby:

In Villanova Monteleone when a child was born a man was called, Tiu Antiogu who had the task of looking at the sky to see if that birth had taken place under a good star or not.[54]

At first glance, these practices might seem impossibly inaccurate to us outsiders. After all, these are types of traditions are usually shrugged off as mere superstitions and not taken seriously by people who don't use them. However, each of the villages who have used these rituals traditionally found they worked for them as well as for their ancestors. Most of them were already in use when Romans began documenting the world around them, and they were considered already ancient at that time in history.

Divination traditions are found all over Italy and her islands, where they are part of a larger cohesive body of traditions which have a consistency of method and result, not only within each individual method, but also between various cures, divination methods, rituals and magic. For example, the spit shape divination: if a mostly circular spit shape is pointed on one side to make the impression of a face wearing a hat, this refers to a male child. So then when this same shape is formed by oil in water used to diagnose and cure **il malocchio** it also indicates a male is responsible for sending the envy that caused **il malocchio.**

Divination methods, cures, and protective magic focused on babies form the largest body of rituals.

"The religious practices; divination and magical practices of propitiatory and apotropaic character, at the crucial moment of childbirth, multiplied."[55]

MOTHERS OF GOD, FEMALE DIVINITY

Italian Magic: Secret Lives of Women

The role of midwives in agricultural communities was not just to assist during the actual birth but also to: use sympathetic magic, to invoke female saints and divinities during challenging childbirths, to care for the mother and baby after the birth with ritual magic and food, to care for the baby using procedures credited with "making the baby." Midwives have their own traditional knowledge, passed down orally to their successors.

In some villages, midwives have been known to help birth most of the babies in their own communities, often with the assistance of their own daughters whom they trained in the midwifery traditions. Many of these traditions were already in use during Roman times when life was being documented by writers, and they continued to be practiced long after the Romans had gone. In other words, this magic, these rituals, and these secrets of nature used by women are much older than Roman traditions. And, they are traditions of non-nobles.

> *"When human nature seems to have exhausted every possibility of overcoming one's limits (such as sterility) or when critical situations (the imminence of childbirth) leads one to turn to divine Providence in search of help."* 56

While women in rural areas relied on each other and their own selves for the operations and care during and after birth process, they firstly rely on and invoke the Divine Feminine through secret prayers that invite her presence into every ritual: from fertility to conception through the birth and into the protection of the child's life. These rituals are traditions handed down through generations on earth, assisted from generations of Divinely Feminine Saints and Goddesses and helpers in the spirit world. Depending on where these communities were located and the dynamic of the social environment, the names and functions of the feminine divinities were adapted. Among elderly generations also, the names of female spirits and divinities are less important than their function.

This is one of the KEYS to rural Italian MAGIC.

In Italy, there is a rich, long history of feminine spirit guides and divinities reaching into the earthly lives of poor women during their daily life chores for the purpose of reconnecting them with knowledge that can better their lives. Oral traditions began in this way, as the Lineage healer cures, but throughout Italy's social and religious changes, connections were lost and feminine communities were broken apart. So, the lineage of goddesses responded time and again in various forms, especially for women outside of Lineage families. They appeared as the Bona Dea, the Signora del Gioco, Donne di Fuora, as Madonnas and female saints and as many more.

Where the church's oppression and abuses and other socio-economic restrictions affected women, these female spirits passed down sacred knowledge, knowledge that was not accessible to women in any other way, such as herbal knowledge, cures, magical means of protection, surviving in sexual autonomy, activating natural fertility rites, and more.

MOTHERS OF GOD: Female Divinity

These particular experiences tended to happen outside closed or remote communities, to women disconnected from family lineages living in bigger villages or cities in Sicily; in cities like Naples, Milan, and Volterra…and onward, wherever the assistance was needed. Within remote agricultural communities, in contrast, they kept their lineages and traditions maintained, being deeply embedded in their valleys, mountain tops and farmlands. Most excitingly, all these experiences happened outside temple walls.

While you can still feel the presence of Goddesses in many of these ancient temple sites, outside of special ceremonies reserved for noble families, the Goddesses were busy making themselves appear to average women, not in the image of glamorous ladies nor fierce huntresses but looking like average women, reportedly a bit more beautiful, and with a treasure trove of ancient wisdom. In this way they could approach average women who were in need of assistance to improve the quality of their lives without scaring them.

This relatability and down-to-earth-like-magic-in-plain-sight is reflected in the people who hold the lineages of curing traditions in Italy and among secret groups like Benandanti: the connections they each have with the spirit world makes sense within their paths: how divinities appear, the forms goddesses take, the knowledge presented to them during their experiences and what they do with it forms a cohesive body of holistic knowledge that comes together on a grander scale, but it's been divided into digestible and separate paths for the purpose of usability and comprehensibility. And, it's the spirits: the helping Spirit Ladies who clearly have arranged this.

> *The confidentiality of the past, the same that required the intervention of a midwife and not of a male assistant in childbirth, advised the woman to address the female saints rather than the male saints".* 57

Some might be tempted to dismiss this as syncretism, but it would not be accurate. And while there are goddesses being hidden under Madonnas, as to which ones…remember that the Romans commercialized goddesses and even remodeled them into warriors and huntresses, completely changing their identities and even names from what they were before. Romans created marketable and streamlined versions of goddesses who mostly served to support male war directives in the way they used gods to support emperor propaganda campaigns. So they adopted the idea of natural spirit beings and made them more fictional. As a result, Lineage healers and secret groups don't relate to most of them as being real at all, and if they are embraced, it's not in the Roman way, but in the earlier historical versions. So as to why the Madonnas and female saints are embraced in rural magic:

With all these daily magic rituals and traditions that looks like witchery….
Why the Madonnas?
Why female saints?
Think: SYMPATHETIC MAGIC
Think: HOMEOPATHIC CURES
Think: RELATABILITY
If you can look beyond the style these traditions seem to be packaged within and

Italian Magic: Secret Lives of Women

look to their roots, with all of these practices, everything makes coherent sense:

LIKE CURES LIKE
and
LIKE HELPS LIKE

The female saints and Madonnas work in this way for women in rural communities. While finding the female Saints mixed with magic can be confusing to some who have escaped oppressive religions and who dislike the syncretized aspects of these practices, make no mistake: the technical reality is that these rituals are performed in partnership with Divinely Feminine beings and the results are miraculous.

It may be helpful to look at the saints invoked by rural women as a tangible type of spirit guide for people in environments who don't have a psychic language nor access to spiritual concepts in a broader sense and who are heavily watched by others, such as in communities where there is a constant vigil by locals against evil witches and simultaneously a heavy church tradition presence and a social necessity for conformity. For those who think that rural magic is just catholic religion traditions with some paganism sprinkled it's necessary to mention that the church did condemn these same "syncretized" women healers as heretics during the Inquisition period for using prayers to cure!

FEMALE SAINTS

A widespread belief by rural women is that the sainted women were once women just like them, who suffered and struggled and survived childbirth and other daily life events that nevertheless placed their lives on the edge of life and death who, above all, continue to live after their souls separate from their fleshy bodies. The stories about saints are generally sad and tragic: most female saints had horrible lives: they were often misunderstood before being sainted, they were oppressed in a way or another or suffered abuse, and yet while on earth they held fast to their faith. In a sort of reward, they acquired superpowers after death; powers that had something to do with their suffering which became strengths that they now used to help those still living on earth. It's like the idea of a goddess-becoming: living the life experience, suffering, and then acquiring knowledge that comes from passing into the big-picture understanding of spirit world.

MOTHERS OF GOD: Female Divinity

For example, Saint Rita, born Rita Lotti in 1381. Her marriage was arranged by her parents to an older man with whom she had her first baby at age 12. He was abusive, but apparently through her faith over time she cured him of his temperament. There is also a legend about her early childhood where, as an infant, bees would swarm around her, particularly moving in and out of her mouth without injuring her. This, along with receiving a sort of stigmata on her forehead after having a visionary experience, she was considered to be a woman of "feminine genius, by living life intensely in both physical and spiritual motherhood" [58] who was sainted after death.

> *"...her condition of bride and mother that makes women feel like one of them, undoubtedly very high, but doesn't change the fact that she was a mother who knows all the sweet hopes and fears of pregnancy, the birth pangs, the joy of holding her children to breast and giving them the abundance of her milk... a [...] holy protector of childbirth."* [59]

It should be noted here, that although Santa Rita's story is embedded in Catholicism the legend of the bees swarming around her is an older attribute of many mother abundance goddesses such as Ecate/Hekate, Diana, and Cibele to name a few. One of Diana's names is "Diana Mellifica" meaning the Diana of the Honeybees, and one of Ecate's names is "Bombo", meaning bumblebee. Priestesses of early goddesses represented as a Queen Bee were named "Melissae". This history is so much more detailed that can be included here, and is a valuable connection between the significance of the Great Mother Goddess, her representations, her relationships with various types of priestesses.

EXAMPLES OF MADONNAS AND FEMALE SAINTS AND THE FEMININE REALMS THEY ARE CALLED UPON TO PROTECT AND ASSIST WITH:

Pregnancy	Childbirth	Milk
Santa Cristina	Santa Cristina	Santa Cristina
Sant'Elena	Santa Rita	Santa Rita
Madonna del Parto	Madonna Dolori	Madonna del Latte
Santa Rita		Nursina
Santa Eufemia		Santa Scholastica
Santa Lucia		

Breast and Breastfeeding	Expulsion of Pacenta
Santa Cristina	Madonna Dolori
Madonna del Latte	

To find a Husband	For Guidance and Answered Prayers during Labor
Santa Rosa	Santa Lucia, Sant'Anna
Santa Cristina	

Italian Magic: Secret Lives of Women

MOTHERS OF GOD

The Madonnas are embraced as the Mother of God, all versions of the Supreme Being, which is definitely a more powerful position of creation than God himself. As a result all over Italy images of the Mother of God are placed in public places. Even if those public places are nestled in nooks of a medieval villages, such as Triora, Italy, where San Bernardino left his graffiti throughout the village, images of the Madonna are found overriding images of a male god. And, in these secret communities of women, the spirit guides they invoke for protection and healing are all feminine: the female saints and the Madonnas and Goddess relevant to personal connections.

The three critical phases of the fertility cycle of women, could not but rely on the patron saints who assisted the mother along a path bristling of dangers, allowing her to complete the pregnancy within the time prescribed by nature; childbirth to have a healthy child; to be able to breastfeed it to your breasts with abundant and healthy milk. Notice how these are only female figures - saints, in fact - delegated to ensure that the woman fulfills her function as the source of life. " [60]

ROMANIZED GODDESSES FROM VARIOUS TIME PERIODS AND IN VARIOUS REMODELED TRANSITIONS FROM THEIR ORIGINAL FORMS

Goddess of Childbirth	Breastfeeding and Weaning	Milk
Giunone Lucina	Edula	Iside
Cibele		
Cerere		
Bona		

Fertility Goddess	Protectress of Pregnant Women
Artemis	Amma Cerealis
Diana	Mater Matuta
Mater Matuta	Rumina
Cybele	

Marked End of Gestation Period	Kept Witches Away
Nona, Decima	Carna

Guided Fate of Child	Goddess of Childbirth Rituals
Fortuna Genitalis	Levana

Protectress of Newborns	Walked Behind Baby During First Steps
Intercidona	Abeona

Cradle Protection, Removed il Malocchio
Cunina

MOTHERS OF GOD: Female Divinity

In our contemporary experience many things that feel natural to us may seem strange to people in rural areas regardless of whether religion is involved, such as how spiritual practices are organized: self-made groups comprised of people who are not family nor neighbors who gather to reenact spiritual myths, hierarchies of learning levels and the rewards of "attunements" and titles such as "high priestess" etc. Other differences between rural spiritual magical traditions and contemporary magical traditions (such as Wicca and ceremonial magic is that the contemporary versions: work with spirits optionally, spirits are often invoked in a unidirectional way, in that prayers may be read, poems and altars may be dedicated, but the live-action communication back-and-forth is not necessarily a part, and interaction in the form of active co-creation with the spirit world often depends on the development of psychic and mediumistic abilities of the practitioner who holds no familial legacy.

Contemporary healing modalities may also seem strange to rural people, being that they are taught outside the family and that they are like school where homework and exercises are prescribed, books are read, and certification is granted to the "graduate". And yet, for many people in contemporary society, they are the only option to be of service as a healer.

While magical and curative traditions enjoy different cultural expressions, looking beyond the "style" makes the foundations of each become clearer, regardless of how the traditions have developed. Very generally speaking we can say traditions fall into natural shamanic origins and conceptual synthetic ones. Neither "natural" nor "synthetic" are used competitively here, they are labels that refer to the marked differences in development between the two general categories.

Specifically focusing on rural lineage traditions/mother magic, it becomes easier to reveal why rural traditions have little in common with Wicca and middle period magic and more commonalities with the oral traditions of shamanism, including both rituals practiced by shaman and rituals practiced by communities where shaman are found. The foundational connection to shamanism, beyond many exactly parallel traditions are these:

- *shamans have played an essential role in the defense of the psychic integrity of the community. They[...] combat not only demons and disease, but also black magicians".* [61]
- shaman in Siberia and central Asia have separate masculine and feminine traditions, relevant here are initiations and spirit helpers just for mothers and their magic and cures to protect and heal babies.
- rural Italian traditions have traditions just for mothers, including feminine spirit assistance and instruction, magic and cures just for babies and mothers.
- rural roles of healers are to combat psychic illness caused by negative spirits, to combat spells and curses made by witches of black magic.
- both have a lifetime role of clearing away evil that manifests in different ways.

Italian Magic: Secret Lives of Women

SHAMANISM

In shamanism* it's the spirits who "make" the shaman (as in, choosing and teaching) and who inform the community of traditions. Shaman are taught by their spirits how to use basic supplies located in their own environments along with specific procedures including words and actions for bringing balance back to health or solving other problems of the soul in ways that are applicable to the needs of the community.

Rituals of this type found in rural Italy, central Asia and Siberia use symbols to express parallels between earth, the spirit world, and the means for ascent. They are all symbols of nature, such as trees and birds. The tools used for curing or other rituals, are often used up: destroyed, burned or in some other natural way transformed from their original state. In contrast, patriarchal paganisms, being based on power and commerce, replaced nature with synthetic representations of nature. Tools are ornate, decorative, designed by human beings and not accessible to the average person (such as made of gold, historically) and cost money to obtain.

Some historical examples of natural versus synthetic:

+ spiritual work in a cave versus spiritual work in a man-made stone temple that emulates a cave except that it's a perfect square

+ using menstrual blood as a representative of regenerative energy of the goddess versus men killing a bull and using its blood in regenerative rituals

+ using a household ceramic cup or bowl versus using a gold chalice

+ providers of magic and cures working in solitude, chosen by spirits versus providers of magic elected by other human beings during hierarchical training

In the rural rituals, there are no certificates of award to the operators, there are no tools of usage on display, there is no pomp and circumstance, no signs of economic success. The rural healers and sorceresses look like everyone else in the neighborhood: they don't wear special clothing signifying they practice magic nor do they wear robes or other reenactment garb when performing cures or protection magic. Like the **Signora del Gioco** and **Donne di Fuori**, they look like an average person in the community, a bit more beautiful, it has been said, nevertheless they look like women.

Therefore, the rituals, initiations and traditions are often called superstitious and shrugged off as dumb, ramshackle, silly, useless, handmade and therefore having no economic value. After all, these rituals look impenetrable in that they can't be sold in a book nor a grimoire aside from descriptions since it is the spirits who activate the cures

---

*specifically here referring to shamanism of central Asia and Siberia and ...of which there are many groups with slightly different traditions operating on a common foundation, and whose traditions find themselves being used in rural Italy (mainland and islands) and vice-versa.

and magical results, and it's the spirits who pull people out of their bodies for astral travel and take them, as spirits, to important places. In contrast, the Roman cults are looked to as powerful and mysterious, having left behind glorious landmarks and high-quality, valued material tools and objects of veneration, made of gold and precious stones along with other material goods and financially valuable assets.

In agricultural life, everything is only partially tangible and fully transient, just like life. Rural people did spend money on **cimaruta** amulets for the protection of their babies (in some places) and other jewelry amulets, but in terms of altars and tools, more than anything they were the basic tools of daily life.

While it's the rural magical curative traditions that have been banned by the church and its healers targeted in the witch hunts and whose midwives were the fantastical focus of the alleged evil witch stories perpetuated by the church, these traditions have no relation to contemporary witchcraft like Wicca nor what the fantastical idea of a witch is, and they only bear a passing connection to some of the various paganism practices. This has nothing to do with religion (as syncretism) and everything to do with the natural root of the traditions. However, they do share parallel rituals, spirit helper groups, and community traditions with shaman and shaman communities of Siberia and central Asia. It's this shamanism of Siberia and central Asia (which has many expressions: male shaman, female shamanesses, each with many subgroups and differing duties) with which rural Italy and her islands have identical practices, beliefs, spirit helpers group systems and even names of divinities.

While it's beyond the scope of this book to mention all the comparisons and parallels between rural Italy and specific groups of central Asia and Siberia, the ones touched upon in this book are related to women and their feminine spirit helpers as: Supreme Being and traditions of ascent (astral travel), The Great Mother of Animals, feminine group spirits for mothers and their babies in practices of magical protection and cures, transmission of inheritance and community roles in death rituals. Of these feminine beings we find the Italian legacy of **La Signora del Gioco**, Demetra and Persephone/Ceres and Proserpina, Ladies of the Hunt, **Donne di Fuora**, **Patruneddi**, the female Saints and Madonnas and their magic walnut tree of Benevento, philosophy of illness being due to negative spirits, and a prevalence of spirits and their affect on the psychic realm. That these traditions are found in patriarchal Italian societies and among catholic religion is a common factor and something shared with shamanism.

The syncretized aspect of these secret worlds of women, whether the lineage healers or daily sacred magic mothers, can be a turn-off for many modern people who realize the church is anti-women, anti-feminine, and anti-motherhood, and whose purpose has been to usurp ancient veneration of feminine regeneration power by creating a male god and claiming he is father parent of all, even though he has no womb and no female partner. The only feminine image in catholic religion is Mary, the virgin who was essentially raped by male god and forced to have his baby: a religious story which has had vastly negative implications for women who continually find themselves under male rule and masculine abuse of their bodies. And yet...

> *"Generally shamanism coexists with other forms of magic and religion".* 62

Italian Magic: Secret Lives of Women

More than the rituals and prayers and magical recipes, this group of spirit world feminine helpers is what's truly significant about Italy's indigenous traditions: female providers whose focus has been to help women in daily life as caretakers and to reconnect them to wisdom when it's been taken from them or when their lineages have been broken. We find this same existence of female divinities reserved for women in shamanism also. For example, in the patriarchal structure of the Turko-Tatars and Siberian shaman, the female divinities *"are reserved for women, their spheres being childbirth and children's diseases."*[63] And while spirit helpers are not limited to mothers nor female identified people at all, rural Italy's traditions reflect this relationship with the female divinities.

Other commonalities shared between rural Italian inherited traditions and community rituals and shamanism of central Asia and Siberia are: mastery over fire, magical flight, techniques of ecstasy specifically where the soul leaves the body, and most central to the existence of shaman and rural healers is their personal relationship with the healing spirits and the spirits who teach them during astral flight. This is also where Italian rural mother magic differs from middle period and contemporary magic. *"In fact, we need only define the shaman's relation to his the shaman's relation to helping spirits"*[64] and *the shaman's relation to "spirits"* [65] in general, being that the helping spirits are the creators of the traditions and they help banish the negative spirits who cause illness in both shamanism and rural Italian traditions.

While methods of rural cures are found in similar forms all across Italy and her islands, each cure is unique to the healer, and it is common to find several healers in a village who cure the same illness slightly differently. In *"shamanic healing: every medicine man is a healer, but the shaman employs a method that is his and his alone".* [66] and their work together *"to defend human beings against diseases and evil spirits"* as enabled to do so by their Supreme Being who came down to earth... [67] is the same arrangement as rural Italian curative traditions from **the signora del gioco, donne di fuora,** Madonnas and hidden goddesses.

POWER OF WORDS AND VOICE

The relationship rural women have with the spirit world can be revealed in various prayers for ascent and astral flight, prayers for cures, and prayers to the female divinities and the moon, and prayers for support during birth. They are not so different from prayers or efforts used in contemporary meditation and healing modalities.

> *"Prayers and invocations became more heartfelt in the imminence of child-birth and during labor. In that critical phase of the reproductive cycle, one provided a picture of the saint before whom a candle was lit, or an image to be placed on the belly of the woman in labor. If the birth presented any difficulty, she tried to make a mass say to the patron saint of the mother."* [68]

MOTHERS OF GOD: Female Divinity

And yet, prayers are not just for motherhood, not only for cures, but also for ascent and astral travel, and are coded with shamanic directives that can also be viewed through a spiritualist lens. The language and psychic procedures for ascent are essentially the same, they are just in bit different in their styles.

The Cult of Sant'Anna (Saint Anne, Mother of the Virgin Mary) was aimed at propitiating motherhood, and was practiced especially by pregnant women and women who had infertility issues. She was also invoked as the protectress of pregnancy and delivery of women and was a helper of poor and oppressed people, often alongside Anna Perenna. Anna Perenna is a slightly different "type" of spirit world helper than the Sant'Anna because she was never embodied in the flesh on earth. She was also embraced by the Romans and invoked for revenge magic, a very different type of magic than is found in the mother magic of rural Italy.

The invocation of female saints and Madonnas is activated through inherited prayers and tone of voice. Prayers and invocations are used in repetitions of 3, 7 and 9, the more significant and common numbers being 3 and 9. The power of the words is in the fact that they are agreements and invitations between the spirit world and the earthly one: saying these traditional prayers are invitations for the divine feminine to channel through the user to whomever needs the energy. It's also notates a relationship of trust: trusting and believing in someone greater than the self. Same type of prayers used in contemporary times to connect with spirit guides and helpers.

AUTHOR NOTE:
The best way to understand if invocations or prayers work for you is to find an already created prayer or invocation and simply try to read it aloud, making sure to be aware of any emotions or sensations you feel in response to doing so. I have personally never had any interest in Madonnas nor female saints, and especially not male ones, but as I read some of these prayers aloud I was filled with intense emotions and tears burst forth. The divine feminine spirits connect to us often through intense emotions, using them to show us a reconnection has been made, even if the emotions brings tears or feels like grief. Divine feminine beings feel emotions too, and many of them have been forgotten, so naturally the emotions they may send to you contain all the joys and sadness of being disconnected and then reunited again after so much time has passed. So, the emotions can be a way for spirit to say "hello, we are connecting you to something that is a conduit for you." The prayers published here are decommissioned prayers, given to the documenters after they were retired from usage

Prayer for Healing

Madonna, ch'io vi vengo a visitare,
So' sempre l'urtima venine,
me ne vergogno piu' di comparine.
Davanti a voi mi vengo a 'nginocchiare,
Madonna, se mi voli perdonare. 69

Madonna, whom I come to visit,
I'm always the last one to come,
I'm more ashamed of it that I seem.
I come to kneel in front of you,
Madonna, please take me in flight and forgive me.

50

Italian Magic: Secret Lives of Women

Prayer to Santa Rita

Tu sposa, madre e vedova,
la donna del perdono,
ottiene aiuto e grazie, per chi e' nell' abbandono.
In malattie incurabili, nei drammi della vita,
ottenga pace intrepida chi invoca santa Rita. 70

You marry, mother and widow,
the woman of forgiveness,
gets help and thanks, for those who are in abandonment.
In incurable diseases, in the tragedies of life,
may those who invoke Saint Rita obtain intrepid peace.

Portate fiori alla dea; a lei piacciono i fiori e le piante...
Tu, o Lucina, ci hai dato la luce!
Tu, esaudisci la preghiera della partoriente! 71

Bring flowers to the goddess; she likes flowers and plants...
You, O Lucina, you gave us the light !
You, hear the prayer of the woman in labor!

Prayer to Lucina for support during Birth

Sii clemente, Lucina,
con le madri in attesa
libera dolcemente l'utero dal feto
giunto a maturazione.

Be merciful, Lucina
with expectant mothers,
gently free from the uterus
the fetus who's arrived to maturation. 72

MOTHERS OF GOD: Female Divinity

Prayer to Diana for ecstatic flight to the moon on horseback

Luna luna, paraluna,
Para mese, uve sese?
-In funtana-
Sa Eirana, s'ebba mia
Mi ch'esportet
Da inoche a Baronia

Moon, moon, hidden moon
hidden month, where are you?
In the spring
Erodias , transport me
on my horse to Baronia. 73

For the purpose of supporting a mother during labor as a method of prevention or cure, whether to ask for a smooth labor, or to improve difficult labor, physical objects representing the Mother of God are used to attract her energy to the scene. This can be likened to the way some people use gemstones and goddess statues during healing sessions and in rituals. These rituals invoking the Madonnas are always used in combination with secret prayers.

MADONNINE, small statues of Madonnas, are used as actual Midwife tools.

Italian Magic: Secret Lives of Women

Method: Midwives place an image of Sant'Anna on the belly of a woman in labor while reciting secret prayers asking for her help similar to this prayer:

"Sant'Anna mia, aiutalar".

"My Saint Anna, help her". [75]

Method: Midwives set a photo of a Madonna with a lighted candle in front of it, repeating prayers.

LOOKING BEYOND CULTURAL EXPRESSION
Into The Red Thread Of Connection

In the Mediumship trainings and teachings of spiritualism, the belief is that there are different types of guides in the spirit world who help us on earth such as: guides for healing, guides for philosophical explorations, guardian guides, cultural guides and more. Much like the existence of groups of guides in found in Siberian and central Asian shamanism, the belief in spiritualism is that the channeler attracts guides-in-spirit with similar interests as themselves, and also that intention can be used to attract specific guides to help solve a particular need. The guides can: join a channeler in creativity, help someone heal themselves, connect them with scientific knowledge, etc. Ultimately the guides choose if they will approach a seeker or make an agreement to heal through a person.

Among the healers in Italy living down dirt roads, within the walls of winding medieval villages and in country homes, likely most of them have never even heard of gemstones nor practices such as "raising one's vibration" nor the terms "grounding" nor even "channeling", but there is an absolutely palpable presence channeling through them when they are healing someone and performing daily sacred magic.

Working with spirits to help others requires a sense of great responsibility and humbleness. In the region of Val d'Aosta, where they call this partnership with the spirit world "the Secret," the belief is that a sincere desire to help must be present. It's a great mothering, no matter what gender person is holding these traditions, and they believe it is their duty to help all who as for it.

MAIDEN, MOTHER, CRONE

Different phases of womanhood are regarded as having different powers in rural Italian traditions, defined as: virgin, pregnant woman, mother and mother of twins. Virgin girls were considered to have the concentrated and potent power of prayer, and sometimes they were payed to make processional prayer walks (sometimes on their knees, a ritual called **ginocchioni** in Roccatamburo 76 to the church to pray for an easy birth. While this may sound superstitious as a small action, it's instead connected to much broader spiritual belief regarding chakras.

Chakras can be defined here very simply as energy centers that work like our physical bodily organs. Our liver, heart, and intestines for example, move fluids through our bodies to maintain health through various operations. Chakras are part of our soul body, and they regulate the flow of energy in a similar way that physical organs move matter. The first two chakras (located near our reproductive organs and just below our belly buttons but in our spirit body) contain energy that supports our daily life concerns about safety, security home, sexuality, creativity, sensuality among other details.

These chakras, the root and sacral, can be concentrated into non-sexual expression as creativity or energetic/spiritual connection, just as they can be focused into sexual expression and physical connection. Therefore, the belief that a non-sexually active female can have a great spiritual power is not far-fetched, but it is individualized of course. An Altaic shaman also wears *7 bells on his collar that were the seven virgins' voices calling the spirits.* 77

> *In Rocchetta di Spoleto, when the birth was difficult and labor pains were longer than expected, we asked seven virgin girls* **verginĕlle** *to go and pray to Madonna del Verde, whose image is located near the local stream.* 78

Virgin girls were also called upon to pray for the gravely ill and to pray for protection over babies to keep **il malocchio** away, and there were special procedures for each situation.

> *In ancient times, virginity was in itself magical power, for example, think of the Persian concept of "mäga", which denotes the intact power of virgin and uncontaminated primeval [...] both the Greek mageia, "magic" and the Latin "magic" descend from the Persian. The magical virginity, on the other hand, is especially focused on the accumulation of power in the person of the magician.* 79

Italian Magic: Secret Lives of Women

Likewise, other states of feminine regenerative energy, such as pregnancy, offer other curative possibilities, as do the physical bodies of mothers of twins, the vagina itself, urine from mothers, and the old lady "crones: The pregnant mother, or the potential for pregnancy in women, is considered a healing force, an *active element of therapy: the fruitfulness of which woman is endowed, a peculiarity understood as a positive power, a generator of life and a regenerator of health.* [80]

> In Umbria, *it was believed that any pregnant woman had the power to cure back pain. For the treatment of lumbago the patient had to be bypassed by 7 pregnant women, one at a time,* [81] *or they must bypass the patient 3 times repeating the operation for 3 consecutive days.* [82]

> *The symbolism inherent in the number three or seven, or the times when the woman must pass over the patient, is also endowed with auspicious meaning, both being the numbers associated with the idea of completeness and totality.* [83]

> *To cure abdominal pain, a mother who had given birth to twins had to climb over the sick man lying on the ground passing over him three times, to cure the back pains, a mother of twins leaps over the sickness.* [84]

An ancient cure for Eryspelas, a fiery skin condition caused by a bacterial infection also known as **fuoco di sant'Antonio** employs the energy of 3 women participants in 3 different stages of feminine energy:

> *"Abbot Bresciani testified to this in reporting a therapeutic ritual still in use in his time:"to ward off the erysipelas and certain pernicious fevers it was necessary that 3 women, 1 very young, 1 middle-aged and one in old age and with some white hair they returned to a crossroads* [85] and performed a specific ritual where they *made some circles with charcoal on the ground and marked you* [the patient] *for the crosses of sant'Andrea* [a way to bind the illness] . *Afterwards they invoke the souls of those who perished from the underworld because they rush to their aid and take away they suffering.* [86]

A belief pervasive in rural Italian culture that finds its match in Peruvian Shamanism is that of menstrual blood being "devoid of life" and therefore a sort of bad luck. This belief may sound in antithesis of all the rituals that honor the female body's ability to be a doorway to the universe.

As regards the general concept of menstrual blood, it was considered impure and contaminating, charged with a nefarious power. [87] *The character of impurity and consequent negativity associated with the blood of the cycle derive from the fact that it is infecund blood not generating life.* [88]

And so other than the celebration of the first period bleed, menstruating women were not wanted near growing crops, fresh plants, near food preparations like cheese and bread because the menstrual blood was considered a loss. This, along with the community watch over young women to make sure they don't lose their virginity outside of marriage are common in agricultural communities where the cycles of life are held in a certain regard.

Regarding the sacrifice of the black hen - used in Valnerina [Umbria] for menarchia and childbirth - the choice of victim regards the relationship between hen and motherhood, expressed by the symbolism of the egg and the symbolic meanings connected to the latter also in the field of cosmogony. [89]

40 days after birth the mother will be considered restored and ready to leave her house for the first time. Prior to this, she must remain in bed for the first 9 days after birth and is considered unclean. During this time the midwives or comare will take the baby to be baptized, often in a dress made in part from part from the mother's wedding dress material.

Italian Magic: Secret Lives of Women

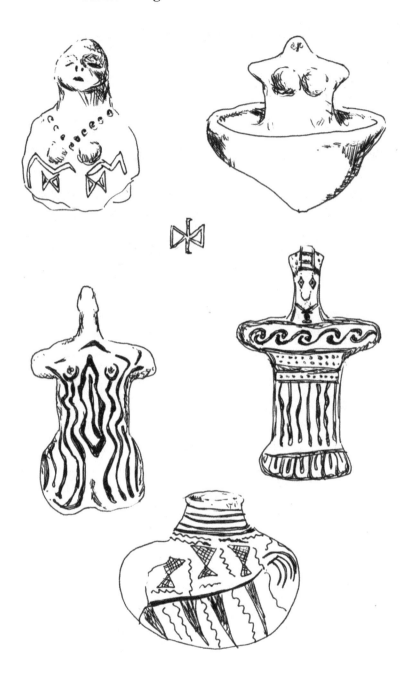

Redrawn and sourced from "The Language of the Goddess" by Marija Gimbutas.
Top row L-r: S. Italian Neolithic near Foggia c. 5700-5300 M.C.; water bowl with breasts from
Romania 4500-4300 B.C.. Small middle double axe butterfly from Bohemia c. 5000 B.C.
Lower row l-r: snake Goddess, Anatolian Neolithic 6000-6500 B.C.; snake Goddess Greece from 6th cent. B.C.
Bottom: Sicilian Copper Age, E of Syracuse 3500-3000 B.C.

SYMPATHETIC MAGIC
to prevent Umbilical Cord Complications
and
SYMPATHETIC RITUAL
for the Placenta and Caul

The connections among women, water, and serpents used in symbolism and spirituality are natural ones. In those realms, they are considered to be positive, life-affirming connections. Who would better know the force, power, purpose and grief of loss of fluids than a woman, whose body is a source of the most important fluids:

menstrual blood (with its regenerative stem cells),
milk (complete nutrition for babies),
and **vaginal fluids** (like a river's waters, maintaining the health of the womb cradle of civilizations. These fluids also tell time.

The other fluid, fluid of the eyes, is one that will be explained in the CURES section, but it is related to these feminine fluids that are conceptualized in magic.

In rural Italy, where women are deeply connected to their bodies and the babies that are birthed through their bodies, there exist many rituals of a sympathetic nature to preserve the function of the Umbilical cord and to prevent its entanglement.

THE NECK of pregnant mothers is an area of the body that is protected from tangles during pregnancy. The belief is that any tangles around the neck would then, in sympathetic parallel, cause tangles to the umbilical cord and possible strangulation to the fetus. In many rural communities therefore, pregnant women removed necklaces, including amulets, during pregnancy, so that the chain has no possibility of being tangled.

Based on this sympathetic magical concept, in Valnerina (the Black Valley in the region of Umbria) threads, cords, and necklaces represent the analogue equivalent of the umbilical cord. For this reason, knotting or twisting them, turning them around the neck or passing them under or overtaking them are dangerous precedents. 90

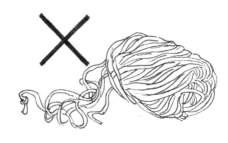

AVOID Tangles
AVOID cords around the neck
AVOID knots

In Perugian territory, to avoid the danger of fetal strangulation, pregnant women avoid carrying around the next skeins of yarn or knotted corbels. 91 as well as sewing thread and needles.

In other areas, to prevent the idea of entanglement of the umbilical cord and the intestines of the fetus, pregnant women avoid weaving on the loom or working with tangled fiber.

In other areas, women avoid crossing legs and arms and fingers and also keep wrapped wires away from their necks. Likewise, they avoid walking under ropes, tangled branches, crossing over hedges, or passing over and under anything that represents a barrier.

AVOID weaving. AVOID thoughts of illness or worry about the health of the baby so as not to attract it.

THE UMBILICAL CORD

The Umbilical cord has been used conceptually in spiritual symbolism as an expression of a conduit between the Divinity's knowledge and human beings. Shamanism practices essentially all involve umbilical cords, conduits, and messengers in both physical forms and in their spirit world parallel form.

In Italy's shamanism, the tree is the conduit: a physical representation of the process of channeling, whereby the Goddess transmits knowledge to women. With its branches reaching upwards and its roots reaching into the earth, the parallels between a body rooting and reaching is simple, and in Italy the Divine Feminine is the consciousness who repeatedly speaks to women through trees, "reaching down to earth" while they "raise their vibration upwards" in the process of channeling.

The tree as axis mundi is not a new concept, and while there have been masculinized

Italian Magic: Secret Lives of Women

tree cults reported in Italian history, the original ones were feminine-centric. Italy's walnut tree of Benevento is one such tree who earned a reputation of being a meeting place for shaman **janare** witches. Though folk tales and church-created myths speak of a devil dancing and romancing women around the tree, in this feminine tree cult there are no men; not as leaders, not as shaman. The tree is a conduit for the many goddesses who support women in their growth towards autonomy. It's the umbilical cord from the Great Mother to all her daughters on earth.

In the way the umbilical cord is a two-way conduit for a baby (bringing in oxygenated blood and taking our nutrient-deficient blood,) it also transmits other information and sensations from the mother's body. The cord opens a conversation between mother and her developing child.

The tree serves this same purpose. Not only does it act as an amplifier of channeled information between the spirit world and earthly one, but in Italy the tree is the Great Goddess Mother's conduit on earth where she manifested herself in vision to gather women and teach them as a group ways to improve the quality of their lives: about cleanliness and organization, the secrets of plants and curing traditions and divinations. It was also a group gathering place for women pulled out of their bodies into astral flight by the Goddess. The Goddess speaks through the trees. These same practices are found in Siberian shamanism.

While the concepts of ascension and astral flight are reenacted by shaman through climbing trees and ladders, the ascension to receptivity of knowledge coming from a higher source is an actual transaction that takes place between mother and her developing fetus through the umbilical cord.

The umbilical cord is also associated with water and serpents. These associations are natural ones, as they are related to the physical parts of the female body. For example, the water content of the human umbilical cord is 88.9% for term cords and 91.9% for preterm cords. [92] The cord itself is a channel, it moves information and vital nutrients back and forth.

Water as a conduit for vital information within the body at even a cellular level is explained in detail in author Dr. Barbara Wren's book "Cellular Awakening" in which she describes how "messages from the macrocosm are transported, via water, through the cell membrane into the microcosm." These messages basically inform the cell when to exchange sodium, potassium, calcium and magnesium in and out of the cells, based on a daily schedule affected by the sun's rising and the moon's appearance. A body dehydrated of water experiences illness due to changes in the structure of the cell membrane that impair the cell's ability to receive operational information vital to their functions.

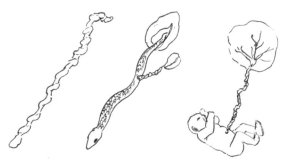

Umbilical cord to baby: delivers information and nutrients, Serpent: delivers information from physical world to spirit world, Water: delivers information to body's cells, necessary to sustain life. Both baby serpents and human babies have a similar (but not identical) system of nutrient transference. Trees have a have similar system of gathering nutrients and transferring information from roots to tree branch tips and what grows there; "ladders".

Likewise, the spiritual serpent is associated with the conduit-like transmission of information. Serpents appear to initiates of specific shamanism traditions in dreams, crossing from one side of the river to another in these dreams, indicating they are messengers from the spirit world bringing messages to the shaman initiate. The serpents appear in slightly changed form in the dreams to indicate the shaman is at the completion of the initiation. The eyes of the serpent are an important part of the ritual, transferring information.

In her book "The Language of the Goddess", anthropologist Marija Gimbutas reports about this deep connection of serpents and water being represented in water vessels decorated with serpents, and therefore associated with the life-sustaining force of water which is vital to life. The shape of the serpent like that of a flowing river, coupled with its ability to shed its skin and regenerate new skin, and its assistance to mediums who learn how to be a conduit from the spirit world to the earthly one, it's also been used magically for purification purposes along with water. The serpent not only has a similar shape to the umbilical cord, but its babies are born in an egg and are attached to a yolk sack by umbilical cord. In Italy, the priestesses of the Goddess Iside (Isis) were known as serpents.

Both water and the serpent have been used conceptually time and again in various magical

and mystical practices. For the sake of this book and magical history, it's important to acknowledge where these concepts come from: they are modeled on nature. The Divine Feminine's expression of universal energy through nature (people, places, elements) is not hidden in concepts that are difficult to understand. Spiritual symbols are built on body parts of humans and animals and plants that have parts to play in such important roles as: birth, regeneration, transference of nurture and nutrition and knowledge through fluids, etc. These are natural processes we can observe on earth which tell us something about how the Divine Feminine energy works in the greater Universe and vice versa.

More specifically, they are related to each other, inseparable symbols of the Divine Feminine's ability to transfer knowledge and information from the spirit world to the earthly one, and in parallel, that the earthly mother transmits important knowledge from her body through the umbilical cord to her fetus. The conceptual use of these ideas comes from the female body.

Images ABOVE: Faces with eyes and mouth of the Goddess emphasized for their significance in protection and generating nurturing fluids of the divine feminine energy: water emanating from her eyes and mouth. Spit is used in the same way in rural Italian traditions.

IMAGE TO LEFT:
Interesting cross-section of the umbilical cord connecting baby to mother's placenta looks like a face, in a body part that is specifically for developing a fetus into a baby..a process taking place in the body of a woman, the goddess' parallel on earth

Before spirituality became patrilineal, water sources such as rivers, lakes, wells and fountains were all associated with the Divine Feminine's life-sustaining energy on earth, and they were often marked with breast-bearing menhirs, directing people towards a source or tributary of the Goddess Mother's gift.

A tradition carried on from these pre-patriarchal times can be found throughout Italy and her islands: in the valleys of rural towns, high on mountain peaks, in all the villages associated with witches and the witch hunts, there are rivers, lakes, and fountains marked with names of goddesses or images of Madonnas, along with witch stories. The traditions of honoring and marking these water sources as gifts from the Goddess are a continuum from Old Europe's breast-bearing menhirs that also marked water sources.

In Italy, this significant link between water, Goddesses, and her parallels (daughters on earth) has played out among women who do the laundry. **Lavatrici**, the Italian word for women who wash laundry, and who gathered at the fountains and rivers were also often **levatrici** midwives. Both of these words are found in rural witch stories. The connections among...

-women who gather at water sources to do their laundry,
-midwives who deliver babies,
-and witches

are not merely conceptual, and though it is believed by some that *"the water that is the fundamental substance of living matter, it is compared to the woman and the moon, both intense symbols of fecundity"*, [93] and that water and women are connected by the idea of life giving water and bodily fluids. That water is a conduit, one that opens a doorway to and from the spirit world, is an advantage taken by the female spirits who passed down knowledge to Italian women, and extraordinary documentations in Italy exist of women being given knowledge while at water sources, doing their daily life duties from the Goddess manifested as regular-looking women with slightly odd characteristics.

It is at these water sources that women often experienced reconnection to lost knowledge that historically has been passed down family lines as psychic-medium arts. The way women were reconnected, or we can say, the way they were given this information follows a pattern: at the wells and fountains where they were regularly doing their laundry an old woman, often known by the village, would be there also. Seemingly this "old woman" was always at the water source, and she was the source of knowledge.

In some villages she would be referred to as the "old woman witch": a grumpy, stand-offish old woman who was feared mostly because she was always depicted as being socially abrasive which was equated with an evil nature. Therefore, there were talks among neighbors that she must be a witch. No one seemed to know where she lived. Somehow she seemed to always be at the fountain or river or well. In other words, she was one of the "good ladies" like **Signora del Gioco** and the **donne di fuora**, the feminine spirits who serve this helpful purpose all across Italy during historical periods where women were cut off from the secrets of nature. In some stories there were several "helper women," and in some stories people were aware of what was taking place and referred to the presence as indeed a spirit. And then, fountains became a place women would meet under the moon before flying to the astral realm to meet with the Good Ladies, such as in Pitigliano, Tuscany.

These stories are common in small villages of northern Italy and even found in France. There are many traditions found in Valle D'Aosta, for example where not only a

Italian Magic: Secret Lives of Women

French dialect is spoken, but magic and curative traditions are found that exist on both sides of the border. It's not uncommon for similarities to bleed over Italy's borders and vice versa. But here we are not talking about the religions of the powers-that-be but rather rural traditions of European shamanism.

Shamanism, for example, is not a practice reserved for ritual moments: shamanism is a way of life and a practice of specific actions and beliefs that reflect the environment. The shaman is dependent on assistance from the spirit world. Witchcraft is something more conceptual and human-created and often uses traditions based on practices found in shamanism. Witchcraft is a collection of things and is defined in different ways by different people.

Shamanism is guided by spirits. Shaman are chosen by spirits, not humans. Shaman must serve a duty to help others improve daily life. While the shaman is taught actions and which tools to use and which particular words to say, these actions are based on working with a variety of specific spirits who are actually in control of whether or not the actions will give a result.

For example in contrast, modern witchcraft can instruct us to conceptualize these ideas and use the tools found in shamanism for magical rituals and the modern witch can make up the rest. It's like using art supplies in a different way than another artist. The human-made magic will have lots of detailed instructions about which tools to use, their colors, under which astrological sign a magical work should be done, how many candles/knots/herbs to use and the specific measurements and quantities and order of actions, depending on who created the spells and who's following who.

Rural Italian tradition, however, would tell us that it uses secret prayers which activates the borrowed power as it channels through the spirit-chosen person while they heal or perform magic. The work : the diagnosis, the cure (whether for physical ailment or psychic illness) is done mostly in the mind and absolutely in cooperation with the spirits who heal. The "healer" or "witch" person is less involved because the spirits do the work, and the cure is used the same way each time for each patient. This has no similarities to middle-period or contemporary magic and many with shamanism. There is also a very real pressure to keep certain workings of traditions secret. Healers don't trade their secrets.

And, this is how traditions are lost forever. They are not written down, and unless they are inherited by someone else, they cease to exist...that is, until and if the spirit creators of the magic and cures pass them down to human beings once again. These traditions were lost to some families during several societal shifts in Italy's history, and those breaks were always followed by assistance from the spirit world. The spirits are alive, so there's always a hope that their traditions will continue to be kept alive as well.

SYMPATHETIC MAGIC: Birth Rituals

Left:
The Fountain in Pitigliano, Tuscany, one of the many fountains where women took flight to the Night School.

Photos of a pagan temple in the center of Italy, originally dedicated to a Goddess. Inside is a natural spring that comes up from underground. The church tried to build on top of the original foundation but right before the opening ceremony the new structure began to crumble and fall.

In the early goddess culture of Italy, everything between heaven (Goddess's realm of energy) and earth (Goddess' physical realm manifested as nature, people, animals and children of the Goddess) is expressed through spiritual symbols which show parallel connections. Water on earth is parallel to the Goddess' ever-flowing energy in universe (the psychic stream). In the Great Mother Goddess' body-doubles on earth (women) the umbilical cord offers the same.

Italian Magic: Secret Lives of Women

Menstrual blood contains stem cells, scientifically recognized to have regenerative properties: the exact attribute of nature that is venerated in the many paganism practices (and the pre-pagan domestic Goddess culture too).

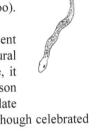

Being that regeneration of all forms of life and the ever present flow of life-sustaining energy of the Goddess was the nucleus of rural agricultural and early domestic Goddess cults in Italy and Old Europe, it was often symbolically venerated as menstrual blood, this is a logical reason why male mystery schools in Italy, such as the cult of Mithra, would emulate this specific blood. In the cult of Mitra, the ritual slaying of the bull, although celebrated as Mithra's conquering abilities, is a masculine reenactment of menstrual blood's release from the uterus.

It's well known that the bucranium (bull skull) has the same shape as the female reproductive organs, and the bull skull is known in Italy as one of the oldest symbols of the Goddess. In the cult of Mithra, this blood was celebrated as having regenerative powers. Subsequent traditions all over Italy venerating regeneration also took on the masculinized version of celebrating regeneration. Also, the christian church used this idea of regenerative blood and attributed its power to Jesus (a man without a womb).

Aside from blood's ability to offer life-supporting nutrients to fetuses, its parallel in the universe is the Goddess' power to sustain the life of consciousness after death of the physical body, which is honored in many Italian agricultural traditions in rituals that celebrate regeneration (of nature and of families) being that these people are intimately linked with these cycles on their farmlands. Life-after-death is also symbolized in the temples of Sardinia. Water offers the conduit for knowledge that sustains life.

The placenta and umbilical cord, deeply connected to the powers of blood and water, are therefore carefully and ritualistically taken care of in rural Italian traditions. The placenta, along with other parts of the body like fingernail clippings, hair, and spit, are carefully tucked away or discarded ritually to prevent damage being done to their owner by an envious person.

*"The umbilical cord has a huge importance for life that it is born
because it binds the mother to the child and, when it is severed, it*

must not fall into the hands of anyone: it could be used, like nails, hair and other parts of the body to the detriment of the ancient owner; and this for that famous principle of homeopathic magic for which the parts of one a person, even if separated, remain in a sympathetic relationship with him. 94

...it was therefore thrown into the fire, a purifying element or, scattered with oil and salt and wrapped in a strip of cloth....or buried at the foot of a tree." 95

The shape of the umbilical cord itself, with tube and veins spiraling, makes a natural serpentine shape. Not only does the serpent bear a similar shape to the umbilical cord and the winding river, but also its babies are born in an egg and are attached to a yolk sack by umbilical cord. While it's not the same function, the resemblance is remarkably similar, and it's easy to see the conceptual usage developed from these comparisons.

The placenta, from the point of view of symbolism, was associated with the generating waters and the Terra Madre. 96

The PLACENTA, like the tree and umbilical cord and serpent, is another source for the concepts of a "ladder between earth and heaven." In fact, we could consider the placenta the ultimate "shaman ladder." Since the function of the tree in shamanism is to be a conduit between shaman and spirit teachers through which knowledge is transmitted, the placenta does the same for the fetus in the womb of the mother. The mother's body and its divine wisdom creates the placenta to assist the fetus during its development. It serves as a conduit of divine biological information necessary for function and growth, it serves as a purification tool, providing oxygen and nutrients and also removing carbon dioxide and other waste, and it promotes circulation through metabolizing substances.

Simply, and literally, it's the original Tree of Life.

All others are conceptual ideas based on original shaman ladder: fetus to mother

Left to Right: Placenta, Placenta, Tree, Cimaruta

Italian Magic: Secret Lives of Women

In Italian rural traditions, the placenta is intimately linked to mother milk production. Given the intimate bond between mother, placenta and child, the rituals are performed to protect from evil that would involve, by virtue of this link, the mother and the newborn. [97]

The navel, called **villicolo** in Neapolitan dialect, has a double meaning: while it indicates the physical connection of a new life to the navel of the mother, it also refers to a greater center connection to the earth. The navel is the connection point between mother and child, and has similarly been used as a concept in Greece and Italy in the oracle traditions of Sybils and Pythia, who are connected to their Goddesses and Gods through trance. Their location of trance divination was marked with an "omphalos stone", which was a representation of this navel, this center of the earth.

Left: Tree in Liguria. Right, drawings by Karyn Crisis, image L and R sourced from "The Language of the Goddess" by Marija Gimbutas. L:Omphalos stone from Ukraine, M: Omphalos stone described by Pausanias; R: carved pebble from near Trento, Italy, Neolithic.

Before statues were concerned with portraiture and therefore anatomical correctness, the figurative work of the ancient statues of Italy and Old Europe depicted the Great Mother Goddess expressed as her physical parallel, the earthly woman. While the eyes, breasts, and pubic triangle were emphasized, also the navel was often marked as place of energetic significance on a woman's body, emphasizing its parallel to the Divine Feminine Universe's conceptual navel: the great universe from which all things are born and return.

On these statues, the navel on human female body is marked as a spiritually significant parallel and not as an anatomical marker. The navel connects the placenta, the umbilical cord, and the baby altogether. This concept of connection runs through Italian rural magic as well. The placenta, and its important function, has traditions to protect its energy in rural Italy in the following ways:

- it is Buried
- it is Consumed
- it is Burned

Ritual BURIAL of the placenta is not a process about honoring the birth, rather it's a protective measure for mother and child. Burying the placenta prevented another animal from eating it. Especially if it were a milk-producing animal, the belief is that through a transfer of energy, the animal eating the placenta would gain the mother's milk and the mother's milk would dry out.

The placenta was also buried to prevent a jealous person from taking it and using it for spells of envy. The placenta, therefore, was buried in the dung piles of animals (to prevent any animal from eating it) [98] or under the eaves, for the addition of purification. In some areas it was buried under trees, like the fig or oak. Sometimes it was buried under the entryway of a house.

> *If the family of the mother-in-law had not enough cattle to justify the existence of the manure, the placenta was buried in a pit. At Rocchetta di Spoleto they buried the placenta in any deep dug in the garden.*
>
> *In Cammoro, it was customary to bury the placenta inside the stable. It is acutely sensitive to a male fetus and that of a female.*
>
> *At Meggiano, the placenta was buried outside the barn, where the manure matured. At Avendita and Ocosce, similarly, the placenta was hidden in the dunghill.* [99]
>
> *In Sicily, even today, the umbilical cord is burned and the placenta thrown into the sea, taking care that nothing is eaten by dogs.*
>
> *In Umbria, the placenta is placed to dry over a fig tree to help the whipping milk; for the same purpose, in Polesine, his father buries her in the yard of the house. In Veneto, if the child does not eat, the father buries the placenta in a deep hole.* [100]

Italian Magic: Secret Lives of Women

Also called **manto delle Madonna** (mantle of the Madonna) in Italy, the placenta is also considered the seat of the soul. Its powers are similar to the umbilical cord. Babies born with the "shirt" (with strips of placenta stuck on their faces) were considered to be destined to be healers and fortunate ones who had powers to work against the types of witches who cast envious spells. It was nature's way of creating a physical marker of a special "otherness" for someone who is psychic and mediumistic, with a propensity towards curing and protecting.

Due to these powers, the placenta was often consumed by mothers in rural areas after adding it to a broth of hen's organs as part of her post-delivery restoration.

When a baby was born in "the shirt" or "caul," often it was dried up and put into a "breve" which means "short", like a little shirt. The **breve** is a little pouch hung and worn around the neck and worn close to the skin, under the clothing. Anyone wearing their **breve** had to be very careful to not let anyone else get the contents, lest they use the placenta in an envious spell. The **breve** is used across Italy from Umbria to Sardinia to Marche and Friuli for protection as well, and has been adopted by the church and banned for rural usage, subsequently, even though the church uses the same ingredients that rural people do.

In Sardinia, **il breve** is called **la punga**. It has a rhomboid shape, measuring 3-4 centimeters on each side. [101] The belief about its power to protect has partly to do with its contents, and part to do with the way it's worn :

> *"by remaining in contact with the body, it was able to ward off evil or at least to act as a barrier to make it less virulent, to prevent misfortunes [...] to preserve from diseases [...] and to chase away spirits."* [102]

LEFT: sa punga

It was also used in Sardinia by mothers of children born in the placenta, who would let it dry out and then sew it into a **punga** to be worn by the child for years, making sure to not let it fall into anyone else's hands.

Something remarkable about this rhomboid shape is that it's a prominent symbol from pre-patriarchal history, found among the goddess statues and temples depicting the Goddess' connection to sacred waters…sacred to the Goddess, the owner of life-water, the giver of life." [103] Water has long been used to cure and purify in Italy.

SYMPATHETIC MAGIC: Birth Rituals

il breve, from Museo Etnostorico della Stregoneria, Triora, Liguria

Friuli is just one of the places where it's believed that a baby born "in the shirt" (in the caul) as they say in Italy is "born under a special sign", [104] meaning that the baby was born with supernatural abilities; a physical marker of psychic and mediumistic abilities. In Italy, when someone has these abilities, it's seen as a serious responsibility that must be used to service the community. Sometimes it means the baby will become a healer, as with the 7th sons...

> A baby born with *"the caul about his neck [...] bound to him a destiny from which there was no escape."* [105]

In Friuli we find the shamans called benandanti. Benandanti are a unique group who have made appearances throughout Italy's historical documents and who still exist today. Benandanti are not found anywhere else in Italy. While historically, in older times, they were known by being marked by the caul, it is no longer a manifestation that is necessary to mark the benandante. When it is time, the spirits bring the benandante to initiation and the subsequent dream battles:

> *"When he reached adulthood, on a Thursday of the Ember Days, the benandante would embark on his 'profession' by falling into a mysterious lethargy.."* [106]

This passage, in the words of its times, describes the benandante falling into a sleep that preceded astral flight; the trance which pulled the benandante out of their body and into the dream realm of the battles. Benandanti don't use **unguenti** (flying ointments) nor plants to enter trance as some people in Italian traditions do.

Also, Benandante didn't just "work" in the astral realm: they also gave messages to their neighbors from departed loved ones. They served as a community Medium, but they also were elected by the spirit world to battle in a team with other benandanti in the astral realm, to keep a balance between light and dark. This election, or initiation, is not something a person can attempt to pursue nor achieve do to hard work. It is entirely decided and initiated by the spirit world.

Italian Magic: Secret Lives of Women

TREE RITUALS FOR FERTILITY

The associations in Italy between the bodies of women and trees become more intimate than just concepts. In the agricultural mother magic communities of the region of Umbria, there is a practice called: **la cerqua furmicusa**.

"This practice, aimed at propitiating the birth when the conception was difficult, took place near the village of Cortigno where grew an ancient oak whose trunk had an opening in the lower part. The ants had established their nests in that dark cavity from which they entered and went out. Many years ago, women who could not have children, went to the foot of the oak to "take" the children:

"Kneeling on the ground, they put their hands inside the cavity and made the gesture of taking something[...] that, extracted their hands from the trunk, they rubbed her stomach so that souls passed inside the uterus." [107]

"And in Valnerina, [Umbria] we will deal with the ancient oak tree where women went to have children." [108] *But central Italy is not the only area in Italy where women went to prepare to receive the souls of their babies and gave birth.*

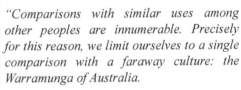

"Comparisons with similar uses among other peoples are innumerable. Precisely for this reason, we limit ourselves to a single comparison with a faraway culture: the Warramunga of Australia.

This tribe believes that the spirits of children - tiny life entities like grains of sand - live within certain trees. The women of the tribe are the trees in which the spirit-children reside and ask them to enter their womb. The spirits fertilize them by entering them through the umbilicus." [109]

SYMPATHETIC MAGIC: Birth Rituals

Radial branch patterns of an oak tree (left) Umbilical cord and veins of placenta (right)

The beautiful radial branches of oak trees look remarkably similar to the umbilical cord and veins of the placenta. **La cerqua furmicusa** is an example of trees not being just a place to receive knowledge, but also to receive new life. For women in this community, it makes wonderful sense that the tree, a natural symbol of the Tree of Life would be the place where prayers are sent and answered regarding fertility: it's the body double of the Great Mother Goddess. Those of us outsiders who are not part of these rituals and beliefs may think this is a flighty idea, but the fact that it has been a repeated tradition for generations means that to the people who use this rite they experience a connection worth repeating.

MILK

Historically, within agricultural communities all across Italy and her islands we find the veneration of waters such as rivers and springs and cave-drippings-turned-stalactites connected to milk, and the belief that both liquids are physical expressions on earth of the Great Goddess Mother's eternal life force. This has also been acknowledged outside of these communities:

> *"Every liquid is water and every water is milk. The sacred primitive moisture that dripped from the body of the mother earth, a perennial source of vital forms, was at the center of the archaic cults of pre-European Neolithic Europe. In the elusive element, rich in germs, fermenting with unexpressed latencies, inexhaustible super-milk, the primordial vital energy, the obscure secret of existence, of generation, of fertility, the damp yeast that presided over the mechanisms of birth, growth, regeneration."* [110]

Both water and milk are also connected with menstrual blood, a TRIO of sacred feminine fluids that support life in the TRIO of: the mother's womb, on the earth (people, animals, nature) , and in the spirit world after physical death (as a conduit along which biological and spiritual knowledge is transmitted). Life and regeneration are inseparable. This concept begins with the earth itself, and for people living off the land, who are intimately connected to these cycles of nature, they understand life comes around again after intimately connected to these cycles of nature, the seeming deaths of plant, animal, and human matter.

Italian Magic: Secret Lives of Women

These beliefs originate back as far or even farther than the temples on the island of Malta, where symbols of bull skulls (symbol of the Goddess' life force on earth because its form is the same as that of women's uterus, ovaries and fallopian tubes), red ochre paint (symbolizing menstrual blood that indeed has stem cells that regenerate) human skulls of the physically deceased, moon crescent and vulture paintings celebrate these energies. These temples and burial chambers use natural symbols to celebrate the belief that while the body is carried away after the soul leaves it, life comes around again through the portal of the Great Mother Goddess' universal womb, just as the female body bears children, a cycle of returning to where one comes from.

There are ancient monuments on the island of Sardinia also embodying these ideas: cave-like temples, circular cuts in the floor, circular structures, water wells, bull skull carvings, menhirs with ancient bee-like symbols, spirals, red ochre colors, identical symbols, water connections, round shapes, columns of life in the center of carved-out rooms. These structures are completely different from Greek and Roman square shaped temples some of which pre-date the Great Pyramids.

Carved circle depressions found inside many ancient stone structures of Sardinia

Just as the woman's power to give birth from her body has been envied by many pagan gods and the christian one (at least by the men who wrote down their alleged biographies), so has the woman's ability to produce food from her own body. Mother's milk is not "just food," it's the original "super food":

> *"the antibodies it is richly endowed with create a precious protective barrier that repels insidious pathogens, while lactoferrin - a protein capable of fixing the iron , which reduces the chances of intestinal infections."* [111]

In fact, mother milk is used for curing in rural Italian traditions. In contrast, breast milk has been written out of masculinized magic rituals and Big Religion as a curative power because it's a body fluid that can't be usurped by men. It has been sexualized in some magical traditions however. Menstrual blood has been substituted with animal blood or blood from self-cutting, on the other hand, and it's been conceptualized in pagan rituals and christian ones as Jesus' blood that regenerates (even though masculine blood has no regenerative power). The ocean has often been given a masculine remodeling as a way to attribute the fluid of water to masculine symbols of life-creation power.

The origin of these fluids attributed specifically to mothers and to the Universe's Great Mother was acknowledged before masculinized pagan practices turned these fluids into pure conceptualization. The 3 fluids of blood, milk and water, are rightfully symbols of the Great Mother Goddess' life force and its movements through the Universe and on the earth through nature (as mother that births more nature) and as earthly mothers (who birth the population).

Remarkably however, or perhaps naturally, in the rural and agricultural communities of Italy, the original symbolic language of a feminine Universe remains. Whether the communities themselves, where women are the sole operators of magic or the secret gestures and rituals that work to restore and maintain parts of the female body that correspond with ancient Goddess statues depicting the life force and regeneration-after-death power of the Great Mother Goddess herself, the life cycles are honored in nature and in the female body. These symbols exist within societies where the male is the head of the family in other ways, referred to even as "king" in some places and rituals of Sardinia.

 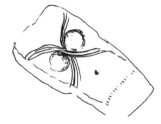

Drawings by Karyn Crisis,images sourced from "The Language of the Goddess" by Marija Gimbutas. L: carved river pebbles from Sicily, early 4th mill. B.C.; R: statue-menhir with breasts from Foggia, SE Italy, 3000 B.C.

In the province of Avellino in the region of Campania, throughout the region of Umbria, in Tuscany, all across Sicily, (and therefore likely anywhere cave systems exist and they are found throughout Italy) there have been deeply intimate rituals that women practiced for attracting the abundance of milk flow to the breasts.

The rituals for abundant breast milk are expressed as propitiatory rituals, in which a sacrificial action is taken in exchange for prayers and invocations made in request for something needed. They are performed not in temples but rather in nature: at the springs, in front of hollow-bodied trees, in rivers and in caves. These are the same symbols of the Great Mother Goddess' life force in pre-pagan matrilineal expression of the universe-on-earth found not only in Italy's mysterious pre-Roman temples, but also throughout nearby European countries.

Italian Magic: Secret Lives of Women

The sympathetic relationship between nature's curative forces and female fluids is found in the curing traditions and spell-breaking rituals of rural Italy: flowing waters release lack and bring a flow of milk. Breast-shaped natural objects sympathetically connect to the breast can be used to promote health and nutritional provision of the breasts. However, these fluids are used to cure more than just the breast.

THE PROPITIATORY RITUALS FOR MILK
Milk Caves, Milk Stones, and Milk Food

The "Milk Caves" of Italy were devotional places of interest for intense mother cults which survived in the countryside from the Paleolithic era until a few decades ago. [112]

These natural caves contain stalactites and stalagmites of white steatite (also known as soap-stone and black pipestone and **pietra ollare** in Italian) which is a soft metamorphic rock composed mainly of talc.

Due to the breast and nipple shape of the stalactites, in their mammellar shape, as they are described, we find another connection between pre-masculinized magic and Italian mother magic communities in the sympathetic methods and homeopathic methods that run through propitiatory rites, domestic magic and lineage cures. These rituals are not just concepts nor superstitions, as outsiders often denigrate them, but have earned the respect of the people for whom they work, and are thus called "miracles of milk."

In addition to mothers coming to the caves as a cure for lost milk, people also brought their lactating farm animals who needed abundant milk flow. People were also cured of headaches from the dripping waters of specific caves and some caves' waters cured eye-illnesses. In these galattorfore traditions, the feminine fluids of breast milk and water are connected to a divinely feminine curative power that returns health to those who need it.

L: One of 2 handmade caves in Triora, Italy with a vaginal shape and honoring the Mother of God. R: Cave in Caserta with notches that hold the sacred water drippings believed to heal eyesight.

SYMPATHETIC MAGIC: Birth Rituals

Also named mamellonary stalactites (**stalattiti mamellonari** in Italian), the stalactites been given names to reflect not only their shape but to mark them as charged places of sacred energy having "the extraordinary virtue of giving milk back to mothers exhausted from too tiring and prolonged breastfeeding". [113]

LOCAL AND GENERAL NAMES OF MAMMELLAR STALACTITES

pocce lattaie (Tuscany)	pietre gattaiole
ogoli delle Tette (Veneto)	mammelle
pietre gattaiole	zizze (Campania , Avellino specifically)

mamme Longobarde (central Italy, Sestino)

Mountains, milk water sources, milk fountains… places with mammellar stalactites in caves were given names indicating their sacred water sources and milk magic. Some of these caves have since had churches built on top of them, of course. Some have since been attributed to male saints or gods where many natural locations, symbols, and feminine divinities were re-modeled with a male-centric perspective as a way of stealing the previous Divinely Feminine power through sublimation. In this way, male spiritual traditions attempt to take away or erase or "evilize" woman's sexuality and the power of her biological functions which are truly miraculous.

Real women have real bodies that produce real living babies, and therefore their needs for health and abundant nutritious milk are connected with female spirits and saints and goddesses of a variety of forms of helpers and not to men, nor male saints nor any other masculine figure who has no ability to produce breast milk, menstrual blood, vaginal secretions nor babies.

GENERAL NAMES of GALATTOFORE POWER
Which refer to Female Body Parts

montagne Lattari

fonti lattaie = milk sources

delle menne in S. Lorenzello

grotte delle zizze = cave of the zizze, Vulturara, Avellino

fontana delle Menne in San Lorenzello (Benevento)

santuario dei lattari = shrine of the Lattari in Caserta

tomba lattaie in Tuscany

=

CULT OF THE DEA MATER
and Caves of the Mater Goddess

There are locations of steatite all over Italy and her islands. For example, steatite

Italian Magic: Secret Lives of Women

exists as **pietra ollare** in the regions of Calabria, Emilia-Romagna, Lombardy, Piedmont, Trentino-Alto Adige, Tuscany, Val d'Aosta and Sardegna. There are galattofore charged caves in many of these places as a result, and therefore histories of the Cults of Dea Mater. caves in many of these places as a result, and therefore histories of the Cults of Dea Mater. A few examples of the caves marked as places of the Dea Mater are:

+ the Irpinia of Mefite, near the ancient colony of Aeclanum in Campania

+ the cave of Matermania on the island of Capri, dedicated to Phrygian Goddess Cybele, the Mater Magna of the Romans

+ the rock churches who've incorporated the caves like S. Angelo in Frosinone and Santa Romana in Santa' Oreste de Soratte where women went to pray and drink water that drips from the walls and to rub their breasts on dripping stalactites

+ cave at Crocetta del Montello known throughout the Veneto

+ in Lombardy, a cave dedicated to San Mama or Mamete

+ In Tuscany La Buca or Tomba Lattaia in the municipality of Cetona, is a cavity that develops for a hundred meters. The name of the cave is derived from the fact that galactofore virtues have always been attributed to the draining waters from its walls, that is, if drunk by mothers during lactation, they will have an abundance of milk secretion. [114]

This cave, which existed in pre Roman times, was consecrated to Phrygian goddess Cibele, who was also embraced by the Romans as their Magna Mater. The cave itself has an altar to Cibele as well as a cavity to collect dripping water. However, Romans remodeled it, adding a square room for resting and relaxation, adapting it to a nymphaeum. It was later dedicated to Mithras.

GALATTOFORE, MIRACOLI DEL LATTE
Sacred Divine Feminine Waters,
Miracles of Milk

"The spring water symbolically comes from the womb of the Mother Goddess in which everything originates." [115]

SYMPATHETIC MAGIC: Birth Rituals

The caves contain white steatite with a milky appearance and breast-like shapes, but they were also revered for their sacred **galattofore** waters that were believed to restore milk to women who were without, but also restore milk flow to nursing animals who were struggling to produce milk, and to cure headaches. Some caves are sources for the springs, and others create their own dripping waters due to the interior climate of the cave.

Many caves have circular carved basins or natural stone bowls and various cavities which collected the springs (and now dried up springs) and drippings. This design is even seen in Sardinia's rock-cut structures that hold water and have a seeming mysterious origin and yet bear symbols like bull skulls, red ochre spirals, bees and other marks of the Goddess' psychic language.

> For example, *"the cave church of the Grotta di Santa Romana in the municipality of S. Oreste (Rome), near the altar there is a small marble basin and the water drips over it from the rock. This water is taken and drunk by devotion by the milk-free women of the neighboring countries: miraculous miracles have also been told of recent events."* [116]

These miracoli del latte or miracles of milk / water, the fact that they were used for curative purposes and also collected to be drunk or otherwise used as cures is something we see consistently within agricultural mother magic and in the Lineage healer path: bowls of water used to cure psychic illness (**il malocchio**), to cure injuries elsewhere on the body as it's used in Emilia Romagna to wash over the body and drain away the illness, a glass or bowl of water with sulfur as a cure for **vermi**, and water thrown on the body from a cup to cure **fuoco di Sant'Antonio** (herpes zoster).

Interior of one of the Domus de Janas in Sardinia, with carved door portals and carved circular depressions that can hold water.

Italian Magic: Secret Lives of Women

RITUAL PROCESSIONS TO MILK CAVES

"...pilgrimages by devotees to the caves which provided stalactite concretions that with their ends full of milky water recall the shape of breasts and the nipple. 117

In the caves, mothers attacked the stalactites by sucking on them or rubbing their breasts against them." 118

It was believed in this sympathetic way, along with invocations and offerings, that abundant milk flow would be given with help from the Divine Feminine.

"In Mignano, in the province of Caserta: at midnight on Pentecost, a procession of women with newborns on the head went barefoot [...] up to the Shrine of the Lattari to pray to the Madonna, protectress of mothers. 119

According to news collected by Alfonso Piciocchi in the Grotta di S. Michele, in the municipality of Liberi (Caserta), [...] numerous pregnant women of the neighboring countries (Liberi, Dragoni and Roccaromana) would go processionally into the cave. These women usually rub their breasts on two dripping stalactites, very similar to their breasts, in order to propitiate the baby's milk.

Similar traditions survive the Fontana delle Menne in San Lorenzello (Benevento) and in the Grotta delle Zizze, in Vulturara (Avellino); in both cases the toponyms, which reflect the local dialects, make explicit reference to the female breasts." 120

There were also ancient lactation shrines hidden in the thickets of sacred oaks, which makes natural sense considering women also go to trees asking to receive the souls of their babies from the Great Goddess Mother. While fertility might not be of interest on your spiritual path, or even if it is, it's important to note here that the tree legends of women dancing 'round trees with the devil are fabricated to deligitimize feminine traditions that are connected to the Divine Feminine. Masculine figures have no place of veneration in these female rituals, and male saints only appear having been stamped on top of sites like caves and springs that were previously, since before Greeks and Romans and the catholic church, venerated as being Divinely Feminine.

Offerings have been found in various caves from different time periods such as bread and beans (foods used in pre-Roman domestic goddess cults by women, connected to Demeter and other earlier feminine divinities, as well as tiny ex-voto jars, wrapped puppets, nipple and udder-shaped figures of 121 terracotta.

SYMPATHETIC MAGIC: Birth Rituals

MADONNA DEL LATTE,
NYMPHS,
GROUPS of FEMININE SPIRITS

Briefly mentioned earlier was a list of female saints who are invoked in times of pregnancy and delivery who are also called upon during the breast-feeding period. The Virgin Mary, Sant'Anna, Sant'Eufemia, Sant'Elisabetta, Santa Maria, are often called as a group **madri di latte** or milk mothers, or as the singular **Madonna del Latte**. Included in this group, and connected to the caves are Cibele (Kybele), San Mamete, Ma, Maria Lactans, and Glalaktotrophusa. And, we also have the nymphs, present all over Italy and with special significance in Sicily.

"Unlike the great deities of the Greek pantheon, whose cults were housed in the great polychrome temples, the Nymphae (the shrines of the Nymphs) are usually associated with natural places and rarely have impressive architectural structures: we find them in the caves and near the water, in places where accumulations of votive objects have been found.

When the Nymphae are in urban areas they are linked to the sanctuaries of the deities of which the Nymphs form the procession, but for the most part they are peripheral, extra urban or rural places, linked to a popular cult." [122]

Even though Nymphs were embraced by Romans, they were used as advertisement in their public temples as a sort of "party welcoming committee" for the noble world.. This is quite a bit different from what we find in rural traditions where Nymphs are of the land and spent their time among the people. Perhaps even more interesting to the Italian story is not only their connection to nature but also to serpents, blood and honey, and of course, water: the symbols of the Great Mother Goddess' regenerative energy on earth. And, that they are considered a **group of spirit beings**, which is a repeating occurrence in the rural history of feminine magic and curative traditions.

The Sicilian Nymphs are linked to the birth and care of the infants as mothers or nurses [123] which frames them in the agricultural mother magic shamanism groups of spirits. Groups of spirits offering specific, categorized assistance to human beings is the essential part of shamanism in Italy and also in Siberia and central Asia. The groups of spirit beings mentioned in this chapter protect not only mothers but also the waters and caves, which

Italian Magic: Secret Lives of Women

are sacred gifts of the Great Mother Goddess. Untangling them from the romantic elite lifestyles of the Romans, in this light it is easier to see them as they operated outside of wealth rituals and leisure parties and aligned instead with the power and forces of nature:

> *The archaic Dea Mater was linked to fertility and therefore to the chthonic world which has death and life in itself; she was venerated then from the most deep antiquity that reserved to her cults of which numerous remain and obvious signs in many caves, and springs, like the Irpinia of Mefite".* 124

Caves, mountains, springs, rivers and tree groves are the places of these women and their helper spirits. The purpose of agricultural magic is to work with the cycles of nature and to invoke her curative powers to maintain a life balance. This is very different magic from the noble families invited into Roman temples.

Incidentally, while the list of caves here certainly isn't exhaustive, it's worthy to note that several of them mentioned (Avellino, Caserta and Irpinia) are located close to the Stretto di Barba river area written about in Italy's Witches and Medicine Women Vol.1, and the terrain of the Janare witches. These places are located also near enough to the alleged site of the original **noce di Benevento**, the magic walnut tree of Benevento that became part of the witch hunt trials documents and a central figure of the "evil witch" myths.

The Stretto di Barba river area is a place that is marked by 3 mysterious early pagan structures that are believed by locals to be protectors / apotropaic charges of the land. Their locations form a triangle shape, the same type seen on early Goddess statues, and it's believed that the Goddess physically manifested herself here, which is truly what the tree story is all about. The **noce di Benevento** is of course a place where women experienced group astral travel / shamanic journeying with the help of the Goddess. The tree is the conduit, just as it is in Siberian and central Asian shamanism.

This interchangeableness is not the easiest belief to explain, embracing a secret feminine world of nymphs, Madonnas, female saints and Goddesses: it's one that's best felt and sensed. For those of us contemporary folks who've survived targeted proselytizing and judgment from the church, trying to embrace the Goddess (who has offered us loving freedom from the church's oppression) in an "outfit" like the dress of the Madonna can feel like walking back towards the oppressors, and that's a sensation that's better left for dead. However, it is also possible to feel equally alienated from Romanized versions of the Goddesses as pro-war warriors and diviners for warlords.

One thing that's evident is that the Goddess can find Her seekers taking any form, and that's the beauty of the Italian traditions: the Good Ladies and Ladies from Outside, who teach women through group astral travel and trance are embraced as much as many Madonnas are, as the Mother of God is, as a variety of named Goddesses are, and for whom nature is also a conduit.

Being pulled along this spiritual path in contemporary times means likely the Feminine

SYMPATHETIC MAGIC: Birth Rituals

Divine will show you Her many ways of connecting to seekers, and thus it becomes less important what form She takes, what name She offers, but only the quality of assistance received through her limitless energy and teachings.

In Sicilian and European practices, there continue to be water sources where sterile women go to bathe or drink water to receive fertility, or where they go to sprinkle their breasts to stimulate milk production; wells in which the sick are plunged to heal from disease or to protect themselves from the evil eye; fountains or rivers that heal.

MILK FOOD

In rural Italy, where people have historically planted, grown, harvested and threshed their own wheat before transforming it into sacred breads, daily food has a magical meaning deeply connected to earth's cycles.

So, here we find rituals that honor the regenerative power of the Goddess connected to women and wheat. The twin-effect here, or parallel, is that wheat goes through a sort of death during threshing, and it's brought to life again as it's turned into breads. Mothers also go through a sort of death as their babies leave their bodies where they've developed for 9 months. That partnership changes as the child is reborn into a physically independent life. So within these worlds of nature and human beings, there is a transformation of one state to another.

This was considered, in the agrarian world, to be the highest power: that of the Goddess Mother's ability to bring to life again that which has transformed, such as with the soul that leaves the physical body after death. Life coming around again is not the only rebirthing idea connected to this however. Being cured of an illness or a disruption in health is also a regenerative process as are the life cycles of curative and nutritive plants that continually grow, die, and are reborn again. Reverence for this cycle was adopted and venerated by many pagan groups and Christianity, where the death and rebirth was usurped by the gods and the Jesus story.

The 4 main Goddesses we find in Italy connected to agricultural communities are: Demeter (the Greek mother) and **Ceres** (the Roman mother) as **Demetra e Cerere** in the Italian language, **Cibele**, and the **Mater Matuta**, the providers of wheat and beans and cereal grains. The connection between Demeter, her healing powers and the mother magic traditions of rural Italy run deep. Significantly, they show direct connections between Goddess associations with plants such as wheat and poppy in artworks with rural traditions carried out by mothers in agricultural communities. In other words, priestesses of Demeter were real, hands in the dirt, living life outside temples, in the temple of nature in active relationship on a daily basis for mother magic rituals.

Italian Magic: Secret Lives of Women

To promote abundance milk flow in mothers, therefore, we find ritualistic wheat recipes used:

Almost everywhere, in Valnerina, the power of increasing the milk secretion was attributed to the wheat flour prepared for it." [125]

Among these preparations there was the homemade pasta with flour and eggs and, in particular, the so-called **frascarelli** *often used, in general, were the* **farinata***: in San Martino.* [126]

In the Val di Narco, was cooked a wheat flour with which it was obtained a **polenta** *that was seasoned with oil and cheese.* [127]

In Fonte Vena, in addition to the **frascarelli** *served in broth, were added to the* **puerpera** *(new mother) farinata obtained by baking flour and wheat in the oven.* [128]

The so-called "washed soup": placed a few slices of bread on a plate, soaked in warm water, once soaked, drained and proceeded to season with sugar.

The name of "washed soup" was used especially in Castelvecchio where boiled bread was served in water flavored with various seasonings. Ldv 366

Everywhere the galactofore quality of soups and legumes were praised, as an old proverb says: Milk comes from the soups, not from the windows that is: if the diet is inadequate, it is useless to hope to have a sufficient amount of milk." [129]

The first meal for the baby, after weaning from mother's milk also consists of wheat. In some areas it is a toasted wheat diluted with milk to make it more digestible, or a bread boiled in milk, or soaked in oil and sugar, and many variants of wheat with a softening liquid of some sort.

Women in rural communities also protected their flow of milk by using "galactophorous" plants such as:

CUMIN - cumino
NETTLE - ortica
FAVA - broad bean
FENNEL - il finocchio
GREEN ANISE - anice verde
MILK THISTLE - il cardo mariano thistle
ITALIAN FITCH aka Goat's Rue - la galega [130]

SYMPATHETIC MAGIC: Birth Rituals

They also ate foods considered to "make milk" and nourish the mother such as lettuce sauce, vegetable broth, milk, ricotta and all those foods that recall milk in the name and color in Turin. 131

MILK SHARE

It was not uncommon for a mother with plenty of milk to help out those who had less or not enough, whether orphan babies or neighbors' children in rural Italy. The nickname given to women who share milk is **mammana**. **Mammana** is also the name given to midwives in Sicily who not only helped the mother give birth, but also prepared the first baths and wrapping the baby.

There is a tradition in Umbria where women who have plenty of milk do a ritual consisting of holding their breasts over a flower-shaped wooden board and letting some drops of milk fall onto the floor in a symbolic gesture that imagines the milk finding its way freely to women who have no milk.

MILK THEFT

Truly, the way to prevent envy in the first place is to not create it. This is a common belief pervasive in Italy, not just in magical practices, and not just in the rural past. Perhaps due to close community living, where everyone is watching everyone else, or due to a reliance on each other, especially in agricultural lifestyles where abundance follows the cycles of nature and therefore poverty or lack can be a very natural occurrence as much as it can be artificially created by governments and commerce. In fact, mothers in environments where there exists a constant worry about the lack of milk do not breastfeed in public so as not to draw envy towards themselves from the less fortunate.

There is a belief that milk can be stolen from a mother who has plenty by a mother who has little, and the way this theft is exacted is in a sympathetic magical nature. The cure for which follows a sympathetic structure as well. The theft works with an intention and an action. In our modern understanding of intention and energy, we'd say that this magic is exactly that: using intention with the flow of an action: taking the opportunity of stealing abundance through something in proximity to whom receives the abundance. For example, when the jealous mother is holding her neighbor's baby knowing its mother has plenty of milk while she has little, she may steal the handkerchief or washcloth the baby is resting on while in her arms, thereby also stealing the energy of the milk it got from its healthy mother through the energetic transference to the fabric.

The mother who is stolen from will experience a loss of milk and have to identify who stole it from her. Usually this is someone who was in her proximity to "take" the energy from her through her baby, so then to restore her milk she has to find the neighbor and likewise be in a close physical proximity to reclaim her energy. This is basically the same steps taken to undo or break a **fattura** spell. In some cases she challenges the neighbor to a sort of western-type "duel of the breast" where she calls out the neighbor after which they have to show their bare breasts to one another and say something like: "what's mine

Italian Magic: Secret Lives of Women

is mine, what's yours is yours", and in similar versions "if milk is yours, come back to you, if milk is mine, remain with me." These are basically the steps of setting energetic boundaries: acknowledgment declaration of space and reclaiming one's energy.

This is, in a way, similar to the process of using oil and water to "put the eyes" on whomever sent **il malocchio** using a sympathetic diagnostic tool of oil "eyes" to see. The **occhi** "making the eyes" cure is done with distance between the victim and the envious person, but with milk theft, the confrontation takes place person-to-person to activate he energetic reversal. In communities where breast milk was the only way to feed a baby, milk was a serious necessity and not only for human mothers, but for the farm animals mothers as well.

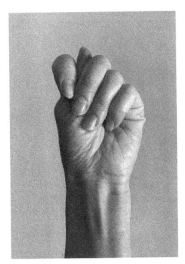

Far left: "hand fig" used to cut the connection to negativity such as the evil eye.
Image left: "hand fig" and crossed arms, defensive, same usage.

PROTECTION AGAINST MILK THEFT

Protection against milk loss due to envy therefore consists of preventative actions such as: concealing one's abundance in the presence of another person who goes without, dissolving envy through the act of sharing milk, invoking the names of female saints while touching the breasts in the presence of an envious person, wearing amulets, and making specific hand gestures.

The **manofica (manufica, figa, manofiga)** is a hand symbol used to deflect envy that is more fully explained in thee Amulets chapter. While the **manofica** is used to protect against spirit attachments and envious spells, it's also used to prevent loss of milk due to envy. While it's mostly known as an amulet, the **manofiga** has been used in rural Italy as an active hand signal, used in the moment akin to touching the breasts in the presence of an envious person, or throwing the hand horns **mano corna** to deflect **il malocchio.**

SYMPATHETIC MAGIC: Birth Rituals

HEN BROTH RESTORATION

The Hen is an integral part of the recovery of each **puerpera's** (new mother's) body, mind and spirit post-childbirth. In some traditions, hen broth and preparations are even used to assist the labor .

> *"to facilitate the delivery, a broth prepared with the head of the hen was administered to the woman giving birth. The law of Magic Analogy came into plan, combining the head of the hen with that of the fetus, favoring its normal release and preventing the dreaded occurrence of paxicality, of difficult expulsion of the placenta [...] the broth was prepared using full-black plumage."* [132]

The 40 days after birth are especially delicate for the new mother, and the black hen traditions are found in many rural communities:

> *"it was used everywhere the administration of broth of hen to give back to the* **puerpera** *the strengths put to test form the separation, from the birth, and from the consequent loss of blood"*. [133]

The **comare** was often required to offer the gift of hen broth or even of the oldest hen to the new mother. The sympathetic relationship between the black hen, the mother and fetus is connected with the symbolism:

- of the egg and its transformative vessel
- the mother her uterus as a transformation vessel for a fetus-to-baby
-and the Feminine Cosmogony as birthplace of all and to whom all return.

The black color associates volatile to the Mother Earth and the chthonic sphere, including the world of which, as happens in all archaic cultures in those of ethnological interest, is linked by a functional relationship with the reproduction of plants. [134]

HEN BROTH RECIPES [135]

Old chicken recipe, "**fa lu brodu bonoslo**"
- a piece of chicken (especially the head)
- water
- salt
- celery
- onion

In Castel San Felice and in Avendita the recipe:
- a piece of chicken (especially the head),
- water
- salt
- marjoram
- tomato

Italian Magic: Secret Lives of Women

"In Meggiano the broth was flavored with a pinch of cinnamon and poured over some slices of bread. 136

In Cammoro he prepared the broth only with water and salt and poured it on the bread. 137

Where bread was not used, broth was prepared by adding home-made pasta, especially short-cut pasta **quadrucch**. 138 *In some areas of Valnerina , as in Cammoro, the people who went to visit gave to the mother a baby chicken for the broth and a little sugar, considered a precious ingredient in the country kitchen of the past.* 139

Regarding the use of the head of the hen, in Sosasso (Ascoli Piceno) the broth was prepared for the puerpera using chicken heads. 140

In Meggiano the gift of the chicken was offered by the mother of the **puepera** *from the mother-in-law.* 141

Scheggino's tradition was to give the hen to some relatives of the female child. 142

While in Rocchetta di Spoleto, although the neighbors used to give a hen to the woman in labor, the tradition required the **comare** *to provide this precious gift. The gift of the hen was offered by all the relatives while the women of the family provided to prepare the "squares" to the egg for the broth."* 143

In Fonte Vena, any friend or relative could to give the hen as a gift, but here tradition dictates that, to prepare the broth, a pan never used in the kitchen before was used **tigama nova**. 144

In Abruzzo the mother-in-law was required to prepare the first hen stock to be administered to the new mother. 145

 In Sosasso (Ascoli Piceno) the broth was prepared for the puerpera using chicken heads. 146

ROOSTER SOUP

"Among the roosters, the best and strongest were considered able to ensure regular reproduction was preserved for the mother. The chicken broth was to the mothers after the birth, together with the egg pasta **"li tajulini"**- *for several days, since the rural medicine attributes to the broth of hen, better if old and even more if black (say the women of Ocosce), a reconstituting power as well as that of favoring or increasing the milk production.* 147

SYMPATHETIC MAGIC: Birth Rituals

MILK WEANING

Breast milk feeding was prolonged for 2 years generally and sometimes for 3. It was widely regarded as the best way for babies to get the nutrients they needed, naturally.

At the same time, mothers also wean one child off their milk if another child is born and needs to be fed. Various methods of weaning:

+ Sprinkle salt on nipples   + Honey and pepper mixture on nipples
+ Honey and vinegar on nipples   + Wiping strong vinegar over breasts
+ Rubbing parsley tufts over breasts 148

The first meal for babies after weaning in many places was a meal of wheat flour mixed with a liquid of some sort: the same type of meal that mothers eat to promote milk flow. The liquids soften the what to make it more digestible.

Documented combinations for first meals: 149

+ Toasted wheat flour mixed with warm milk   + Boiled wheat and milk
+ Toasted wheat flour with goat or cow's milk (even donkey)
+ Boiled bread crust in milk or water, seasoned with:
-teaspoon sugar or -oil or -sugar and oil together

SYMPATHETIC LABOR MAGIC

Italian Magic: Secret Lives of Women

Regarding labor, both midwives and husbands had a role in the sympathetic rituals to support smooth labor.

MIDWIVES

COOKING - In addition to the secret prayers that midwives whispered under their breath to support labor, along with special massages that helped adjust the fetus, often midwives used cooking methods in magical ways:

> *"when they felt that the pains were coming, they grabbed the rolling pin and drew the dough for the pasta with special lena: the rapid movements forward made to spread the* **sfogliala** *on* **spianatora** *facilitated the contractions of the uterus. In addition, if the woman was able to complete the culinary operation, there would be noodles ready for the traditional broth of soup to ingest after delivery and for the lunch of relatives cheering."* [150]

CANDLES - Much like the tradition of using a secret prayer with a Madonna statue or over a series of statues, midwives also used a sort of candle spell where secret prayers were whispered over a group of candles, one-by-one. The increasing energy of burning flame combined with the heated intensity of the prayers coincided with the last bit of candle being extinguished as the baby is expelled.

SCISSORS - In some places, such as Alghero (Sardinia) women recited prayers or special magic formulas and waved a pair of scissors on the woman's belly. The scissors were used to alleviate the pains of childbirth. The practice was also useful for mitigating post-partum pain. [151] In some places scissors are used to cut the umbilical cord. Often the new mother will suck the blood-soaked scissors [...] because the blood of childbirth is considered pure and good blood. [152]

In Caligari, Sardinia, and likely many other places, scissors were placed under the mattress of the pregnant woman to protect both her and her baby from **il malocchio** the evil eye. Traditionally, the scissors were open, with both blades "up", similar to the moon crescent, horseshoe usage for protection, and the hand horns **le corna, mano cornuto.**

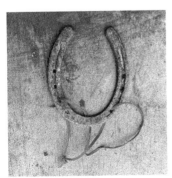

BELLS - In Umbria and elsewhere, the movement of the bell is used for the support of

SYMPATHETIC MAGIC: Birth Rituals

a happy outcome of birth, by using the laws of sympathetic magic. Here, the free flow of sound from the dark bronze cavity is propitious for the exit of the fetus: The use of bells here has a double meaning because they are also traditionally used to clear the air of negativity most specifically by pushing away negative spirits, thus having an apotropaic efficacy.

> "The bells are rung with the mouth pulling on the rope instead the hands to establish a more intimate contact between the operator and the means used when elements are involved that are especially "charged" with the power and identity of the person such as saliva and breathing. The number of strokes is associated to the symbolic meaning of the number 3."[153]

PHOTOS OF FEMALE SAINTS - Kept within view during delivery as a focal point for labor assistance, photos of female saints are used like any depiction of a Goddess for support. The female saints, however, have a relatability factor for mothers due to the fact that many female saints once had marriages and babies and suffered through and survived hardships supported by the strengths of their beliefs.

VIRGIN GIRLS - In Rocchetta di Spoleto, when the birth was difficult and labor pains were longer than expected, seven virgin girls **verginĕlle** were asked by families to go and pray to the Madonna del Verde, whose image is located near the local stream. [154]

HAIR- The tradition around hair in these communities also follows a sympathetic nature. The hair is kept loose and free during delivery of the baby to promote a smooth birth. In these mother magic traditions, knots are used to stop the flow of negativity and to "tie up" illness so that it finishes, and so hair is not kept tied up or tied back during delivery. This is consistent with the belief in preventing knots in necklaces and in knitting yard to keep the umbilical cord free-flowing during pregnancy.

HUSBANDS

In these rural communities, women were the sole operators of magic. Husbands were believed to have a passive apotropaic function: the energy of their clothing or personal affects could serve to protect a wife in an urgent situation.

PANTS - In the case of labor, husbands would lend their pants and place them on his wife's belly during delivery. [155]

In some areas of Sardinia during the birth it was used to hang the trousers in front of the house and the wives beat them and they ranted with great noise, as if the pants were accomplices or actors of some serious fault. They were clubbing their trousers in place of their husband and father as the one responsible for the pains that the mother gave her motherhood. [156]

HATS - Hats specifically were used to help expulsion of the placenta. The hat was were placed on his wife's belly during delivery. [157]

WOLFPACK/ SYMPATHETIC EXCHANGE - In many places the husband would lay down in bed either next to his wife during delivery, or in place of her as she leaned on a chair to give birth.

In other places, the husband would lie down next to the wife in labor and scream, in the ways wolves howl to join in the suffering of their partners, this "joining in" was believed to help alleviate labor pains and difficulties and also prevent negative spirits from claiming the child.

Mater Matuta statues with wrapped babies

WRAPPING and MATER MATUTA

The concept of "wrapping the baby" is an interesting one found in rural Italy. It has continuity to a mysterious period in Italian history: that of the Mater Matuta, a Great Mother Goddess given a re-naming by the Romans but not a complete re-modeling.

The Mater Matuta was an archaic divinity in Rome who represented material maternity. She was preceded by the older Aurora, Goddess of Light. She was honored the 11th of June during the festival of Matralia with a procession of women carrying children in their arms who asked for protections from this divinity represented [in statuary] seated on the throne with newborns on her lap. The newborns she holds are wrapped in strips of fabric.

This mother protectress Goddess is depicted in roughly carved and humble, yet naturally powerful statues, marked by their largeness: largeness of the female body, largeness of the throne she sits upon, the largeness of her strength, as she is depicted holding several wrapped babies. It's an artistic style not well loved due to the lack of anatomical perfection and polished smoothness that Greek and Roman statues offer, and so the Mater Matuta statues are largely ignored. And yet, they depict a tradition that is practiced in rural Italy and is not relegated to the past of temple culture. And it's just one of many traditions seen carved into stone that yet live in the flesh-and-blood daily rural life, also largely ignored.

These statues and depictions are wonderful because they reveal a time period of spiritual transition that was making movements away from the earliest matrilineal expression of the Goddess on earth as mother and provider of all. Spiritual stories we rewritten to take focus away from the expression of the divinity of motherhood and the direct connection between the role of Goddess and mothers on earth. Rituals also moved away from depicting the regenerative power of plants as connected to the feminine. Among the people, Mater Matuta was also honored as having gifted grains, the same grains used in rural Italian daily sacred food rituals. This movement away from the feminine was focused into the masculine paganisms. At the same time, these particular statues aren't settled into the masculine vision of remodeled Goddesses. So they capture a freeze-frame of sorts, a testament to the connection between domestic mothers and the function of the Great Goddess Mothers who support them in their magical domestic duties that revolve around keeping life in balance. In other words, the original magic is that of the Mothers: both earthly and spirit world Mother Goddesses.

The wrapping involved strips of fabric starting at the feet and spiraling upwards to the chest, keeping the legs locked together. This is a tradition carried on until the 1970s in rural Italy and possibly longer in remote areas. This, like many other rural birth traditions, have been reported as already being in use when the Romans began documenting the world around them. In the areas of birth traditions, milk theft, midwifery and the like, a woman did field research in the area of Turin as recently as 2005. What emerged from her research and testimonies is that:

> *"The traditional oral knowledge of the last sixty years that have remained alive and passed as such to the new generations of mothers. Furthermore, the investigation took place in a hospital, the Sant'Anna Hospital in Turin, where it was possible to find young women and also inter view the mothers and grandmothers of these, in order to verify if, and how profoundly the oral tradition on pregnancy had been maintained and handed down."*[158]

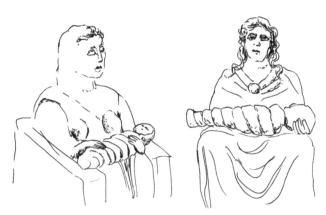

Mater Matuta statues with wrapped babies

The specific tradition of bandaging the baby is one that also took place in

Italian Magic: Secret Lives of Women

Umbria's Valnerina until the 1950s, where :

> *"[...]the newborn was wrapped tightly from the chest down.*
> *There was no child who was not subjected to this constraint*
> *that prevented any movement leaving only the arms free.*
> *It was firmly believed that the bandage prevented the child from*
> *growing up with his crooked legs. Regarding the time the bandage*
> *was maintained, it varied to a minimum of 7-8 months to a year or*
> *more. Among the bands, as protection, they used to pin a blessed*
> *medal [...]Even the Etrurians bandaged the children including the*
> *chest and arms."* [159]

> *One of the midwives also told of having "learned from another*
> *midwife who, when she was going to give birth to the children, had*
> *to take the urine of the first bandage and put it on the door of the*
> *house because it's said that this was necessary to not let the* **bruxas**
> *witches enter at home".* [160]

Keep in mind Italians in these communities think of "witches" as women who make **fatture** harmful spells against others rather than ones who do healing and magic for positive benefit.

FIRST BATH, FLOWER BATH, WINE BATH

All the "firsts" for newborns are important-from the first nail and hair cuttings (whose pieces had to be carefully protected so as not to get into the hands of an envious person), as well as the first bath.

> *The first bath is treated as a purification ritual: it's the first time the*
> *baby "comes into contact with a liquid other than the amniotic one*
> *and, therefore, this event represents a further ritual of separation*
> *from the mother's womb.* [161]

Newborns were put into baths of:

- walnut leaves to reinvigorate them [162]
- wine to make them grow strong
- waters ritualistically infused with wildflowers
  (the same types used in protective magic)
- bran and scrubbed with salt to toughen their skin

Another interesting parallel here is the ritualistic throwing of the bath water, which is an idea found in water cures, especially in the region of Emilia Romagna:

> *"It is thrown into the hearth of the house if it is a female, outside*

if it is a male." This ritual underlines how different the destinies of children are and reproduces the peasant social structure according to which the woman competes for domestic work, while to the man outside the walls of the house." 163

There is another ritual water is commonly called **l'acqua di san Giovanni** and also called "100 herbs water". Many things can be said about this water, which can loosely be compared as an Italian version of Florida Water. A much deeper description of this water, its ingredients and its significance is shared in the chapter on Water. In brief, this is a water used for purification. An uncovered bucket of water is left to soak overnight on June 23rd, collecting the dew of the morning of June 24th, with specific flowers and herbs left to infuse the water with their energies. On the 24th of June, the plant parts are strained out, and the newborn baby is the first to be washed in this water to ensure good health and to also transfer it's good luck to the water. The remaining water is used by family members to wash their face, wash their bodies, and wash their homes, to *"acquire health, strength and fortune."* 164

ABORTION HERBS

Herbs used for abortions are the same ones used for cures. There are risks associated with using herbs for abortion, and careful preparations of dosages are required to avoid complications that can include death. Herbs for abortions were used in decoctions, infusions, and also pushed into the vagina.

+ PARSLEY - Prezzemolo
+ HELLEBORE - Elleboro
+MANDRAKE - Mandragora
+ SAGE - SALVIA
+ PHEASANT'S EYE - Adonis
+ GOAT'S RUE -Galega
+ MALLOW-Malva
+ CLOVER - trifoglio
+ HYPERICUM - Iperico
+ WILD ROSEMARY - Rosmarino Selvatico

+ RUE - Ruta
+ ARTEMISIA - also as Mugwort
+ TANSY - Tanaceto
+ LAUREL-Alloro
+ CELERY - sedano
+ CYCLAMEN-Ciclamino
+ CHICORY - Cicoria
+ BROOM - Ginestra

The mallow incorporated in goose fat, spread on the female genitals, promotes abortion. 165

Parsley was used crushed: it was boiled until it became a thick mush to be gulped down. An alternative herb was the rue that was introduced in-to the vagina. 166

Chicory was used as a purifier of the body, but it was believed that its liquid, after a long boiling, caused an abortion. 167

During the post-partum period, at Fonte Vena, the **puerpera** *new*

Italian Magic: Secret Lives of Women

mother used to drink an infusion of mallow, fasting for about a week, because of the strong decongesting power possessed by the plant, which was used to say, "La malva de 'gni male salva" **The mallow cures of all evil.** 168

GROUNDING OF DESIRES

The basis of these Italian rural traditions is an ancient one: in our modern times we call it "Law of Attraction" and use expressions like "thoughts become things." The careful actions and thoughts around cravings and desires is similar to the sympathetic correlation found in many other birth rituals.

The illustration above illustrates the timelessness of this idea. It's a pose used in yoga, and it's also been advertised the past couple of years by the new "biohacking" assortment of alternative methods for healing the body.

This exact pose has been traditionally used generation after generation in rural and agricultural communities of Italy who have no modern psychic language and who are unaware of modern metaphysical ideas. This is just one of their traditions of "grounding". The practice is used when a mother is craving or desiring something that would not be beneficial for the fetus to receive, thereby moving their desires and cravings out of their body, preventing the desire from imprinting into the child.

"In Abruzzo and in the Marches, to avoid the feared effects of the "pregnant women's wishes", similar methods were used. Those documented in Valnerina A Collesolio say that **to send back the "desire", one must stretch the legs upward.**" 169

"The reflux would allow you to send back the **rogla** *until it is receded to the head, that is, to the place where the intense desire had been*

conceived". 170

Also, when women felt an intense desire or craving they shouldn't act on for the same reasons, women avoided touching their bodies, due to belief that the act of touching the body at that moment would create an "imprint of desire" that would have manifested in the fetus.

These beliefs were based on actual occurrences in the communities; they weren't ideas "up in the air". In addition to mothers believing their babies would receive their transferred craving were it not sent back, they also believed touching themselves during a moment of desire would leave mark, such a deep red birthmark, like the color of wine.

While this ritual cures a specific type of desire, at its root is a broader concept of thought: that cravings and desires of this nature are an unnatural feeling of being "in need", which, according to the Law of Attraction is an affirmation of need (whereas a desire of a creative, passionate nature affirms a desire to expand and express more of oneself). Considering that Italian traditions and cures of these communities are about bringing life into balance and working with the flow of energy rather than denying or resisting it, it can be said that this type of cure settles a battle within the mind: rather than succumbing to an addictive-type feeling behind a craving, instead taking an action that shows the possibility of exerting choice over the desire rather than helplessness.

Another modern metaphysical idea at play in these birth traditions is the specific aspect of Law of Attraction that is often explained in these words:

"you get what focus on, so focus on what you want."

"Next to the bed, a picture was used to depict a child or a graceful face so that, upon awakening, the woman would be favorably impressed. 171
In order to have a positive imprint, one would say today. 172

This gives a little more foundation to the practice of pregnant mothers of avoiding to look at things they find ugly while pregnant, avoiding to look at people with illness and deformities, avoiding to feel undesirable or unattainable desires. The mother's body is considered a transmission vessel, and transmitting negativity of any kind was consciously avoided.

To counter these possibilities during pregnancy instead women focus on photos of beautiful babies and the beauty of nature, rather than allowing their minds to worry about what could go wrong during birth and with the coming child's health.

Italian Magic: Secret Lives of Women

"An essential grounding ritual that women used was simply, and naturally to touch the ground with their hands in order to transmit it to the earth." 173

L: cobblestones in the mountains of Rieti, Lazio.

KEY DIVINATION
+
HORSE SHOES

While this topic might be better placed in a chapter focused solely on divination methods, keys are a part of the mothers' duties, and they are connected to the hen house, which is an important part of rural communities' home units. Chickens are a valuable inheritance within families, and often brides are responsible for their inherited hen and rooster's health as they are taken to her new home. There are birth divinations and beliefs about the birth of chickens and symbolism in regards to chicken eggs that have parallels to the way the sex of a woman's fetus is divined by the moon phase.

The chicken coop is protected with amulets and fertility is promoted by laying an iron horse shoe under the straw, just as horseshoes are used in the same way for human mothers "to promote the expulsion of the placenta. 174 Donkey iron is also used.

"like the barn, the **pollaio** *chicken house was also the theater of ritual operations performed by women and connected to the exercise of the "daily sacred".*175

Among the simplest and most widespread magical practices, to reach the discovery of objects lost, there are those called:
'de su sedazzu,' *(of the sieve),*
'de is ferrus', *(of the scissors), and*
'de sa crai', *of the key*

The latter, sometimes, used hanging from a string as a pendulum. 176

In all these practices are present [are secret] words or ritual verses.

*The same results are obtained with the key, whose tip is supported by the "seer", on the plane of the table and from the same estate perpendicular with a slight pressure of the index finger on the ring of the same key.*177

The horseshoe was used to help smooth childbirth. 178

CIMARUTA

While various opinions can be found about what flower is featured in the **cimaruta** amulets, a quick look at older charms shows a consistency about the flower: its center. The center of the flower in these amulets is unique. The only flower that has a center like this is the RUE flower.

Top row l-r: Iperico flower, Verbena flower, Malva flower
Bottom Row: Poppry Flower, Mandrake flower, Rue flower

It makes sense that the rue would be used on the **cimaruta** since the **cima diruta** "tree" on which all the charms are hung is a rue plant branch and that rue is a panacea plant i.e. a "cure all plant" : used in magic, in curative healing for so many ailments, for abortions and for protection by rural women. It was traditionally a very important plants that was also widely available. **Cimarute** amulets are traditionally bought in silver. For rural families they were quite an expensive investment. Cimaruta is not an actual word, but rather a composite made from the words **cima di ruta** meaning: top of the rue.

Closeup sketches of Rue flower petals and centers. This is the only magical flower with the puffy and segmented center seen on most and on the oldest cimaruta charms (which are all derivatives)

Italian Magic: Secret Lives of Women

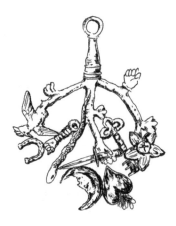

The **cima di ruta*** amulet as it is called in Naples is a composite of symbols. It is more popularly known by the name **cimaruta** which is a word composite. The **cimaruta** itself has very little connection to the fantastical ideas written about it with the exception of its obvious representations of very real rural rituals and protection magic, often overlooked considering rural traditions have not been elevated to the importance of Roman ones and have been slagged off as being syncretized (mix of Catholicism and magic) and of no real value to contemporary witches. Americans seem to largely rely on Roman sources for magic, missing the more longstanding indigenous traditions altogether in doing so. In fact, Roman documentations of **cimaruta** don't exist, neither do medieval records, which is noteworthy here considering it has been rumored that medieval witches used the **cimaruta** as an amulet, and that the medieval period's magic was well documented, the good, the bad, and the very ugly.

This is consistent with the fact that Romans did not adopt many rural apotropaic rituals that they nevertheless acknowledged as having existed prior to their documentations. Romans rather enjoyed re-styling magic discovered from other ruling-class sources and remodeling pre-existing divinities into a visual form and workable shape that supported their directives (mostly power, opulence, and conquering).

It's important to note this for research purposes, because when something seems an eternal mystery which no one can quite put their finger on, it's because it's a synthetically created mystery. In this case, there is a truth to the **cimaruta** although it may be less glamorous than you desire. It is made of symbols which have daily sacred significance for rural people and their mother magic way of life where amulets were either for: the children and/or their mothers, and also inherited by new wives and mothers-to-be from their mother-in-laws. The symbols themselves confess this.

For example, while serpents have enjoyed a conceptual expression in many magical traditions and are also connected to many Goddesses, in rural Italy snake-charmers are healers who used parts of the snake to cure poisonous bites. They became identified with serpents in a sympathetic way based on magical-medico cures. This serpent connection is not an isolated one: in rural traditions, the poison is associated with the cure. Sympathetic connections along with homeopathic remedies are pervasive in rural Italy, while conceptual ideas based on a synthetic replication of this idea are pervasive in other types of magic.

As with all symbolic items that become stylized, the original meanings get lost in design and decoration, being that design is about visual balance and therefore done with a broad creative freedom and adapted to the cultural meanings of the time period for the sake of appealing to commerce. With jewelry and amulets, a symbol may begin as one thing and come to mean something else in a different province or region or time period.

Roman traditions and documentation are quite different from rural life and its longstanding traditions: Romans were avid learners and collectors of spiritual practices and magical rituals from their many invaded and conquered territories, having access to sources not available to rural people, for example. Roman documentation was done by philosophers and well-read historians with the ruling elite's vision in mind, and it can't be counted on as a general view of all of Italy and its multicultural imprints and lifestyles.

Inquisitive and tolerant of many different practices, Romans would use any magic that would give a result, and this is also how the general population took to magic as well: life and health were urgent, crops and food were needed, relationships were wanted, and people were not picky about which ritual was used to get what they wanted. This is vastly different from longstanding inherited traditions that are part of a framework based on continuity of preserving and protecting life through the support of nature and helping spirits connected to those needs and to nature.

At ground level, consistency is found where people were connected to the earth, and slower, more gradual changes took place: among farmers, harvesters, food producers in rural places where nature and maternity are forces that can't be controlled. In these rural places, whether remote or non-educated in reading not writing, they certainly had to submit to ruling powers like the church at times, and yet they maintained the traditions of their ancestors above and beyond the ruling powers.

Nevertheless, Italians will tell you that magic has always been everywhere in Italy: it was not reserved for a secret group of alleged witches. Italian people who are healers or have inherited magic traditions from within their family are secretive anyway, and don't need to be part of a cult, ancient or modern, to be so: it's in the nature of their work, which is different to many contemporary people who want it to be known that they are witches or do magic. For protection's sake, the Italian attitude is to keep secret.

The only historical piece to loosely resemble the now very designed **cimaruta** is an Etruscan one, housed in the Bologna Museum (below left), which is a very sparse design of the bare plant of rue and not entirely natural. Progressing to the very designed and "charm" laden **cimaruta** is a big jump. A more natural progression is found in Sardinia where red coral branches decorated with apotropaic bells compose this amulet.

Italian Magic: Secret Lives of Women

(below right, sourced from "Gioelli. Storia, linguaggio, regligiosita dell'ornamento in Sardegna", p.351).

The longstanding tradition of using and inheriting amulets made for mothers and babies is pervasive in rural Italy. Many of these amulets began as natural sympathetic designs: teeth, animal hair, red coral, white coral, seashells, nipple shapes, flower shapes, bells, particular woods, pieces of iron, carnelian and obsidian, broom/branch shapes that emulate trees.

Naturally, they were also part of domestic goddess culture that revolved around women's duties to their babies and community and to the Goddess who provided to them what they needed. Romans embraced and reused some of the symbols found on **cimarute**, but these symbols have been ever-present in rural culture: they neither came into fashion nor went out of fashion. They are rather a tribute to the woman's work:

+ hen house key inherited at her wedding and protection from Ecate Hekate;
+ rooster restorative soup;
+ horseshoes and donkey shoes used to push out placenta and to protect the home;
+ fried fish left as offerings to spirit helper **Signora del Gioco** and **Donne di Fuora**;
+ the rue flower itself, one of the panacea plants used for medicinal and magical needs,
+ the mother's love heart and its parallel to Divine Feminine love;
+ the serpent's medicine against poison;
+ all tied to a rue branch resembling the fertility tree where women went to receive the spirits of their babies and to give birth.

Considering the vast collection of rituals of daily sacred magic used by rural women to protect and feed their families, to bring balance to an imbalance (curses, blights on crops, weather, psychic illness, physical illness), the continuity among rural protection work finds amulets used pervasively, and mostly for : newborn babies and small children, mothers, and farm animals. In this light, perhaps it's easier to see the origin of the cimaruta as protection for babies, tied around their necks with the symbols of the magic of their mothers who protect them and the Divine Feminine parallel who in turn protects mothers.

ancient **pagghiara** structure, Puglia

Daniela Scaglioso makes a doll with a
poppy flower and her hair, Puglia.

Italian Magic: Secret Lives of Women
DEATH
La Morte

"Terraddóssu, paradisu santu," si suava dire.
"The body to the earth, the soul to the sky" [179]

"The most crucial moments of life, that is birth and death, now hospitalized, took place once in the family and were managed, except for some rare exception, always by women." [180]

"Until the fifties and sixties, the idea of giving birth in a hospital was not even considered, and births, even in cities like Alghero [in Sardinia], took place at home with the help of a midwife."[181]While this quote refers to Sardinia, the same can be said for mainland Italy and Sicily.

"Birth seemed intensely connected with the fertility of the earth" [182] and because these events occur according to a time clock, the natural way to tell time was according to the passage of time they mark and tell: the cycles of earth's fertility for nature and light (sun and moon), the feminine cycle for fertility of humanity. The earth's clock of the recurring seasons moves in accordance with the passage of light of the universe's clock of the recurring solstices and equinoxes. The parallel in humanity with these cycles are the menstrual cycle of blood-clock and the maternity-womb clock.

The divinity, the source of power of the Universe, was naturally honored as a feminine power that was able to give life and to regenerate life after death in a circular continuum "on earth as it is in heaven" because that was evident in nature: the miracle and mystery of life that has inspired religions around the world to seek an explanation and a source for, physically takes place through the human feminine body. Therefore the divine feminine was a stronger power than the church's male god who was created in relatively recent times, and who was introduced into Italian culture long after spiritual traditions had been established honoring the feminine and nature herself. It was not necessary to view the divine feminine as a specific person but as a much larger source of all.

Even though most cults that were documented in history (by men) were male-centric or written from a masculine perspective, they do nevertheless leave a trail of theft that can be traced backwards in time towards the point where they usurped what came before them. Doing so brings back natural meanings of many symbols that have taken on a frightening meaning or ones that seem indecipherable. They are only so because they were given synthetic meanings connected to masculine concepts, whereas their original meanings had a parallel relationship to something in nature which pointed to the meaning of the symbol.

In this way we can see how a male-centric view was established by superimposing

DEATH: La Morte

upon a naturally feminine one. The masculine-centric myths often lack a sense, but this is because they are disconnected from nature and can only be understood as purely conceptual ideas that have no reflection in nature. Their preceding foundational beliefs, which, in their early stages, embraced such ideas as regeneration, life after death, nature as a conduit, and reception of knowledge from the spirit world, were not limited to binary gendered couples only, nor were they seen as being part of a masculine-centric cosmogony. The shift towards patriarchy and man as the progenitor of all life coincided with the invasions of male warring tribes.

Italian rural traditions however, being deeply rooted in the earth's cycles and cycles of women's bodies, incorporate daily sacred work to restore balance to what is out of balance through a sympathetic understanding of emotion, thought, motion and flow. The agricultural rituals of Italy are not about dominion over nature but rather a partnership with it. Naturally, these traditions are found in the domestic female world, though many have been taken over by men, as most things have in the world. The ones that remain are the lineage cures and mother magic, handed down from Goddesses such as **Ecate**, **Demetra**, **Cerere** and **Cibele**.

ACCEPTING DEATH

Left to take care of themselves without hospitals nor doctors until the 1960's, and even then maintaining family traditions, Italian people in remote rural areas also had to deal with the complexities of family deaths and the process of dying all on their own. Death was considered natural however, as it has also been unavoidable in rural life. Life, death, and regeneration have always been linked together for agricultural communities. Outside of rural communities death is often seen as a failure: a failure of man to exert control over nature.

What is considered "unnatural" death in rural communities is the struggle to die. This agony, as it's called, during the death transition is seen an unnatural state believed to be the result of guilt of some sort, such as for an unconfessed theft. And, something out of balance is always approached with natural remedy for restoring balance.

The belief that death is a natural part of life is a common belief among oral traditions who actively engage with the spirit world in daily sacred rituals of various kinds. Whether through veneration of goddesses, madonnas, female saints, and other divinities, these traditions maintain relationships with spirits for whom death is not an end to life. In fact, the curing traditions and magical rituals are working partnerships with spirits: for performing exorcisms, cures, and magic, and these relationships are daily-life ones; they are not reserved for group nor public ritual.

Many oral traditions, if not all, consider death to be a natural end of a phase of life and that it can occur without struggle. To illustrate a very ancient belief taking place in our modern days, here is a story shared by the author:

"While training as a Spiritualist medium in 2012, our teacher was

Italian Magic: Secret Lives of Women

explaining a Spiritualist belief that death can occur without illness, accident, nor struggle; that it is simply a transition of the spirit from the physical body (where it's temporarily housed for the purpose of physical life on earth) into the spirit or energy world. A classmate illustrated this by telling us that her grandpa had been living with her family after her grandma had died some years ago. One day, her grandpa had been laying in his bed when he suddenly stood up, took off all his clothes, walked one lap around the house and then said, 'it's time now,' before he climbed back in bed. He said, "I see your grandma", and then he passed away, just like that. No sadness, no illness, no struggle."

"In Sardinia, death should be natural. If is unnatural and an agony is experienced, there are means to end the agony: take away things from the room that keep the soul in the body: protective amulets, medallions, crosses, photos, etc...then call **s'accabadora**.*"* [183]

Various ways to find **accabbadora** spelled in print:
-**s'accaddabora** -**sas accabadöras** (plural) -**s'accabadure** (plural) -**acabadura**

S'ACCABBADORA

In remote Italian villages, the woman who served as midwife for a baby's birth into this earthly world is often the same one who helps him pass out of his body and release his soul into the spirit world. In Sardinia specifically, but said to have existed in other remote areas of Italy, this is the role of **s'accabadora**, the angel of death on earth. She is one who helps bring the moment of death to a suffering person who has no other release and after all other remedies have been tried. She is referred to as "the Euthaniser", but one of compassion, feared only by outsiders (like the church and male historians) but not by those who seek her assistance.

Sas accabadöras

'This word comes from the verb to come to life ...' [184]

and also...

aggabbàre in Sardinian means "put an end to something" so

a proper translation for **femmina aggabbadora** could be: the "**woman who finishes.**"[185]

But it's also been said that the word "**accabbadora**" is from Spain, probably derived from the Spanish **acaba**r (finish). [186]

As you can imagine, having the power to bring life into the world as a midwife, to develop it in one's body as a mother, and then also to be invited and entrusted to end life for someone else, this power is a direct threat to the alleged power of the male dominant catholic world and its male god-and-son partnership. Because even though in Italy we find the Madonna revered, she is revered by the church for being a virgin (raped by god however) and her birth process is considered an unclean sin for which she has to be purified. Women of rural Italy, on the other hand, relate to her as a mother, and a mother who can help them with her wisdom and healing power from the spirit world.

Italy's male church clergy have killed, tortured and molested countless people throughout its history, but these behaviors are not criticized by their organization, nor is their unnaturally all-male divinity story criticized, which serves to continually remind humanity of the masculine power over life (with force).

Therefore, there are not so many reports about **s'accabadora** outside of local testimonies which fortunately do exist. Historical documents have been made, and of course they have been written by outsiders visiting the land who offer criticism and denigration of a tradition they don't understand:

S'ACCABBADORA in SARDINIAN HISTORY

"The first author who took an interest in the figure de **s'accabadora** *was General Alberto Della Marmore when he published his book Voyage en Sardaigne, in 1826. Two years later, an English traveler's book appeared: William Henry Smyth who, during his trip to Sardinia, noted in his diary, appeared in 1828: "In Barbagia there was the extraordinary practice of suffocating, in hopeless cases, a person. This gesture was performed by a person in charge of it, called* **accabadora** *that is,* **the one that ends life***, but the custom*

Italian Magic: Secret Lives of Women

was abolished 70 years ago by Father Vassallo, who visited these places as a missionary."[187]

After these initial publications received some attention and grandly claimed Vassallo had the power to abolish this tradition, the authors rewrote their findings "with the clear intention of wanting the controversy that arose from it" [188] such as 'that the Sardinians, in ancient times, had the habit of killing their old men', even though the falsity of this statement has already been demonstrated by several writers". [189]

This is often the case of indigenous traditions or ones that are deeply embedded in agricultural worlds: outsiders visit and put their own perspectives on the traditions they find (far different from the insider world of experience). In these cases the **s'accabdure** were referred to as "barbaric", and despite testimonies that **s'accabadoras** helped people avoid terrible suffering during death, Bonaventura Licheri chose to not only depict them as "as a sort of Erinni ready to finish the dying, in expectation of compensation," but he also compared them with Sardinian "Janas intanadas." While the figure of the Jana in Sardinia is ambivalent outsiders often associate them with evil witches and bloodsucking creatures. In this arrogant way, it can be seen how people connect real women to fantasy ideas to stir up controversy, as happened in Sardinia with the advent of writers making their own stories up on the findings of **accabadure**, such as in this poem:

> *The* **accabadora** *witch*
> *God's adulterer*
> *Demon in a true land*
> *hits the mortal, mortally beats*
> *They celebrate the crow and kill him*
> *before burying it*
> *They are hell's daughters*
> *daughters of the bad luck.*
> *Death's merchants they follow the smell,*
> *then they ask to the* **accabbadora** *the price.* [190]

Through more recent documentations and even current day online blog forums where people share their own family experiences with this figure and her invited mercy, it's been proven that the nasty, death-seeking version of **s'accabadora** never existed. This tradition, one based on need, existed until very recently (and perhaps still does) and not just in Sardinia, but also in Umbria, and there are testimonies of people talking about their own family experiences with a figure like **s'accabadora** in many other rural places as well. In the Italian tradition, she isn't "named" in distinction.

> *"The last episodes are more recent than you think, one dates back to 1952 in Orgosolo and one just in Luras in 1929. Curious the report drawn up by the carabinieri on the last "euthanasia" in which the death of the patient is justified with the fact that "the family members gave their consent".* [191]

DEATH: La Morte

Author Dolores Turchi who has written extensively about the shamanism of Sardinia published "Ho visto agire s'accabadora" in 2008, and in this book she interviews Madame Paolina Concas, at this time elderly, who said when she was 22 years old she saw "with her eyes **s'accabadora** in action". The book comes with a cd of the video interview, so this was very recent activity. And, personal testimonies concur that these are mercy killings and there is no old woman roaming around bursting into homes to kill old men.

SILENT BURDENS OF S'ACCABBADORA

It's fair to say that generally on earth the enjoyment of killing has been expressed by the masculine population. Whether hunting, war, domestic abuse, serial killers, and genocide, tortures in the name of religion, for example, the majority of killings are by men. Still, the idea of a woman killing someone, even with their permission and as an act of mercy, seems to shock people.

For women generally, the enjoyment of killing is not part of the feminine history. History's scars shows women overwhelmingly being the victims of male violence. Also, women have birthed the entire population of the planet through their bodies. So, to call the **s'accabadure**, who are also often midwives and mothers, "priestesses of death", is ignorant and also denial of the truth. The rural Italian philosophy of health and life, where life is embraced, death is accepted as part of life...but death is not worshiped as a point of focus. The cycles of nature are well known because lives are lived in utter dependence upon them.

Outside of agricultural communities and in contemporary societies people have created joyful killing traditions, such as humans who do hunting as "sport" rather than as survival, which is killing for an artificial need. So the alarm towards women who offer mercy killing after all other attempts to cure must come from some other deep-seated fear of feminine power. Why? Because men historically have cut off women from knowledge and banned them from learning institutions, stole their magic and re-wrote their spiritual creation stories into masculine-centric ones...and yet, women still remain connected to the secrets of nature, of life, of death, and rebirth. It's an unstoppable connection in feminine blood, and it's not something men can "get at" and control.

These **s'accabadure** were accused of being evil by outsiders and the church, the same was done to healers and midwives during the witch hunts. Perhaps you're noticing a trend here: midwives, healers, euthanizers all targeted by a masculine-only religious institutions who took over these duties. When people have bad things happen to them and sometimes scapegoat others (which was the advantageous technique of turning neighbor against neighbor, creating a frenzy in the witch hunts) scapegoating is often "up in the air" and not based on evidence but on strongly convincing words that incite fear and obscure a clear view of reality.

While it's true that women throughout history have known the secrets of how to use poison plants to kill, no women were killing suffering men with plants in the cases of **s'accabadure**. The difference here between public fear of **s'accabadure** and witches seems to be that one fear is rooted in reality and the other fear is rooted in the imaginary: the witch concept created by the church is full of romanticized ideas; the **s'accabadora** is dealing with a much harsher reality that is less glamorous: death of a person already in agony from some other source having nothing to do with her.

S'accabbadure were dealing with a hardcore reality that people in her community are well aware of: that people don't always die naturally, which means your loved ones are in the family home, struggling, possibly crying out in pain or fear. It's very real and tangible. People don't want to see their own family members stalled in the turn towards death.

The **s'accabadure** have a truly haunting burden to bear and one kept in silence: the somber moment of assisting someone to die through physically interacting with the person in agony, surely an enormous weight to wear on one's shoulders, and one honored by all, considering she wore a black hood to separate her personality from the duty at hand. Imagine the inner fortitude and strength it must take to not be able to prolong the life of someone you know, maybe even someone you delivered into this world, watching their eyes full of suffering, and then knowing with your action the light will go out of those same eyes. Because it's not just about assisted death, it's also about helping someone be released of their guilt and struggle, those terrible emotions that reveal weaknesses during an already most vulnerable moment.

None of us want to see our friends and loved ones suffer. But can we also imagine having to administer a touch that the final goodbye and not keep prolonging that moment our of our own selfishness and desire to keep them living just a little bit longer? This is the neutral position of **s'accabadure**.

> *"The intervention of* **s'accabadora** *was very reserved and, when requested, was done in the most secret way possible: nobody had to see and nobody had to come to know it...The figure of* **s'accabadora** *is not an invention."* [192]

> *"It was family members who called these "expert" women [...]but very often, if the dying man was conscious, he himself requested the intervention of these people who, according to many they did not do it lightly. In other words, these women practiced a kind of euthanasia."* [193]

> *"It was considered an act of piety to shorten the suffering."* [194]

> *"The* **accabadoras** *are always females."* [195]

> *"In Luras in 1929 the* **accabadora** *was also the midwife of the country, and also in Orgosolo in 1952. It was not just a technical task, but was part of a complex magical ritual of which* **acabadura** *was the extreme ratio.* [196]

DEATH: La Morte

So the question really is, when has compassion been considered sacrilegious? And why is the church, for example, allowed to kill and torture people for perversion's sake and not be criticized for it ? It seems religion is without compassion and in need of checks and balances, rather than the small rural communities and their **s'accabadoras** who truly take care of each other, selflessly, until their end.

TOOLS OF s'ACCABBADURE

> *"We are led to believe that the figure of s'accabadora was typically Sardinian, in documents of the past centuries it is discovered that everywhere, to shorten the long agony, the same objects were used and everywhere. It is clear that even in other countries* there was a figure that these instruments put into action, even if it was not called by the name of* **accabadora**.*"* [197]

YOKE (**jualeddu, julai, juvale, juale** in Sardinian, **il giogo** in Italian)

HAMMER (**su mazolu, mazzolu, sa mazzocca, su mazzoccu** in Sardinian)

STONE (**scojo, pincia**) and STONE DUST

COMB

BLACK HOOD OR SCARF

BRICK

BORDER/BOUNDARY STONE (**cippus**)

CERAMIC TILE (**coccia**)

PIECES OF TILE (**guardiole, guandiole**)

*Here "countries" means other Italian regions.

Image left: Miniature yoke.   Image right: olivaster hammer

Italian Magic: Secret Lives of Women

THE WEIGHT OF GUILT

Before explaining the tools and rituals of **s'accabadora**, it's necessary to explore the belief in natural-versus-unnatural death. As mentioned, when a person is so near their death that they are bedridden but unable to die and they are stuck in the agony of the unnatural in-between, it is believed to be caused by an unresolved guilty conscience.

The guilt could be about an old theft never confessed, but there are more serious crimes considered worthy of his agony: the illegal moving of border stones that define peoples' land boundaries and the burning of a yoke (used for oxen), even a yoke that is no longer usable.

The profound respect and fear towards these things is something we can't understand in modern times, but they are beliefs so ancient their origins are difficult to pinpoint, and yet applicable symbolism can be found around them that falls in a connective line to all the other domestic goddess symbols, pre-patriarchal paganism spiritual beliefs and certainly pre-christian oral tradition beliefs about life and death: where one realm is a parallel for another. Therefore, in the sympathetic connection, the object the guilt is connected to is placed under the pillow or under the neck of the person in agony to hasten death.

> In popular belief, troubled agony was the punishment of sins committed by high material and symbolic value for the subsistence of the agro-pastoral society. Among them, having cheated on the boundaries of the fields to appropriate the land of others, or having thrown or burned a yoke (**juvale**, **juale**) for the oxen, an action that was not done even when the tool had become unserviceable". 197

DEATH: La Morte

In Abruzzo it was believed that a particularly long and painful agony was due to the fact that the dying had burned a yoke for oxen: and sometimes a yoke that had never worked. [198]

In the Marche, when the agony became exceedingly painful, supposing that the agonizing person had guilty of burning a yoke, to release the blame they used to uncover the part of the roof above the dying man. [199]

*The association of the yoke with the agony was also found in other Mediterranean areas (Abruzzo, Romagna, south of France), probable sign of a ritual similar to the **acabadura** spread outside Sardinia.* [200]

DUAL FUNCTION

"a sort of bridge between one life and another." [201]

The associations between the yoke, its sacred importance, the ancestral terror it evokes in people who have stolen or burned one and the resultant guilt which prevents a natural death that must be reckoned with at the end of life are associations that we outsiders can only conceptualize upon. For those who live in this world, however, this belief exists in the realm of experience. This is one of those traditions many people will shrug off as superstition. But for people who live this experience, it is real. The imbalance is real and the cure is real.

While the origins of the profundity of the yoke have been lost in time, the respect towards it has not (for the border stones also). It's been suggested:

> *"whatever the origin was, it had to be treated with great respect, therefore those who burned it were in the most serious sacrilege. This belief is not only Sardinian, it was present both in the north and in the south of Italy. Numerous synods mention it as a vain superstition, which, however, at least in Sardinia, has resisted until the twentieth century."* [202]

"What is real, is that *"that the yoke has an ambivalent function: it presides at **birth** as a protective and apotropaic symbol and at **death** as an instrument of punishment and as executioner. In Oliena, when a child was about to be born, the yoke was placed behind the door; it would have facilitated the **birth** and removed any evil influence.* [203]

The function of the yoke is understood by someone as an acceptance of the dominion of others and therefore as a humiliation to be suffered at the moment of death if one is guilty of serious faults. In

Italian Magic: Secret Lives of Women

this case, however, it would not be explained why this instrument also presided over birth with apotropaic value and because even today in some old restored houses (for example in Nughedu Santa Vittoria) you can still see walls, yokes or deer horns." 204

The yoke, *"in the peasant world, had risen to the symbol of the most knowledgeable thing with which man came into contact,"*205 *and that this knowledge comes from the spirit world, the divinities. Due to likely connections to the Orphic cult which had reached Southern Italy, expanding more and more into the surrounding regions which was based on the dualistic concept of soul and body, of death and rebirth."* 206

In cults such as Orphism, which were spread by itinerant teachers who traveled from place to place, we often find the oral traditions of passing down knowledge. The knowledge is memorized in connection to the actions that represent it and, as often happens with the passage of time, the meaning is lost but the action is kept, having strong enough resonance to have an meaning that is felt, rather than one which can be described in specific ways.

Orphism is *"characterized by dualism, which holds two lives together: that of the soul, and that of the body. It could be hypothesized that the symbol of this union was represented in the agrarian world, representing a sort of bridge between one life and an-other* [in the yoke]. *The yoke could serve as a tangible image to facilitate the understanding of Orphic theology at the popular level. The Orphic conception* [...] *gave hope beyond death.* 207 It is pre-Christian, and is certainly based on a pre-patriarchal paganism as evidenced by tombs of Malta and Sardinia where tombs depict symbols of death and regeneration connected to the moon and the vulture Goddess.

Without spending more time to express the gravity of the yoke through gathered testimonies, it's interesting to share that in these areas of Italy, murder is not considered as serious a crime as stealing or burning a yoke. This is due to the fact that murder, killing, and revenge can be traced to the hands that did it..so a man can bring the killer to accountability. Justice can be served in some way.

The yoke however, is believed to have "supernatural" origins, a gift from the divinities that improved earthly life in a dramatic way as are all shaman tools and knowledge that comes from the spirit world. Therefore if something is done to it, the only way someone can be brought to justice is through the god(s), and this is activated by **s'accabbadora** using the sympathetic act of surrendering to the yoke.

YOKE UNDER PILLOW

From the testimony of Signorina Paolina Concas (born 1918) interviewed in Dolores Turchi's book on March 25 2008, describing her experience watching **s'accabbadora** help someone pass out of agony with the use of the yoke:

"but we did not see it when she pulled it out, because she had this **jualeddu** *[yoke] under her apron, but it had to be very small. It was put right here, under the head of the dying person; when this* **jualeddu** *put under the head.. soon after...she was just it was only a little, a little...(spreading out the hands shows the size)...a small yoke...similar to the great yoke that they do for oxen.*[208]

It was big enough to be slipped under the neck and that's it... and then she's dead. When we saw this we were afraid...we asked ourselves:'how, how did she die so fast.?' Immediately, no more than minutes, after she [s'accabbadora] has done it [put the yoke]... because it was an absurd thing to die so fast, it seemed to me [209] *it's secret! Put this thing under the neck and* **bòmboro**, *on the ground!* [210] *this was in 1938, 1940...*

"In Leonessa if instead it was suspected that he had trespassed on the property of others during plowing, the yoke of oxen was placed under the pillow." [211]

PROCEDURES

When a person is found to be in agony, one of the very first efforts made to ease their release into death is the procedure of removing objects from their bedroom and their body: anything that would keep them tied to the earthly realm or keep them fearful and too sentimental to leave it:

"The room had to be stripped of everything that had the task of protecting the sick (amulets, sacred objects) and what he had most dear (family affections, objects of material value and sentimental). [212]

Italian Magic: Secret Lives of Women

"...about the Sardinian **accabadoras***: 'They were women endowed with special virtues, or considered as such. Taking from the neck of the agonizing sacred amulets, such as scapulars, medallions of saints or patenas, it seems they hastened the earthly end, reducing agony, allowing the soul, as it was popular superstition, to separate more easily from the body."* 213

Amulets are removed from around the dying person's neck, family photos removed from the wall, all personal objects are taken away. This belief is found in spiritualism as well, where it's believed the soul of a dying person can often linger long after it's ready to leave out of guilt for leaving surviving family members.

In modernized environments, when people are visiting a dying relative in a hospital, a common occurrence is that their loved one passes the moment they leave to get coffee or fall asleep for a short while. A common feeling of the surviving relatives is guilt that they weren't there for the dying moment, not realizing that the dying person was politely waiting for them to leave so their soul could leave their body, knowing it was time to pass and that waiting any longer was just unnatural.

In rural Italy, there is an understanding of the dying process and what hinders or helps.

"The same is true of family members [...] because with their affection they prevent the soul from detaching from the body and attachment to earthly things, which in a sense hinder a good death" 214

CLOSURE

A personal tradition documented in Sardinia is practiced to release any emotional connection (psychic cords, we might say in contemporary terms) with someone who is in agony is by *going to the [former] lover's house and touched the door to cancel any form of hatred that could still exist.* 215

Similar to the guilt associated with the yoke and its procedure for relieving it through a sort of confession and death brought into balance, there is a parallel procedure done with a piece of STEEL or a SCALE WEIGHT:

"...that certain sins would be paid at the time of death In Friuli, for example, those who weigh very often "will struggle to die will have a very painful agony". To be freed from this torment you must place under the guilt of the dying a steelyard or any weight of the scale!" 216

The belief, as well as trivial, would seem even ridiculous, yet this belief was widespread in Italy. But the presence under the pillow of the steel yard or even the weight of any scale, that is to say of a hard and heavy object with which one could easily hit the back of the head, is the spy of a custom spread almost everywhere. 217

RECITING MAGIC FORMULAS

"To recite spells or magic formulas before an agonization was not a custom that concerned only the areas of the Alpago; also in Sardinia, in some places in the Trexental, there is talk of mysterious spells that usually, according to Gino Cabiddu, 'were pronounced to hasten the end' of the dying man." 218

The magic "formulas" as they are called, are part of the system of lineage healing where there exist also magic "signatures" or marks that are made with the hands. The combination, along with the secret words, are what activate the channeled cure, even in the death transition process.

When the spells and fumigations weren't enough to help the person in agony pass into death, **s'accabadora** was called.

SUFFUMIGI

Suffumigi, or "fumigations" used in rural communities are a resin-less loose incense made of plants, herbs, and sometimes flowers. The power of the plant being released through fire and as heavy smoke is used to cure psychic fright and other ailments (physical and psychic). There are specific recipes for specific issues.

"For agony, a mixture was made and burned with various aromatic herbs, such as rosemary and mint, with the conviction that the spread of that smoke would have benefited the patient by putting an end to his torments, as well as prayers invoking death." 219

If this didn't work, **s'accabbadora** was called. She also tried prayers and sometimes herbal remedies to bring the person back to life or to pass, and if these didn't work, she used the yoke, the comb, or the hammer.

NOTE: Both rosemary and mint are considered apotropaic plants in rural communities. Their properties protect people against negative energies and spirits (in similar but slightly different ways) and also replenish the body after an attack form envy or spirit attachment energy drain.

GUILT for BOUNDARY STONES

"The connection of the boundary stones with the long agony was a known and feared belief throughout Italy." 220 *An ancestral fear surrounds the boundary stones, the so-called terms; their removal reaches a gravity that does not only imply the injury of the rights of others."* 221

Italian Magic: Secret Lives of Women

STONES

The boundary stones marking the corners or edges of land property are deeply respected and their tampering elicits a punishment at the time of death that is deeply feared. There are various beliefs around the border stones: some believe the are watched over by spirits, for example, but everyone believes that moving the border stones, as a sneaky way of stealing more land will surely result in an agonizing death, and therefore there is a similar tradition to the yoke hold one accountable: a stone, or several, were placed underneath the bed of the dying person, or next to the bed, to relieve the agony as well as to serve as a confession to the onlookers that the agonizing person was indeed guilty of moving border stones as he would quickly die after the stones were placed. Stones were placed under the pillow in some areas.

While this may sound superstitious to us outsiders, the reality of this method was profound, so much so that we have evidence of "the Synod of Benevento of 1723, condemning the practice of *'putting the stone on the bedside of the dying man, so that he immediately dies'*". 222 That this practice was condemned by the church meant that it is a cure used by the people that really worked, so it is in competition with the church's god who is supposed to be in charge of these things (whom people should be dependent upon).

> *"The same episode, with a variant: dying, in the presence of the woman he implored: take this stone from my chest!' And in response, she said: 'stone you gave, stone you take, and no one takes it away.' The epilogue is then the same: the man ceased to live."* 223

STONE DUST

Because the idea behind these rituals is to restore balance, the ritual sometimes includes taking something from the criminal in order for the person who committed the act to be released from this debt and pass away:

> stone, a fistful of dust or other from the bed of death." 224 It's the sympathetic act of taking off the burden of the secret, taking off the weight of a crime committed. *This would have been enough to stop the agony and move to a better life."* 225

BRICK

In some areas, a brick was placed under the pillow for border-stones agony.

CERAMIC TILES

In some areas, a ceramic tile is broken in half by two neighbors and placed under a boundary stone in the presence of witnesses to freshly acknowledge the boundary markers. If one of these neighbors is later stuck in agony during death, the ceramic tiles are searched for to check if the agonizer has in fact moved a border stone. If he has been found guilty, the sympathetic ritual is made by placing a piece of the ceramic under the pillow to ease death. The pieces of tile were called **guardiole** in Valnerina, and in the Cerretan, and **guandiole** was the name used in Sellano. [226]

Vulture Goddess from early 7th mill. B.C., in the Anatolian Neolithic Catal Huyuk shrine seen on next page.

Combs from 4000 B.C. Switzerland

Images inspired by "The Language of the Goddess" by Marija Gimbutas

COMB

> *"For extended agony a comb was placed under the agonizing [person's] pillow. Giving an explanation of why it was considered so bad to burn a comb is not easy. Certain beliefs, as we have seen for the boundary stones, start long ago and have been transmitted until quite recently, they had to be well rooted and closely related to the sacred. The comb was in ancient times a symbol of death and regeneration."* [227]

Reading about a comb being put under a pillow to bring death to a suffering person is the kind of passage that can summon criticisms like "this is just a primitive superstition, it's weird" unless you broaden your perspective all the way back to the Upper Paleolithic era where vulture birds and their comb-like wings were found painted and engraved on the walls of caves, specifically in Spain in 13,000 to 11,000BC. [228] to symbolize an important cyclical passage of life and death being infinitely connected. Even before this, burials of vulture wings that had been carefully cut off in the same point and carefully placed (also with other birds who eat only carrion, depending on which birds were living in the area) have been found carefully placed in tombs in a repeated non-random manner in the proto Paleolithic era in various areas showing the same tradition.

The tombs and wings come together again in Catalhoyuk's Neolithic site from 7500 BCE, where symbolic paintings accompany tomb arrangements that show vultures carrying a decapitated body away from the earth and towards its life after death. The vultures are painted red, the color symbolizing the regenerative life force of the Goddess-in-effect. This is where the shape of the comb has not only an earthly and heavenly symbolic meaning, but also serves as a representation of the movement of this energy: The comb/wing as a symbol of energy regenerating, expanding, and therefore, protecting, says in effect "life continues after death of the body," which is a belief found in all oral traditions who honor and communicate with the dead or rather, the living who are no longer on earth.

Italian Magic: Secret Lives of Women

The vulture wing is unique in that it takes a different shape from many other bird wings when spread out and consequently looks like a comb and a flat broom brush at the same time. It's been embraced as a symbol that shows the energy movement, a movement that represents the universal divine feminine energy in the way it moves through the earthly world: in this case, as the sweeping change of physical death that leads to continued life in the spirit world.

And, the vulture is a bird that only eats carrion…it's not a bird that hunts and kills. This is significant because all the birds found in these ritualistic burials in tombs of this pre-Great Pyramid of Egypt era tell a story that shows the bird goddess is assisting already dead people and animals: she is not attacking and killing them, but giving wings to their spirit after death, like the role of the psychopomp.

The transformation of the Goddess into a vulture is well known in Egypt and Greece. The vulture as down-to-earth-goddess-regenerative power, who carries away the flesh, freeing the spirit in the body, is also found together with breasted statues often also decorated with serpents and built into water jugs, tying in those sacred symbols to the divine feminine life force over and over again. Not just as the life force, but also as the psychopomp who helps the cycle of life regenerate.

In the history of ancient art there have been many Goddesses depicted either wearing vulture parts or changing into vultures, and also at the same time being represented as rivers and mountains and crows, combs and brooms. From Athena to the Celtic Triple Goddess in Ireland, found in Gaul, Greece, Egypt and in the Germanic Valkyrie, many unnamed feminine divinities from the earliest spiritual practices were considered death goddesses of regeneration. Outside of myth is the very real, rural-on-earth **s'accabbadora**.

As patriarchal male-centric paganisms began to rewrite spiritual stories, they kept the central theme of regeneration but stole it from the goddess and gave it to male gods. The invented male gods who took on this feminine divine power of being connected to death and rebirth had no parallels in nature, so the mythical language was created by usurping the previously feminine symbols and attributes onto masculine gods.

The bird goddess was turned into the evil witch who harms babies and steals blood, she was now the baba yaga, the vampires, harpies, sirens, death demons, and other creatures modeled after women who prey on new born life especially. Even though men were invading with weapons, this figure was never conceptualized into something evil.

The original goddess symbols connected to death told a different story: that the Goddess accompanied people on their soul-separation journey from their bodies after their natural deaths, helping them continue their lives in the spirit world. This was the original meaning of Diana as "goddess of the hunt": the female psychopomp who led night time processions to collect lost souls and lead them to the afterlife.

These stories were just one of many turning points in the historical re-writing of women's history of delivering babies, curing, divining, and sometimes euthanizing by request. These stories were attacks by men on societal and spiritual fronts. The patriarchal stories say that women kill and take life for a self- serving, vindictive purpose. Not only did this turn-of-tales create fear of women, but also a fear of life and death.

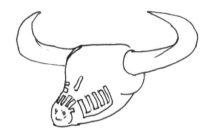

The comb, like many of the symbols of the divine feminine, is a symbol of purification and protection and a combinaation of other meanings all representing representing the energy body of the Goddess in her parallel on earth: the woman.

The comb has traveled from the earliest spiritual artwork in caves, to adorn tombs and decorate statues, and it has touched down in some important places throughout time's stretch away from the beginnings of divinely feminine recognized universe, leaving marks at: Gobekli Tepe, Catalhoyuk, in Celtic artwork from 4000bc, in the Ukraine from 4000-2500bc and into rural Italy.

> *"In the Friulian and among the Ladins obviously the object [...] was used as a propitiatory object to exorcise, since we see it hung around the neck of so many little idols belonging to that period, as well as depicted in pottery from the Bronze Age. The symbolism of this object has crossed thousands of years among the Roman populations, with the conviction that it would have placated the goddess of death or would have accelerated the passage."* [229]

It's maintained the same usage in rural Italy until the 1950s-1970s, and a symbol in physical form like the yoke, found in both birth and death rituals, it is still found in practical use in modern days in the peasant world in Barbagia:

> *"For Ollolai [in Sardinia] for example, until a few decades ago, it was used in the chicken coops, for the hatching that lasted three*

Italian Magic: Secret Lives of Women

weeks, they placed underneath (the hen) from 9 to 13 eggs and covered it with **una corbula, sa quorve,** *and under it were placed 3 white stones and an old tooth and toothless comb to protect the chicks from thunder and lightning. In this case the comb has a protective and apotropaic function."* 230

Outside of Italy *the comb is still worn by European peasants for healing and protection in the same way as shown on this old European figurine *from 4000-3500 B.C.* 231

Writes Marija Gimbutas, *"the European peasants use the comb for protection against diseases or other evils and for healing purposes. Children and women after childbirth wear a comb pendant on their front or back, a custom inherited from prehistory when it was considered necessary to appease the Vulture Goddess (Death), during the period of her rule to secure a safe and healthy life."* 232

Above : Old European figurine wearing comb 4000-3500 B.C., Ukraine.

So, returning to s'accabbadorra *it is not risky to think that this belief [in the comb] comes to us from the prehistoric period and that, without interruption, it has been transmitted underground to our time,* 233 as are the rites of the border stones.

BLACK CLOAK

The **accabbadora** is said to wear a black cloak, the type that covers her face. So even though the family and the dying person knows her, she assumes an anonymous role for the death ritual, one of neutrality, rather than one of a familiar and personal nature. Sometimes seeing her in this way was enough to frighten someone back to life for a period of time.

Even though **s'accabbadora** isn't written about so much, people all across Italy and her islands are aware and accepting of her existence, from the Veneto to Umbria to many villages in Campania who are very different from each other, to people living on the far reaches of the coastlines.

"They were dressed in black and wore a cape, a macabre coincidence makes them 'resemble' Death, and when you saw one, in fact some one had to die." 234

DEATH: La Morte

"it was like calling Death in person, arriving at night, wrapped in a black cloak, only in her hand she had the hammer instead of the scythe. It sometimes happened that he recovered due to the fear of ending up in hell and the desire for revenge. We returned to ourselves by a sort of desire for expiation and to chase a second chance. And sometimes it worked!"[235]

L-r: The ziggurat of Monte d'Accoddi , Sardinia, euthanasia olivaster hammer, white alabaster lady

HAMMER

Perhaps the most shock-inducing tool of **s'accabbadure** is the hammer which is used to give a quick and precise blow to the head of the dying person. The purpose of this tool is to end suffering, but the image of the hammer does have a rather imposing look to it: with a large top end, sensibly weighted to create a quick and fatal blow. Its design is exceedingly simple-looking, which is probably the reason it makes people gasp uncomfortably; it is blunt and bold. Perhaps it's also due to the beauty of its somber wood.

"The very heavy hammer is made of olivaster wood, 42 cm long and 24 cm wide, with a short handle that allows you to grip it with confidence to facilitate its aim so that you can give a strong and sure shot. [236]

*"**Su Mazolu**, [a local name for the hammer] was used, a sort of hammer made of olivastro wood, of which only one specimen is known, preserved in the Ethnographic Museum of Luras.[in Sardinia].* [237]

*"A single, firm hit was given in the temporal bone, causing a painless and instantaneous death. The **mazzolu**, as well as the skills to perform this 'job', **were inherited from mother to daughters or nieces**, taking care of keeping the identity of this figure the least known possible."* [238]

Italian Magic: Secret Lives of Women

OTHER GODS + GODDESSES WITH HAMMERS

In addition to the most ancient Vulture Goddess (**Dea Avvoltoio** is the Italian translation but not the original name) being connected to these traditions, there are other later-period gods and goddesses who have also similarities to not just the tools used by **s'accabbadora**, but to her figure herself.

However, most of them have been turned into male gods accessorized with the original divinely feminine symbols of regeneration and life force power. This is what "paganisms" are essentially: a vast group spiritual practices formed during varying degrees of separation from the original divinely feminine cosmogony, and built "on top" of pre-existing matrilineal spiritual beliefs, symbols and concepts. Naming all these practices "paganism" really doesn't work: many of them are not related to each other at all and have fundamental differences with the exception that they all mark periods in time where men, as they established the patriarchy, placed themselves not only at the center of society but also at the center of the universe, taking over the regenerative life-giving roles of the mother goddesses.

For example, some practices lumped into the "pagan" category are oral traditions which share identical compositions to shamanism around the globe, other "paganisms" are based on masculine savior-gods that don't include any feminine figure of fertility in similar ways to Christianity, and on. Ceremonial magic and Wicca-type binary god/goddess practices have noting in common with Mithraism, and this is subject that needs to be untangled at a greater depth than will be done here.

Therefore, in myths of the psychopomps we mostly have stories about masculine roles who nevertheless are decorated with and who use tools and symbols that were originally connected to the goddess and were an expression of her life force's movement through the universe and its parallel earth. These stories are nevertheless important because they show theft of what came before…whereas Goddesses in later time periods were remodeled into the masculine ideal and stripped of their original symbols, which essentially cuts them off from the historical trail.

Since men were the ones who re-wrote the spiritual myths and then documented them and documented history itself (while women were forbidden to write and read), we therefore only have their side of the historical story in written records.

DEATH: La Morte

KARUN, known in Italian as CARONTE, is a masculine figure depicted assuming the previously feminine role of psychopomp; a figure whose role is to guide new spirits to their afterlife. Mentioning the name Caronte to most Italians illicits a terrified facial response, or at the least a head shake "no, no".

The role of spirit figures in death processes are much more specialized than simply "guide to the afterlife" and "god of the underworld" (who was previously a goddess, by the way). A psychopomp is actually a helper. In the Greek tradition, Charon also called Kharon, has a different role. In the Italian tradition, Caronte's role is positive. In Sardegna there is a different figure whose role was definitely terrifying, which you will read about shortly.

The specific role of a psychopomp is to take a newly released spirit (one who just detached from a dead body) and lead the spirit through purification, awareness of death rites, mental states, opportunities to face a "life review", and things of this nature which take place before a spirit even goes to the light or is able to travel towards the rest of its life in the spirit world. These processes begin even before the physical death transition has been completed and have been considered an essential post-death condition where the new spirit is reliant on guidance to make the right steps towards its afterlife.

For example, a human being's spirit knows when it is ready to die, but, as already mentioned, mindsets of guilt or attachment to physical life can cause a struggle between the smaller will and the greater wisdom of the soul. The psychopomp can help, by bringing loved ones and friends who are already in the spirit world to come be envisioned by the dying person (often at the literal foot of their death bed) so they feel more at ease to pass over. This same technique is often used by Mediums who help spirits lost in the astral realm cross over into the light, and it brings an ease to spirits who are otherwise afraid or resistant to complete their death transition.

In Italy's villages, stories survive about goddesses who, before they were turned into huntresses and war-supporters by Romans, had the same roles we find for feminine spirit helpers in many central Asian and Siberian shamanism groups. In these stories goddesses such as Diana and the Signora del Gioco were reportedly seen leading processions through the forest with a trail of lost spirits that were being taken home to the spirit world.

These same goddesses and spirit women were also documented as having served the helpful purpose of reconnecting women with: divination techniques, secrets of herbs, cures, and more, often in the forest or around the fountains and rivers where women were doing their laundry. Additionally, these spirit women were reported as being able to bring to life again animals that had just been killed for food.

The role of the psychopomp in Siberian and central Asian shamanism is a dual one: there are spirits who are psychopomps (in Italy, for example, Ecate/Hekate takes this role) and there are flesh-and-blood shaman who are psychopomps (in Italy, **s'accabadure** take this role). Also in Australian shamanism, (where tree fertility rituals bear a striking similarity to ones practiced in rural Italy), we find specialists in the realm of the spirit as

126

healers or psychopomps and keepers of the land or community. The Tungusic shaman's **saman** mission is to ensure that the spiritual equilibrium of the entire society is maintained, [239] which is also the role of **s'accabbadora**.

In these worlds a shaman is indispensable in any ceremony that concerns the experience of the human soul [240] which of course applies to the release of the soul from the physical body during the death transition. Performing exorcisms against **il malocchio** (the evil eye) and the **s'accabbadora's** rituals with herbs, amulet removal, and magic words all fall into this category.

In Italy there are ancient traditions kept by women, which are inherited mostly within family lines, and to a lesser extent but also absolutely present there are traditions inherited by men in the same way, sometimes being passed from female family members to male ones. These traditions, which remain unaltered as they are passed to a new healer, are cures for what Italians believe are ultimately ailments caused by spiritual imbalance and *according to the principle that diseases originate from bad spirits.* [241] Most Lineage cures release the physical body of symptoms and in parallel release the spirit of negative energy attacking it, from other spirits or from spells and are, in effect, exorcisms. And, the cures are activated with the channeled energy of the divine feminine and helper spirits.

SHAPE-SHIFTING INTO ANIMALS

The idea of anthropomorphism tells us that humans see themselves in animals, claiming that the historical images and statues are expressions of "the attribution of human traits, emotions, or intentions to non-human entities, but this is truly a short-sighted view, one likely developed from the outside; that is, someone who hasn't experienced a spiritual practice where and understanding of other people, places, and consciousness is achieved through communication with other conscious beings.

In oral traditions, from shamanism to spiritualism, the knowledge passed down from teacher to student initiate is knowledge received from the spirit world, and not the other way around. This spirit world knowledge includes the wisdom and teaching of consciousness in the forms of animals, plants, and all nature, from spirits who lived on earth in bodies and from high guides and divinities who were never embodied; knowledge from consciousness.

The spirits teach the people these methods. In shamanism, the methods are created by the spirits who instruct the people on which materials and actions to use...and this is why these methods look "uneducated, messy," and not glamorous and polished as they do in Roman style temples. It's also the spirits who create the cures and rituals. The anthropological stance claims, in contrast, that men create their own meanings and place them upon nature and animals...and yet this is simply not true for insiders.

The materials used by the shaman are made by hand and from whatever is available in their accessible neighborhoods. Therefore, the materials used as tools are not made of carved and polished marble and ornate poured gold: they are herbs, animal parts, plants, tree branches, spit and blood, sounds of voices both human and animal, etc. And, it is the same for Lineage healers, who use pebbles, spit, vines, discarded bird feathers, tree branches, stones, moonlight, oil and water, fire, etc. In the traditions of Sardinia especially, there are masks and bells and rituals around the cycles of nature that echo shaman traditions that are not part of a current shaman practice any longer, are still celebrated around the island.

Images of costumes specific to villages in Sardinia. There is a large variety of masks and costumes incorporating bells of different sizes. They bear striking similarities to many other shamanic costumes from around the world.

> *"It is the shaman who turns himself into an animal, just as he achieves a similar result by putting on an animal mask...a new identity for the shaman, who becomes an animal-spirit and "speaks", sings, or flies like the animals and birds."* [242]

The Pomo and Menomini shaman, among others [243] learn bird languages which become part of their secret shaman language, therefore also assuming a new language. The shaman doesn't turn the animal into a human and give the animal a new identity: the shaman's viewpoint, abilities, and powers and methods of movement become that of the

Italian Magic: Secret Lives of Women

animal he turns into for the purposes of astral flight, for curing, protecting, aiding in the death transition, etc. Also, it's the spirit teachers of the shaman, along with the animal spirits, who choose the shaman and help the shaman shape-shift: this ability does not come from the shaman herself.

This shape-shifting tradition exists in Italy as well, among the wolf-shifters of the Benandanti, and the women who shift into owls, cats, and foxes as they fly to the dreamworld to learn from the Ladies from Outside **donne di fuora.** Early descriptions of Diana in Italy were not as a warrior but as a psychopomp who changed into wolf form as she was helping spirits find their way into the afterlife during nighttime processions through the forests. Then there are an array of bird goddess statues from 5000 BC depicting female bodies mixed with bird parts, both water birds and vultures and owl shapes.

The rural Italian Lineage methods look strange and superstitious many people would say, but they are arranged by spirits and spirits channel energy through them, using the healer or **s'accabbadora** as the conduit. Those cures and the euthanasia are activated through the quiet mumbling of their secret prayers and invocations which often sound nonsensical to outsiders, themselves representing an idea represented by words that are a spirit language.

TOOLS OF THE PSYCHOPOMP

Tools and physical attributes of the "death-assistant" who also protects the spirits of people who are passing, as seen in illustrative depictions of the historically documented psychopomps are: The Hammer, The Hammer marked with an X, Snakes, Vulture parts, apotropaic teeth that are protective against negative energy and negative spirits.

THE HAMMER
THE HAMMER with X SYMBOL

Karun/Charon/Caronte/ Charun have been typically depicted in the spiritual myths wielding a hammer with an X on it. These beings are also considered protectors and psychopomp-helper-guides. While their depictions are mainly found in spiritual myths and spiritual artwork, which stretch back into an unknown ancient origin, the hammer was (and perhaps still is) an actual physical tool in the very physically real embodiment of the earthly psychopomp, **femmina s'accabbadora.**

Interestingly, this X symbol has historically been used to mark the place of life-nourishing breast milk and breasts of the mother as the divine feminine's parallel on earth in statues from 5000 BC for example. The X as a symbol of the most ancient Goddess also survived throughout the many masculine makeovers of pre-Roman Goddesses and can be seen in statues where either straps (and straps decorated with bells) create an X across a Goddess' body, or as the "Isaic Knot" as it was known (The knot of Isis) created by tying two straps of fabric into a knot between the breasts.

DEATH: La Morte

Iside, as Isis is known in Italy, is often seen by people there (and anthropologists acknowledge this peasant-born belief) as one-and-the same as the Madonna and the Great Mother, and she is venerated still, even if she is hidden in Madonnas. These beliefs vary by village and region, but Iside is well-beloved in Italy, and this X has long been associated with her and shows an important link to the function and offerings of this Goddess…but did not begin with her. The X associated with the Great Goddess Mother is much older than even Iside.

While there doesn't appear to be a hammer in this body of spiritual symbolic language that expresses the feminine life force energy, there is a "double axe" which looks similar to the olivaster hammer of **s'accabbador**a.

SNAKES

Charon is depicted with snakes wrapped around his arms or in his hands, and he is not the first masculine figure to be drawn or sculpted with serpents in the imitation of female divinities who came before.

Snakes have historically been used to symbolize a spiritual connection to the Goddess' regenerative life force of life-giving fluids, of life-after-death, as a symbol of transformation of a spiritual initiate, and as messengers between the world of spirit and the physical world.

Italian Magic: Secret Lives of Women

The regenerative fluids often drawn in serpentine shape are: vaginal fluid, blood of the placenta as well as the stem cells of menstrual blood...all natural, active, living symbols that indicate life is continually renewing itself.

These powers have been expressed as being energies whose nutritive value is parallel to water sources like rivers and oceans and fountains and wells. These waters have been connected together in spiritual art marked with images of snakes and breasts together on water jugs, rivers have been marked with breast-bearing menhir, fishnet/snake skin patterns along with undulating lines that mimic both the serpent's movements and the flow of waters are found on feminine representative art, along with water bird Goddess figurines.

The regenerative life force of the Great Goddess Mother has been expressed as phases and movements of energy since the earliest of representations of spirits. The Bona Dea and other divinely feminine figures who were messengers to people, passing down esoteric knowledge and healing methods, were depicted as having serpents wrapped around their arms or marking sacred places on their bodies It was not until much later in time that men used the serpent symbol with male gods of healing such as Asclepius, or with male psychopomp figures. Serpents, whatever gender was imparted to them, have long been considered messengers to the earthly world from the spirit world and vice-versa.

VULTURE PARTS

Caronte is depicted as having a vulture face and hooked nose and is often paired with Etruscan winged goddess Vanth. Another known name for the psychopomp in Italian history is Charu, the Etruscan figure depicted as escorting spirits to the afterlife. The figure Caronte, in the Romanized history, bears only a similar name to the Greek version of this psychopomp: their purposes, accoutrements and representations differ. The Greek figure stands at the helm of a boat, equipped with an oar, and serves as a death-ferry man of souls who takes coins for payment to cross into the afterlife, whereas Charu serves the dead as protector up to a certain point on their journey towards completing their death transition.

It has been the feminine vulture goddess who was the original psychopomp, regenerating life by taking souls into the spirit world to prepare for life after the disconnection from their physical bodies as depicted in the tombs of Catal Hoyuk in the early 7th millennium B.C. The vulture was not the only bird associated with the divine feminine's supernatural universal powers on-earth. She was also depicted as water birds as a nutritive force, and as night flying birds, as astral traveler who could travel from the physical world to the spirit world and back again. These early beliefs celebrated the connectedness of death and life, life and death as a continued, unbroken cycle. While these beliefs are found in rural Italy and in Sardinia's celebrated ancient rituals, they are also found in the shamanism and communities of shaman in central Asia and Siberia.

DEATH: La Morte

APOTROPAIC TEETH

Karun's face is depicted in a frightening manner, often with long wild boar teeth for the apotropaic purpose of protection. The wild boar was originally associated with the Goddess. So even here, in earlier myths about the masculinized vulture goddess, the action was one of assistance and protection, and not about vampirism nor greedy death. The Medusa has a similar history which is too detailed to mention here, but it's worthy to note she's another Divinely Feminine protectress who was remodeled into an evil temptress role by men for the purpose of turning people away from her protective power, through fear tactics, so they would seek the protection of men instead, both on a spiritual level and an earthly one. It's a way of corralling people socially into the new order. Medusa's power lingered, however, and was used on Roman armor.

Italy's stories are rife with these social directives to turn people against feminine power and towards masculine power which ironically, has proven evidentially to be much more evil than the allegedly evil witches they created.

"With the face of vulture and with snakes in hand, and we conclude with Charun who, like the **accabadoras,** *put end to life with a hammer."* 244

ASSISTANTS

Caronte and his earthly counterpart **s'accabadora** were seen as HELPERS and not as DEATH GIVERS-TAKERS as the later anthropologists or writers would try to sensationalize them to be. **S'accabbadora** helps to ease deaths already in-process and stuck to the point of agony by bringing a spiritual balance; whether trying to bring the person back to life with curative methods, or helping the person release their soul into death. The difference between Caronte and **s'accabbadora** is that **s'accabbadora** exists in real life (not in myth), and the role of **s'accabbadora** in Italy's rural villages is one held exclusively by women.

SARIDNIA, ZIGGURATS, AND HAMMER GOD

On the Italian island of Sardinia there is a mythological figure whose name has gone through several etymological changes over time, but whose role has stayed the

Italian Magic: Secret Lives of Women

same: an masculine executioner of sorts, albeit with an evil attitude who punishes people guilty of committing serious sins (or what were considered serious at the time and place and whose type varies greatly) by giving them an agonizing death…to which the **s'accabbadora** must be called to finish by bringing mercy and an end to the agonized life.

Both Micidissu and Ningirsu have gone through name changes over the passage of time, but it's suggested by Sardinian author Dolores Turchi they each have etymological developments that may have originated in the same place: Minzitissu, Minzidissu, Ningirsu, Mingirsu, Mincissu, Mincidissu, Mindicissu. [245]

This figure, as expressed in the story of Micidissu, has connections to the Sumerian god Ningirsu: both figures are depicted using the accessory of a killing "bat" or hammer.

> *The talk of Mindicissu is not the talk of a devil, but rather that of a strict executioner who applies the penalty without reductions, forcing a sinner to return what he has stolen. Only in this way will it make it easier to pass away. For now, it's in no hurry to hit.* [246]

Both of these gods share an identical description, in that they both appeared to dying people who were in agony and they did not relive the agony, instead letting the dying person struggle as a punishment for crimes such as theft. The struggle was meant to be a payment for the debt of the crime. And both of these figures carried large bats/clubs. It's as though they were applying pressure from the spirit world, asking for a payment due…while s'accabbadora was taking the payment, rewarding the soul with release, so it would enter the spirit world in a state of balance, without any debt to pay.

Another curious connection between the Mincidissu of Sardinia and Ningirsu of Sumeria is that both were worshiped or honored in temples that are ziqqurats.

> *In Sardinia there is the ziqqurat of Monte Accoddi near Porto Torres, dated around 2500 a. C. We do not know if the worshiped divinity was called Ningirsu, but it is possible that the name reached up to us is the corruption of which Ningir-su may in time have been transformed into Mingirsu and subsequently into Mincissu, Mincidissu.* [247]

DEATH: La Morte

As mentioned, Ningirsu was always depicted with the bat in his hand. Ofelia Pinna writes in 1921 of the people of Sassari, where she remembers a tradition that remotely resembles that of the **accabadoras** that had just disappeared:

> *When a dying man was plagued by the throes of a slow agony, those*
> *of the family thought that he, when he was alive, must have burnt*
> *some old club built from the yoke of oxen; they then ran to look for*
> *one of these clubs from a neighboring house and put it between the*
> *bed and the mattress of the bed where the dying man was planning*
> *with the certainty that his life would soon be shortened.* 248

This ties together not only a history of "paying for a crime" but also the bat and the yoke and bringing a soul to "balance of debt" during an agonizing death so it can be released and pass into the afterlife. There are also reports from villagers explaining how their **s'accabbadora**, after putting the yoke under the neck of a dying person, would then "make some formulas* and then slam" 249 meaning that the **s'accabbadora** would say her secret prayers or invocation and then strike quickly with her hammer. So In the Sardinian tradition, the **s'accabbadora** pays the debt and releases the dying from agony.

And yet, in Italian style, people with these Lineage (inherited) traditions, are not marketed nor advertised . And yet, for those who need these things like the assistance of **s'accabbadora**, magic, and other cures, everyone knows who to go to. Someone always knows where the healers can be found. If you have a particular ailment, you can be guided to the healer who heals that particular ailment. And yet no one talks about it, because the attitude is that the healers are for those who have needs: they are not to be studied nor marketed. So, everyone keeps it a natural secret. Resources are made available to those who seek, when they seek. Other than that, the mysterious and supernatural are not talked about, nor analyzed, nor sought.

FEMALE SAINTS OF BIRTH AND DEATH
AS THE SPIRITUAL COUNTERPARTS TO MIDWIVES AND S'ACCABBADURE

The connection between female midwives assisting young life to be born from womens' bodies, and **femmina s'accabadure** assisting spirits in departing their old bodies finds its parallel in the realm of female saints as well.

Sant'Anna *Saint Anna the same Saint called upon for labor also called upon for death [Sant'Anna also of a pagan origin]* 250 and to Anna Perenna, a goddess of the country people who protected them from abusive societal powers. More than that, Sant'Anna and Santa Marta together were prayed to in a early pagan conjuration in popular magic formulas, appealed to like the Fates for matters of life and death:

> *"they always went together, they tied and cut the thread together,*
> 251 *so that the thread of the life of the creature in agony was cut off.*
> *There exists a little conjuration spell asking for their help as well."*
> 252

Italian Magic: Secret Lives of Women

This may shed some light on the connection rural women feel towards female saints being inspirations to them in their daily lives, and why they view female saints as accessible spirit helpers who understand their plight and can help them with their needs. The spirit world, in turn, offers validation for the parallel role of "midwife for life and death."

COMMUNITY FUNERAL RITES

To gain some insight into the impact of death in rural communities, the following passages written by author Emanuela Tocci about her traditions from Acri in Calabria are presented:

> *"Unlike the Greek and Roman tradition in which the kingdom of the dead is considered a reality in itself and distant, death in Acri and throughout Calabria, is a continuation of life in a different dimension, a very close dimension, at times almost palpable, as if it were only a veil to separate them. In the "Acrese" funeral ritual there are many points in common with the funeral dimension of antiquity.*
>
> *The loss of a loved one breaks the dynamic balance of collective life, and this "social void" depends on the intensity of the position that the deceased had in the life of society and its groups: death destroys not only the "physical person" but also the "social person" and therefore the relationship of the individual with his group. With the death of a person being itself a ritual, a way of acting is set in motion, and with it the tradition is perpetuated, and therefore, in many ways, the identity of the community.*
>
> *For this reason, death is experienced by the community as a threat to social cohesion. Here then comes the rites of the funeral, the last greeting to the corpse, the funeral vigils, the anniversary masses, the condolences and expressions of condolences from friends and acquaintances."*[253]

The ensuing rituals, also found in other villages in other regions of Italy, are comprised of various duties that look quite humble but reflect ancient beliefs in the continuation of life of the soul after it departs the physical body in the transition we call death. The greater rituals are performed by women.

> *Rituals that not only help in the elaboration of mourning, but transform the negative state of the deceased into the positive state of the dead.* [254]

DEATH: La Morte

BODY PREPARATION

It's common for the midwives to care for the dead bodies, whether ones of children or adults. From rural villages on mainland Italy to the island of Sardegna, there are threads of connection among funeral rituals based on the same essential idea: birth and death are a cycle of life, and therefore sacred preparations must be done to both new bodies coming into this world as well as for the old ones from whom the soul has detached. Life continues, and it is the woman who is the central figure of assistance for the soul in whichever body it is contained.

With baby traditions, from first baths to the first cutting of fingernails and first haircuts and more, these seemingly mundane practical actions are performed as rituals, imbued with intentions and prayers whose purpose is to instill, at this very first ages, a foundation of good values in the personality of the baby. For example, the nail cutting ritual focuses on preventing the baby from becoming a thief. Other rituals such as protecting it from envy, preventing it from holding onto cravings the mother had during pregnancy and others focus on other guided intentions.

Concerning death, the rituals revolve around preparing the soul to have every object or condition it needs to continue life in the spirit world and to do so free of encumbrances or remnants of the past, as well as having actions that bear resemblance to a rebirth into the afterlife. A common procedure from the island of Sardinia illustrates the woman's role, who is often a midwife or midwives:

> ...for the sick person, there was still the woman to assist him during and after death. Her task was to wash the body of the deceased, put it into the coffin (and before it existed, on the litter). Although such operations required a more than feminine force, the women in the family never turned to the men, but they called three women involved in these operations, relatives or neighbors. [255]

BELLS FOR LIFE, BELLS FOR DEATH

As was mentioned in the BIRTH chapter, bells in rural Italy were used to announce the arrival of new life, with differing rings announcing the birth of a girl or a boy. In death, bells are also used to let the community know about the transition of a loved one the gender of the person who has transitioned, thus setting a boundary:

> "Two strokes were played at a time to announce the death of a male; three at a time for the female[232] In Santa Anatolia, in the event of the death of a male person, the largest bell in the church was played, which produces a darker sound; in case of a woman's death the bell was sounded more clear and shrill. In the first case it was said "sonà 'a uominiom, in the second" Sona' a femmina". [256]

Bells were also used to mark the transition from day to night, and to set a boundary between *the period of activity and the rest period.* [256] For example, it was often used as a call to return home from work in the fields, and certain chores were not done after the bell sounded.

Bells also marked an even more important separation: one acknowledging the significant shift between day to night, not just as a demarcation between time for work and rest, but also to call attention to the opening doors between the visible world of the physical and the unseen world of spirits. This boundary is of acknowledgment and not of denial, of the possibility of worlds intersecting through apparitions and chance meetings with spirits during the nighttime.

> *The deceased could cross the barrier that separates the dead from the living and return to do visit to his relatives, or appear in certain places.* [25]

Since death in the rural world doesn't mean the end of life but rather a transition, there are many rituals honoring the transition rather than just the "end" of something or someone. Everything has it's place: the physically embodied people live on the physical earth, and the people who have died have not ceased to live: they have just detached from their physical bodies and are living as spirits elsewhere. This "elsewhere", while related to the theme of nighttime and the realm of the invisible, is nevertheless not a wall but a door that can be traversed by the spirits to visit the embodied living, whether relatives, scary demonic spirits and devils, and friends:

> *The popular saying warns that: the day is made for the living, the night for the dead".* [259] *The harmless presences of the family members should not be removed: it is their right to return to the places where they lived, without disturbing the development of the life of the living.* [260]

Spirits of relatives and loved ones can also be asked for help or for guidance, and spirits ask those living on earth for help too. People will ask ghosts and ancestor spirits for help with guidance in community issues and daily life needs or curiosities, for example. While many of rural Italy's rituals and beliefs were more cohesive in rural communities, many of the beliefs are found throughout a broader culture, even if we can't say Italy is "one unified culture". Beliefs about the spirit world in places like Italy haven't changed much over the passage of time, as people are deeply connected to their vast and ancient histories whether in practice or in education, and beliefs haven't changed much over the passage of time. Rural Italy's deculturalization (as Italians call it) began not too long ago anyway, starting in the 1970s...10 to 20 years earlier in some regions' villages and 10 to 20 years later in others.

Outside of the mundane, spirits of the female saints, the Madonna in her many forms, and goddesses of nature were all implored for assistance during childbirth, for protection of newborns, for promoting fertility, and cures.

DEATH: La Morte

PROCESSION RITUALS

Another ritual which has parallels in both the physical world and spirit world and that is used to celebrate moments of birth and death is the procession. Processions are rituals used to mark transitions between life and death, they are used to implore spirits (as saints, as Madonnas, as goddesses and as nature spirits) for various types of assistance, and processions are used by the spirit world as well, for their own rituals often observed by people living in the country and in forests. Most processions of these rural ritualistic efforts are led by and performed by women.

Some examples of Processions made by flesh and blood people asking for assistance from the spirit world are:

* Ones led by particular numbers of virgin girls (4, 7, or 9) wearing white. Virgin girls are hired for their ability to deliver effective prayers requesting healing for an ill person still suffering after other methods to restore health have failed and also for escorting the bodies of dead infants and small children to the church. In the case of dead children, girls are used in the processions of baby girls, and boys are used in processions of dead boys. They all wear white. Some girls walk, while others make their way in a slow march on their knees.

* Processions of women wearing black and carrying rosaries were used in some regions, but more often than not, processions of women wearing black were believed to be spirits in mourning rather than physically embodied people, due to the ritualistic color of death (in the transitional phase) to be white. The use of white as a color related to the rituals of death in Italy goes back to end of the 5th millennium M.C.

* Infertile mothers asking for fertility have long made processions to Birth Trees, asking for the spirits of their babies to come into their wombs through the hollow of the birth trees.

* Processions by groups of women to **galattofore** caves asking for the abundance of breast milk production, processions to mountaintops asking the feminine divine in one form or another for help in various ailments and for successful childbirth, and processions to other naturally charged locations are all examples of ancient rituals performed by rural women.

* Processional rituals led by spirit people can also be found throughout Italy's documented history (and even more sightings exist in the shared stories of locals), appearing in many diverse regions and yet consistently reported as: processions of spirits being led through the forest by a singular female figure who often flies through the sky and sometimes takes the form of a wolf. It's also commonly reported that animals spirits are among the people spirits in these processions. When this type of procession is seen by people at night, they run away, due to the common fear that the procession might grab them up and take them along, and thus take them from their life on earth. The female psychopomps who lead these processions are seen also as fairies,

Italian Magic: Secret Lives of Women

as a type of angel of death who is really acting as a protectress of lost spirits, gathering them, along with spirits of animals, to take them home to their place in the spirit world.

* Processional rituals led by spirits themselves who are vising other spirits in graveyards and walking familiar roads:

> *The procession of Fosso Iaccone (Cerreto). Near the cemetery of Vallerio [...] During the whole month of November, at one time, a nocturnal procession of ghosts could be seen which, in the light of candles, chanting, emerged from the ravine and headed to the cemetery8 The theme of the procession of the dead, at least in the current situation of deculturalization of tradition rural, appears little widespread in Valnerina. Comparisons with the neighboring territory of Leonessa make it possible to suppose that, long ago, legends in the Umbrian territory were much more numerous.*

> *In the legends of Leonardo, midnight struck, the dead go in procession, from the cemetery to the church, passing through the deserted streets of the villages, in the light of dim lights.* 261

And in Val D'Aosta, spirits in processions were commonly seen with flames coming out of their fingers, as if they were candles.

The processions for the newly dead organized by flesh-and-blood surviving relatives and community members are more like a send-off to the spirit world with detailed actions whose efforts honor and release the spirit of a recently deceased person rather than to fight against this transition in life.

There are rituals for clothing, food, doors and windows, sweeping, and mourning using the voice, all created with the careful consideration that a soul is departing and its path to the spirit world should be uninterrupted by the living. Every effort is made to prepare the spirit with familiar things it might need during its journey to cross over. Truly, it is an acknowledgment that life continues on for a person after they separate from their physical body in the transition we call death.

PERSONAL ITEMS PLACED IN COFFINS

In Acri, Calabria, coins were often placed in coffings to pay for transport until the afterlife, which is a ritual that takes after the Greek Charon tradition. In Sardinia, *it is still common to lay objects in the funeral bed, of a comb, a needle and a piece of cloth [...] ."* 262

In Sardinia we find a type of spirit called **panas** or **pantamas** which are the spirits of women who died in childbirth. *The word pana, as V. Diószegi has shown, is a Manchu-Tungus term [language found in East Siberia] meaning soul-shadow.* 263

DEATH: La Morte

In the popular belief, the spirits of these women who died in tragedy will be restless unless, for a period of 7 years, their spirits visit the river or spring or fountain and perform a combination of daily life rituals such as: washing their bloody clothes or the clothes of their baby, sewing, and combing the hair of their husband. They must be able to do these things for 7 years uninterrupted before their souls can reach peace and move on. It is believed the things that can interrupt the **panas** are: being distracted from going to the river to do their chores and, being distracted by the newborn babies of their former earthly neighborhood.

To assist them on their 7 year journey, specific items are buried with them, which is a practice performed until 50 years ago in places:

> *A piece of cloth, a needle with a knotted thread, a pair of scissors, a petine and a tuft of her husband's hair were therefore placed within the coffin, so that they would have the sewing equipment the clothes of their child. In some countries a piece of soap was also added.* [264]

These efforts and beliefs are focused on keeping these spirits in their place, which is doing their duties in the spirit world so they can move onward from these tragedies. *"Good or bad, glorious or damned, a ghost is always a ghost and, like any otherness, it's an intrusion in the order usual of life ."* [265] Because in rural communities, people are very aware of restless spirits and experience the negative effects, which is basically what all the fearful "folk tales" about vampire witches are about: the restless spirits who envy the living and act like succubi on them or their children at night. This is why people leave brooms outside their doors and bowls of salt grains at the doors and windows: to catch up the spirits (of the former town folk) in the act of counting grains that they will surely be unable to do (for lack of education) and thereby be distracted from their envious mission of haunting the flesh-and-blood living: keeping things in their place.

Placing locks of the husbands' hair in the coffin of the women who died in childbirth is also something practiced by female widows:

> *At the death of her husband, the widow tore off a large amount of hair and laid it on the body, a custom common to all of southern Italy.* [266]

Another example of keeping a spirit in its place and holding onto it in some way is from *Onani, Lula and Orune, [in Sardinia]:*

> *When a mother died, her nails and part of her hair were cut so that the fortune of the house was not taken away; sometimes these were carried by the widower.* [267]

This is a comprehensive extension of the practice of putting placenta pieces (from babies born wearing it) into a little protective pouch that only the child can wear. This keeps the baby's special energy with it, and keeps it away from anyone who'd want to use it against the baby magically. The idea that personal "parts" hold a charge are found in

Italian Magic: Secret Lives of Women

magical practices worldwide. This is just one more example of how that concept has actual roots in daily life rather than being born from a conceptually created practice of wealthy people and their temples and magic schools.

It's worth mentioning here, since these rural communities whose magical works are often overlooked due to an appearance of syncretism, that *the use of putting objects in the burial is denounced by various synods, which have always forbidden similar practices But the custom had to be well established.* [268] In fact, most daily magical practices (meaning all the rituals regarding death, life, fertility, and food) have been criticized by the church at one time or another, so it's not appropriate to consider rural Italy to be in a "subservient" relationship with the church even if symbols of the church are as much as part of the communities as their magic.

CLOTHING

From Acri in Calabria:

> *"The sad funeral rite begins with the composition of the corpse, which is stripped of the cloths of everyday life and covered with the best clothes. The shoes must necessarily be new to symbolize the long journey that awaits him.* [269]

And yet we find the opposite in other regions' villages, such as Trognano in Umbria, where they don't put shoes on the deceased, only new clothing.

> *"The day after the funeral, in Ogliastra, until the sixties some relatives went to the house of the dead with basins on the head, in a row from the oldest to the youngest. The women washed the clothes of the dead with 7 pieces of soap given by the closest relative of the deceased. They then returned the washed clothes but not the advanced soap that was divided by the women, otherwise the dead could not have entered Paradise.* [270]

CLOTHING : WHITE AND BLACK

It's tradition in many rural places for the color white to be worn for funeral processions and proceedings, whether worn by children escorting the body or worn by the men carrying the coffin or pushing the sled for the coffin. White is worn during the during the death transition, whereas post-death, the widows (if they were women) wore black for the rest of their lives. The purpose of these clothing rituals for the community are to acknowledge a shift between the dead person's life on earth and living their continuation of life in the spirit world.

DEATH: La Morte

In Acri, Calabria:

All relatives dressed in black during the funeral and also later ,for a period of time that varied according to the degree of kinship and sex: men for some years, women even for a lifetime. Children and boys were exempt from mourning. [271]

Many older people tend to conform to residual social habits, dressing with particular sobriety or even black for a period of time, depending on the drama of the mournful event and the degree of parental or sentimental closeness with the dead. [272]

Always men, until the 70s wore a long beard until the thirtieth day and, as an exterior sign of mourning, wore shirts with black buttons and black stockings. [273]

In Nuoro, Sardinia:

After the funeral, once the condolences were over, all the clothes were dressed in black. In other regions there are similar traditions with varying lengths of time for the male widow to wear his beard until it's cut. For some widowed women, they must wear their grieving shirt until it falls apart.

In Acri, Calabria:

Today, however, the dress of mourning is no longer considered the measure of pain by the majority of the Acris population: "The mourning is carried within". [274]

Another tradition is one that runs threads of connections also in BIRTHING traditions and CURING traditions which is an attitude of using intention blended with the natural movement of a natural force:

*to help free the **pana** from her fatigue* [from wandering eternally along the streams to washing her clothes eternally], *after dying in childbirth, people entrusted expert women (who were not mere laundresses, but experts in certain rituals) to wash the laundry of nine women who had happily given birth to their own child. Naturally this work had to be carried out by the same people who had started it, just as the washing had to take place always at the same stream. Who offered herself for this operation did not have to look at the water when her work began, but turned her back to the stream so as to throw the first cloth behind her, keeping her eyes closed and without saying a word. In short she had to behave as if she herself were the spirit of the deceased.* [275]

Italian Magic: Secret Lives of Women

If you read "Italy's Witches and Medicine Women Vol 1," then this act of "throwing something into the past" will be familiar from the pages where curing traditions with water from the Emilia-Romagna region are described. The clothing aspect, of holding a bonded charge between mother and children, is expressed elsewhere in Italy when a mother sews a piece of her wedding gown into her baby's baptism dress or other item of clothing, signifying a loving link between the two.

BODY ADORNMENTS ON THE DECEASED

From Sardinia:

"Around the 1950s in some Sardinian villages, it was still common to cover the dead man with basil, [and] in Muravera with paper flowers. In Perdas, direct testimony of a woman of 1907, the dead were covered with long colorful ribbons, brought by visitors.[276]

A Calabrian tradition taking place before the body is redressed in new clothing, put into its coffin and decorated with plants as it is in many places, is to first cleanse it with wine, and after...

Promptly the eyes were closed, because the mouth and open eyes could infect and attract to death the survivors: it is said that if the dead man stays with his eyes open he waits for another. [277]

Cleansing the body with wine was also done in Cerreto, Abruzzo [278] as well as other rural villages where people took care of their own births and deaths. In parallel, when a baby is born in these same rural areas, it is bathed for the first time in wine, with alternative baths of salt, walnut leaves, and other herbal washes that strengthen the skin. Prior to burial, other items left next to the body are: blessed olive leaves, blessed water, pieces of bread, and candles.

RITUALS OF THE HOME

In rural communities, ones where midwives and mothers served as the only doctors available (until the 1950s-1970s), the home was the central place of sacred daily magic: for ritualistic food preparation and production, for births, for cures, and for death rituals.

The home environment is charged. You've read about the removal of photographs and amulets and other personal items during a family member's death transition (that took place in their bed in their home), you read about just a few tiny rituals enacted within the home of a woman giving birth in her own bed and some of the practical items used for birth magic. You will read about more items used to protect the home in the Amulets chapter. Arrangement of the home is done according to beliefs and necessities, to both prevent negative interference and to restore balance.

DEATH: La Morte

The house has a very important role because besides constituting the family identity it is also a place of protection. In Acri there is a strong belief that the spirit is linked to the place of death, so the dead "outside the home" frighten. Family and friends are arranged around the coffin. 279

In rituals made by the living to prepare the deceased's body for its journey and to both honor and mourn her/his/their passing, many of the daily life affairs are reversed. This is a tradition held over from more ancient times in the earliest of **carnevale** celebrations where people enacted going into the spirit world to communicate with spirits by wearing masks and dancing backwards. The masks signified they were not themselves but transitioned into spirits, and the backwards dance signified leaving the physical world to journey into the parallel energy/spirit world.

The reversal helps signal to the spirit, if it is lingering, that they are no longer connected to their former home in the same way. Reversal also prevents the new spirit from lingering in the home rather than moving towards its transitional journey beyond, so it can come visit her/his/their family at a later date once all is well and balance is restored.

WINDOWS and DOORS

After the body has been washed and dressed and put in the coffin by the women and family members, *the body is oriented with the feet facing the door to facilitate the beginning of the journey.* 280 The body is surrounded by friends and family in the home while a reversal of daily duties are performed before and after the funeral procession takes place:

Often windows and doors are kept open during the mourning period before the funeral so that, in the words of locals, *"the soul could go out"*. 281 In contrast:

In Abruzzo, the front door was left open so that the souls of the deceased relatives could come in and visit their relative, or descendant, and could bless him in waiting of the transfer to the cemetery, to which the deceased relatives participated together with the living. 282

Then, in Sardinia for example, after the funeral is completed, the home where the person died must keep the windows shut for an entire year to prevent the soul from returning back before its transition into the spirit realm is complete. In other rural areas, the time period for keeping doors and windows open or closed is as little as a few days, in keeping with ritualistic numerical repetitions such as 3, 7, and 9.

The traditions are based on making the opposite action than would normally be done. So while they vary slightly from rural place to rural place, they work within their community's traditions as a comprehensive group of rituals with a specific aim. They are not haphazard. In fact, they reveal a system: from birth rituals to death rituals, from the love
144

Italian Magic: Secret Lives of Women

rituals to the cures and what we would call "law of attraction" or "mindfulness" attitudes, to the sympathetic and homeopathic nature of operations, the same root concept is in place, and no matter how strange the rituals may seem, they are interconnected and based on a macrocosmic/microscosmic view of life. We should say this is extraordinary for groups of people all across Italy and her islands who are often denigrated as "folk, uneducated or merely syncretized", terms that distract from the profound spirit-world mark in these traditions.

FIRE

In many rural places across Italy, the fire in the hearth, where meals are cooked and the home is heated, was extinguished for a determined amount of time. In some village homes this last for 3 days after the funeral, or longer in others, *because there should not be any sign of material life.* [283] Therefore food is brought from outside the house, for a time, provided by neighbors or other relatives to the family in mourning. The favor is, of course returned at the appropriate time. Often friends or relatives would bring food for 7-9 days after the funeral, being that daily activities were carried out in normalcy outside of the home of grieving.

> In regions such as Marche and Umbria, *wherever the burial took place, the custom of burning the dead man's straw mattress was observed.* [284] *The burning of the* **paglione** *straw bed meant that the dead man had gone away forever* [285] This is another signal to help the spirit pass on into its new "home", by reminding it that previous comforts can no longer be used.

MIRRORS

Mirrors, normally used by flesh-and-blood living people to check their appearances during the day were covered during funeral days to prevent the spirits from peering back and, even more, to prevent them from using it as a doorway back into the house. There is not a fear against a beloved family member's spirit reappearing, but this action is a choice, no matter how personally heartbreaking, to ensure the spirit of the recently deceased keeps moving onwards, towards their fuller life in the spirit world...so that they are not in a state of unrest. Then, after the transition is completed, visitations can be expected and appreciated.

FURNITURE

The house of the deceased, where family and friends gather around the coffin before the funeral procession and ensuing burial, marks itself for the death transition by arranging furniture in the reverse, especially furniture and accessories normally used for eating meals. Rural homes are situated in traditional ways to begin with, and while the surrounding terrain of course alters the composition of the rural village, in general similarities can be found in each rural area:

DEATH: La Morte

The suspicious, reserved farmer does not willingly open his house to the outside. And this is an aspect to the character that is reflected in the house. [286]

The home is in the center of the farm, set either high on a hill or among the surrounding trees, most commonly olive trees and the vineyards. These trees and shrubs do not offer much protection from the elements, only some insulation from outsiders,

and therefore with regards to the orientation, the house is generally influenced by climactic reasons, and turns its back to the north and the facade facing south or south-west. Stairs, flowered balconies, and entrance doors this receive the sun throughout the day, with north-facing walls completely without windows to avoid the north wind. [287]

In more isolated fields or outside the perimeter of the villages, homes are grouped in farmhouses typology [288] as a protection.

Within the homes, barns, and chicken coops are arrangements aligning with the elements of nature as well. In contrast to American homes, space is arranged sparingly with decorations and more to be functional for a life that includes daily food and farm production. With family members, aside from mothers, spending most of their time outdoors, everything is in its place and everything in the home has a use.

So in the events of birth and death we find special arrangements reflecting those transitions revolving around the house as a center of activity and protected place for the ones living within its walls. In the house of a deceased person, traditions in Acri, for example, move the furniture to the walls [289] or upside down, along with extinguishing the fireplace and ceasing many daily activities which are done for living people as a marking of a soul's transition from the house to its new home in the spirit world.

Mealtime is such an important ritual in not only rural Italy but also in contemporary Italy. It's a time of nourishment, connection, abundance, and most importantly: community. Particularly in rural Italy, where people grow and harvest and then produce their own food, mealtime is imbued with a sense of ritual, magic, and connection to the cycles of nature and life.

Therefore, in the home of a deceased person, traditions with ritual aspects regarding food (and there are many) are done in reverse. While there is a funeral meal for friends and family, they do not gather as normal at the meal table. If the usual table is used, it is covered with black cloth, as are the baskets of food that are brought by neighbors. Often it's forbidden to spread the tablecloth on the table. For some, the chairs were used as a table for the food and covered with a white tablecloth. Normally the tablecloth is essential to mealtime, as it is used to gather crumbs. During funeral meals, it's forbidden to throw out crumbs due to a belief that it is "throwing away abundance" or *attracting misfortune to the house."* [290]

Italian Magic: Secret Lives of Women

In another widespread tradition, and in a literal physical reversal, instead of a table or chairs an agricultural symbol of regeneration is used:

The "cup" of wood perched on the ground upside down so that the bottom served as a table top 291 and the people sharing the meal would then sit around the upside down cup and use their laps to hold their plates, enacting the reverse.

> *The custom was called "making the cup" and the funeral lunch "the cup". The cup,* **la coppa** *in Italian, is a name derived from the wooden container used to contain the seeds to be sown, which also served as a unit of measurement. The association of the funeral meal with a container intended to contain grains to be sown is explained in the archaic cultural context, pre-ext, present everywhere, which relates the dead to the seeds, the earth and the production of vegetables* 292 *From this perspective, the foods placed in the "cup" acquire the value of a propitiatory offer.* 293

FUNERAL MEAL

Death is a sort of rebirth, and in matrilineal cultures, these transitions are eternally linked and not separate from each other in any way. Thus far you've read about many death traditions that involve preparing a person's soul for its journey into the afterlife and towards its new "home." So, it's important to note here the full-circle connection between birth and death rituals in the common funeral meal: *the typical lunch offered to relatives of the deceased consisted of chicken broth with homemade pasta.* 294 The chicken broth, preferably made with a black hen, is also used to restore the body of a mother immediately after giving birth.

While a funeral meal is eaten in the home of the deceased and shared by family and friends, food is not cooked in the home. People living outside the home bring food to nourish the remaining ones in the home, and there rituals incorporated into this process involving every aspect of the meal regarding operating in the reverse and in keeping things in their place. In the south of Italy, the rural name for this meal brought from the outside in due to forbidden fire in the funerary home is **consòlo,** 295 keeping in mind there other names in the different dialects of other villages and regions.

> *At Villa Collefegato (Norcia) the meal for relatives of the deceased was carried for a whole week, in turn, by 7 families.* 296

We also find, in other regions, the traditional number of days a food is brought to the family in mourning to follow ritualistic numerical patterns: days of 3, 7, 9 and in some places even 40 days (a number you may remember from the BIRTH chapter about the traditional rest period for a mother to remain in her home after giving birth.

> *In Padule di Cascia, [Perugia, Umbria] the use of the fork was forbidden and only the spoon should be used.* 297

DEATH: La Morte

At the end of the banquet[...] by order of rank, the dishes were placed in the same basket in which they had been brought, without washing them and taking care to leave each leftover in the house in mourning, even the smallest, otherwise we would risk "bringing back the dead".

A black cloth was spread over the basket. The plates of the funeral lunch could not be washed in the house of the deceased, but in the house of those who had prepared lunch. The same custom in Popoli di Norcia. In some countrysides, it was allowed to bring back only the bread, taking care to leave three slices on the table. Each of the relatives who participate in the **recùnselu** *were required to offer, in turn, a* **recinselu***, so these funeral banquets could last months.* 298

SWEEPING

The ritual of sweeping that is found throughout rural Italy involves the belief that once the deceased has been moved out of the home and towards the funeral procession, only then is it safe to sweep the house. If you were to sweep while the dead person is still in the house, the action risks to sweep the soul away without giving it proper ritual attention. *"When the dead man comes out, the rubbish comes out."* 299 After the deceased was removed from the house, *to be transported to the cemetery as prescribed by the funeral rites,* then *a member of the family was in charge of following the coffin sweeping behind it up to the threshold of the house* 202 and carefully because *it will take away the misfortune of the house.* 300

The broom has many protective, purifying, and other magic ritualistic uses in rural Italy from birth rituals, to death rituals, love rituals and protection traditions. The specific rules of sweeping are understood in an energetic way, in their sympathetic action of purifying by removing what's old or transformed. This is in line with the tradition after the funeral meal that forbids shaking of the table cloth and removal of the crumbs of food until the deceased person has been moved out of the house and begun funeral processions that move the soul towards its new home.

MOURNERS, LOOSE HAIR AND WAILING

Death rituals in Italy are connected to rebirth, and this is not a mere conceptual idea, as evidenced in the rural Italian birth traditions which are repeated in rural Italian death traditions. The cheers of the midwife and family for the new mother and baby are paralleled in the beholding of death by the wails of the female mourners, whose public displays of emotion and narrations of grief not only mark the deceased's spirit's transition, but aid in guiding the spirit away from its earthly family and towards its journey into the afterlife.

This is a journey which can be fraught with challenges just as the journey for a new life coming through the birth canal can be. Therefore we find in rural Italy and in shamanism rituals that are carefully performed not just for those living on earth, but also

Italian Magic: Secret Lives of Women

for those passing away from life on earth. In fact, the rituals are focused more towards the recently deceased than they are for the flesh-embodied. These rituals keep everything in its place on earth and in the spirit world.

The many death rituals are part of a holistic preparation effort to ultimately guide the newly freed soul towards its new home in the afterlife and to prevent it from losing its way. In rural tradition even something natural like crying and the vocalized expression of mourning takes on a ritualistic tone and they are an integral part of the process. The rituals in rural Italy surrounding the death transition are twofold: one, the part that the survivors experience, and two, the continued life journey (in the reverse, the spirit world*) that the spirit of the deceased must take.

The duties of shaman in Asian and Siberian shamanism also play a dual role in the community's death rituals: 1) the shaman acts as a ritual leader, operating many rituals signifying, as in Italian traditions, the end of the deceased's former connection to earthly belongings and property, and 2) as a psychopomp who actually travels with the spirit to its destination in the afterlife, ensuring the spirit arrives and does not become lost.

In between these duties, the shaman is aided by a professional female mourner in Borneo, Indonesia, for specific example, whose vocalizations narrate guidance to the spirit assisting its path before the shaman will meet and ensure the transition's completion. Interestingly, for the shaman of the Sea Dyak, *almost all the* [helper/guide] *spirits are invoked under the name of Ini: "Great Mother".* [301]

> *A professional woman mourner sits beside the corpse and performs a vocal recital without music [...]and recounts at great length (sometimes for as long as 12 hours) the vicissitudes of the deceased's journey in the beyond...The purpose of the recital is to keep the soul from going astray in its journey in the underworld."* [302]

> *Indeed, the mourner plays the role of the psychopomp, although she does not herself escort the soul [...], she has really guided the deceased to his new home.* [303]

While the examples above were in regards to the Sea Dyak, in the rural Italian tradition of women mourners we find a parallel in their mourning songs, called **sos attitidos** in Sardinia: *The main purpose of* **sos attitidos** *in addition to that of praising the dead was above all to accompany him on the journey he was preparing to make.* [304]

> *"Only women could be* **lamentatrici** *mourners. They were a fundamental part of those rituals designed to face Death, which yesterday was a group and not a private one."* [305]

Professional mourners are hired to join the family mourners. Sometimes they hardly know the deceased at all. They often wear black heavy shawls, and in Sardinia the professional mourners partially covered their faces by the black and yellow bandages of mourning. They enter the room of the dead body, whose feet are towards the door, and they encircle it.

The Italian mourners work in groups, occupying a visible place within the community group by howling in a circle. In Calabria, they do so with hair loose and emotional wails and vocalizing. In these same communities, the hair of a mother giving birth is also worn loose, so that nothing impedes the flow of energy helping the baby come out of the mother's body (and therefore to prevent any entanglement with negative challenges). It is the same loose, flowing hair that we find in the death transition rituals:

> *"In the front row the women who, with their hair loose, start the wake, during which prayers are recited, often interrupted by screams and crying. They also remember merits, virtues and particular anecdotes of the life of the deceased."* [306]

The wailing takes a particular course, starting high-pitched and painful, and after a variety of emotional outpouring, the mourners began to sing about the life and lineage of the deceased, describing the positive attributes of the deceased, and generally documenting the life line through song. Depending on the cause of death, the songs may even call for **vendetta** revenge.

> *They sang one at a time, to each verse the women answered with a chorus of groans, sobs and cries ...*[307]

> In some places, *people even tore their hair and scratched their faces in celebration of pain.* Sometimes *this practice was so intense and violent that the women who practiced it had to stay several days in bed to recover from their injuries. The torn clothes and hair were thrown on the deceased as a sign of respect and which the dead would have interpreted as sincere pain.* [308]

> *There are rare testimonies that report the habit of placing a basin full of water under the coffin during the waking period, with the consideration that, being a sort of means of connection with other dimensions, the water would have allowed the passage of the soul to the afterlife.* [309]

SEND-OFF OF THE BODY AND SPIRIT

The mourning continues for hours, often until the very late night, followed by the funeral procession to present the body and coffin to the community:

> *The funeral procession does not follow the shortest route between home and church, but generally follows the path in relation to social status. The deceased left his home and now leaves the countryside, and members of the community greet him. The funeral mass is*

celebrated, then [again on] the 7th day, month and year. 310

In parallel to this send-off into the community we find rituals to not only ensure the spirit also finds its way to its new home in the spirit world, but also which serve to close-off the deceased from it's earthly life to prevent any out-of-place spirit hauntings.

In some villages of Italy, this ritual begins when family members place coins in the coffins to pay the Greek version of Charon/Kharon for passage on the boat of the dead as is done in Acri, Calabria and other villages who have been influenced by Greek traditions,which are separate from traditions established by Etruscans and other groups who influenced other regions and villages. Some people believe the boat of the dead is the transportation vehicle that the spirit takes on its journey to become part of the greater afterlife community, after the body takes its journey through the funeral meal, the mourning rituals, and the funerary process in the village community.

In Indonesia and parts of Malaysia we find a magico-religious practice that involves the use of the "boat of the spirits," which carries the soul of the dead to the beyond. 311 On different planes, all these funerary rite and customs pursue the same end: escorting the deceased to the beyond." 312 This same holistic belief system about the death transition it very much the same in Italian rural culture.

COMMUNITY BREAD

In rural Italy there are many occasions, both private and public for ritual breads. The culmination of funerary rituals arrives at the sharing of bread among the community. This follows the sharing and reception of the body of the deceased among the community.

In Acri, Calabria:

> *The funeral mass is celebrated, then the seventh day, month and year. In some fractions of Acri it is used to give a bread to the participants of the seventh day. This is not an Acris tradition, but a contamination of nearby Corigliano. In Acri, on the other hand, the "gift" of bread is linked to the days of celebration. The realization of ritual breads made from a mixture of flour and sometimes honey is typical of many festivals in Calabria.* 313

In Nuoro, Sardinia::

> *After the funeral, once the condolences were over, all the clothes were dressed in black. In the homes of wealthy people, after some time from the funeral, the "bread of souls" was made and distributed to the poor.* 314 *The preparation of this bread made of semolina in the shape of a crown* in Sardegna, for example, with other forms of bread used in villages, *ritual gestures such as signing* and reciting prayers.* 315

DEATH: La Morte

"bread of souls" pane delle anime

These rituals and traditions are carried out with reverence for their purpose, in keeping with a belief that it's possible for a spirit to become lost during transition on their journey to the afterlife (and therefore haunt others as an unsettled spirit), as well as a fear that some newly deceased spirits may try to come back and bring their loved ones with them. There is a dual feeling towards the dead, that their existence, or co-existence with the living is ok as long as it's not disruptive:

"The harmless presences of the family members should not be removed: it is their right to return to the places where they lived, without disturbing the development of the life of the living. 316

This is a community way of thinking Italian rural traditions have with Central and North Asian peoples' as well beliefs found in Siberian communities where shamanism exists:

Feelings towards the long dead are ambivalent: on one hand, the long dead are revered and [...]in time they come to be regarded as tutelary spirits of the family [...] and are expected to act as protectors; on the other hand, the[..] recently dead are feared. This fear of the dead is due to the fact that [...]at first, no dead person accepts his new mode of being; he cannot renounce "living" and he returns to his family [...] to live among his kin. So what is feared [by living people] is the dead's refusal to forsake the earthly world. 317

In other words, it's human nature to not want to continue life without the familiar around: especially in the absence of family, friends, and loved ones. This human condition is at the heart of all ghosts stories, such as the **pana**, who, in order to find peace, must wash their clothes and the clothes of their deceased child in a river for 7 years without interruption. It's a compulsion to find normalcy in the supernatural.

Therefore, in rural Italy and central and northern Asia, Oceania and Siberia we find the many rituals whose to ensure a successful death transition for the spirit to move forward without struggle, for the good of the entire community, *such as the funerary banquet that is held in their honor 3, 7, or 40 days after their decease.* 318 In some villages, such as Acri, Calabria, there is the tradition of leaving 3 pieces of bread on the nightstand along with some water for the deceased's spirit. In other villages, food is left for 3 days after the death because it is believed the spirit can linger for this amount of time.

In central and north Asia, death rituals take place over the period of 3, 7, or 40 days rather than immediately after death due to the community belief that *or 3, 7, or 40 days the soul lives in the cemetery, and only after that period it is believed to take its departure for the underworld.* 319 These numerical patterns are also adhered to in rural Italy: both in death rituals and in birth rituals, yet more connections between Italian rural birth rituals and death rituals: the 40 days of significance for a new mother. After the transition of birth, it's said her body is *"40 days the open grave"*320 until her blood rebalances itself in the biological process of post-birth repair. The actions of these rituals show a deep belief that death and life are transitions of a regenerative nature and not transitions of finality.

FINISHING RITUALS

To prevent things being out of place, there are a few finishing rituals, and they are similar to the finishing rituals we also find in some of the inherited Lineage cures, especially ones for psychic ailments caused by: envious spells, psychic fright, and spirit attachments. In death traditions, these rituals prevent unsettled ghosts or untimely deaths for relatives of the recently deceased.

FIRE

Fire is something used in the death rituals to signal a cut off; a sealing of the action. For example, in rural cures against the evil eye, often a hot piece of charcoal is used at the end of the cure to "burn" any remaining connection to negativity between the victim and the spell-sender. In death rituals, the often the crumbs of the funeral meal, always forbidden to be thrown away, are instead thrown into the fire as a sort of offering, *equivalent to the ancient offers of food to the Lares and domestic Penates* 321 to ensure the deceased does not return to take family members. Also in Central Asia at the funeral banquet food is thrown into the fire as an offering to the deceased. 322 It's a form of closure and a purification (a reversal of the normal).

The leftovers or crumbs are burned in the fire after the dishes are placed back into the basket of whomever provided the funeral meal. The dishes are placed back into the basket in a specific order and any leftovers and small crumbs are left in the home of the deceased otherwise we would risk "bringing back the dead". 323

WAX SEAL

Whereas a stone or stone dust was used to help a struggling person die, by adding a certain weight that would open the heart's doorway to the soul, here in the post-death rituals we find the wax being used like a seal to shut the doorway to the soul at the heart center, thus preventing the dead person to enter his body again (or close enough proximity to it to affect the physical world) and take other living family members with him into the afterlife.

> *In some areas of Sardinia a wax doll was placed in the shape of a cross to prevent the dead from taking someone from the family.* 324

Yet one more ritual based on the idea of keeping things in their place and working with the flow of energy, which are ideas conceptual magic is based upon. In places where shamanism is found, such as just a few mentioned here, the community has a holistic set of rituals and traditions based on their interconnected beliefs about life, death, and illness. The shaman plays specific roles in these communities. There are also different duties for different types of shaman. While these roles deserve an entirely different conversation, this environment is mentioned to shed some light on the types of community beliefs being connected to but separate from the lifestyle and duties of a shaman. Shamanism is for the shaman; holistic community rituals expressing beliefs in the interconnectedness of life, death, and regeneration are for the community. Everything in its place.

PASSING OF BORROWED POWER

Another mysterious and sacred death ritual is one that takes place between a dying healer and the chosen healer-to-be. The ritual of initiations itself is quite simple, but there is a supernatural event that is the key to not only the effectiveness of the inherited cures but also to the passing of the power. This is more evident in some initiations than others.

The initiations themselves take place on one of only 4 dates per year, so even the clock of initiations operates on the feminine clock: the solstices and equinoxes. These dates in Italy are not on the 21st of said month, they occur on the 24th of 4 months: December 24 and July 24 being the 2 most widely used.

The Lineage healers in rural Italy are ones who receive an "inheritance" from someone in their own family usually, someone who is a healer. The inheritance consists of one or more cures which require a ritual transmission of energy. The energy is the key to the success of the cures, and it is a channeled energy that is activated by other parts of the inheritance:

-secret prayers or invocations that are handed down orally,
-specific actions used with...
-specific matter...

to cure specific illnesses that work on the body, mind and spirit. Each inheritance consists of these 3 parts. The actual cure that takes place is aided by the channeled energy (the divine feminine) who moves through the healer. This ability to channel healing energy is not referred to as channeling, but as holding a "borrowed power. This borrowed power is usually (but not always) transferred from a dying healer to a healer-to-be, since it withdraws from the elder healer and moves to the new healer. Sometimes a healer is initiated and waits years to practice their healing inheritance because the elder healer is still alive and healing people. When the elder healer either gives permission to the new healer to heal or when they die, the new healer is given permission to begin healing people.

TYPES OF ILLNESSES
TYPES OF HEALERS

The types of cures found in rural Italy, referred to here "lineage cures", must be approached with a psychic viewpoint, one that includes the acknowledgment of the influence of spirits (both helpful and harmful), an understanding of animism, and clarification of some shamanism practices.

The cures are not simply "the Italian version" of other healing practices brought into contemporary times from a much older period of time. They do contain usage of the laws of energy, such as affirmative thought, and they bear resemblances and shared ideas of other orally transmitted indigenous curing traditions found around the world.

Perhaps a curious significance is the way they are received through an "inheritance" from an elder healer to a healer-to-be. These fully-formed cures, along with their components (which could be sealed envelopes with written words, secret prayers that must be whispered, marks/signs made with the hands, plants and liquids used for diagnosis), are loyally adhered to and not altered. Their active component, the mysterious part that brings the miracle cure about, is the channeled energy of a higher consciousness, the divine feminine lifeforce. The inheritance includes: a ritualistic transmission of energy which then activates the other inherited parts of the cure which will be the healer's tools for the rest of their lifetime.

Typically these cures are handed down through the family lines which sometimes include in-laws. Usually females hand-down cures to females, and males to males, but if there is a need for a healer to be replaced, these lines can be crossed: a mother may initiate her son. It is also common for a healer to not pass down their cures if they are not guided to by spirit and if their relatives are not interested.

The cures are not taught through training alongside a teacher nor elder healer, with the exception of a very minute few, such as some specific muscle massages and some specific herbal preparations. There is no learning of theory, no meditation practice, no education about energy systems. Italian healers are solo workers: the curing procedures are a special event that occurs between them and their healer spirits.

Materials used in the cures are: plants, gold and silver rings and medallions, oil and water, scissors, thread, spit, blood, urine, fire, specific moon phases, secret prayers, feathers, sealed envelopes with written words inside, ash, stones, vines, sewing needles and thread, medallions, nut shells, mummified animal parts, and magical ideas such as: doubles to transfer the illness to, burial, tying/knotting, cutting and burning and more.

TYPES OF ILLNESSES , TYPES OF HEALERS

There are pranotherapy healers in Italy, even in rural places, who have discovered their healing abilities in unusual ways and have subsequently combined this gift with training in various modernized modalities, but they are not part of the lineage tradition.

While these cures are found all throughout rural Italy, there are variations not only village to village and region to region, but often from street to street, neighbor to neighbor, healer to healer. The lineage cures do exist all across rural Italy and her islands, and generally a consistent body of cures are found in all these places. However, there are also other types of cures concentrated in certain villages.

For example, some areas of Italy are known for their herbal remedies due to the vast variety of flora growing there. Valle Argentina in the province of Imperia in the region of Liguria boasts a tradition of plant cures and healers who have an astounding knowledge of an enormous body of curative plants. In the region of Emilia Romagna a large number of water cures are found. Some villages in Sicily use sea mosses not found anywhere else. Some Sardinia healers use obsidian and carnelian in cures and also in protective amulets, along with seashells called "the eye of Santa Lucia." Then there are specific cures using silver medallions, the laying of hands, and there are people whose specialty is seeing spirits and speaking for them for the purpose of enacting cures that use no nature at all. Some plants with a magical reputation no longer grow in some areas where they used to and are considered "extinct", while they grow elsewhere, thriving. An abundance of flora grow on Campania's mount Taburno, 608 varieties including many poison plants such as belladonna and stramonium. In Puglia and Sardinia there are varieties of the magico-religious rite called **tarantismo** which cures a variety of spider bites.

There are so many cures, this book cannot attempt to contain them all, but presented here is a collection of some of the more intriguing ones, with comparisons of various versions to show continuity of concept, thought, and practice.

Triora, Italy in the region of Liguria. **Il paese,** the countryside 2,560 feet up in the mountains.

Italian Magic: Secret Lives of Women

ILLNESSES

ILLNESSES in rural Italy can be classified into 2 categories:

1. Illnesses of a physiological nature: a lung issue caused by cigarettes; a back injury caused by farm work; an intestinal issue caused by malnutrition, etc.

2. Illnesses of a psychic nature: anxiety and stomach pains caused by psychic fright; lethargy and depression caused by an envious spell; brain fog, severe malnutrition, suicidal feelings caused by a hex, a symptom caused by some invisible outside force.

Some illnesses are described in a way that make them sound imaginary to those of us outside rural life and have therefore been accused of being simply superstitious such with lycanthropy or werewolves or "wolf men". Keep in mind though, there are cures for these particular illnesses, which means that for the people experiencing these illnesses, they are very real. And, if you are able to look beyond the cultural expression of what they are called, you can find the universal meaning of the illness at the root, the technicality of what it is. Some such illnesses we'll explore within these pages are: fallen soul, **striadura**, and the invoice or bill.

In matters of the universe, whether describing supernatural experiences, illnesses, spiritual beliefs and anything non-physically tangible, we must grapple with language to express our ideas are about them. Language evolves with the times, so this means we are continually developing ways to express our inner world, something that has been attempted since the earliest of times, but with great difficulty. What a symbol means during a certain time period may lose its meaning completely during another. So, in attempting to describe our experiences through language choices we make may limit someone else's understanding of our description because we are in fact limiting our own expression by squishing it into symbols (language) while the experience itself is bigger than symbols and language in the first place.

This is the challenge all spiritual practices experience in attempting to express their inner workings: languaging. The other challenge is understanding how someone else processes their own experience. For example, a small child may not know that a "ghost" is not visible to other people. To the child, she is interacting with a spirit in the same way she is interacting with other adults and children around her. So how can she explain that to someone who can't see when she doesn't realize the other person can't see the same way she does? So when it comes to expressing illness as related to negative spirits, to spells and a loss of soul, or even in describing astral flight or sensations experienced in miraculous cures, language can fail and confuse.

There is a belief about health in Italy that is pervasive among the older traditions and generations. This belief runs through Lineage cures, magic, protections and even the ingredients of the after dinner digestive drink called **amaro**. The belief is that an unhappy soul makes for unbalanced health. If the soul is unhappy and it's connected to a body, then it stands to reason the body will suffer. In our contemporary psychic language we can say this is the potential energetic environment that can be taken advantage of by a spirit attachment to drain energy and affect the health of the unhappy person in one way or another.

In these rural communities, for the healers and the healers it is believed that illnesses are in fact caused by negative spirits: either the spirit of the ill person or an external spirit focused on the ill person such as a spirit attachment, or as sent by another negative person through a **fatture**. The people of central and north Asian communities and their shaman also believe *"disease is provoked by the evil spirits of the dead."*[325]

TYPES OF MALEFICI

Below is a small collection of names of the illnesses caused by negative spirits, spells, and hexes or the act of causing them.

+ **la Jettatura-** the act of sending the evil eye through the eyes, or visualization, an energetic spell based on envy that causes physical suffering.

+ **il Malocchio-** the evil eye, the result of the **jettatura**, negative energy targeting the mind, thoughts, energy, creating a disruption to whatever is envied by the sender. Sent intentionally through a spell. Also called **occhiaticcio, uggia** and **aduggiare.**

+ **l'Iinvidia -** envy: received like **il malocchio**, often sent unintentionally by a person who chooses to have a victim complex mentality or passive aggressive anger towards the world that they think owes them something. A general daily envy that is transmitted to others and can also be sent through a spirit attachment with an unaware passive aggressive person who doesn't just behave in a passive aggressive way but lives this way as a mental construct.

+ **la Striadura -** a psychic illness caused by a specific type of negative spirit.

+ **la Fattura -** a negative spell, often sent by way of a poppet simulacrum.

+ **le Mazzine -** Sardinian word for **la fatture,** negative spell that can cause death.

+ **Umbra** Sardinian word for frights or "the scares", received as a result of a negative ghost experience.

+ **s'Azzicchidu** Sardinian word for frights or "the scares", received as a result of a flesh-and-blood person, animal, or event that can lead to serious physical or mental ailments.

+ **lu scantu** Sicilian name, means "jitters" for psychic fright that affects intestines .

+ **l'anima caduta** "fallen soul"; psychic illness where a person has lost themselves.

Italian Magic: Secret Lives of Women

+   **l'Ammaliature** -love spells, bindings.

+   **la Legatura-** binding spells using words, string, knots.

+   **i Vermi -** a psychic illness mostly affecting children.

+   **lupo mannaro (lycanthropy) -** a psychic illness, a frenzied state affecting men.

SYMPTOMS OF ILLNESS

A brief list of symptoms of illness caused by negative spirits and spirit attachments: helminthiasis (parasitic worms), fright, jitters, brain fog, anxiety, jaundice, depression, peeling skin, obsessions, auditory and visual hallucinations, disorders of the gastrointestinal functions, circulation issues, anemia, shrinking of the limbs, listlessness, fainting, high fever, severe headache, vomiting, dizziness, feeling of disconnect and loss of soul, panic, overall decay of health. In short, all strange interruptions to health and mental clarity which continue in deterioration that are not caused by any known factor such as ingested food or chemical reaction.

The symptoms resulting from a **fattura** (invasive hex) or **il malocchio** (spell based on envy) are ones that fall in line with anemia, which we can generally say involves a loss of personal vitality and power, both energetically and physically. The **fattura** is a spell that works its way inside the heart chakra, solar plexus, and sacral chakra areas in a parasitical way, often amplified by the help of a spirit attachment. For example, a **fattura** can feel like a sudden and utter despair a disabling loss of hope, and the heavy inner weight and depression, a loss of self, a sense of alarm followed by a sinking feeling or the need to hide, and a shrinking of the self. A **fattura** can kill.

A **jettatura** is not as skilled, and its actions hover like a negative bubble around the recipient, waiting for a weakness to present itself and then invade that weakness, amplifying it through influence, and its effects are nothing to be taken lightly. For example, if someone is about to do something positive for their goal, and the goal is envied by someone, the person who is envious will try to interrupt that goal by sending negativity. As a result, the negativity can affect the person with the goal by causing little accidents and transportation issues when they are doing work for their goal: a little bad mood can suddenly balloon into one that attracts more negativity until the person is distracted from their goal and caught up in a downward spiral of little negative issues that can build. Car accidents, allergic reactions, trips and slips, suicidal thoughts, lethargy are common ways this energy affects someone. Often negative spirits join in **jettatura**, increasing its effects.

The **fattura** and **jettatura**, being invasive, often work on their own as sent by the spell/hex worker, or they are enhanced by a spirit attachment (intentionally and unintentionally). Spirit attachments are simply disembodied people who haven't completed their death transition and look to find extra energy to keep them going. Because they haven't completed their death transition they are living a limited energetic life. Living vicariously through humans gives them opportunities to push emotional buttons through influence and drain that energy to use for themselves. Also, hexers can employ negative spirits.

When a spirit attachment is involved, the sensations of fear and alarm are increased dramatically. Attacks are often felt in the intestinal area because this is where spirits plug in to communicate emotions and sensations (being that our "gut" senses these things in our solar plexus and sacral chakra areas), so it's natural to feel nausea and cramping. The spirits use this tactic to disarm the victim. When the victim feels fearful and shrinks into themselves the spirits deplete iron from the blood. In a strong enough attack, or as a result of attacks over time, an imbalance such as a loss of iron in the blood is the result. Iron is a protector, both spiritually and energetically which is why negative spirits attempt to deplete it, making the victim vulnerable to a parasitic energy drain.

Thus, most of the cures for these types of illnesses in Italy include herbs high in iron, or actual iron itself. Iron is one of the most used tools in rural Italian preventative magic and psychic cures. Iron keeps negative spirits away and immobilizes them.

TYPES OF HEALERS

Healers in Italy are called many names by people with differing relationships to the healers: outsiders, those seeking healing, community members, anthropologists, historians with an agenda to discredit them, builders of folk tales and so on. Of course we have to consider even more names in different dialects and the fact that who is known as a healer in one village is known as an evil witch in another, or a miracle worker in the next.

However, within rural communities, there are and have been a variety of names specific to the duties performed by the person, the greater variety of which are found in Sardinia. This definitive naming is also found also in central and north Asian shamanism communities, in Siberia and among the Turko Tartars.

Is praticas is the name used in Sardinia for seers: people who can release someone else from **il malocchio** and hexes **(le fatture** in Italian and **le mazzinas** in Sardinian). They are able to see the psychic connection between victim and hexer and do the serious work required to sever those draining ties. **Is practicas** also make protections.

I guaritori and **le guaritrici,** (masculine, feminine) are Lineage healers who use a combination of: secret words or prayers, matter (oil, string, medallions, water, wheat, etc) and inherited actions to cure illnesses of the body and soul. **Sanadoras** is the Sardinian name.

I segnatori Lineage healers whose specialty is marking the body with signs, sometimes a bit of oil, and secret prayers to heal illnesses of the body and soul. For example, a healer from Campania who removes **il malocchio** from a victim through marking the forehead with olive oil in the shape of a cross while uttering secret prayers. Or, the Sicilian version where marks are made on the forehead, ribs and wrist with oil and while uttering secret prayers. The signatures made by the healer are always connected to charged words.

Italian Magic: Secret Lives of Women

Le majare/ maiare are found in Sicily and are experts in using plants to heal physical ailments and canceling **fatture**. They also use Lineage healer tools and inherited prayers that have a nursery rhyme style and sound like a patchwork of words and ideas, making their secret meaning far less immediate than other prayers that neutralize **il malocchio**. These words, **ro ciarmu,** activate their channeling ability to cure. Their magic and healing works are done with a channeled energy. Their expertise, aside from plant magic, is the power to remove the presence of negative opposing force and they also attack back, invoking malice against the attacker, so, protecting people against spirit attachments and hexers. They are astral travelers, lineage holders, have often been **lavatrici** and **levatrici**.

Le janare Like the Sicilian Lineage majare healers but from many villages in the region of Campania. Gifted dreamers, traditions of flying to the moon with horses and trees (typical shamanic symbols of flight), they use bread magic and perform other fertility rituals and protection magic of rural Italy. Experts in spells, lineage cures, and herbs.

I ciarmavermi Sicilian rural healers whose specialty is to rid people of helminthiasis (worms) trough recitation of spells that push out negative spirits who caused the worms. Their rituals use charged words and variety of rural tools including plants. Their name means "worms charmers." The worms illness is considered one due to psychic fright caused by a spirit attachment who is sending intense negative energy that plugs into a victim's intestinal area (solar plexus chakra and sacral chakra) creating severe digestive upset, fear, and shrinkage of vitality. Helminthiasis is a magical illnes and cured as such .

Is bruxas A **bruxu/bruxa** is considered a healer, a diviner of future events, and also someone who does black magic (a **fattucchiere**) who can also harm through poppet spells. But really, this is a Sardinian generalized word (like strega/streghe) for witch. So, it's laden with the sensationalist fear mongering the church created through anti-female healer propaganda of the kind that alleged witches were women who were under the guidance of the devil and were like vampires and owls of the night who invade homes and suck energy from babies and people: a superstitious fairy tale based on real spirit-attachment experiences but blamed on healer women. As a result of a more complicated socio-economic war by the church (as discussed in much greater detail in "Italy's Witches And Medicine Women Vol. 1") the names of midwives, healers and laundry women became synonymous with witches and hexers. There has been woven into the culture a confusing idea about these roles of women.

Lo stregone / i stregoni Is a term (singular, plural) used for male sorcerer whose work is of a curing nature mostly through protection work, neutralizing magic spells and also making magical works that can harm. Used in the same way as **strega** is used but for men. Sometimes these healers are associated with the church. Note: **stregoneria** is just an historical name to broadly identify witches: it's not a term for a specific type of witchcraft or a "path." It's a word created by historians.

Lu sconniuratore The "Interruptors" from Umbria. [326] Diviners and exorcists. Their specialty is neutralizing black magic. For the diagnosis, they used a basin full of water in which they revealed the figures of the witches responsible for the crimes then neutralized the **fatture** with channeled energy. In Ocricchio, people still remember the last of these soothsayers-therapists nicknamed **Birichicchin**. [327] They cured lycanthropy and other spirit attachment illnesses of psychic frenzy where the blood is affected by negative spirits. [328]

La sconnin- ratora is another name for "Interruptors" in the Umbria region near the village of Valnerina.

Ciarauli Sicilian experts in "Like cures like"..sympathetic magic cures with homeopathic power, specifically the power to heal wounds from the bites of snakes, vipers, tarantulas and poisonous insects using parts of the poisonous animal (such as mummified serpent heads and insect parts) dipped in oil to cure the poisonous bite in a victim. They would recite their secret words and trace marks on the body of the victim with the mummified parts. Also known for using laurel and lavender for snake protection charms. *The* **ciaraulo** *was the 7th child, born January 25th, who would have had the ability to enchant snakes and knew the secrets of curing viper bites.* [329]

Sa spiridadas Sardinian trance channelers similar to the oracles. Their name means "the spirited, the ones invaded by spirits". [330] Their procedure was like that of Edgar Cayce: they would lie down, enter a trance state where their own consciousness was asleep, and their spirit helpers would give medical advice for people whose illnesses were mysterious, they unveiled the dark magic workings of **fattutre** in especially difficult cases that other healers couldn't cure, and *they had the purpose of knowing secret existential plots, birth times, travel outcomes; equity investments, as well as news on precious lost or stolen items and missing loved ones and they made predictions about the future.* [331]

Cogas Sardinian diviner of future events, a reader.

Femina de mexina, Uomo di Medicina. Medicine Woman / Medicine Man. Sardinian names for healers, **sa mexina** is the general name for Sardinian medicine, not of the pharmaceutical kind but of the Lineage magic kind. There are different types of **mexina** such as **Acquas de mexina** (medicinal waters) and many more. Interchangeable with the names **guaritore** and **guaritrice** on the mainland.

S'Affumentadora/ Suffumigatrice A healer specializing in the art of **affumentu** (Sardinian word for **suffumugio** which means fumigation. She heals a victim of fright and psychic scares and lifts depressed moods with **sa mexina 'e s'azzicchidu,** the medicine of fright whose cures are fumigations: burning combinations of plants on a tile, creating a heavy smoke that is moved over the victim in a specific way along with secret prayers. Fumigation experts are also on the Italian mainland.

And there are those who **heal with hands**, using a special gift, an ability to move magic through their bodily fluids and spiritual energy called **umbra de caraou** in Sardinian. This power can be used positively or negatively.

Italian Magic: Secret Lives of Women

NAMING

The biggest variety of specific names given to healers can be found within Sardinian culture, perhaps because of the careful documentation of a few writers such as Ugo Dessy and Dolores Turchi. Mario Polia and his student Fabiola Chavez Hualpa have carefully collected the same type of information in Valnerina the region of Umbria. This does not mean there isn't a wide a variety of names on the mainland or in Sicily. It is the author's personal experience while traveling into countryside villages that most names and information about healers, cures, and magic can only be found in-person and in direct contact with the lineage holders, and often times people living all around the healers don't even know they exist, depending on the age range of people in the area, how deeply into deculturalization the village has moved, and whether or not people in the environment seek healers. So it's safe to say that the vast majority of knowledge has never been documented.

Perhaps this documentation also exists because Sardinian traditions resisted church intervention and outside influences moreso than the mainland, and Sardinian people still celebrate their customs such as processions, indigenous clothing, food traditions and more, and as a result people felt safer to uphold traditions and even been proud of them. This definitive naming is also found in central and north Asian shamanism communities, in Siberia and among the Turko Tartars.

As a result of a more complicated socio-economic war by the church (as discussed in greater detail in "Italy's Witches and Medicine Women Vol. 1", the names of midwives, healers and laundry women became synonymous with witches. There has been a confusing idea about these roles of women woven into the culture, that these names are for evil, blood-sucking children-killing women. The reach of the Italian church is something we don't experience in America and the church's usurpation of rural magic can't be overlooked either. Both the church and contemporary magicians have stolen ideas (but not the spirit helpers) from rural traditions and then turned around and either banned rural people from using them (the church did) or accused them of stealing from magical traditions (as some American writers claim) which were developed much later than rural traditions and were themselves a mix of traditions and cultural imprints.

For example, a **bruxa** is considered a healer and also a sorceress who does black magic. The same goes for the **streghe**, the **majare**, and **stregoni**. There are names in every dialect, and most have a negative connotation towards female sexuality also, such as **bajiue**, from Liguria meaning witch and bitch, and even the word broom **scopa** also means "fuck". These are generalized "witch" names that are part of the church's fear spreading that have become embedded in community beliefs, often perpetuated through "folk stories,"* used to imply people who are part of the evil witch fantasy created by the church and don't refer to a specific structured path: women who heal but who also harm and who meet with the

---

* the word "folk" is also a denigration, a word that implies stupidity and a reflection of rural culture as being "dumb and confused". While these "folk stories" are well known in rural Italy, they were not created by rural people. Sadly, the rural illnesses and cures are connected to these stories, which was part of the church's doing in their tactics to denounce rural traditions.

devil and do his works and receive instructions and ointments...rather than technical terms for the work they do such as was presented in the abbreviated previous list. However, there is no such word as **stregha** in the Italian language nor is there any word with "gha" at the end due to Italian language grammar rules.

With all these names, some people do embrace them and are currently reclaiming them. This languaging also depends on the village, the region, the collective fears of each community and its history of vulnerability to the church's power, whether or not people embrace their history and can talk about witches without fear, or those who love the idea of witches.

The subject of witches as healers, and of "good witches versus bad witches" in Italy is a very complex one and there are various beliefs towards these words and roles. There is denial, there is acceptance, there is fear and love towards those whose names are often interchanged with both positive traits and evil ones. In some villages, where magic is a daily sacred operation such as in the countryside, witches are only considered to be the type of people who do negative magic against others in works such as: sending the evil eye to someone, casting a hex, competitive magic, and anything harmful that is against the free will of another that will affect their health, wealth mind body and spirit. Whereas magic is used to undo these negative works by people who aren't considered witches. This is the prevalent definition in rural places.

At the same, in some villages that are medieval in structure and in cities where all these ideas exist, women who cure using plants are considered witches. Some people consider these to be the only real witches, such as with Antonietta from Triora whose interview you can find in "Italy's Witches and Medicine Women Vol 1", and yet historically, a witch who cured people with plants is one who was targeted by inquisitors during the witch hunts for their partnership with the devil, and were considered different from people with other spiritual powers.

Most commonly, healers don't call themselves healers nor witches nor does their community either. In the Italian way, they are called by what they are, often they are just known by their name and what they can cure. Sometimes they are known as **zia** aunt, nodding to that community mother figure who is both a mother and a medium. Or, men are known by their name and maybe as the man who heals whatever ailment he inherited the cure for. Sometimes they are known as **zio** uncle referring to them being of service to the community as well. Since they are known to cure specific ailments, you search for the person who cures backaches, herpes, or psychic fright, for example, rather than a general "healer" who doesn't exist, because the cures are specialized.

> *The principal function of the shaman in central and north Asia is*
> *magical healing.* [332]

The lineage healers of Italy serve this same shamanaic function. Futher, the link between what we can define as mother magic or feminine shamanism in rural Italy has been undeniably copied, remixed, and adapted by people using the ingredients solely for magic of a negative spell/hex nature rather than for curing. Essentially all magic outside of shamanism is conceptual and are largely varied practices taken on by individuals who have different beliefs from the people in their community. In both shamanism and Italian rural life however, there is a continuity between the rituals of the healers and the rituals upheld by the community in which they live: while the healers have their private rituals, they share the same basis of beliefs and concepts (and materials used) as do the community rituals performed by the community (for example, as have been briefly mentioned here regarding birth and death rituals and in the coming chapters protective magic).

Whether contemporary ideas, rural realities, witch hunt confusions, and languaging issues, personalized ideas, family specific magic...the best way to understand the variety of ideas towards witches is to experience Italy while talking local people and spending time feeling out their way of daily living, their love of their land, the communal way of life, and more. Museums and tours can also be helpful to offer outsider views or broader perspectives. Generally speaking the American viewpoint is so different from Italy's daily life that a mere intellectual examination is not enough to bring a full understanding. To understand Italy, one must travel around Italy and mingle or live among local people.

There does exist a practical fear of ghosts, spirit attachments, and succubi-type nighttime experiences, and there is a fear of harmful magic because in Italy the effects of these negative experiences are so real and common that they need cures. This is something learned from local people- just how prevalent the spirit world enacts upon theirs.

BORROWED POWER OF LINEAGE HEALERS

The lineage healers in Italy are holders of legacies: they inherit secret knowledge received hundreds of years prior by their ancestors that continues to be handed down through family lineages to perpetuate its use and availability for the people who need the cures. This knowledge is transmitted orally and energetically.

A legacy is: a body of advanced knowledge created by a higher consciousness (instead of being something developed through trial-and-error over long periods of time), which has been structured into actions that serve a need, such as improving the quality of life. Legacies are handed down from person to person in already completely developed form that can be utilized by human beings but not necessarily be completely understood by them. The legacy is not just mental facts and actions: there is a conscious power present in these legacies, a divine feminine power operating through the healers. This power activates the inherited legacies when a new healer receives them, and this power withdraws from an elder healer when they approach death.

To ensure the efficacy and continued existence of the legacies, there are agreements made between the people in the lineage who hold this knowledge. The agreements revolve around loyalty to the cures, always being available to whomever needs the cures, not charging a fee, keeping the prayer words secret while they are in use. The main agreement actively lives in the secret prayers/invocations that the healer uses during the cures: this can be likened to passive channeling. In rural Italian traditions, there are no techniques of "opening oneself to becoming a channel": the secret words do that, they are the invitation and the agreement between healer and channeled conscious energy. Some healers receive the transmission of just one cure, and yet others receive many cures.

There are safeguards built into the legacies so they cannot be stolen or misused. For example, there is a specific procedure to pass the knowledge from one healer to another. If this is not done correctly and it is not approved by the spirits who created the legacy, the cure won't work. Also, the legacy is a bit mysterious even to the healer: while there are secret prayers that activate the channeling, many of them are fragmented and symbolic, and they are so old that meanings have been lost. Therefore they are not prayers that can be stolen and used in a way they are not meant to. The life of the healer is one lived in partnership with the higher power. The power is borrowed and independent from the healer: it cannot be used creatively in ways unintended for use by the spirits who lend it.

This is the borrowed power. The borrowed power is where the healer's relationship with it looks like both spiritualist healing and shamanism, because the healer's abilities rely completely on the spirit world, in this case, the divine feminine in various forms. In the way a trance-channeler is a conduit for spirit helpers, the Italian lineage healer is as well. There is no practice to get into trance for lineage healers however: the prayers and procedure are the activation necessary. The channeled power does the rest. The healer is very aware they are not the power, that the power does not belong to them and it is something they must honor. It works when people need it, but it's not something to have and to hold. There is even often a sensation of being forbidden to talk about the curing ability, for fear the healer might lose the ability to cure. It's a strange balance of knowing that you have a service to offer and yet it's only there when a person appears who has the need for the service, and knowing a higher consciousness is ultimately in charge of the cure.

In contrast, for many of us Americans, becoming a healer is a process we seek out. Becoming a healer for many contemporary people is a process that's about the healer first, then the clients second. In Italy, becoming a healer is more about the people who need the healing. The healer will live a humble life, largely away from any fanfare and recognition, have a daily open-door policy, and traditionally not get paid at all, though some do accept an offering, but they don't ask. Healers often give up whatever their own goals or dreams are so that they can be of service to the community around them who are in need of the cure. They remain in their community so the people know where to find them.

Traditionally, these legacy cures are passed down a family line. Most often, a woman passes down her inherited cures to a female family member she's guided to give them to. A woman may inherit cures from her mother or grandmother. Sometimes, a female family member will pass down her cures to a male family member, such as with Ottorino and his mother. Sometimes a female family member will pass down her cures to her daughter-in-law (and also protective amulets). More rare are male only family healer lineages. They are not as numerous as the female lineages, but they do exist.

Italian Magic: Secret Lives of Women

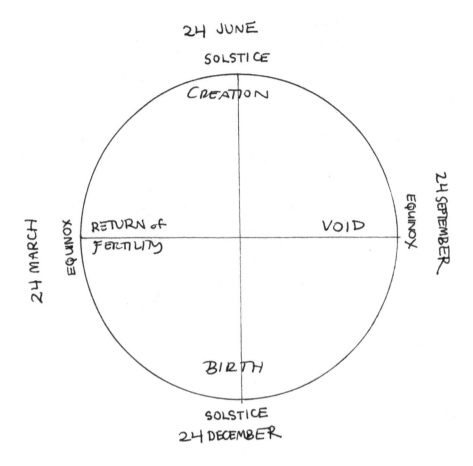

24 JUNE

SOLSTICE

CREATION

24 MARCH EQUINOX

RETURN of FERTILITY

VOID

EQUINOX 24 SEPTEMBER

BIRTH

SOLSTICE
24 DECEMBER

RITUAL INITIATIONS OF HEALERS

There are ritual initiations that healers must participate in to receive their transmission of energy and knowledge. The rituals take place on 1 of 3 specific dates in the year. A transmission of knowledge containing the secret prayers or invocations or spells along with ritual actions are passed orally from elder healer to the new healer. Depending on the tools used for the cures, some healers inherit bowls, teacups, copper pots, rings, sealed envelopes with secret words inside, or another object that has been used solely for curing.

It's uncommon for a healer to undergo any type of training or preparation before this ritual takes place. In contemporary times many people study, travel, practice yoga, do fasting, and otherwise engage in purification efforts or meditations to prepare themselves for work as a healer before becoming initiated/attuned/etc. In rural Italy, the moment takes place naturally, although for some healers there were preparatory efforts made on their behalf when they were infants, as you'll find in a few of the examples here.

TYPES OF ILLNESSES , TYPES OF HEALERS

Photo: Bajardo, Liguria.

MARKED AT BIRTH

Among some healers is a belief that they are marked from birth with a indication of their special gifts that will develop later in life. Traditional physical markers of innate healing abilities are:

+ being born in the caul
+ being born with umbilical cord wrapped around neck or surviving a traumatic birth
+ being the 7th born son born after a daughter OR the 7th son of a 7th son in line of males
+ bring 3rd born female
+ born December 24th/25th or January 24th/25th

People born in the caul have, in rural places, traditionally been celebrated for having a natural connection to something otherworldy, be it luck, a connection to the spirit world that enables them to cure, and having an ability against witchcraft namely for breaking spells or battling against black magic. In Friuli specifically, being born in the caul was a guarantee to be called on as a **benandante** when they came of age. Referred to as being "born with the shirt" or born with the "mantle of the Madonna", their dried placenta in part or in whole was dried out and then worn by them in a little pouch as a protective amulet for the duration of their lives. *The color of the membrane was significant: if it was white, the child was destined to have luck, if red would become a witch or a sorcerer.* 333

Physical markers are nature's way of calling attention to something, to notice a correlation and a pattern of significance. Spirit also makes efforts to call attention through

168

Italian Magic: Secret Lives of Women

correlations to marks or sounds or movements. These physical indicators are less prevalent than they used to be, but this makes sense considering the changes in societies and cultural attitudes towards spiritual possibilities. In the culture of the past, such as during the 1800s, "I'll believe it when I see it" was more prevalent, and therefore spiritual experiences of levitation, spirit sounds, and other physical phenomena were occurring to turn attention towards the spirit world. In our current times of over-saturation from technology, information and availability we find "I don't believe it even when I see it" and also attitudes of belief that everything is possible, so physical markers are not needed...people know of healing, people believe in the spirit world, so the connections and evidential support appear in more individuated ways, and some people just are not ready to explore these realms.

BENANDANTI

Benandanti are people who are elected by the spirit world to be part of a shamanic tradition unique to the physical regional location of Friuli in north east Italy. Being a **benandante** involves traveling in the astral realm and being very aware of what occurs there: whom you see, recognizing with whom you are traveling, being aware of what form you might shape shift into (wolves, for example) and what you are doing there specifically within the battles for balance between light and dark. While the main battles for **benandanti** are called "the ember days" and take place 4 times a year on the clock of the solstices and equinoxes, during the period when a **benandante** is active they will frequently have participatory dreams...as frequently as every night.

The initatic age range for **Benandanti** is between 20-28 years old and the duty period lasts for a span of 10-20 years or so. There are a variety of ways a person discovers they are being called into action as a benandante, but they all have one thing in common:

The call, being "called out" as in called out of the physical body to travel as a spirit. This call or initiation comes from the spirit world. In the beginnings, the call out is more attention-getting, and some people will find themselves in the presence of a figure (like an angel or a spirit person) helping take them out of their body, some hear the sound of a drum and others find themselves being taken into the dream world mid-action and being to recognize what's happening to them.

"He is a man just like us, [...] who is placed above us all [like a rank] *and beats a drum, and calls us"* testimony of Battista Moduco, reporting what happens to him when he's wearing his caul at night and being called out of his body, 1580s. 334

The testimony of Paolo Gasparutto from the same time period explains that a golden angel took him out of his body to speak with him *"It came out because in the body it cannot speak"*. 335 While psychic communication can happen between spirits in-body, conversing fully clairaudiently back-and-forth and moving in the astral realm happens when the spirit body is out and fully operating in that realm.

For some, when the dream ends they begin to put the pieces together about what took place and understand, in a sort of reverse order, that they have been initiated into the role of a **benandante**. Commonly **benandanti** report that the place in the astral world they are taken to is already full of activities of the battle and that there is no one central figure directing everyone although there is a perception of rank and the skill level of other people they engage with, either as team members or as fighters they battle with. For some there are 4-6 people they regularly battle with on their team but report seeing thousands of others involved in the astral battles. Everything is somehow in its place and the **benandante** learn as they go from their experiences in the spirit world, and also from their daily dreams.

The attitude of **benandanti** is very much like that of rural healers in the sense of a loyalty to the duty they are called to. This is not a path someone can choose.

NOTE *For a very detailed interview with Benandanti living in this current time period themselves, refer to "Italy's Witches and Medicine Women Vol 1.

INITIATIONS OF WORMS CHARMERS

There are several initiatic rituals for worms charmers (as they are called in Sicily but exist on the mainland also) for adults and children. In Sicily, the rituals involved in worm- charming are referred as being comprised of "*incantation, oration and genuine exorcism*" which cut the cords of negative energy that allowed the parasitical worms to fester.

In a uniquely Sicilian tradition, a healer can be "made" years before their elder healer dies, but they can only begin to heal once the elder healer passes or if their elder asks them to begin sooner (such as if the elder healer becomes ill and can't keep up with the needs of people seeking the cure) . This is considered to be a medico-magical heredity. *To be able to cast a spell* [for curing], *outside of worms charming, you would need to visit the trustee of that spell every Friday for 7 consecutive Fridays* [in Sicily] 336 in agreement with the spell-holder and thus become activated to do the spell-work yourself.

> "*On Christmas night or Easter day, whomever wants to acquire the "gift" should go to church with someone who nows which spell should be recited. Then in May, on the night of the full moon, she should go into the countryside, find a thistle caterpillar, rub it between their hands, then have their hands bound by the spell-sayer, and lastly have the remains of the caterpillar pushed in between her hands. 3 days later, the hands unbound, the person now has the power to heal others from worms.*" 337

There are other variations on this theme where other worms are used such as earthworms cabbage caterpillar, bait worms, but the same ritual remains: the hand must be bound with the worm inside and unbound *on good Friday. If, on that day, when the hand is opened the worm is dead, then that person has acquired the gift of the saintly hand.* 338

The ritual for a baby follows the same theme of the worm in the hand and wrapping it, opening it later to find out if the worm was killed or not. Firstly the mother, must recite

Italian Magic: Secret Lives of Women

a part of the initiation spell *"I held the worm in my hand as a pagan, now as a christian I kill it."* 339 and then the healer would mark the child with some crosses traced on the baby while reciting another part of the initiation spell *"On Easter day the worm will fall."* 340 If the worm dies while wrapped in the baby's hand, then the baby will be able to heal others when they are older. Almost the exact same formula is used on the mainland in Roccaporena, Umbria and other villages in Perugia.

FIRE MARKERS

In Arezzo, Tuscany, there is a magico-medical cure called **segni del fuoco,** which means "the signs of fires" that are used for curing burns. This cure's initiation is also unique in that it can be given to several people at once and it *must be renewed every 3 years otherwise it fades* [the virtue to cure]. 341 Also, a healer can pass the cure to anyone he feels wants to use it, and each healer can cure people in their areas simultaneously without passing the power through death of the elder healer. In fact, the vows would not be able to be renewed if the elder healer had died. This is a healing tradition held by men.

The initiation is *transmitted on December 24,* on Christmas Eve, at the stroke of midnight and the formula (the words used as part of the signatures) consists of 8 words.

> *"On Christmas Eve a fire is lit in the fireplace or outdoors and at midnight the person who gives the instructions and the adept (but they can also be more than one) stand in front of to this fire and they recite the Pater Noster; then they pick up a burning stick, make the sign of the cross and say the formula. That's all."* 342

MAJARE INITIATIONS IN SICILY

The **Majare** of Sicily have a reputation in some local myths of being witches in league with **il diavolo** the devil much like the **Janare** of Campania. In truth, they know the secrets of nature, the secrets of healing, and how to make and undo **fatture** and **il malocchio** *using mostly family objects such as oil, water, salt, a plate, keys, golden wedding rings or very common and widespread herbs [...] such as rue, the parsley and mallow* 343 combined with secret word formulas, ones with rhyming characteristics much like that of the Janare of the mainland's Campania region. And their name's witch connotations is associated with both midwives and washerwomen, just as the **lavatrici** and **levatrici are** as well.

The initiation of a new **majara:**
> *"took place by the work of other women (the godmothers), who in the night of Saint John (June 24th, i.e. 3 days after the summer solstice) or on Christmas Eve (December 24th, i.e. 3 days after the solstice in winter) "consecrate" the new* **majara**, *bathing her with water, at the confluence of 3 streets* or 3 waterways.* 344

* a crossroads in Italian tradition is the place where 3 streets meet not the intersection of 2 roads making 4.
* **Le storte** means "crooked" and refers to an illness that makes the stomach feel twisted and crooked, described in "Italy's Witches And Medicine Women Vol 1" in Filomena's interview, in reference to negative spirits...it can also refer to crooked muscles elsewhere.

TYPES OF ILLNESSES, TYPES OF HEALERS

INITIATION OF BABIES IN EMILIA ROMAGNA

Babies born marked as healers or born into families with healing lineages were prepped by their mothers in a ritual that charged them to their healing tools and even snuck a little charge secretly from their baptism ceremony. This preparation is similar to the story of Yves whose grandfather began his initiation when he was a baby and completed it at a later date when he would be ready and aware of the responsibilities and could retain the knowledge.

A ritual initiation tradition illustrated here with testimony from Emilia Romagna shows a link to the cimaruta's charm for babies along with the ancient tradition of wrapping:

> *"When I was baptized, my grandmother hid what she needed to inside the bands for* **segnare** *signing: a vine shoot for* **le storte****, the flowers for the* **occhi** *eyes, the grains of barley and rice for the* **porri** *warts, a black thread threaded into a needle for* **orzaiolo** *the stye. All these instruments hidden in the bands have been baptized with me, and I think that my brothers also had them. As far as I know, this custom occurs only here in Romagna. If this had not happened, the child could not receive virtue, which was transmitted to him later on Christmas Eve, so the virtue begins at baptism and is completed later, when the child is old enough to keep the formulas in mind and be sure that he does not reveal them. Age naturally depends on one subject to another."* interview with *Vittorio Tonelli* 345

INITIATIONS OF 3RD BORN FEMALES

There are few references to the "3rd born females" yet many documentations of rural women and their night time schooling relationship with female divinities. The myths of Ceres/Prosperina and Demeter/Persephone come alive here in the very real astral travel experiences of women in Italy. This is the feminine form of learning from the spirit world which is in stark contrast to the very masculinized and hierarchical Roman temple studies with laws and rules operating under the patriarchy. The Roman temples often had inner learning centers or ritual spaces that were inaccessible to regular people. Elite, noble people studied in the inner chambers of the temples. These temples were also designed and built by men, even the ones venerating various Goddesses, so they were all built in a man's vision of female divinity. While Romans allowed many freedoms, even in the temple of the Vesta virgins there was a giant wooden penis statue of protection. The penis, or the male version of genitals, was an apotropaic method employed by Romans. This idea of curing with the "male" is also found, in a more limited way, in rural magical cures.

For a deeper look, see the chapter called IL VOLO/FLIGHT. For the purposes of this section on Initiations, the 3rd born women in rural Italy refers to women called out of their bodies for the purpose learning from female divinities in the astral realm. The testimonies of women being called out in spirit by Diana are part of this tradition, in earlier time periods the female figures were called **Signora del Gioco** Lady of the Games, or even

Italian Magic: Secret Lives of Women

The Good Lady. In Sicily and Naples there were female spirit teachers called **Donne di Fuora** Ladies of Outside, and other names such as **Satia**, **Abundia** and **Perchta** were used before the Romanized names such as Diana ever made their appearances.

The 3rd born women had a similar duty to **benandanti**: they *were obliged to go out thrice weekly[...]in the company of dame Abonde.* 346 *they had the duty, imposed on them by destiny, to secure prosperity and abundance"*347 Therefore they were taught how to take flight to do this in the north, it was with the mind and the help of the female spirits. Considering the suffering of women historically, the ritual of connecting women to abundance is truly radical.

IL MALOCCHIO INITIATIONS

Initiations or transference of the power to both diagnose and cure **il malocchio** the evil eye are the most commonly known, perhaps because almost every **nonna** grandma performs their version, and perhaps because December 24th is the traditional night to pass the method from one holder to another. And, **rimedi contro il malocchio** remedies against **il malocchio** are the most pervasive cures to survive outside of wholly rural traditions. They are a part of a greater whole of rituals from the rural world that are still in use today.

Some initiations have a religious aspect to them, some have absolutely none. There are many different variations. Generally speaking, the transference is quick and simple. The requirement is a mental and emotional preparedness, because the healing work is often challenging. The invocations or words, in whatever form, must be kept secret or risk the loss of their power. They are not written down, and they are passed with discretion.

LE GUARITRICI + I RITI TERAPEUTICI
Healers and Therapeutic Rites / The Medicine

Ottorino (pictured above) , a healer who lives near San Giovanni Valdarno, Tuscany. He was a farmer until he was 20 years old, then had a career in glass-making. When his mother was close to death, she asked him to carry on her curing traditions, because she was the only healer in their area, and people would still need these cures. So he agreed. His sons are currently uninterested in learning his cures.

His TOOLS are:

+ a silver medallion
+ a variety of herbs: blessed olive leaves, **erba della paura**, mallow, hypericum, several other local plants.
+ **vespa** wasp nest
+ oil, blessed water
+ secret prayers
+ making the sign of the cross
+ sulfur

Italian Magic: Secret Lives of Women

What he CURES:

+ Psychic Frights that cause muscular contractions in humans and animals
+ Stomach inflammations intestinal inflammations, other inflammations
+ clearing the kidneys, constipation
+ bedsores
+ wounds
+ external hemorrhoids
+ **orzaiolo** (eye styes)
+ **il malocchio** (the evil eye)
+ **fuoco di sant'Antonio** (shingles)
+ **vermi** (psychic fright induced worms in adults and children)

Ottorino gives cures out of a small adapted room in his house (the equivalent of a small laundry room in American houses) on street level with a door to the outside, so patients can arrive when necessary. Patients come to him, and this is the common procedure for healers in general. Ottorino can also cure some illnesses at a distance, such as **vermi**. This is helpful in the case of a very ill infant for whom travel can be a challenge. In cases like these, a "double" is used to cure such as an item of clothing that is infused with the infant's energy. He performs the same water, sulfur, medallion, prayer ritual but instead of performing it over the baby, he performs the ritual over the clothing, which is then taken back to the baby. This ritual act also brings the cure to the baby.

*Ottorino's extended interview will be included in "Italy's Witches and Medicine Women Vol 2.

Tuscan views

LE GUARITRICI + I RITI TERAPEUTICI

Mastitis Cure, from the Aplini sisters near San Giovanni Valdarno, Toscana.

Symptoms: Mastitis is a condition where the breast feels like it's burning.

Ingredients: + a wasp nest **vespa** with larvae taken from the window frames on the outside of their house + salt + egg yolks

Procedure: The vespa is mashed into a paste with lots of salt and 2 egg yolks. The mixture is placed wet onto the red part of the breast for a time. It is used it 2 or 3 times until the breast can give milk again. The details of this cure are in their memory: they don't have a written-down recipe. They said they are not witches and they don't do magic. They learned these cures and the plants from their mother in law **suocera**. (think: fire of the wasp sting for the sympathetic connection)

L-r top row: Alpini sisters Anna and Marisa, land near their home.
L-r bottom: wasp nest with larva, used for healing; their windowsill where they collected it

Italian Magic: Secret Lives of Women

Hemorrhoids Cure, from the Aplini sisters near San Giovanni Valdarno, Toscana.
Ingredients: + proper olive oil only + big pieces of the herb
Procedure: gather these herbs fresh [above] and dry them slowly. Make an oil infusion, let it set until the herbs settle in the bottom, then strain and put in bottle to use topically.

The sisters didn't know the name of the plant, they only knew where to harvest it (at the end of their road), which is common for many rural healers. They know plants, when to harvest them, how to use them, but they don't know the technical names, often they just know the dialect name or a type of nickname.

Filomena dropping oil into water to diagnose and cure **il malocchio** for the author

LE GUARITRICI + I RITI TERAPEUTICI

Filomena lives in Guardia Sanframondi. She inherited her mother's cures for physical and psychic ailments when she was 15, and she is in her mid 80s now. She trained alongside her mother for some time to learn the physical cures before curing patients on her own. She also inherited her mother's cure against **il malocchio** the evil eye and began using it immediately.

For example, she learned a pointy-finger type massage from her mother to cure arm muscle twists and ankle injuries. It's not a regular massage, but it feels as though her finger points are pushing into the body. She rubs some olive oil on the body part and then does this specific type of massage there and heals sports injuries, for example, miraculously taking away both the pain and the injury. For this particular cure, she worked alongside her mother for a period of time after she received the oral transmission, before she was able to cure on her own.

In contrast to this training, the **occhi** diagnostic cure she inherited was able to be used immediately. Her particular **occhi** cure works on headaches caused by envy, personal power loss due to past life envy, and some spirit attachment envy (specifically, spirits who cause hyperactivity, distractedness, and ungroundedness. Both In and near her village there tare other healers who perform the **occhi** cure against **il malocchio.** Each healer has a slightly different cure, and these differences are not just in "style". Because there are different types and sources of **il malocchio,** there's a need for differently focused cures.

+ **Filomena's occhi procedure:**
+ she makes a plate of water and places it in front of the patient.
+ she asks them to watch their own plate of water.
+ she moves her hand, spread flat, over the plate of water while whispering her secret prayer and also making the marks of an equilateral cross.
+ she takes a cup of olive oil, and with her pointer finger she drops 7 drops of oil into the water and then observes their movements.
+ she throws away the water and oil into the sink, down the drain.
+ she then repeats this 2 more times, for a total of 3 repetitions.
+ depending on what she finds, she may repeat this another day, or she may end the procedure by placing open scissors in the water with a pinch of salt while whispering another secret prayer.

Her TOOLS are: olive oil, water, scissors, hands, fingers, secret prayers
What she CURES: il malocchio, sciatica, sprained and twisted muscles

*Filomena's extended interview can be read in "Italy's Witches and Medicine Women Vol 1. where her treatment of 2 different people is described in detail. Filomena has not passed on her legacies to anyone.

Italian Magic: Secret Lives of Women

Antonietta is healer, born in Puglia. She moved to the village of Triora in 1947, after spending time in Arma di Taggia where she experienced WWII. She's known and honored as a **strega**, a true healer, in Triora, and some people say she's the last person who holds this curative plant knowledge in the area.

She is now 92 years old, and the first time she has even been to the doctor was a just a few years ago. She has always been a harvester as well, which she learned how to do from her father who had a high knowledge of herbs, and other older farmers. Until just a few years ago, when she started to slow down a bit, she would harvest all her own plants from the surrounding mountain, and her house's living room was bursting with whatever her current harvest contained: plants, both fresh and dried; fruits, dried fruit skins, fruit stems and seeds and fermented drinks, flowers, snail shells and oil infusions.

Triora is 2,559 feet up on a mountaintop in the Ligurian region. It experiences a heavy winter, and the available nature is at the mercy of the seasons and weather. The large variety of plants Antonietta uses are gathered from: fountains, the surrounding mountain paths, she takes large snails from the graveyard at the highest point of the mountain, and she grows some of her own. Her supply varies depending upon the season.

Mostly Antonietta cures with plants and edible nature, but she also cures **colpo delle streghe** (painful hunched spine) with the moon and prayers and offers this cure over the telephone when the moon is in the correct phase. She also cures erysipelas (shingles) using a silver ring.

LE GUARITRICI + I RITI TERAPEUTICI

Her TOOLS are:

a silver ring, moonlight, secret prayer, herbs and plants that she infuses into oil, tea, ointments, compresses, steam baths, amaro. Herbs: maidenhair fern, strigonella/herba da madonna, passion flower, elder berry, hawthorn, 9 types of chamomile, calimedro, St. johns wort, calendula, stinging nettles, olive leaves, horse tail, mallow, dandelion, lime leaf, linden flower, thyme, sage, rosemary, pulmonaria leaves, tarragon, laurel, oregano, juniper leaves and berries, lavender, orange juice and skins, lemon, eucalyptus, wild fennel, artemisia absinthum, cherry stems, large snails from the graveyard (only the large ones) ,

Italian Magic: Secret Lives of Women

pomegranate bark, honey, red plums, apple, cabbage leaves, raw potato juice, spiderwebs, and more.

What she CURES: lumbago, lung issues, sciatica, heart issues, psoriasis, liver issues, lymphatic disease, muscle twists, bone issues, **colpo delle streghe**, herpes zoster, cystitis, sunburn, dysentery, kidney issues, blood pressure, diabetes, colds and flu, sore throat, cough, sleep disorders, insect stings, warts, sprained ankle, various types of inflammation,

Antonietta's herb supply is different every time I visit, even if it's just 1-2 months between visits, due to nautre being her supply. The seasons bring different options. Sometimes she has 5 types of chamomile and large snails from the graveyard, sometimes a large amount of **strigonella** and **capelvenere**, other times, not.

toothaches, indigestion, psychic fright, erysipelas, to name a few illnesses.

*Her extended interview is in "Italy's Witches and Medicine Women Vol 1, which lists many of the plants she uses and what she uses them for. She has not passed down her lineage to her children.

Triora view from below, alcove in the village whose history is written about in "Italy's Witches and Medicine Women Vol 1".

PASSING OF POWER FROM THE SPIRIT WORLD

Yves, a Sicilian healer living in France whose interview is in "Italy's Witches and Medicine Women Vol. 1", is part of a masculine lineage of healers. His grandfather (his father's father) was a well known but secretive healer in their village. Yves' father knew his father was a healer, but there was no talk about it ever. In fact Yves' father would not inherit grandfather's healing lineage at all...it would be passed to Yves from "the beyond."

When Yves was a very small child, his grandfather placed his hands on Yves' head, but didn't explain what he was doing to any of the family members. It was a preparatory move. His grandfather died before explaining any of this to Yves. After, Yves began having a variety of experiences that lasted into his adult years: levitating, astral travel, and being able to sense his grandfather's presence in spirit form. His grandfather used to wear a ring with a black stone when he cured people, and it was an item Yves' family members fought over in the wake of his death. Everyone who tried to wear it became ill, except for Yves who eventually tried it on and then kept it. After, Yves' grandfather's spirit appeared to Yves' father on Christmas eve and demanded he place his hands on Yves' head to make him a healer, and after a year or two of refusal the father eventually did and Yves became a powerful healer, "made" by his deceased grandfather's spirit, who used his father as a conduit to pass the power.

Yves' grandfather continued to teach and train him from the spirit world. Yves currently heals people in a French hospital and has been photographed with red and blue lights coming out of his hands. He is in France's official National List of Healers. He is also a Medium, gives card readings, and cleanses his own energy daily by embracing particular trees in the forest and taking several showers while rubbing himself with coarse salt. His grandfather was a pranotherapist, so Yves' range of cures is broad and this is unusual for the younger generation of rural healers (healers back a generation or 3 held many cures, as in the case of people who live out in isolated areas where healers were few.

His TOOLS are: His grandfather's ring with a black stone, pendulum, hands, prayers, incense, coarse salt. He uses photographs to release **il malocchio** at a distance or on himself.

What he CURES: varicose veins, brain seizures in dogs, a large variety of ailments experienced by people in the hospital as well as **il malocchio**.

*Yves' extended interview is in "Italy's Witches and Medicine Women Vol 1, which contains details about how his grandfather communicates with him, how he cares for his own energy, and more about his journey to becoming a healer.

In contrast to our contemporary lifestyles of being on-the-go, where healers are willing to make appointments for clients and travel around giving services, healers in rural Italy are stationary. The cures they offer are tailor-made for the ailments that affect their community. Yves' case is unusual because it is contemporary, and he has also embraced other modalities such as reiki. Pranotherapists and healers who work with angels are also found these days in Italy, but this is distinctly different from the rural traditions. Rural healers remain in their villages. The patients who come to be cured by them are also sometimes doctors and nurses, and some healers are even visited by sports teams.

It makes sense, therefore, that some cures are not passed on: if the spirit world is aware that people are no longer suffering from illnesses resulting from conditions that no longer exist, the cures will likely be allowed to die out. Likewise, a lineage may be discontinued if the only possible recipients are either uninterested in being of service, if they are planning to move somewhere else or take a different career, and other factors that the spirit world and the elder healer takes notice of. The purpose of the gift of the cures is that they provide for specific needs. It is not common to find a "one-cure-cures-all" healer in many rural places, although there are exceptions such as healers who use only their hands and secret prayers, herbalists like Antonietta who treat a variety of illnesses, and healers such as Yves who have also trained in a variety of contemporary modalities.

This is why the tradition of healers in Italy is to remain in the same village for the duration of their life as a healer: they were made for their environment by the spirits. And, healers in rural places tend to have an open door policy on their days of work, where anyone can come by during their hours, and often they have lines of people waiting, depending on the area and depending on the variety of cures they offer. A healer who offers **su contravelenu** (as it is called in Sardinian dialect, meaning "poison cure") for example wears his medicine pouch 24 hours a day, even while he is sleeping , so he can help anyone who needs it. **Su contravelenu** is a "contra-poison", a sympathetic magical cure for poisonous snake bites and poisonous insect bites that uses a mummified piece of that creature dipped in oil, marked onto the puncture site and accompanied by secret prayers. It takes time to procure the creatures that are then mummified, so they are more rare than other supplies. Snakes, in certain areas, are a common cause of illness, and their bites can occur at any hour.

Another significant factor that prevents charlatans from taking advantage of poor and urgently ill people seeking cures is that there is no fee to get a cure. Being that there are no fees and cures are free, there can be no economic competition. Healers will take donations of things, such as food or flowers and of money if offered, but they never ask.

That being said, some keep an offering plate out, and while they do not ask for a set fee, there is a certain pressure to leave money. These healers tend to be more modern-minded, fashion-forward, world-aware, have experienced some fame such as being interviewed on television. It is the personal experience of the author that these types of healers are a bit possessive of their cures and fame and are less welcoming to people interested in their work, not out of a protective nature of the cures but of something a little more ego-centric. They will speak endlessly about all the healings they've done in a bragging sort of way. This is quite strange for an Italian person of any village, considering the great hospitality that Italians are known for. And, this stands in stark contrast to older healers who also may not want to talk about their cures but still offer an unconditionally loving warmth.

I RITI TERAPEUTICI
Therapeutic Rites/CURES

The foundation of the beliefs and rituals in birth, death, and curing traditions of rural Italy are the Laws of Energy (the Law of Attraction being one of those laws). Therefore, there is a belief in personal responsibility for one's health. This means a person has choices and can be empowered by those choices, for example, by going to a healer rather than "waiting on god." This, perhaps, is the real power that the church has fought against, because the beauty of rural cures is that they are available and they do work, which is why people still seek out these cures. In medieval times, the church attempted to turn people away from "witches" and instead seek cures from monks, but more people died than

Italian Magic: Secret Lives of Women

were cured by the church. It's the same with the church's still unsuccessful exorcisms and prayers. And with many of Italy's rural areas going without doctors and hospitals until the 1950s-1970s, the tradition of going to local healers is a very ancient one.

Medicine is originally founded on magic. [348] While there is not a general word in Italy to categorize this type of medicine, on the island of Sardinia once again we do find a name for the body of these types of cures: **sa mexina** (the medicine).

There are 3 parts to rural Italian cures just as there are 3 parts to rural magic.
The 3 parts are:
+ **the matter** (oil, water, plants, silver medallions, sulphur, etc)
+ **the actions** (marks made on the body, marks made over water, specific movements made and actions taken)
+ **the words** (secret prayers or invocations whispered during the healing session)

photo: Davide Tiso, 2020. Author's medallions used for healing

LE GUARITRICI + I RITI TERAPEUTICI

These cures are all based on channeling. The channeled energy of the divine feminine is the key to these cures. The words activate this agreement between the divine feminine and the healer, as curing energy flows to the healer who also must be willing to receive it. The channeling could be termed "passive" because the healer is transmitted the energy through the ritual agreement and then "unlocks it" each time the secret prayers are said during the curative process. The healers do not actively meditate or use psychic abilities to prepare to consciously channel. And yet, the sensations received during cures are palpable and otherworldy.*

The channeled cures use simple tools that have a homeopathic/sympathetic nature. The basic idea looks like: LIKE CURES LIKE. This is also where conceptual magic draws its inspiration from. Conceptual magic often uses some connection to nature, but one that has been synthesized in some way. Conceptual magic will use the concept of a cure or ritual (without the key piece channeled energy) in a way that suits a contemporary need such as: for a goal, for a financial gain, for "getting something" beyond just improving health or removing a spirit attachment. The synthesis comes from a bastardization of an action meant for one thing yet stolen and re-worked for another. For example, knot magic. Knot magic originated as a cure for both human and farm animal illnesses and has been copied, in concept, by conceptual magic users who, for example, have turned it into binding spells to acquire lovers or to harm am intended victim.

In rural culture, we find an absence of psychic language and a reliance on orally transmitted tradition. Therefore their lineage cures are not adapted by them, nor added to in a Do-It-Yourself way. The inheritances are loyally kept in the same condition they were received in and passed it along in the same condition.

So, many of these cures look weird and are uninteresting because they can't really be written down into a collection nor a grimoire unless they are being documented by ingredients or concept, because the mechanisms are kept secret. In fact, they work based on "the secret" as it's called in some regions as Val d'Aosta. The "secret" is the partnerships healers have with the spirit world. Some healers will be able to verbalize this to you and others not, depending on their vocabulary and ability to explain.

**There are CURES for physical ailments,
and there are CURES for psychic ailments.**

This means there are cures for illnesses affecting the physical body, like twisted muscles, eczema, styes, sore throat, cystitis...and then there are cures for illnesses (which may be affecting the physical body) caused by negative energy or spirit attachments that affect the mind, body and spirit of a person, i.e. illnesses with a psychic cause.

The materials used in CURES look much like the materials used in magic spells. A healer has one cure per illness: a mixture of matter, words, and actions that is performed

---

*To read about the author's experiences receiving healings, refer to "Italy's Witches And Medicine Women Vol 1", and more coming in "IWAMW Vol2"

Italian Magic: Secret Lives of Women

in the same way whether the client is old, young, masculine or feminine or other gender. And, **there is preventative magic and curative magic.**

PSYCHIC FRIGHT

+ **azzicchidu** - fright caused by people, animals, living souls (Sardinian)
+ **azzicchidu de anima morta** or **de umbra** - fright of a dead soul or ghost.
+ **azzicchidu de anima bia** - fright from living soul 349
+ **arrisagghiari** - a surprise fear (Sardinian)
+ **scantu** - jitters, indicator of worms/fright magical illness is present (Sicilian)
+ **paura** - the fear (mainland Italy)
+ **spavento** - the fright (mainland Italy)
+ **umbra**, fright received from a dead soul (Sardinian)

Symptoms of s'azzicchidu: insomnia and ravings; loss of appetite, vomiting; emaciated pale face; fixed absent gaze (**spriau** shocked); furunculosis, especially on the head; restless sleep; high fever with delirium, paralysis. Repeating of symptoms on anniversary of fright. 350

Taken seriously in rural Italy, psychic fright caused by trauma or negative spirits is believed to be the precursor to other illnesses, so cures revolve around releasing the fright. There are curative methods done by healers such as **suffumigi** fumigations to lift the emotional moods of fright and the more serious exorcism spells of cord-cutting when spirit attachments have taken a strong influence over someone, and more. On the preventative side, there is a body smudging technique that anyone, even children, can do for themselves to release the fright immediately or at a later date when its accumulation has created nightmares for example, called **s'imbrusciadura.**

It is believed negative spirits can enter into the body through the breath: the inhale or gasp taken in fear. It's the equivalent of saying, that a weak boundary allows a spirit attachment to hook in. Likewise, a trauma that causes a person to shrink into themselves deprives them of vitality and balanced energy.

Psychic fear makes "frightened blood", as it's known in Sicily or "spoiled blood" in Umbria's Valnerina. Blood instilled with fear from a shock or from negative spirits is therefore weakened blood, which leads to weakened health. In these rural traditions, the affect of the spirit world on the physical one is real, and *a strong "fear" could "spoil the blood" and cause damage to health and the sphere of personality, to the point of inducing insanity and death".* 351

In contrast, an in-keeping with this philosophy is the belief that strong blood can fascinate the weaker, and this is what gives power to throwing the "evil eye" at someone else. The power to send **il malocchio** to someone else is rooted in the force of the blood as a conduit fluid.

Spiritually, energetically and alchemically we find that iron represents protection,

187

stamina, strength, alignment with the soul's purpose, and we find that a lack of iron presents itself as anemia, lack of strength, lack of red blood cells, lack of stamina and an absence of protection. The idea of a vampire is relevant here, also the parasite, the spirit attachment and the energy vampire. Technically, negative spirits try to empty the blood of iron through bullying and perpetuation of fear-inducing tactics. Spirit mediums in contemporary environments can and do develop anemia as a result of dealing with negative spirits (if they do) repeatedly.

Iron is found used as protection throughout the rural world in the form of: amulets, horse shoes and fish hooks protecting the home and chicken coops and persons. Iron as aloex ferox and other iron-rich herbs are essential ingredients in the digestive drink called **amaro**. This drink is connected to the Italian philosophy about the importance of the spirit's health as related to health of the physical body, and digestion playing an active role in this balance between spirit and physical body. Iron creates a barrier between you and negative spirits, whether used as a horseshoe or ingested and turned into energy.

In the local stories of succubi who disturb sleeping people at night and who suck blood from babies, iron also makes an appearance as a ritualistic protection, particularly in stories about **janare** witches who have been being accused as the shape-shifting spirits who attack people in their beds..There is a ritual, among the local people, regarding what to do in this instance:

> *"When you wake at night to find a ghostly figure on top of you, trying to smother you, you must try to grab her hair. She will ask you what you have in your hand. If you reply 'I got your hair', she goes away. If you reply 'I got iron', she stays, she can't move [...] if you keep her, when the morning comes, you can recognize who she is, maybe she is your neighbor or someone you know."* [352]

PSYCHIC FRIGHT CURE

> *"With the* **azzicchidus** *the scares, you should not joke: an* **azzicchidu** *held inside can also bring paralysis [...] One can even die."* [353]

The self-help method taught to people in Sardinia is similar to a grounding technique on the mainland. The Sardinian version is called **s'imbrusciadura**. It's used when someone freezes in fear in a place, and the name translates to "smudging". It's a method anyone can do immediately, even children, in a moment of fear. This is similar to something animals do in nature: when you see some water birds tussle with each other only to separate and shake their feathers. Or if a dog has been sitting inactive for a while, he may get up and stretch.

> *Some make also distinctions of place:* **logu opertu,** *open place, and* **logu serradu,** *closed place. These distinctions determine the variants in the* **s'imbrusciadura** *ritual, especially in the number of times that must be accomplished: from 1, to 3, to 9.* [354]

Italian Magic: Secret Lives of Women

Psychic Fright cure -s'imbrusciadura- to smudge the body by rolling the self on the ground, from Sardinia.

Ingredients: + just the self

Procedure: Used immediately and often by children when they are playing and become frightened, they often drop themselves and roll on the ground to smudge away the fear.

Psychic Fright cure- s'imbrusciadura - to smudge the body by rolling the self on the ground. Sardinian.

Ingredients: + Blanket or Towel + Location where trauma or fright occurred.

Procedure: return to the place where a fright occurred, or have friends wrap you in a blanket and take you there. Lay yourself on the ground, wrapped, and roll around in the place where the fright occurred, returning the energy back to the earth, whether at a grave yard, the beach, or forest. In this tradition, if you are the person affected and are too weak to take yourself to the place of trauma, then your friends will come to wrap you in blankets and then take you to the place.

+This cure is used when a fear haunts someone, for example when it repeats in one's dreams, or the fear revisits someone on the anniversary of their frightful event.

Psychic Fright cure "s'imbrusciadura"- to smudge the body by rolling the self on earth taken from the location of the fright: in the special case of not being able to return to the scene of the psychic trauma or not wanting to roll in public (such as if the smudging has to be done naked or if the location might be crowded, of if intense fear of returning to the place).

Ingredients: + some soil/sand/earth from the location of the fright + blanket

Procedure: Have someone collect a handful of land of the place. Spread this earth over a blanket previously laid out at home. The patient rolls in the soil and therefore transfers the fright energy into it. Collect it without touching it, and either throw it in a pit beneath the ground, so that no one puts your feet on it, or you throw it in one well that no one drinks from, throw into the fire of the fireplace or in a place where nobody can come in contact. 355

Psychic Fright cure "s'imbrusciadura"- to smudge the body by rolling the self on earth taken from the location of the fright: in the special case of not being able to return to the scene of the psychic trauma or not wanting to roll in public (such as if the smudging has to be done naked or if the location might be crowded, of if intense fear of returning to the place).

Ingredients: + some soil/sand/earth from the location of the fright + blanket

Procedure: Have someone collect a handful of land of the place. Spread this earth over a blanket previously laid out at home. The patient rolls in the soil and therefore transfers the fright energy into it. Collect it without touching it, and either throw it in a pit beneath the ground, so that no one puts your feet on it, or you throw it in one well that no one drinks from, throw into the fire of the fireplace or in a place where nobody can come in contact. [355]

The author collects earth from each place she visits in Italy so as to be able to revisit those places if desired. This earth is from a temple ground in Lazio.

Italian Magic: Secret Lives of Women

SUFFUMIGI / AFFUMENTU

Suffumugi are used throughout Italy, Sardinia and Sicily, to cure fright, **il malocchio, fatture,** post partum depression and other psychic disturbances. **Suffumigio** means "fumigation". **Suffumigi** (plural) are used in rural Italian curing traditions and there are secret recipes and prayers that are inherited, but there are also suffumigi that everyone can use at certain times of the year for general energy cleaning and more.

Suffumigi have a common thread among all material items used in rural cures: they are composed of accessible natural items found nearby within walking distance, and so they are made of fresh plants and dried plants and a very few extra items. All the ingredients are gathered by hand and prepared by hand to use in a natural, balanced way.

This type of fumigation incense is not ground in a mortal and pestle nor are binders used nor any other process to turn the plants into another product. The natural items used are in their natural state, although some are used after being dried.

Suffumigi are also burned in a specific way: on a ceramic tile, such as a terra cotta roof tile. The material items used (terra cotta tile, or other such items used for other cures like teacups or bowls) are often inherited from an elder healer and in any case are reserved specifically for this curing purpose. Traditionally, a healer takes an ember from the fireplace and places it on a terra cotta tile. On top of this tile, and around the ember, are placed the herbs and other ingredients. They are burned to create a heavy smoke which is then passed over and across the patient.

The smoke should be heavy enough to envelope the person receiving the healing, or at least for their body part (or whatever the focal point of the cure is) in heavy smoke. Due to the smoke factor, windows and doors are kept open during this curing ritual. But this is not the only reason: as with all rural Italian cures, each action taken in the physical world also has its parallel intention in the energy world. So, work done on the physical body also means that work is being done on the spirit body. In this light, open doors and open windows don't only allow for the smoke to move out, but they symbolically allow for the energy being released to move away.

S'affumentadora is the name for the fumigator in Sardinia, but fumigations are used all across mainland Italy as well as Sicily.

PROCEDURE

The **s'affumentadora** fumigator sits below her client, who is often raised above her in some way, such as on a chair. She speaks her secret prayers over the patient, and she moves the heavy smoke in a specific way over and across her patient, starting from the patient's feet and moving up towards her head, then from one shoulder to the other, repeating this entire procedure 3 times. The specially chosen burning herbs do the work to release the patient of imbalance along with the channeled energy. There are always 2 windows or doors open because "**s'affumentu** *can not take place - it would not be worth* *doing - if not in a room with two doors. This is because the sick person should not leave from the same atmosphere where he entered or he would recover the evil he had."* 356

The suffumigi, being part of the Lineage cures, work successfully with the assistance of a channeled energy from the Divine Feminine, which means the recipes are inherited along with secret prayers which activate the channeled energy. Lineage cures are inherited and never altered by the healer who inherits them. It's the duty of the healer to protect their integrity and their composition and usages, along with protecting the secret prayers which activate the channeled conscious energy.

S'affumentu is the name of the specific **suffumigio** therapy used to cure psychic fright. All the **suffumigi** are meant to create a very heavy smoke, whether around the patient, if the suffumigio is for curing an illness or state of mind, or through the entire home, if the suggumigio is being used to clean out the air or the previous year's energy of the home.

Italian Magic: Secret Lives of Women

Psychic Fright cure "s'affumentu" - therapeutic name for a cure involving fumigation/ smoking of the body by a **s'affumentadora** (the fumigation healer).

Ingredients: + a common Tile of terra cotta + a small pile of Embers alive from the fireplace + a bundle containing consecrated Palm on Sunday + pieces of Wax and Flowers taken from the high altar after a religious function + small bottle containing Holy Water + Secret Words

Procedure: The **s'affumentadora** sprinkles holy water on the child's face, then gathers embers and puts them on the concave part of the tile. She takes a pinch of the blessed **suffumigio** mixture, holding it between fingers suspended over the embers while reciting her ritual words. She traces 3 signs of cross on the embers letting fall the last of the **suffumigio** mixture held between the fingers. As smoke emanates from the tile, the healer raises it towards the face of the patient; as the smoke wraps around the immobile and fascinated child. S'afumentadora speaks other incomprehensible words, finally pouring the holy water bottle onto the embers, which are extinguished. The steam is also insufflated by the **s'affumentadora** on the face of the **azzicada**, the child who got a scare. New embers are put back on the tile and the same operation is repeated 3 times. In conclusion, holy water is sprinkled on the face and on the baby's hair.

Psychic Fright cure: s'affumentu and maurreddinu for **umbra**, a fright received from the soul of a dead person, which is different from **s'azzicchidu**, the fright caused by people or animals, living souls.

Ingredients: + Black Shawl + Ceramic Tile + Embers + **Suffumigio** + Secret Words

Procedure: The patient is seated on a chair and her head is covered with one black shawl. At the feet of the patient, on the floor, the tile is placed with the embers. The woman officiates the standing ceremony. 3 times the sign of the cross is made, then she reads the secret words. She recites the verses 3 times while letting the blessed aromatic herbs drop onto the embers, incense and wax. Then she imposes the palms of the hands on the head of the patient, exerting continuous and strong pressures. She bends down to touch the patient's head with her lips and traces with the lips three signs of the cross. In conclusion - she frees the patient from the shawl that covered her, and the healer spits 3 times on the hair of the patient.

Italian Magic: Secret Lives of Women

Psychic Fright Cure: **l'anima caduta** Fallen Soul from Romagna. Both diagnostic tool and cure. Has the same spiritual causation of symptoms as **vermi** but instead of panic and jitters, the emotional state is low: stomach pain accompanied by a sense of emptiness, depression, tiredness. From Ms. Gilda.

Diagnostic Procedure: *"I give myself the patient's belt, I tell him to hold it at one end with the hand and then I measure it with my arm, from the elbow to the fingertips: if with the last measurement I don't touch the patient's hand, it means that the soul has not fallen, if instead I touch it or even go beyond, it means that the soul has fallen."*

Curing Procedure: Having established this fact, she proceeds to raise the soul, which occurs through a light massage from the top to the bottom carried out with the fingertips and then bandaging the stomach with a band for children [the kind midwives use]. If this treatment is not enough and the soul continues to stay low, Ms. Gilda does not hesitate to implement the extreme remedies: she greases the disturbed part with oil and applies a Bertelli plaster. She also always says secret words without which her all her efforts would be useless. 357

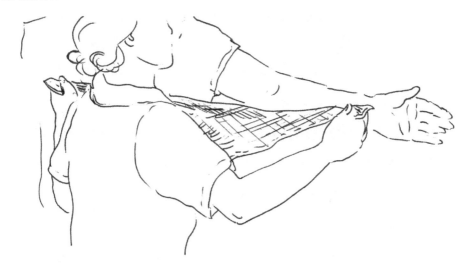

Psychic Fright Cure: the **erba della paura** (the fear herb) from Ottorino, healer near San Giovanni Valdarno, Toscana.

Ingredients: + Erba Della Paura (also called erba della Madonna and Strigonella) + blessed Olive leaves + Water + Hand made marks + Secret Prayer + Amulet

Procedure: Ottorino combines **erba della paura** medicinal herb together with the blessed olive tree's leaves and water to make an infusion. He lets it boil and make a sign on it with his amulet, *"a little medal like one of our **nonnas** grandmas used to have. You have to sign both the water and the person who need to be cured. Then, with this water, you bless (by making her/him wet) the person who needs to be cured 3 times a day, for 3 days, on the articulations (like arm joint, leg joint ecc.) This fear, really, is a muscular contraction and this blessed water pushes the fear away."* 358

LE GUARITRICI + I RITI TERAPEUTICI

photo: Davide Tiso 2020, **la Edera.**

Psychic Fright Cure: fright vine, from Cefala and Catania, Sicily.
Ingredients: + Vitis Vinifera, a small common grape vine + cup of Water + Prayers + hand made Marks on body of patient
Procedure: A healer uses a small vine shoot enlarged at one end (to simulate a head) with 2 small holes as eyes to mark the sign of the cross over the patient's mouth, forehead and shoulders. Reciting a prayer, the vine shoot is pressed onto the mouth and stomach. After, the vine is thrown into a glass of water while reciting the lord's prayer with the patient. If the shoot opens in the enlarged area even more while in water, it means the patient has worms. So, the patient must drink a little from the glass. The remaining water is thrown out of the house so no one else can catch the "fright". [359]

Psychic Fright Cure: **u cuppitieddu du scantu** (fright cup) from Sicily.
Ingredients: + vermicidal herbs: marine absinthe (artemisia cretacea), alsidium helmintochorton (Corsican moss), sargassum vulgare (brown seaweed) , digenea simplex (red sea broom) + Corallina officinalis (coral moss) + Delphinium staphysagria (larkspur) + sweetening foods: honey, cream, to make the medicine more palatable.
Procedure: An old lady healer collects the right kind of vermicidal herbs and prepares a mixture for the patient to eat [360] while saying the magic spell words.

Psychic Fright Cure: **Cugghiuta de vermi** (collection of worms) Ragusa, Sicily.
Ingredients: + Parlsey + Curse + symbolic cut
Procedure: (apotropaic) The healer uses a particular curse against the appearance of worms, while tickling the patient's navel with a parsley stalk [to gather them to this location to be cut]. [361] Activating this cure with the spell words, she enacts a psychic cut once the worms have been drawn to the navel and uses various methods to seal off the cut (placing ash in the navel, placing wax in the navel, or having the patient drink some liquid with a bit of the cut thread.

Italian Magic: Secret Lives of Women

photo: Davide Tiso, 2020. **La Edera**

VERMI : WORMS

Vermi means worms. **Vermi** is an illness whose physical symptoms occur as a result of psychic fright caused by a negative spirit, such as an experience of fear or shock in the presence of a ghost or spirit attachment that takes one by surprise. Psychic fright, in general, is believed to cause several types of illnesses that affect people and animals.

Vermi is found affecting children most often. It is blamed on unsanitary conditions, such as eating meat or food that's been out in the sumer heat too long with hands that have been playing in the soil, thereby acquiring tapeworms or parasitical worms who causing the symptoms. But this is shared with other beliefs such as: people already have parasites in the intestines which remain unharmful until something makes them active. It's believed that the experience of spirited fright creates a moment of weakness in the body when the defenses are down and therefore the worms begin to "jump", as it is said.

The physical symptoms of the illness manifest as: muscle cramping, physical pain and discomfort, nutrient deprivation, intestinal inflammation, choking and suffocation (if the worms arrive to the throat) and lung issues (if the worms arrive there), anemia, jitters.

Due to the psychic causation **vermi** is cured both naturally and magically. The physical cure expels the worms from the body in various ways. The symbolic work using rituals, spells, and plants command the spirit parasites away and cuts cords of connection with them. This is considered exorcism work and there are varying degrees of severity.

Presented here are a variety of **vermi** cures, some focusing just on natural components, others on magical actions showing a sympathetic connection between materials used and the body part they are working on physically and psychically. Among the natural components you'll notice associations with mythological concepts and the nutrient components or medicinal nature they hold. With the magical components, you'll find things such as threads and cord cutting, sulfur compositions resembling both intestines and worms, plants with high iron content used to restore energy after spirit attachment drain, and a focus on the realm of the belly which is also the psychic receptor (clarisentience) that spirit attachments plug into causing feelings of anxiety, twisted muscles **le storte**, nutrition deprivation, iron depletion and the realm of fearful sensations.

The words used in the spells also describe the actions being taken, in the typical Italian rhythmic **filastrocche** nursery rhyme style, which is a sing-song type of oracular series of phrases that are embedded with symbolism and numerical magic. In the way the filastrocche hold meanings for 2 different realms, the cures in general, with their spell words, symbolic actions, and ingredients often bear a resemblance to both the physical illness being cures as well as the energetic counterpart of causation in the spirit world.

Tuscany view from Volterra.

One of the many owls you can find throughout Tuscany, near the front doors of businesses, healers, and homes, keeping eyes on the energy entering and exiting.

Vermi Cure, from Ottorino near San Giovanni Valdarno, Toscana
Symptoms: muscle cramping, jitters, fright, anemia, digestion troubles, pain
Ingredients: + powdered sulfur + iron spatula + glass of water + secret prayers + medallion of a Madonna
Procedure: Over the gas stove flame place the long- handled iron spatula. Place a heaping amount of powdered sulfur onto spatula, melt with wooden ladel. When liquified, pour into glass of water where it takes the shape of intestines and worms. Bless the glass of water and sulfur with medallion of the Madonna and secret prayers.

This works for children and adults. It also works at a distance: if an ill child can't travel to him for treatment, one of the parents can bring an item of clothing belonging to the child and it will serve as a link between the cure and the child.

Italian Magic: Secret Lives of Women

Ottorino takes powdered sulfur and melts it on an iron spatula over the stove and then pours it into water, several times. The sulfur takes the form of both worms and intestines.

After he makes this transformative preparation, he blesses it with his secret prayer and silver medallion.

This can cure someone who comes in person or at a distance.

For **vermi** parasitical worms.

Vermi Diagnosis from Sicily. Variations are found of: the little worm cup **ciacaredda:** *when worms are suspected, a small coffee cup whose rim has been coated with garlic and oil is placed rim-down on the patient's navel: if the cup sticks, the patient has worms.* 362

Panata Water Cures

While bread in itself may not make sense as a cure, consider that in rural Italy wheat is honored as a sacred grain, a gift from the Great Mother, and one that *undergoes a "Passion", tortured, beaten, put to death, is the first divinity that rises again, it is the wheat that inaugurates the triduum of the passion-death-resurrection, then transferred to new gods,* 363 the synthetic non-natural ones like Christ.

Acqua Panata Panata Water (Breaded Water) is a cure where wheat is "undone" and reverted back to its primal regenerative force, and consumed to counteract psychic fright.

LE GUARITRICI + I RITI TERAPEUTICI

Panata Water Cure, from the border area between Valnerina, Lazio, Leonese territory:
Ingredients: + Bread + Fireplace Coals + Water
Procedure:"Toasting the fright" involves toasting a slice of wheat bread on the embers of a fire, then leaving it to create an infusion in a jug of cold water until the bread was almost completely unmade. Then the patient drinks some of the water. [364]

The Panata Water cures, of which there are many variations, work to alleviate the acquired fear. The sypmathetic notions of burning and dissolving are at work here and are connected to the sacredness of bread. Panata Water alleviates, *in addition to the violent or traumatic impressions due to physical causes, the terror deriving from the nocturnal manifestation of immaterial entities (a malevolent spirit, a specter) metamorphosed animal: dog; cat; nocturnal bird, etc.* [365]

Vermi Cure, from Valle Argentina, Liguria
Ingredients: + Pumpkin seeds + Honey + Sugar + Castor oil
Procedure: Crush 60 grams of peeled seeds together with 20 grams of sugar or honey to obtain a paste in a mortar.
Take in a single dose, reduced by half for children. After 5- 6 hours purge yourself with castor oil, checking that the head of the tapeworm has been expelled. If not, the operation is repeated after three or four days. [366]

Vermi Cure, from Valle Argentina, Liguria
Ingredients: + **Bumegu**/Absinthe + Garlic + Olive oil
Procedure: Make a decoction of 15 grams of absinthe plant for about 5 minutes in a liter of water, sweetening with honey.
Procedure: with the juice of the crushed absinthe plant add a little garlic and administer with a teaspoon of oil. [368]

Vermi Cure, from Valle Argentina, Liguria For Babies
Ingredients: + bulb of Garlic
Procedure: a bulb of garlic tied around the neck [367]

For Children
Ingredients: a decoction of Black Mulberry rind
ALSO
Ingredients: +Absinthe + Milk + crushed Garlic
Procedure: chop and boil a little absinthe in the milk with a few cloves of crushed garlic and then spread it on the belly as a paste.
Procedure: + Rue can also be used the same way. [368]

Italian Magic: Secret Lives of Women

photo: Davide Tiso, 2020. Inherited fabrics.

Vermi Cure, from Valle Argentina, Liguria
Ingredients: + contused Onion + Garlic + white Wine
Procedure: make a vermifuge wine by making 4 grams of contused onion, 1 gram
of crushed garlic in 400 grams of white wine, squeeze for eight days. Pour 2 or 3
tablespoons of this preparation into a glass of water, stir and allow the fasting children to
drink. 369

Vermi Cure, from Valle Argentina, Liguria
Ingredients: + Santolina herb + Water
Procedure: an infusion of a few grams in a cup of boiling water, left to rest for about a
quarter of an hour, is powerful
in treating the intestinal parasite. Administer with caution, especially to children. Can
have aphrodisiac properties. 370

LE GUARITRICI + I RITI TERAPEUTICI

Photos Top row l-r: Lettuce, used in flying ointments and for protection invoking an ancient god. Mint, used widely for protection against negative spirits and envy (and to cut the connection to them). Here, gathered from the countryside by author Gianfranco Mele of Sava, Puglia.

Photos Bottom l-r: Helichrysum gathered by the author with Doriana on her mountain at Agricola Castellarone in Liguria. Wild fennel gathered from the countryside by Gianfranco Mele. Fennel is widely used in rural magic to make magic white circle of protection with the invocation of Santa Lucia. It's also used for healing the eyes.

Italian Magic: Secret Lives of Women

Vermi Cure, from Ruscio, Umbria and also Perugia
Ingredients: + bulbs of Garlic
Procedure: Hang a garlic head or a necklace of segments called **coroncina** around the baby's neck. The smell would have forced the worms to leave. The same is used by the farmers of the territory of Perugia. [371]

Vermi Cure, from Roccaporena, Umbria
Ingredients: + **Nepitella/Mentuccia** [Lesser Calamint]
Procedure: Juice of **mentuccia** was given to the child with worms (Polia 2009, II: 670). LDV401

Vermi Cure, from Fonte Vena, Umbria
Ingredients: + Garlic + Bread + Egg + **Nepitella/Mentuccia**
Procedure: In addition to the garlic necklace, cooked bread with garlic was eaten; slices of toasted bread in the crumb of which bits of garlic had been placed; egg omelette flavored with the **mentucci.** [372]

Vermi Cure, from Vocabolo Sant'Angelo, Perugia
Ingredients: + Garlic + Rue
Procedure: a piece garlic was placed on the child's chest. The rue was crushed then the child was given a teaspoon of freshly squeezed juice. Another version was to put garlic under the pillow and rub the hands and feet of the child with the garlic. [373]

Vermi Cure, from Scheggino, Umbria
Ingredients: + Garlic + **Mentastro/mentuccia/nepitella**
Procedure: In addition to hanging the garlic necklace, they pounded garlic and **mentastro** leaves between two stones; the pulp was placed in a cloth bag that the child would wear.

Vermi Cure, from Perugino, Umbria
Ingredients: + Garli + Rue + Rag
Procedure: Crush together rue leaves and 5 garlic cloves and place in fabric rag. The rag containing the pungent smell was placed on the belly of the child. [374]

Vermi Cure, from Umbria
Ingredients: + Breve + Garlic + Protections
Procedure: In the **breve** [little pouch worn against skin] that the children wore [for protection against magic], together with religious images was inserted a clove of garlic. It should be remembered that garlic is effective also against the fascination [**il malocchio**] and ambushes of witches [black magic] as well as against the worms. [375]

LE GUARITRICI + I RITI TERAPEUTICI

Photo: Davide Tiso 2020. Inherited terra cotta bowl from Caserta, Campania

SYMPATHETIC CORD CUTTING CURES

Within the body of the **vermi** cures from Sicily to Sardinia the mainland, there are a wide variety of rituals, all based on idea of severing the parasitical spirit/worm invasion on the spirit/physical body of the victim.

The cures used by the Worm Charmers in Sicily are considered to be, in no uncertain terms, "spells," even ones that use religious words, and the healers refer to them by several names in dialect. Both **cirmata** and **pircantari** are medicinal spells recited to *keep a-way the bad spirits which carry disease.* 376 **Ciarmari i vermi** refers to the magical ritual works used to cure worms comprised of the spell, the words, and the actions. It means literally: charming the worms.

Worms Charmers **Ciarmari i vermi** both diagnose people and cure them, which is something found in **rimedi control il malocchio** (remedies against the evil eye). They are able *to quantify the parasites, localise them and identify their orientation whether curled up or ring- shaped.* 377 Some cures focus on the use of ingested remedies, some on external pressures to expel the worms (garlic, garlic parasites), and the next few presented are from the category of **ciarmari i vermi** using magical practices involving cord cutting and word spells, as they are referred to in Sicily.

Italian Magic: Secret Lives of Women

Ciarmari i vermi use rituals like tracing 3 crosses on the body to mark the illness and to cut the connection with worms and spirits who brought them. In addition to these symbolic sympathetic cuts they make physical cuts of vines and strings ritualistically in conjunction with word spells.

Vermi Cure, from Campania.
Ingredients: + Water + Threads + Scissors + Prayers
Procedure: Make 9 strands of thread of the same length as the circumference of the person's neck, but 1 must be longer. Recite a prayer over each thread, then break the head of the strings with scissors. Cut the tip of the strings, put them in a glass of water, make a cross on it with the finger saying:

"and for every thread, I'll throw you in the fire and you'll burn." [378]

Say this 3 times, while also repeating other secret words.
Then burn the threads in the stove.
This must be done for 3 mornings on a fast and the patient must also drink some of the water from the glass, it does not matter that he drinks it all, just a little. [358]

Photo: Davide Tiso, 2020. Inherited needles set and thimble

LE GUARITRICI + I RITI TERAPEUTICI

Vermi Cure, from Sardinia

Ingredients: + Water + Breath + raw Wool + Virgin operator

Procedure: In the presence of the ill person, the virgin healer must breathe on a plate full of water to add its purity to this very pure element. Immediately afterwards, lay 7 pieces of raw wool on the water and observe the way they float for a while; the threads, filling with water, swelled up and twisted with sinuous movements similar to those made by worms when worms are present. By interpreting these displacements, the healer is able to understand how serious the infestation was how to act accordingly. Then she collects the 7 pieces of wool, divide them again obtaining small fragments which she places back on the plate and the observation resumes.

Repeat.

As the threads finally remained inert, it is interpreted so also the worms that infested the patient would have swollen up to burst and the cure is complete. The water and the pieces of wool were then dispersed by the same healer in distant places. 379

Verbal Spells Cures + Signatures (Segnature)

The **segnature** signatures are type of cure that are also inherited and passed down on a solstice or equinox date. They can be used in-person or at-a-distance. There are different ones for different illnesses, and there are signatures to cure both people and animals.

While they do refer to gestures or marks made by the hands, they are also absolutely dependent upon the secret words...so the gestures and marks are just a small physical symbol of the words, which are the actual signatures.

> *The males and females are dedicated to the treatment of "pains"*
> *through the "signature" of the painful part [...] the operator uses a*
> *ring on the patient's skin - generally the true blessed marriage -or*
> *a string, tracing a cross with it and then tying the part and ensuring*

Italian Magic: Secret Lives of Women

> *it with three knots. In the latter method, the true "signature"* **la segnatura** *precedes the "binding",* **la legatura** *which "symbolizes the magical ligament of malice".* 380

They use words interconnected with specific ritual markings made on the body. The emphasis is on the way the illness is being "marked" or identified for healing. For example, a healer would say "I mark the worms." The body is marked with the healer's fingers tracing specific signs and the words and actions the healer uses thereafter target the marked place.

The recitation of special formulas, transmitted by an operator to an apprentice operator and kept secret, is an inseparable part of the procedure. 381 The signatures cure many ailments: from toothache, **vermi**, warts, eryspelas, and **storture** (muscle twists). They signatures can cure at a distance as well.

> *"...it is a small, very light massage, it does little. They are the words [that cure], but they are not witchcraft, they are real things, it is the Madonna who helps. And then people heal even if I don't touch them: if the person is far away [...] , I boil the water, I say the words and the prayers and that heals the same."* 382

Healing with the hands is another form of healing found in relation to several illnesses. It is used to cure headaches from **il malocchio**, for example. The hands are positioned in a way that their polarity allows the energy to flow through, and it is the secret words that accompany the hand positions which activate the channeled energy that actually enacts the cure.

These are different from word spells called **scongiuri**, even though words are integral. Presented next are **segnare i vermi signatures for worms** cures which mark the worms and also employ cord-cutting.

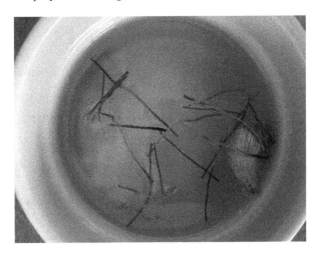

LE GUARITRICI + I RITI TERAPEUTICI

Vermi Cure, spell casting for children with worms from Sicily
Ingredients: + Linen Thread + Garlic + Water + Words
Procedure: The healer chops garlic and puts it in a glass of water. She anoints her hands with oil, marking the sign of the cross on child's belly then diagnosing through circular massage. She recites a verbal spell 3 times such as:

> *"Holy Monday, Holy Tuesday, Holy Wednesday, Maundy Thursday, Good Friday, Holy Saturday, Easter Sunday, the worms fall to earth".*

In Dialect:

Luni santu, marti santu, mercuri santu, jovi santu, venneri santu, sabatu santu, duminica di Pasqua, u vermu n terra casca. 3

Measuring:
Next, she cuts a piece of thread with the left hand, measuring the stretched-out span of the patient's arms and hands at their side and then their overall span. She cuts a second thread to measure the person head to foot. She takes both threads, knots them together and winds them around her index finger and thumb. This represents the entanglement of the worms.

Cutting the connection:
She then removes the from her hand, cuts them up with scissors as if cutting up worms. She places the cut threads with one finger into a glass of water with garlic. She will then observe: if the immersed threads remains straight, there are no more worms. If the threads curl up and intertwist, worms are still present.

Call and response:
If so, the healer must do a call-and-response verbal spell with the child's mother (if the patient is a child). Then, the patient must drink the garlic water (without the threads) for 2-3 consecutive days.

Vermi Cure, from Valle Argentina, region of Liguria
Ingredients: + hand-made marks on body + words
Procedure: A healer named Amalia makes signs of the cross from the lower belly upwards, pronouncing, at each sign, the following words:

> *"Holy Monday, Holy Tuesday, Holy Wednesday, Holy Thursday, Good Friday, Holy Saturday."*

> **"Lunedi Santo, Martedi Santo, Mercoledi Santo, Giovedi Santo, Venerdi Santo, Sabato Santo."**

The final formulation was: "O Lord, free this man from the worms but **leave one that goes to the heart!"** There is another prayer that adds a command to make the worms **descend**. And different healers have other prayers and parts to their rituals. 384

Italian Magic: Secret Lives of Women

Vermi Cure, from Valle Argentina, region of Liguria
Ingredients: + hand-made marks on body + crushed garlic + oil
Procedure: Put crushed or chopped garlic in a saucer with oil, allowing to macerate for two or three hours. With this ointment marks are made under the ears, at the temples and at the wrist of the right hand. 385

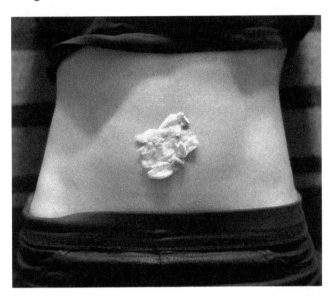

Vermi Cure, from Sicily
Ingredients: + string + spells + fire + scissors + marks on body
Procedure: These words are said in Sicilian dialect while marking 3 cutting crosses on belly and sides of belly:

> *"Blessed Monday, Blessed Tuesday, Blessed Wednesday, Maundy Thursday, Good Friday, Blessed Saturday, Easter Sunday, Easter Monday, falls the worm face down. Cut 1, cut 2, cut the worm which thou has, cut 3, cut 4, cut 5, cut the worm from the belly, cut 6, cut the worm from the bile, cut 7, cut 8, cut 9, cut the worm from the heart, cut 10, cut the worm which has a hold on you."* 386

This or similar spell is recited in Sperlinga, Valaguarnera, Castel di Lucio, Gangi, Ispica, Acicatena, Prizzi, Partinico, San Biagio Platani, Noto, Tortorici, Mistetta, all in Sicily. Several varieties of this exist where, to conclude the cure, the strings are cut and burned in the fire; burned ashes of the string are put into the navel; other spells are recited naming body parts that are being exorcised, and words used to restore the blood. It's been documented by Mariangela Napoli that **vermi** cures are still used in at least 40 cities in Sicily.

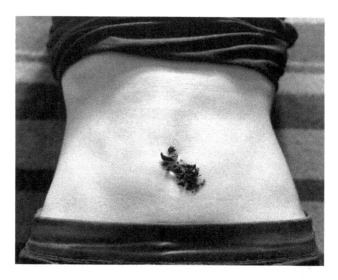

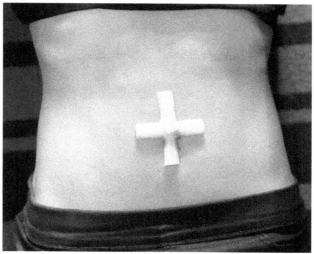

Vermi Cure, from Roccaporena, Umbria
Ingredients: + **mentuccia/nepitella** calamint + hand-made marks **segnature**
Procedure: The healer marked the child with signs of the cross and then passed her hand over the body while saying special prayers. Then, the child was given juice of the calamint plant to drink. 387

Vermi Cure, from Sicily:
Ingredients: + hot wax + hand-made marks + word spell to cut worms
Procedure: As we've also seen in death rituals, where a wax scross seal was placed on the heart to keep the spirit from returning... to cure in Sicily marks are made with a finger dipped in hot wax over the stomach and various body parts to cut the connection to the worms.

Italian Magic: Secret Lives of Women

STRIADURA

Striadura is the disease caused by intense negative magic that results in a variety of illnesses. It's also a condition whose cures look less connected to the physical body and more connected to the magical cause of the illness. The types of illnesses resulting from striadura are:

1) **azzicchidu** *or mild fright;*
2) **spreu** *or* **assustru***, grave fright;*
3) anemia, characterized by pallor;
4) exhaustion, characterized by lack of
muscle tone, listlessness, depression
(typical symptoms also from **il malocchio**
the evil eye or certain **fatture**
invoices);
5) shrinking of the limbs;
6) jaundice;
7) favism.
388

Jaundice and favism, it should be noted, are characterized by haemolytic anemia: a deficiency of iron and red blood cells. Iron depletion is a common characteristic of illnesses caused by negative spirits.

In order to understand the cures for **striadura**, its name and associations must be mentioned. **Striadura**, from the point of view of the healers who cure it, means something similar to "bewitched," but not exactly. The idea of "bewitched", for which there are different terms in Italian, refers to being under the effects of a spell performed by a flesh-and-blood witch. The **stria,** however, is the sorceress who has the power to oppress someone with **striadura** (the illness of the **stria**) from the realm of spirits.

The **stria** is the embodiment of deep, dark negativity whose omen is the "**striga**" or owl (both la **civette**-Athene noctua-a nocturnal bird of prey without ear tufts and **il gufo**-Asio otus-a bird of prey with ear tufts both from Strigidae family). And, it is believed the **stria** shape-shifts into owls who are used for the purpose of imposing their negative magic on others. So rather than through physical acts of magic, **striadura** is transmitted from spirits to spirits. The name **stria** means something even less tangible and more rooted in the world of harmful spirits and energy than the physical world. It's a name that must be sensed and felt to be understood rather than a name that is specifically tied to the images it conjures: due to the antiwitch stories incorporated into nature by the church and coupled with myths of the vampire, owls took on an ill-omen affect, but it is not believed the owl itself causes **striadura**. The **stria** is her own being, not entirely physical, but rather like a spirit attachment who is a source of negativity, in contemporary terms.

In the Italian way of not naming things other than by describing what they are, this name is held in the realm of imaginary concepts created around the witch who does black magic coupled with very real physical symptoms of suffering such as jaundice and loss of self, and even death. And, its symptoms bear tell-tale signs of interference by negative spirits.

PREVENTION

There are preventative actions taken against **striadura**. Preventative cures are used after "reading the signs", which is done for example after experiencing an owl fly directly over one's head and receiving a premonition about incoming negativity directly after. The cures intervene after the illness has taken shape within the body, which include exorcism.

Striadura Preventions are similar to preventions used against **il malocchio**, and basically serve to prevent the **striadura** from attaching; to confuse the stria while a person is sleeping, to wear something charged with energy against it:

1. Boundary prevention:
+ *keep your legs or arms crossed in sleep.* 389
This is another form of "breaking the circuit" like the **mano figa** hand sign that psychically cuts the connection between a person and a negative energy vampire. This is a technique also taught in many contemporary psychic workshops to help empaths protect themselves.
+ wearing amulets with specific writings
+ wearing a pouch with protective items
+ keep a sickle point towards the door.

2. Reversal:
This is another form of "shape-shifting one's energy"... not the act of shape-shifting, but of changing one's energetic location, to confuse the negative spirits and is a common

Italian Magic: Secret Lives of Women

apotropaic technique used for protection in rural Italy.

+   sleeping head-to-toe across short side of the bed rather than the usual position
+   hold the trestle of the chimney upside down with the feet up

3. Spellwork.

photo: Davide Tiso 2020, **Coppi** Italian terra cotta roof tile, Striadura cure ingredients

DIAGNOSIS

If outer symptoms, such as yellow skin and yellowed eyes are not apparent, then there are specific ways of measuring if a patient has **striadura.**

Striadura Diagnosis: Nuoro, Sardinia

+   With a thread of wool, the healer measures the patient. The patient must stand with arms opened as much as possible.
+   *First from the top of the head to the tip of the feet,*
+   *then from the end of the middle finger of the left hand up to that of the right hand.*

If the two distances are equal it is not the disease of the **striga** *"sa maladia 'e s'istria". If the height of the sick person is less than its width, the evil is present.* 390 The more disparity in measurements, the more advanced the disease.

LE GUARITRICI + I RITI TERAPEUTICI

STRIADURA   CURES

Striadura Cure: from Nuoro, Sardinia
Ingredients: + Linen Thread + Owl Feathers or White Hen Feathers as substitute only in extreme emergency + Rosemary + blessed Wax + blessed Palm + **Timanza** (incense grains) + **Coppi** terra cotta roof tile + Hands + Secret Words

Procedure: The healer takes half of the thread with which she has measured the patient and cuts it into tiny pieces. Then she adds some rosemary, a piece of blessed wax, 2 or 3 pieces of pure blessed palm and a few grains of incense and a pinch of white Strix feather.

All of this is set on fire, in a tile that is especially kept for this use only.
While the strange specimens burn and create a smoke, the healer, full of faith and concentrated in her work,
+   takes in hand the tile and make a cross sign with it above the patient's head.
+   then she moves it 3 times around the patient's neck
+   then she performs 8 other cross marks:
    -on the humerus -on the elbow -on the wrist -on the hand -on the side -on the knee -on the instep -on the foot.

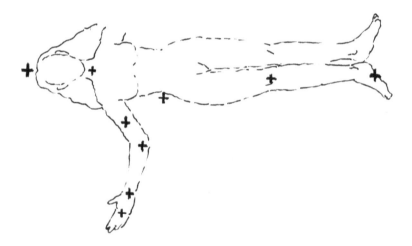

Then she lays the tile on the ground and recites 3 Ave Marias to Our Lady of the Remedy for the cure to be valid. While the healer is praying, the patient jumps barefoot or in stockings 3 times, through the smoking tile, and finally she warms her feet to the sacred fire and rubs her hands in the smoke that comes from it.

In contemporary modalities, something similar can be seen in the method of EFT Tapping (Emotional Freedom Technique) where specific phrases are said while tapping a specific series of points on one's own body. The purpose of the phrases said in conjunction with touching points on the body is to release the trauma held there energetically.

Italian Magic: Secret Lives of Women

Striadura Cure: from Campidano di Oristano, in Marrubiu in Sardinia
Ingredients: spells focused on exorcism
Procedure: The healer, practiced in the art of these spells, speaks the words aloud over someone who just experienced the **striga** fly over their head:

> *"Istria istria / chi passas sa bia / chi passas su mari / aundi est binu / aundi est cabi / e ddus ous tundus / chi hant fattu is puddus ... "* 391

Striadura Cure: from Campidano di Oristano, in Marrubiu in Sardinia
Ingredients: spells focused on exorcism
Procedure: The healer, practiced in the art of these spells, speaks the words aloud over someone who just experienced the **striga** fly over their head:

> *"Istria istria / malaitta sias / malaitta de Deus / no tocchis sanguni allenu / finzas a contai / arena de tres maris / and perdas de tres montis ... "*

> *"Strige strige / you are cursed / cursed by God / do not touch other people's blood / before having counted / sand of three seas / and stones of three mountains ... "* 392

Striadura Cure: one of many **Is mexinas de sa stria** (medicine of the stria) of Sardinia
Ingredients: + Owl Feather + Coffee + String + Secret Words +Lunar Cycle
Procedure: The healers, who use many variants of this serious medicine, generally:

- Burn feathers of a nocturnal bird of prey (owl) reducing them to ash
- Pour into the coffee that will be given to the patient while the healer uses charged words over them
- often performed during the last phase of the lunar cycle

Variations:
+ sometimes also burning the thread used for diagnosis and adding to the coffee with their ash +marking crosses above the patient while saying magic formulas + adding particles of blessed wax in the church and nails and hair of the same patient to the coffee + the special coffee that the patient will have to drink (made of ash, etc) will be taken on an empty stomach the following morning. 393

Striadura Cure: s'affumentu de sa stria: the fumigation of the **striga**
Ingredients: + Roof Tile that owl flew over + blessed Wax + Rosemary + Embers from fire + Owl Feather + Magic Words + Shirt boiled in lye + Rumex Patientia herb
Procedure: The healer prepares the curative fumigation by placing embers from the fire in the concave terra cotta roof tile along with the owl feather and other ingredients. The patient must suck up the smoke while the healer recites the spell. Then the patient must jump 3 times over the smoking tile wearing a shirt soaked in lye. The patient must then get in bed, covered abundantly so that she sweats. The shirt is soaked in a yellow liquid (the substance of the **striadura**, created homeopathically here by rumex patientia, commonly called patience herb which is a deep yellow color very similar to the yellow of the jaundice. Then the healer makes the sauna, with the vapors of a basin of boiling water, in which medicinal herbs have been immersed; the root of **lampazzu** (romice), taken both in decoction, and cut into floppy disks and applied to the skin. 394

It's worth noting here that for healers who perform variations of **Is mexinas de sa stria**, their medicines are deeply respected and all preparations are t*aken with extreme caution and attention, and as with certain modern chemotherapy products "under the direct control of the healer"*. 395 The symptoms of **striadura** are also considered extremely grave, cause by evil and affecting the body with *pallor and exhaustion - considered serious, as "typical" of death.* 396 Whether or not this makes sense to our contemporary minds, these illnesses exist, and the belief in their causation being connected to spirits and physical conditions are prevalent enough to need cures, and for those cures to not only exist but also be relied upon.

Perhaps a note that might make things clearer is that a **fattura** is also a black magic spell that can be deadly for a victim, but, the possibility of finding the **fattura** before it "takes its due"means that the **fattura** can be undone by someone who knows how. This requires the "interruptor" to know who sent it, or to at least see how the **fattura** was composed. While spirit attachments are part of **fattura**, Stiradura, in contrast, is executed solely by a negative spirit, which can make the "undoing" considerably more difficult. The fact that the negative spirit, without a human channel, can inflict damage on a physical body is also revealing about the power these spirits have to reach into the physical world.

Italian Magic: Secret Lives of Women

Photos: Above left: by Fabio Toti, 2018. Mandringa stone in Volterra, Italy. Above right: Back of stone which seems to have the face of an old woman. This stone has a river flowing under it, and women used to gather here to wash clothes and share knowledge. It's also one of the locations where women were visited by **La Signora del Gioco**, in the form of Aradia, Abundance Goddesses who reconnected women with magic.

SUGATURA

Sugatura translates to "decayed" or "exhausted" and refers to a type of anemia that affects small children. The physical marks of **sugatura** appear as a bruise called a "blackberry"most often appearing behind the ears of the "dead" child. And the symptoms are: *a pale color; weight loss; an extreme weakness that manifested itself in too prolonged and almost lethargic sleeps alternated with states of extreme restlessness; loss of appetite; slow and listless movements; faint wags.* 397

The healers of this traditional medicine believe anemia happens as a result of blood drawn by the witches at night who sneak into houses through keyholes at night and use their lips as a suction cup, removing blood fluid from the baby. It is believed that this feared vampiric activity is done by shape-shifting witches of the common stories found around Italy (such as the Janare) wherein the witches fly into homes at night through key holes and chimneys, often in the forms of animals like cats or insects, *projecting their double soul without assuming a specific form and therefore remaining invisible.* 398

Just as common as the stories of night time vampyric witches are stories of preventative protections against them that are widely used throughout rural Italy such as **saggina** brooms at the front doors with many tiny fibers, bowls of salt by windows, and other protective objects that would cause the shape shifters to be caught up in counting the endless grains (because they can't count..and therefore the sun would rise before the count ended, thus causing the vampyric witch to flee) or to filter their negativity out, preventing them from coming into the home, or using iron to fortify the home's entryway to prevent vampires from entering.

And yet, we find the real existence of the illnesses that are part of these folk tales in rural Italy. Perhaps most interesting is the fact that these illnesses are types of anemia, wherein the blood is damaged and lacking in iron.

CURE AND METHOD TO REVEAL THE WITCH

Illustrated in the **sugatura** cure below is a type of method that was used to help babies with **sugatura**, but it was also a type of method used to reveal the sorceress. There are many versions of this method, which is always interactive in 2 parts: the victim makes a ritualistic action and the sorceress responds. It's similar to the 2 part call-and-response method for dealing with night time succubi. An action will be taken by the victim or intended victim, and the sorceress will unwittingly respond: perhaps she will knock on the door first thing in the morning asking to borrow flour, or if a ritualistic injury spell was performed, the next day a woman in the village may have a wound in the corresponding spot.

Sugatura Cure: from Umbria: Valnerina: in Casciano; in the Monteleone di Spoleto territory; in the Nursino, Perugia, Torre di Cammoro, Sciedi, Fogliano
Ingredients: + Laundry Cauldron + Fire in the hearth + baby's Clothes
Procedure 1: The baby's clothes, including swaddling, are removed and placed in the water in the cauldron used for laundry and boiled for a long time in the flame of the domestic hearth. 399

> *During the boiling, the witch was forced to show herself knocking at the door of the house. The rite of boiling clothes has been documented in various places in Valnerina, Casciano, the Monteleone di Spoleto territory, in the Nursino. Everywhere has documented the conviction that the ritual forced the witch to reveal itself knocking at the door, perhaps to borrow, something: in the latter case alms (a piece of bread, or lard, or cheese, salt).* 400

> *The heat of the fire is transmitted to the witch; this, in order to stop the torment, is forced to reveal its identity. The vehicle of transmission is the garment used which is magically linked to the owner as impregnated with its fluids. At the same time, the same garment binds the witch because her saliva (or breath) at the time of sucking, is mixed with the victim's blood.* 401

Revealing the black magic witch is a common procedure found throughout rural Italy in similar ways. For example, in the region of Campania Janara witches are alleged to be shape-shifters who creep into unprotected homes at night in the form of black shadowy eel shapes who can pass through keyholes and cracks in doorways. These shadowy eels act as succubi on sleeping people, but the people know to grab the hair of the shadowy eel and recite little phrases about iron in a call-and-response that the witch must participate in. This call-and-response also causes her to reveal her identity the next morning by knocking on the door and asking for sugar, or similar things of this nature.

Italian Magic: Secret Lives of Women

Grabbing the tail of a shadowy black cat running by is also an action taken. The shadow cat is believed to be the shape-shifted form of a sorceress with negative intentions who is psychically spying in that moment. The act of grabbing or trying to grab the tail of the shadow cat will also reveal the identity of the person behind the shadow: either in a psychic intuition in that moment, or as a neighbor approaching asking to borrow something. This is an older form of a contemporary practice of looking into "shadow figures" to see beyond the shadow and discover who is psychically trying to affect another person. The simple acknowledgment and observation begins to reveal the true identity behind the shadow.

There are also numerous stories by locals in rural areas that take place during strange atmospheric phenomena, such as when a lone person is out walking in a field or other natural place and a sudden dark fog cloud approaches along with the arrival of serpents or frogs. In these strange moments, often the lone person will throw a knife into the fog or stomp on a snake only to find both the fog and animals suddenly disappear. Always, within the next week and often within a day or 2 the lone person will find themselves in the village somewhere, buying a meal or drink or in some way connected to another person who reveals a wound from a knife, from a boot stomp, or in some way correlating to their supernatural experience in the atmospheric phenomenon, thus revealing the person behind the shape-shifted form.

This is simply an experience of a person using a "double" to move about in a hidden way, traveling not in the astral realm but in the physical one.

The relationship with nature in rural Italy is a deep one. In Sicily, for example, there are healers who pray directly to Rosemary the herb, invoking its healing power and protection, and there are others who pray to the rainbow. Others also pray to the water itself and others to white light. The world is alive for them, messengers and helpers are everywhere according to a universal code. Further, the "folk" or village tales that speak of spirits and strange happenings are all consistent stories about these universal codes, so that humans and spirits all obey the codes, which is what the Natural Laws of the Universe, as they are called in more contemporary times, speak about as well: that the laws are always operating. There is no escaping the laws, there are only passive actions or co-creative actions. All of the spiritual teachings that can be found on contemporary times, which of course are expressed in more contemporary language, can be found in rural Italian traditions, because rural Italian traditions were not created by people but by the spirit world, and so the fit together as a holistic system that makes sense and is constant and nothing is out of place.

FUOCO DI SANT'ANTONIO

Herpes Zoster is called The Fire of Saint Anthony **Fuoco di sant'Antonio** in Italy which references the burning pain the condition can cause the skin. The cures use a sympathetic connection to fire, often using the idea of "fire fighting fire" or "water putting out the fire".

Fuoco di sant'Antonio Cure, from male healer near San Giovanni Valdarno, Tuscany. His mother passed it to him just before her death.

Ingredients: + Water + Hand Horns gesture **mano cornuto** + Prayers + Cup

Procedure: Healer makes the sign of the horns with his left hand. He dips the 2 extended fingers into the cup of water and flings the water in a cross pattern over the patient's left eye and face area. He makes the corss horizontally then vertically and repeats 9 times while whispering his secret prayer.

Fuoco di sant'Antonio Cure, from Ottorino, near San Giovanni Valdarno, Tuscany

Ingredients: + Wasp Nest with larvae + Olive Oil + other Plants such as **Timo Serpillo** (serpent thyme).

Procedure: He collects a common wasp nest with tiny the larva in it from the countryside and makes an infusion by boiling with other plants in olive oil, then let it rest for 6 or 7 months. He then applies it when needed, marking a sign on the patient with his silver medal (with a Madonna on it). *"If you don't sign it with the medal the process of healing cannot reach its total power, but just the half of it."* *author interview 2019*

Fuoco di sant'Antonio Cure *dugi di San Antoni,* from Sicily.

Ingredients: + Spit + verbal Spells

Procedure: The healer casts out the herpes by saying the secret prayer and spitting on the infected area. Here, and many other rural places in Italy, the saliva is believed to have healing properties. 402

Fuoco di sant'Antonio Cure, from Valle Argentina, Liguria

Ingredients: + Gold object + hand made Marks of Crosses

Procedure: The healer makes a circle around the swelling with a gold object or with crosses from top to bottom, so as to let the evil vent; otherwise if the circle was closed the face [where the skin condition is present] would burst. The healer Amalia repeats a particular prayer 9 times in (known as precedents of Saint Brigid and Saint Apollonia). The healer specifies that, after marking herpes, it is necessary to refresh and disinfect with a decoction of **parietaria** herb. 403

Fuoco di sant'Antonio Cure, from Campumavue, Liguria

Ingredients: + Oak tree Branch + Fire + Water

Procedure: A large branch of this plant was placed on the fire. When the affected extremity becomes fiery in a sympathetic way, the person submerges themselves in a bucket of water as a healthy bath against herpes. A common cure used by men in this area. 404

Italian Magic: Secret Lives of Women

Orzaiolo refers to an eye stye, which takes the shape of a piece of barley, or **orzo,** a short grain pasta shaped like a piece of rice that's wider in its center. Most of the cures for orzaiolo involve a sympathetic sewing ritual over the eye where the stye is. The sewing motions are made while the healer recites inherited secret prayers.

Orzaiolo Cure, from Ottorino, a healer near San Giovanni Valdarno, Tuscany.
Ingredients: + Silver Medal with Madonna on it + Secret Prayers + Marks **Segnature**
Procedure: + Ottorino moves the medallion over the stye, saying the specific prayer for stye. "For every sickness there is a specific prayer," he says. *author interview 2019

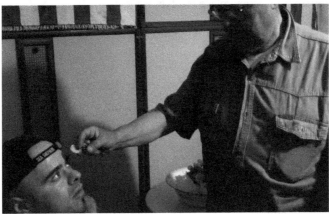

Ottorino demonstrating the movements he makes on a patient to cure **orzaiolo**.
He is demonstrating on Fabio Toti, who lives in San Giovanni Valdarno.

LE GUARITRICI + I RITI TERAPEUTICI

Orzaiolo Cure, Emilia-Romagna
Ingredients: + Needle + Black Thread without a knot + charged Words
Procedure: The healer passes this thread over the eyelid and the stye 3 times, always moving outwards so as not to transmit the evil to the other eye. The eye must be kept closed and the thread must run well on the eyelid, all the way down, holding it tight with the other hand because it flows better, as the healer says in an intense tone *"run away, stye, I sew you!"* [405]

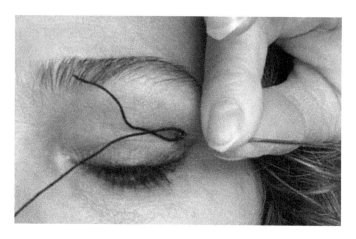

Orzaiolo Cure, various locations in Perugia, Umbria
Ingredients: + Wheat grains or + Barley grains (9 of them)
Procedure: Shift the evil onto some grains of wheat with which the operator touches the patient's eyelids. [406] The wheat or barley absorbs the evil from the eyelids. Repeat 9 times.

Orzaiolo Cure, from Valle Argentina, Liguria
Ingredients: + false Rue seeds (common scrofula)
Procedure: Prepare a decoction, place on stye [407]

Orzaiolo Cure, from Preci , Umbria
Ingredients: + Needle + Thread +charged Words
Procedure: Use needle and thread pretending to sew the eyelids. While "sewing the stye", it was said: *"Comma', che fa'? Cucio l'orzolo"* [408]

COLDS, BRONCHITIS, SORE THROAT

Cold Cure, from Perugia, Umbria
Ingredients: + Mallow leaves + Water
Procedure: Make an infusion of mallow leaves, bring to boil, breathe the steam. [409]

Italian Magic: Secret Lives of Women

Cold Cure, from Preci, Umbria.
Ingredients: + Brick + Fire + Juniper berries + Honey
Procedure: Heat a brick in the fire, place under the feet of patient. Make an infusion with juniper berries, sweetened with honey, and leave it on the patient's chest for a long time. [410]

Bronchitis Cure, from Scheggino, Umbria
Ingredients: + Pig's Bone Marrow
Procedure: Rub the chest with the marrow contained in the bone of the ham. [411]

Photo above: Davide Tiso 2020. Mallow and juniper berries.
Photo below: the countryside of Campania

LE GUARITRICI + I RITI TERAPEUTICI

Photos: Pitigliano, Tuscany

Italian Magic: Secret Lives of Women

Olio ferrato, which translates to iron-infused olive oil, is a special type of oil made by immersing 3 different spiked irons (such as ones used in the heart and ones used to shoe animals), sometimes in the quantity of 3, sometimes 7, into the oil until the oil comes to a boil. The irons are previously heated to incandescence (glowing red) before they are immersed in the oil. From here, the oil is like a "mother" batch, from which remedies can be made. It is use for sore throat cures. Considering the connection iron has to negative spirits, and that sore throats take place in the throat area whose energetic chakra counterpart is the "place of speaking one's truth," and the fact that this energy center is plugged into by spirit attachments, it's no surprise that we find an iron-infused remedy for a sore throat here. Incidentally, there is a type of aloe, aloe ferox, used in Amaro, created in a similar way with the infusion of an iron instrument.

Sore Throat Cure, "olio ferrato"
Ingredients: + Iron-infused Oil + Handkerchief
Procedure: For treatment of sore throat, grease throat area with **olio ferrato**. [412]

For **colds, bronchitis and pneumonia**. In Preci and Ancarano [Umbria], the neck and chest are greased with "iron oil"; then a handkerchief containing hot ash wrapped around the neck. [413]

HEADACHES

Cure for Headache, Migraine, Neuralgia cure, evil caused by trauma from Monte-Littu, Sardinia
Ingredients: + Magic Circle + 2 Healers + Words Spell call-and-response
Procedure: 2 healers, **"cummari di foccu"** had to work simultaneously. They were positioned one in front of the other with the arms extended and, holding hands, formed a magic circle in which to enclose the sufferer. Then began the operation which was a [call-and-response] performance alternately said by the two in an almost narrative tone of voice. The first one began, the one in front of the aching person, reciting a symbolic poem about a little goat who came from the sea, dragging her head in pain, including the numbers of days the pain has lasted. One person recited the story, the other spoke as the goat. After the spoken formula was complete, the ritual resumed: both women bathed their right hand with blessed water and placed it on the head of the sufferer. They recited, this time in a low voice, the prayers necessary to obtain a definitive disappearance of the pain:

Una capruledda da mare venisi/ cu lu capu in tarra traendi/ cu' la linga muggendi/cosa e' lu chi hai?

A goat came from the sea, dragging her head on the ground and complaining. "What do you have?"

Capruledda mea/ chi sei cu' lu capu/ tarra traendi/ e cu' la linga muggendi?

225

LE GUARITRICI + I RITI TERAPEUTICI

My little goat, who drags his head on the ground and bellows?

Cosa dia hae'?/ Soccu caranta notti/ e caranta di/ chi no' drommu pa lu dolori/ di lu capu folti. "What do I have to have? It is forty nights, and forty days that I do not sleep with severe head pain."

"Anda a gjesgia manna/ e pidda un pocu/ d'ea beneditta/ ponitilla in capu cu la manu/e lu dulori di capu/ ti sara' paltutu." "Go to the main church, and take a little blessed water, place it on your head with your hands and the pain in your head will disappear." [414]

Photo, Davide Tiso 2020. The author's inherited gold wedding ring used for healing.

Headache Cure, from Badesi, Sardinia
Ingredients: + Gold Wedding Ring + white String
Procedure: A gold wedding ring is borrowed because it has been repeatedly blessed. Poor people couldn't afford one often, so people would lend theirs out for healing. Then the healer ties it with a white cord, swings it slowly in front of the face of the person in pain, saying prayers. The sacredness of the **medicinosu** jewel, the faith in the strength of the prayers seem to have the power to chase away the malaise immediately. The slow

swaying ring and the sense of tranquility infused by the whispered voice almost ended up hypnotizing the patient who fell into a good, restful sleep to wake up healed.

Headache Cure "mal di testa" from Valle Argentina, Liguria
Ingredients: + **Vitalba Leaves** (clematis vitalba)
Procedure: chop up **vitalba** leaves, put in the nose for the most stubborn headaches 415

Headache Cure " mal di testa" from Valle Argentina, Liguria
Ingredients: + Rosemary + **Vedovella** (wild widow) + **assenzio** (absinthe).
Procedure: make a decoction, use as footbath 416

Headache Cure "mal di testa" from Valle Argentina, Liguria
Ingredients: + Vinegar + Lemon juice + Arnica + Lavender
Procedure: make distillate from arnica or lavender, add lemon juice or vinegar and bathe the forehead. 417

Headache Cure "mal di testa" from Valle Argentina, Liguria
Ingredients: + Potato + Lemon + Handkerchief
Procedure: Apply sliced potato or sliced lemon around head, holding tightly in place with a handkerchief. 418

Headaches of a nervous origin Cure: from Valle Argentina, Liguria
Ingredients: + **Erba Mela** (agrimony)
Procedure: Make a decoction herbal tea of **erba mela** by placing 1/2 oz herbs in liter of water, boiling for a few minutes. 419

Headaches of a nervous origin Cure: from Valle Argentina, Liguria
Ingredients: + Chamomile or + Linden or + Betonica or + Primrose roots, flowers
Procedure: Make teas made from fresh decoctions of chamomile, linden betonica. Primrose flowers are a flower sacred to the moon 420

Photo: Davide Tiso, 2020.
Inherited hand-made olive spoon from Campania.made olive spoon from Campania.

Migraine Cure, Ruscio, Umbria 422
Ingredients: + shed skin of a viper
Procedure: Tie the viper skin (shed in the springtime) to the forehead to relieve the pain.

Conjunctivitis Cure, Valle Argentina, Liguria
Ingredients: + Rue + piece of natural Straw
Procedure: Chew a little bit of rue, then blow with a straw on the affected parts to relieve redness of the eyes. 423

Conjunctivitis Cure, Valle Argentina, Liguria
Ingredients: + Wild Fennel seeds + Water
Procedure: Take no more than 10 wild fennel seeds, put into a liter of water and boil them for a quarter of an hour. When the water has cooled, make compresses. 424

Conjunctivitis Cure, Valle Argentina, Liguria
Ingredients: + Elder flowers + Plantain leaves + Nervus grass (27 leaves)

\+ Mallow + Chamomile.
Procedure: after a short boiling, the preparation must be allowed to cool before applying it to the eyes yellow [425]

Conjunctivitis Cure, Valle Argentina, Liguria
Ingredients: + Cornflower flowers + **Rosolaccio** (red poppy) flowers
Procedure: make a decoction, use as compress on eyes. [426]

Conjunctivitis Cure, Realdo, Liguria
Ingredients: + Rose petals
Procedure: Boil rose petals for about five minutes, then use the water to wash the eyes. [427]

Cupping Cure, "suzione e ventosa" from Emilia Romagna
Ingredients: + Cup/Glass + full Moon + Coin + strip of Gauze
Procedure: For muscle tear or inflammation, stagnant blood: light the gauze on fire inside the glass. Then slide the coin under glass, flipping it onto the area of pain, knocking out the fire. The smoke takes the oxygen and fills the glass with the skin, pulling out the toxins.[428]

L'OS DEL COR /Sternum/ Breastbone

To "do the heart or breastbone" called **l'os del cor** in Sardinia, is a ritual that releases anxiety and chest pains. Some methods focus on using a handkerchief to measure and to dissolve the anxiety represented by knots. Other methods use a form of "cupping". Formulas and prayers are part of all rituals.

L'os del cor Handkerchief Cure, Sardinia
Procedure: The handkerchief was folded several times measuring from the wrist to the elbow by the healer, as she was facing the patient. Finally the two people were in contact [as the measurements became smaller and smaller and hugged each other. This cures shortness of breath due to anxiety.

L'os del cor Handkerchief Cure, Sardinia
Procedure: Ritual payment. The healer removes the handkerchief from her head and gives one of the tips to the patient who them must touch it to the pit of the their stomach. Then the healer takes the other kerchief tip in her left hand. Then she stretches the kerchoief and measures it from the elbow to the wrist, reciting prayers and making the cross for every measure. The operation is repeated 3 times repeating the prayers in Latin, Sardinian, Algherese, and using incomprehensible words. Finally the healer throws the kerchief on the ground and the patient says: *"Deu ta'l paghi!"* [429]

L'os del cor Handkerchief Cure, Sardinia
Procedure: The handkerchief to make l'os del cor was knotted and the medicine was successful when the knot "melted" and the anxiety released.

L'os del cor Cupping Cure, Sardinia
Procedure: A crust of bread was taken where a hole was made. Some fringes were pulled from a towel in the hole. *"The towels that our grandmothers made were very long fringes."* The bread with the fringes rested on the bare belly, at the level of the stomach and the fringes were lit with a match. Then the flame was covered with a glass. At this point if the skin was sucked out of the glass then the evil was defeated. If the flame instead went out, the procedure had to be redone. [430]

Photo: Davide Tiso, 2020, inherited fabrics from Caserta, Campania.

L'os del cor Cupping Cure, Sardinia
Procedure: For chest pains. The healer used an empty glass that fitted over a small light placed on the patient's chest. The air contained inside the glass burned and the muscles of the chest were pushed into the glass by the pressure of the outside air. [431]

Italian Magic: Secret Lives of Women

L'os del cor Handkerchief Cure, Sardinia
Procedure: The healer puts a handkerchief on the patient's shoulders and pulled the nocks with particular movements while reciting some formulas or prayers.

To calm the nerve centers, Triora, Liguria
Ingredients: Mugwort
Procedure: A powder, obtained by stepping on the dried plant and taken in very small doses during the day, calms the nerve centers due to its ancient sedative properties. [442]

To calm palpitations and anguish, Triora, Liguria
Ingredients: + Thyme + Sage + Valerian
Procedure: 1 tablespoon per plant infused for a few minutes in a quarter of a liter of water. Take 1 cup early in the morning and another one in the evening before bedtime. [443]

To calm sleep populated by nightmares, Triora, Liguria
Ingredients: + Hawthorn + Valerian + Passionflower
Procedure: 1tablespoon per plant infused for a few minutes in a quarter of a liter of water. Take 1 cup early in the morning and another one in the evening before bedtime. [434]

Toothache Cure, Poggio di Croce, Umbria
Ingredients: + gold wedding Ring + words Formula
Procedure: Mark crosses on the cheek with the gold wedding ring by reciting this formula:

"S'e dolore te sse passa, s'e tingola te sse casca" [435]

Tignola Cavities **Cure,** Leonessano, Umbria
Ingredients: + gold wedding Ring + words formula
Procedure: A series of cross marks are used on the patient's cheek using the wedding ring. If the tooth is sick, the real **sattaca**, does not flow. In this the operator repeats the signs of the cross until the true flows freely. Throughout the operation, the same formula us-ed to ward off the evil eye murmurs in an imperceptible way. [436]

BETWEEN MAGIC + MEDICINE

Shamanism approaches life and illness with an acknowledgment that physical matter and energy are inseparable. Spirits who live in bodies on the planet are just as present as inhabitants of the universe as are spirits who exist outside of bodies (the dead). In order to maintain health and balance of a physical body, it's the spirit who must be healed. For those who can't soothe their own spirits through self-responsible action, a shaman and the shaman's spirit helpers can be called upon to do this work for them. This is the service Lineage healers of rural Italy offer.

Masculinized medicine moved away from this belief of interconnectedness and catapulted the male doctor as the one with power to use instruments and or drugs that treat symptoms only. Masculine religion is a parallel of this as well, especially in Christianity where a male priest or preacher is the one with salvation power. Both male doctors and male religious leaders (who don't have all the answers and certainly can't relate to a female or non binary gendered body as doctors and can't relate to spirit experiences outside the social control of their organized religious system) nevertheless require a devoted adherence, disempowering the ones they are mean to help. Both the masculine medical establishment and the masculinized dominance of spiritualist and religions caused a great historical disruption in our relationship to the natural world and the spirit world.

Shamanism as Lineage cures of rural Italy is a way of life based on the inseparableness of our life on earth from that of the spirit world and its laws of energy. No Lineage healer will take the credit for themselves, honoring instead the power that cures through them. Magic, especially middle period magic (medieval) revolves around "Do-It-Yourself" methods of gathering information from available sources, re-creating and re-conceptualizing spells made by other people, reworking previously documented ideas or teachings of others, often with revolving door or spirit experimentation, meaning that practitioners will say an invocation to various gods, goddesses and beings but not necessarily the same ones each time and often using whatever spirits are available including negative ones who bring harm invoked by people who don't have a grasp of the workings of the spirit world at all. In fact, many forms of paganisms (and there are many, and they shouldn't be categorized under one "lump" name when they have different foundational systems) are based on an entirely independent way of functioning within magical realms.

In contrast within both shamanism and Lineage cures there exists and essential "spirit marriage" required between healer and the channeled spirits who enact the cures, and this marriage is instigated by the spirits and not the humans. This applies to all rituals, whether physically enacted cures or ones that middle-period magic based its ideas upon and which look more magically crafted than curative. Often called "medico-magical" by

Italian Magic: Secret Lives of Women

anthropologists, or simply "spells" by healers in Sicily, the power to enact change comes from the inherited spirit world partnership always, no matter what the actions.

This brings us to the practice of using "doubles", in later periods called "simulacrum".

DOUBLES

BETWEEN MAGIC + MEDICINE

MAGICAL CURES USING DOUBLES

Cures specialized in healing specific ailments using doubles are found throughout rural Italy. They are part of the Lineage curing traditions. These cures employ a double into which negativity that has caused illness is transferred or alternatively, whose energy is absorbed into the body through ritual to replace the illness. A double is simply a substitute, a representation of something enacted upon to bring about a curative change.

The idea of the cure is that the double absorbs the illness and then its destruction coincides with the release of illness from a person's body. The natural motion (decay, decimation, rotting, death) is bound to the double through magical absorption or transfer and used as a catalyst for removing the cause of illness. When an animal or insect is used, the masculine one is used whenever possible. Many of these cures are also carried out only under specific moon phases. Similar actions are used for the transfer of helpful energies into the body such as from curative flowers. Reading through the following examples makes shows the foundation inspiring medieval magic's spells and curses or other non-healing acts of conceptual magic.

TO TRANSFER THE ILLNESS

Warts Cure, from Leonese territory, between Valnerina and Lazio
Ingredients: + Snail +Long thorns
Procedure: Rubbing any one of the 3 ingredients listed along with a magical ritual: the method consists of rubbing a snail on warts and then piercing it with long thorns leaving it stuck to a tree, or to a pole, until it is completely dry. Once dried, the warts (which in the meantime have reduced in their size) disappear completely.

Warts and allergy rash Cure, from Campania near Caserta
Ingredients: + fresh Meat
Procedure: Bury the meat while saying a few special words indicating that as the meat rots, the rash is released or the warts fall away and are healed.

Warts Cure, Sant'Antonio di Gallura, Sardinia [437]
Ingredients: + coarse Salt
Procedure: The healer chooses a grain for each wart to be removed, then kisses them. One salt grain is rubbed on each infected area with movements that formed small crosses. Once this operation was completed, the grains were wrapped well in a cloth and then left in a difficult place to access [so that no one else would acquire the illness]. At the end of this practice the ugly excrements that had afflicted the patient had disappeared almost immediately and had no longer occurred.

Warts Cure, Sardinia
Ingredients: + Sheep's fat + Magic Formula (words)

234

Italian Magic: Secret Lives of Women

Procedure: The healer anoints the warts with sheep's fat while saying magic formulas, then throws the fat into a ditch (which absorbed the evil that caused the warts). As long as it takes the fat to melt into the earth is how long it takes the warts to heal. [438]

A NOTE ABOUT WARTS

The belief behind the psychic causation of warts is that they are an expression of negative energy that has seeped into the mind of the affected person from a source of evil. This negative energy convinces the affected person that they are ugly just like the negative energy, and a match in energy is achieved. So, warts are an expression of this negativity and ugliness, or an agreement with it. Interestingly, in our contemporary usage of affirmations (positive words to change the negative thinking of the mind), warts are "Little expressions of hate; a belief in ugliness," [439] in the words of Louise Hay, author of "You Can Heal Your Life", a book about discovering the underlying thoughts behind illness.

Fever Cure, from Preci, Umbria
Ingredients: + Walnut or Hazelnut shell, deprived of its contents + a live Spider
Procedure: Place live spider in nut shell. Close the spider in the nut shell. Tie it to the neck of the feverish patient, and expect the spider to die. [440] The spider absorbs the fever.

Spleen Cure, Naples
Ingredients: + Tree Bark
Procedure: The healer cuts a shape as big as a foot out of tree bark. The bark absorbs the evil that caused illness during the magic formula. The bark is destroyed by fire. This is repeated 3 times. [441]

Warts Cure, Liguria
Ingredients: + Apple + Beans + Willow leaves +Linden leaves + small stones + water
Procedure: Section an apple (Malus domestica L.) into 4 sections, then bury it away from home with beans (Phaseolus vulgaris L.) and willow leaves (Salix viminalis L.), which are then made to rot in a pool of stagnant water [442] with leaves of linden (Tiglio) which, then put in a bag with small stones, are rubbed on the affected part by reciting a prayer [443] In any case, to get a positive result, the healer must take care to throw the plant used far from the home of the person marked. [444]

Pains Cure, Emilia-Romagna
Ingredients: + Cotton ball + Signatures/Marks + verbal Formula
Procedure: To eliminate pain this healer (now dead) from Romagna used a practice of pure magic: using a cotton ball and that was placed on the patient's painful area, the healer made certain signs [marks] and pronouncing certain formulas [secret prayers]. The cotton was seen to then penetrate by itself under the skin according to the witnesses, and

after a short time it emerged naturally loaded with all the pains of the patient. In this way the cotton removed the pains. It is the same practice that is part of the patrimony of rites of the Filipino healers- an impressive testimony of these natural "emergencies" of similar remedies despite the profound differences of the operators and their countries of origin. 445

Warts Cure "segnature", Opagna, province of Perugia in the region of Umbria
Ingredients: + branch of Juniper + Personal Information + Fire + signs of the Cross + Secret Words
Procedure: The healer traces crosses over warts with the branch of juniper while reciting her secret words formula. She also stated the person's first and last name, date of birth, and place of baptism while marking the warts with juniper. At the end of the operation, she threw the branch of juniper into the fire, saying, *"As the juniper decays, the wart is taken away."* A negative influence. [...] is transferred to a material element that acts as a "scapegoat" - in this case, the juniper with marked apotropaic virtues - and is eliminated by destroying the support: as the juniper is consumed in the flame, so the warts disappear. 446

Sciatica Cure, Oristano, Sardinia
Ingredients: + wild Fig Branches + waning Moon + Secret Prayers + Fire
Procedure: The cure must be repeated 9 times, for 3 moons in a row, every month 3 days, in the period of the good moon (the waning one); if there is also osteoarthritis, it takes longer. Wild fig branches must be used, the ones born the countryside: if it is not wild is not good. The "patient" detaches all the leaves from the two fig branches, then one gives it to Aunt Angelina and the other wraps it around her waist. Angelina takes a chair and sits next to the patient, who remains standing. "It takes 2 of these branches every time," she explains, "so 6 a month, 18 for all the treatment. The cure begins. While the patient continues to hold his branch around his waist, Angelina leans the other against his leg and begins to recite the prayers: she says them to herself, barely moving her lips. The cure lasts about 20 minutes, during which Angelina never takes her attention away from the patient and does not stop praying. As she murmurs the prayers, she breaks part of the branch in a specific procedure: she first recites the prayers for the hip and then breaks the part of the fig that has been in contact with the hip; then she says the prayers for the thigh and breaks the corresponding part of the branch, and so on up to the foot. The twig that the patient held around his waist is then delivered and he repeats the whole operation, always continuing to pray. Finally he makes a great cross sign with both branches broken and stands up. "I burn them in the fireplace," she says. "The evil has passed through the fig branches and when I break them and burn them, the evil goes away." 447

Warts Cure, Olbia and rural areas of Sassari, Sardinia
Ingredients: + fig twig + natural latex from fig twig + prayer
Procedure: Wild fig twig **su caprificu** was engraved at the base with a cross cut. The latext that gushed out was used to wet all the warts at the same time while a prayer was said:
Abba e' latte beneitta, leadicche su signu, de su Malignu" translated to: "Blessed milk juice takes away the sign of the Evil One." The formula and procedure could be repeated

for a maximum of seven days. 448

Warts Cure, Various.
Ingredients: + Just the healer himself
Procedure: It has been reported that there exist some male healers who only have to walk towards a person with warts for the patient to receive healing, or for the patient to receive just a light touch from the healer's hand.

Fuoco di sant'Antonio (herpes zoster) Cure, Villafranca,Tuscany
Ingredients: + bramble sprigs (elm leaf blackberry) + fire +
Procedure: For the fire of sant' Antonio (herpes zoster), the healer will make signatures with sprigs of bramble (rubus ulmifolius schott), which are then burned. 449

Inflammation Cure various, Villafranca,Tuscany
Ingredients: + Sage + Water source
Procedure: Inflammations are marked with 9 leaves of sage (Salvia officinalis L.), close to a water source. The healer who scores the patient's back who is turned to the source and repeats the ritual 3 times (9 total) while reciting a propitiatory prayer; everything will be repeated for 8 days. After this time the leaves will be thrown into the river, behind the sick person. 450

LIKE CURES LIKE

Curing Kidney Stones with a Stone, Sardinia
Ingredients: + Millstone + Fire + Prayers + Cloth
Procedure: A healer named Zio Palmerio learned from a female healer to take the "heart" of the Sardinian millstone (which is even more ancient than the Roman one), and warms it inside an open fire. *When the flame goes out and only the embers remain, the sick person, man or woman who is, cloaks himself with a cloth and puts himself on the stone, with his legs open on the embers. The cloth must also 'cover' the embers, and this embers, with smoke and stone, heals. For less than half an hour.*
Zio Palmerio recites the specific prayer 3 times and traces the cross 3 times before placing the heart of the grinding wheel on the ground. If a patient is not completely cured by this, Zio Palmerio can take the heart of the grinding wheel to the patient and simply heat it, without putting the patient under the cloth, ad they will be healed completely. 451

Curing a Burn with Fire, Valnerina, Umbria
Ingredients: + Fire
Procedure: An ancient method used when you burned a hand with the flame, consisted in exposing it to fire: in this way, the excess heat responsible for the burn makes it 'drink' from the fire. 452
Curing a Scorpion sting with Scorpion oil, Valnerina, Umbria

Ingredients: + Olive oil + Scorpion
Procedure: Against scorpion stings, there was a time where scorpion oil was used almost everywhere. It was obtained by soaking various specimens of these insects in olive oil. 453

Curing a Toothache with a Gold Wedding Ring
Ingredients: + Gold wedding ring borrowed from a couple truly in love
Procedure: Healer marks the cheeks of the person with a toothache, making equilateral cross marks while saying the specific secret prayer, repeating the procedure 3 times.

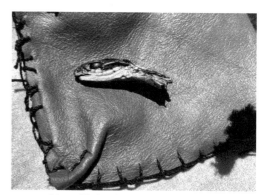

Mummified snake head, used in healing.
Collection of the author.

Curing a poisonous bite with poison, "su contravelenu" Oristano, Sardinia
Ingredients: + mummified piece of the poisonous insect/reptile + leather bag
Procedure: The healer prepares this cure by going to the countryside to look for and to take a head of viper, frog, toad, a gecko, etc. The pieces are left to dry with their tongue out and closed in bag. This must be done under the right moon, when the moon is about to end. The mummified parts are kept by the healer in a leather bag hanging from his neck and never takes it off, especially in the countryside someone may urgently need it.

Then, to cure a person bit by a poisonous animal, a healer rubs it 3 times in a cross formation, first on the ground and then in the hand or in the face or in any other part of the body where the poisonous animal has bitten. 454

Curing a burn with fire, Arezzo, Tuscany
Ingredients: + Match or Wood + fire + 8 secret Words
Procedure: On a fresh burn wound received within 24 hours (prior to the healing, no ointment must be put on the burn, neither oil nor water, nothing). The burn is then marked

238

Italian Magic: Secret Lives of Women

by the healer: *"With a burning match, or with another burning wood, I pass over the burn and on each burnt point I make two cross marks with the match saying the 8 words of the secret formula, one for each arm of the cross...they are secular words, a kind of chant accompanied by the gesture of disappearing, and in any case it considerably diminishes."* In half an hour released the pain, even heals 3rd degree burns. [455]

TO TRANSFER THE HEALING

There are also cures which use doubles to transfer healing energy into. In the case of a person who needs healing but can't go to the healer, a piece of their clothing is brought to the healer. In the case of a farm animal who can't travel to the healer, a tuft of fur is brought to the healer. In either case, the healer performs the entire formula over the substitute, transferring the healing energy into it, which can then be transferred back to the person or animal when their personal item is placed back over their body. This procedure is also carried out when making protections against **il malocchio**. A double is also referred to as a simulacrum, especially in cursing magic.

Liver Cure, Naples
Ingredients: + yellow Flower + stocking
Procedure: For 3 days, petals of a yellow flower are put into a stocking and the stocking is placed over the liver. The yellow of the liver passes into the stocking and the liver heals. [456]

Pain Cure, from Nerina Toni a healer who lives in Soliera, Emilia-Romagna
Ingredients: + Pan + Salt + Secret Words + Match sticks + Canvas bandage
Procedure: *"I boil water in my little pot, I throw in 3pinches of salt, saying the words and making the sign of the cross over the water. Then I make 3 crosses with matches, throw them in the water and reite the creed. When the water boils, I turn off and let it cool. Then I wet my fingers in the water, massage the diseased part a little and meanwhile repeat the same words I said while the water was on the fire. Then I bundle the sick part with a white canvas and inside I leave the wooden crosses, for 3 hours. After these 3 hours the pain diminishes and after twenty-four hours it completely disappears."* She says it's not the massage that heals, it's the words *"but they are not witchcraft, they are real things, it is the little Madonna who helps."* [457]

Photo: Davide Tiso, 2020.
Crosses, collection of the author.

Pain Cure at-a-distance for twisted muscles
Ingredients: + stem of wheat
Procedure: Healer looks at the wheat, which is a double for the person in pain. He looks where the knots are and identifies the point in the body where the muscles are crooked and transfers the healing to the wheat stalk, at which point the patient receives the energy.

LEGATURA DEI DOLORI
Binding the Pains

Bindings in rural Italy are cures performed as a "tying off" the flow of negative energy towards an illness. They involve a string type object to make knots in and also secret prayers. However, there do exist bindings that work in the opposite way which "glue" someone to someone else, such as in a love spell where a desired person is "bound" to someone who desires them through the same procedure: making knots that "tie" them together or using menstrual blood in the victim's drink or food so they consume the "tie." However, the "love bindings" are obviously not a cure and not perpetrated by healers. The synthesized form of binding copied the cure and used it as a template in the case of sorceresses using knots who also use a prayer twisted into something it was not intended for.

The binding formulas for curing pains and illness like warts (and painful ones nicknamed "leeks" for the way they grow under the skin) involves "signatures" and "ligatures" (or marks and bindings).

The "signatures" involve marking of the illness, often with a gold wedding ring and secret word formula received on Christmas eve, after which the healer binds the pain and/or illness, stopping it from spreading and to stop it altogether.

The "ligature" bindings involve tying knots into strings or long vine-like plants. These cures are used on people and animals. Often the bindings are thrown away in the same way **occhi** water which absorbs **il malocchio** is: somewhere far from the patient's home, in some location where no one else can absorb the negative energy.

Binding Knot Cure, for muscle tears and sprains, Casale dei Frati, Umbria
Ingredients: + hemp String + 3 knots + word Formula
Procedure: The healer forms 3 knots on each end of the hemp string, then grasping it by the ends and keeping it taught in a loop that forms a cross, she rests it on the injured part (repeating this 3 times) while reciting the following:

"Virgin Mary, first your most held hand then mine
[asking the Virgin Mary to make signatures]
There were 3 sisters who looked like 3 spinsters,
carrying 3 bowls: one of **water***, one of* **blood** *and one of* **salt***."*

Italian Magic: Secret Lives of Women

Continuing in the therapeutic ritual, if it was a sore limb, the operator tied the part with the twine keeping the ligature until the pain stopped. [458]

Binding Knot Cure, for warts, Sardinia
Ingredients: + Straw + Salt + Wheat grains + Spit + waning Moon + Almond tree
Procedure: The **sanadora** Aunt Bissenta, lent herself for these things, always free of charge and provided that the moon was waning. The rite started with the lighting of a little straw in which she had thrown a handful of wheat and as many crystals of salt as there were warts to make disappear. Immediately afterwards she placed herself near the patient, marked the affected part by making small crosses, then spit on it and had started to mumble in a very low voice. At the end of this phase, she took a small string of thread which she had knotted quickly (as many knots as there were leeks). After the long operation, during which she continued to whisper prayers, she wrapped this thread forming a tight skein which she had buried at the foot of an almond tree in a hole she herself had previously dug in her own courtyard. The whole thing was then covered with a smooth stone so that no one would step on it. The intervention ended when she said to the patient with a reassuring smile: *"Go with God, my little son, you will see that with the new moon your hands will return as clean as they were before."* [459]

Binding Knot Cure for warts, Pula, Sardinia
Ingredients: + long rush stem + knots + name of patient + prayers
Procedure: The healer must take the medicine, the rush vine, at dawn before the sun comes out. He must visit the patient and count the warts. Then he must make the exact same amount of knots.

> *"For every knot I make, I say: that the leeks go away to that person, and I pronounce his name. Then I throw the medicine on the ground and before I pick it up I make a cross on it. Then I put it in my pocket and go to a place where that person who has warts will never have to pass, I take out the medicine and if there is it is a ditch I throw it into the water, or I bury it in the ground or I hide it under a stone. The rush begins to rot and as the leeks rot it goes away. It takes about forty days.* [460]

Binding Knot Cure for warts, Ozieri, Sardinia
Ingredients: + long river rush + knots + spit
Procedure: The healer takes a long river rush, which is a green and elastic stem on which she, using only her right hand, had made as many knots as there were leeks to be removed from the patient. Immediately afterwards she spit on the patient's limb and rubbed each leek 3 times with each knot of the reed which she immediately loosened "inviting" the growth to disappear in the same way. The first part of the ritual ended here and the healer moved away with the rush, being very careful not to touch it in the central area (the one where the knots were before) as it had "charged" with the evil. Then she threw the stem

in a place known only to her so that the healed patient would never need to come see her again for treatment. In fact, before disappearing, the old woman had pronounced words of an averting nature. 461

Binding Knot Pain Cure for animals
Ingredients: + thread or string + specific prayers
Procedure: For animals in pain, healers often gently tie their legs together and lie them down during the procedure so they don't run away. Knots of differing quantities are tied into threads or ropes and looped around the ankles of the animal while prayers are recited and sometimes water is sprinkled.

DANCING CURES

Dancing cures or cures that use movement of body parts employ sympathetic methods for releasing immobility and pain due to: poison from animal or insect bites, atrophy and injury of muscles, pain in tendons and nerves affecting movement.

The expression of sympathy with the injured body part or with the vehicle for illness (the poisonous animal, for example) is part of the cure. As with all rural cures, there exists a symbolic language encoded in the essential ingredients of action, word, and matter, which invite problem solving with spirits (helpers) and against spirits (the ones who harm) to begin. In the dancing cures:

- the words invite the healing in, imploring help in a coded way from the spirit world, as well as often commanding or describing a healing action.

- the actions, here as dancing in circular movement coinciding with words and circular music or moving like the animal who either poisoned or whose movement is desired and..

- the matter is the body itself. Here we truly see the meeting of the spirit and the body, acted out soulfully on the physical plane in the entranced dance which is not just about the movement of the body but using the body's movements repetitively to escape the illness...to travel into the spirit world and bring back balance to the earthly one. As with all rural cures, there is the intervention or assistance of spirits.

In the first cure presented, there is a recognizable sympathetic formula expressed:

Dancing Cure for muscle tears, fractures, sciatica, Sardinia
Ingredients: + rabbit Foot + words Formula + circular Dance
Procedure: The **sanadora** uses the hind leg of a hare which, thanks to its extraordinary mobility, is called **ossu balladore** (dancing bone) and places it in close contact with the painful part of the immobile patient (thigh, leg or foot) and, keeping it so as to leave the

joint free, made the leg "dance" according to a circular path along the patient's limb and at the same time recited this formula: *"Balla, balla, ballerino, a me la clausura, a te la sventura"* (Dance, dance, dancer, the cloister to me, the misfortune to you). [462]

In contrast, these next cures are of a variety where the victim of a poisonous bite must actively participate in their own healing. In fact, they become the spirited vehicle for it.

IL TARANTISMO / Tarantism

The spider dance cures, known collectively as **il tarantismo** tarantism are actually a variety of cures based on the sympathetic principle for a variety of spider type bites and even for scorpio and snake bites.

Tarantism has been a longstanding tradition of the region of Puglia, and it's also found on the island of Sardinia. Tarantism manifested itself mainly in the summer months, the period of wheat harvest in Puglia. It's been documented there were as many as 21 themes [for cures] corresponding to 21 species of tarantulas in villages such as Melendugno, Sava, Manduria, Martina Franca, San Giorgio di Taranto, Monteparano, Lizzano, Montemesola, Castellaneta, Grottaglie, Francavilla Fontana, Brindisi, [463] deriving a Greek influence in the region of Puglia, and a variety in Sardinia as well in such places as Nuoro, Oristano, and Cabras.

The themes are essential to each cure which is based on the type of spider who poisoned the victim. Each type of spider has a poison that expresses very specific symptoms of behavior in the victims who can't help but act out, while the community participates in a cure for the theme. For example, some of the spider theme classifications are: the widow, the maiden, the new mother, and the paralytic.

> *"The pinch of the tarantula was easily recognized by the reactions it provoked; and from those reactions were understood which tarantula had pinched him, whether unmarried or widowed."* [464]

The curative process, the **tarantella** (dance) for the **tarantata** (bitten one), involves music, movement, trance, and interestingly sometimes gazing at the colors green, yellow or red [465] to induce the frenzied energy needed in some cures in sympathetic connection to the tarantulas *with spots yellow, red or brown on the back, depending on the species.* [466] Noteworthy here is the color yellow, also used by **sos attitidos** mourners who act as psychopomps for the spirit of the recently deceased, bridging a journey between the earthly world and the spirit world.

DANZA DEI TARANTOLATI / SU BALLU
dance of tarantulars / the dance

The phenomenon has a ritual complexity in Manduria [in Puglia] and its surroundings up to the early 1900s. [467] The tradition was that of community involvement with the exorcism, in the way the community was involved in other dances (for courtship and joyful celebration) and comparable to the way the community was involved with death rituals and funeral processions. In the case of tarantism, it wasn't just believed that the spider infected a person with poison, but that there was a spirit condition taking place, and while the victim had to actively engage with their healing process, the community surrounded them with their presence and assistance: specific musicians who were keepers of the traditional songs would play their role depending on the type of spider bite at hand, and people were gathered to be part of the dance or lend their energy to the victim.

In tarantism, women take the leading role in aiding the victim to heal, similar to their roles in the death mourning rituals. While **tarantata** victims must also participate, women dances are gathered from the community based on corresponding life phase of the spider who bit the victim (as maidens, mothers, or widows) to dance alongside the victim, along with other community members who are willing to dance for 3 days. A majority of victims of the tarantula's pinch were women anyway, simply due to the fact that women were harvesting the crops. Of course, men were bitten too.

The dance of Nuoro, Sardinia:
Il tarantolati dell'arza nuorese -*according to the descriptions that have been made, they found a remedy in a sort of dance of which they were conductors 7 widows, 7 brides, 7 spinsters.* Here the tarantula *mainly affected male subjects, aged 20 to 40, who showed a possession of a female entity, losing its virile identity [...] taking on feelings and behaviors proper of the woman.* 468

When a man was pinched by the tarantula in this area, the community got to work: men dug a pit in a dung heap where they'd place the victim, stripped down to his underwear. Women (young, old, married, widowed) and men were gathered for the dances who took an active part observing the ritual healing. The crowd formed a circle around the victim who was buried up to his shoulders in the pit while they made a comedic scene, clanging pots and pans and clowning around making jokes to and about the victim who *became in the course of the ritual ceremony, a bit the laughing stock of the community.* 469 In this emotional burial, the victim *is returned to the womb; he is alone. When he has managed to laugh - evidently of himself together with others - he is reborn, having extracted his healing.* 470

The dance of Oristano, Sardinia:
Il ballo della tarantola nell' oristanese- *The pinch of the tarantula was easily recognized by the reactions it provoked; and from those reactions were understood which tarantula had pinched him, whether unmarried or widowed.* 471 So when a man was pinched, the family began to gather help from the community by gathering the people necessary for the dance.

> *"When one was pinched by a widow, they were looking for a young man dressed in black to give relief, when he was pinched by a maiden they were looking for a brightly dressed young woman or if the victim herself was very young, they dressed her in white."* 472

Italian Magic: Secret Lives of Women

The musicians and people gathered and eventually the victim, who at first was paralyzed to a point of only being able to writhe on the ground, would get up and dance with the young man or maiden-whomever the victim was obsessing over, seemingly inspired into action by the double, the stand-in partner from the community who'd play-act to east the loneliness felt by the theme of a widow who'd lost their partner. They would both dance for 3 days along with other community members and the musicians. In any case, whomever was bitten and danced for 3 days was left to do their dance but at the same time a bit feared because *"..they were not completely conscious in those moments."* 473

The Cabrarese tarantola, Sardinia:
La tarantola cabrarese- *"In Cabras there are four species of **argias** and tarantulas: the widow, the maiden, the puerpera, the paralytic. Here, it is not clear well if the spider is always the same, since this distinction is made exclusively by the symptoms of the bad that results from the bite. the community of* **su ballu de s'argia** (dance of the tarantula) *no longer exists.* 474

La Tarantola Vedova, Sardinia
The widow tarantula- For the widow tarantula's symptoms there is a *group therapeutic ritual: 3 days and 3 nights of dances led by authentic widows or simulants, in mourning clothing, which insert funeral lamentations into the dance. A mass scene prepared by experts with the participation of the neighborhood. The ceremony takes place normally outdoors. While we change around the* **tarantolato** *suffering, in the representation of a widow's pain, to which the* **tarantolate** *itself is urged to take part."* 475

La tarantola puerpera, Sardinia:
The new mother tarantula- The "new mother spider" bite poisons the victim to feel distraught to the point of suicidal destructiveness. They are focused on killing themselves in a hot oven unless their intense need to cradle a baby is met. So the cure uses a double, a doll made of rags mimicking a newborn baby, while also a dance is done to bring a tarantula to the mouth of an oven or to actually place one in the oven, ritually playing out the suicidal death. . [...] *by placing a doll in the patient's arms, which is brought to pour affection and maternal care on that simulacrum of newborn. For the ritual 3 days and 3 nights, the* **tarantolato** *is assisted by the neighbors, while cradle, fondling, caring for the newborn.* 476

La tarantola nubile, Sardinia:
The maiden tarantula- The **argia bagadia** species, the maiden tarantula, makes a victim jump and dance like crazy, with an abundance of energy. *"To relieve the evil we danced, playing and singing together for 3 days and 3 nights."* 477

These symptoms are uniformly felt by each victim, and the theme of the rituals are an integral part of the cure for each victim. *"In the area of Taranto and Brindisi, where paganism was highly developed, the exorcism ended with a long procession of musicians in the place where it was believed the encounter with the animal and its poisonous bite had occurred."* 478 This act of returning to the scene of the bite is similar to the **s'imbrusciadura** cure, where the victim of a psychic fright returns to the place where they felt fear and grounds it into the earth by rolling their body on the ground, thereby leaving the trauma where it occurred.

Illness in rural Italy is not just a collection of symptoms but also a result of negative energy often referred to as "evil." As with all rural cures, there exists the intervention of helping spirits (and the banishing of harmful ones), present in the dance of the tarantula in the acquired trance state, which is not unfamiliar to other spiritual paths. Called "being ridden" in some pagan practices, or expressed in trance mediumship of Edgar Cayce, and posing similarities to shamanism as well:

"The Yamana shaman [...] commands a helping spirit, as long as he is possessed by it he is insensible, But this insensibility belongs, rather, to his shamanic condition, for he can play about barefoot on fire and swallowing burning coals. 479

This same "insensibility" of **tarantolate** is noted by observers of the spider dances, who seem "out of their minds" and at the same time are performing specific functions that are part of the cure. Often referred to as "hysteria of an unknown origin" by outsiders, consider this: if rural people were wearing ceremonial costumes during their trance dances, perhaps like the sufis, would they be considered less hysterical and more seriously spiritual? Writings about the rural world tend to denigate and insult the intelligence of the people using their traditions, claiming that they are not only poor in cash but also in comprehension of knowledge. Whereas viewpoints towards Romans, sufis or other people who perform rituals dressed in costumes reserved for that tradition and in temples or temples reserved for that purpose are considered deeply spiritual and expressing a profound connection to the universe.

In rural Italy, these trances were done out of urgent need: they solved very real poisonous problems such as excruciating pain and paralysis and emotional turmoil resulting from spider bites. Tarantism was performed as soon as possible, gathering community members, kitchen items, and specialized musicians and making the arrangements necessary for the type of spider theme, but the ceremony and rituals look poor, regular, dusty, ugly, crazy...certainly not ornamental nor opulent...only very real. The trance allowed in the helping spirits to temporarily possess the tarantolate. This procedure is perhaps frustrating for outsiders since there is not spiritual practice involved that is preparatory: the trance exists in these moments and not outside of them. But this was the true usage: trance for cures, in a real and immediate urgency, not used for the sake of spiritual expansion or enlightenment. While some paths offer growth for a seeker's curiosity's sake, others use spiritual tools to solve immediate problems where there are not other solutions.

THE POWER OF WORDS

Words are an essential part of rural cures. They are the key to not only the cures but to the effectiveness of the healer, because in rural traditions, they literally open the pathway for channeling. Rather than practicing the skill of channeling, in the rural world the words begin this process automatically, allowing the divine universe to channel through the healer. So these words are an important inheritance, and many of the secret words are in

Italian Magic: Secret Lives of Women

themselves eternal secrets to those who inherit them. In this way, the cures are protected.

Words are also essential parts of community ritual, whether they are parts of music for tarantismo cures or courtship rituals or even nursery rhymes for children which contain spiritual ideas, they even find their way into magic of course, based on the charges they hold.

The secret prayers follow general patterns: as lyrical poem-like stories or requests; as encoded numerical symbolism embedded in words or phrases; and also as words that are never read nor heard because they are sealed in a pouch, and yet they still have the power to cure. Sometimes the words involve saints and Madonnas, sometimes they feature fish, goats and herbs, some are commands towards energy, sometimes singular words have a charge. Prayers of the lineage cures tend to be the encoded and fragmentary, composed of just a few words or in seemingly non-sensical sentences used in repetition that seem to have nothing to do with cures nor religion or anything related to the illness at all, but they are secret symbols of something else such as astrology, numerology, and initiatic rites. In this way, in their strange symbolism, they keep the secret of the cure. The more sensible sounding a prayer is, the more likely it is to have been created recently, or made just for spellwork and derived from a curative prayer, or part of a community healing ritual but does not have a lineage behind it.

Words can hold a charge and transfer that charge, just as an object can, through psychometry. Some people believe words are the real magic.

Words that are never seen, and yet they cure from within an envelope:

In Caligari, Sardinia, there is a healer named **Zio** Uncle Palmerio who inherited *2 sealed envelopes which contain some writings. Zio Palmerio does not know what is written on those sheets, first of all because the envelopes are sealed, then because he cannot read. However on each envelope there is written what they are for. If they are opened, the envelopes are no longer needed,* [it means they have been retired] *and neither can they be shown to others. Palmerio got these envelopes from his mother-in-law, who must have been a little sorceress too: one is for women, to ensure them a good birth, the other is for men, to save their lives in case of danger.* 480

During the war, Palmerio was enlisted and he brought an envelope with him to "protect his life" while he fought alongside his fellow soldiers, but he realized he accidentally brought the envelope for "a good birth" One night they asked for hospitality from a man who allowed them to stay in the haystack. The man told the soldiers that *his daughter-in-law had been in labor for more than forty-eight hours, but that the baby was unable to be born and that the doctor could not come because it was raining too much. "Then I took the envelope for the good birth out of my pocket, I threw it on the ground, I made the cross on it, then I told Atzeni to put it under the shoulder blade of the daughter-in-law. After a quarter of an hour a boy was born, male and healthy. This envelope with the words for the good birth served to give birth well all my children and also many other children."* 481

BETWEEN MAGIC + MEDICINE

Traditional Affirmative Words used as a call-and-response:

In Collegiacone, mothers replied to their impatient daughters to marry. [482] These words were performed as a sort of call-and-response and share the same attitude of pregnant mothers who affirm the health of their coming baby by surrounding themselves with good thoughts and photos of beautiful children.

> Mamma mmia, vojo marito, che lo crognale ha gia fiorito!
> Fija mia, te pija 'n malanno: lo crognale fiorisce tutto l'anno !

> Mom, I want a husband the crognale has already bloomed!
> My daughter, you are ill*: the crognale blooms all year round!

*As an expression, the equivalent of saying "you're crazy" or "you're not thinking well"

Words that describe curative actions embedded with numerical symbolism and astrology:

> "Holy Monday, the newborn child is frightened,
> Holy Tuesday, the worm is in his guise,
> Holy Wednesday, the worm is in his corner,
> Maundy Thursday, the spell is cast,
> Good Friday is torture,
> Holy Saturday is delightful,
> and on Easter Sunday the worm falls whole." [483]

Words that describe a curative action embedded with numerical symbolism turned into a love binding spell:

> "Cristo e' nato, Cristo e' morto, Cristo e' resuscitato,
> Portami il tizio che lo ho legato". [484]

> "Christ was born, Christ died, Christ rose from the dead,
> Bring me the guy that I tied up".

Words that create a boundary of protection:

> "Santa Lucia, va' la' a casa tua
> prendi 'n po' de finocchi
> e puliscime quest'occhi" [485]

> "Saint Lucia, go there to your home
> take some fennel
> and clean these eyes"

This prayer has an apotropaic character: the passage of the holy martyr is requested to enclose the house within a protective barrier that prevents negative forces from crossing it. Here "home" is to be understood as the paradise where fennel grows...[the supernatural place it comes from, i.e. Source/Universe]

Italian Magic: Secret Lives of Women

Words that create a boundary of protection and invoke magical healing:

"Santa Lucia, santa Lucia,
passa 'ntorno a casa mia:
co' 'n mazzo de finocchi
puliscime bene l'occhi" 486

"Saint Lucia, Saint Lucia,
go around my house:
with a bunch of fennels
clean my eyes well"

Fennel, on the other hand, besides its pharmacological power used to heal the eyes has a parallel functions of apotropaic quality: fennel has the power to drive away witches.

Words that invoke a protection and describe an action:

"Of ferro di quadrupede,
tu che sei tanto forte
d'ogni nemico guardami.
Scaccialo e dagli morte, distruggila,
distruggila questa genia d'arpia,
con la tua forza magica,
guarda a casa mia."

Of quadruped iron
you who are so strong
of every enemy look at me.
Cast it out and kill it, destroy it,
destroy this harpy genie,
with your magic force,
look at my house.

This prayer invokes the power or iron that is used throughout rural cures against spirit attachments, in amaro herbs and spices that protect the digestions, and is found in the apotropaic amulets used for the home and the body. 487

Filastrocce Rhyming Words that tell the story of a protective action:

"Occhiatura, scarpiatura, vatinni da 'sta criatura"
and
"Malocchio, calpestato a terra, lascia questa creatura"
"Evil eye, trampled on the ground, leave this creature "

Words combining rural apotropaic nature and saints:
This is the type of prayer considered heretical by the church.

Acqua e sale mia Signora, per levare ogni fattura,
acqua e sale San Giovanni, per spegnere questo fuoco grande
acqua e sale per le magiare, và fattura e non tornare.

Water and salt my Lady, to remove every invoice,
water and salt San Giovanni, to put out this great fire
water and salt for magiare, go [away] invoice and do not return. 488

BETWEEN MAGIC + MEDICINE

Curative Words that tell a universal story and describe an action for vermi:

"Saint Agata cries many tears...The Lord passed by and said: Agata, why are you crying?
Because the 'Master Worm' is come and is eating my little daughter!

Worm 1, worm 2, worm 3, worm 4, worm 5, worm 6, worm 7, worm 8, worm 9
falls thus from the heart"

"Sant'Aituzza assai lacrimi chianceva, ...
Passau lu Signuri ecci rissi: -
Aituzza, pirchi' sta chiancennu? -
Pirchi' vinni lu vermu mastru e si sta manciannu la me figghiuzza."

"Vermu unu, vermu-ddui, vermu-ttri, vermu quattru, vermu cincu,
vermu sei, vermu setti, vermu ottu, vermu novi, casca stu vermu di lu cori" 489

LE MALEDIZIONI

EVIL EYE, HEXES, BINDINGS, WORD SPELLS, and FILTERS
Malocchio, Fatture, Legature, Scongiuri, Filtri

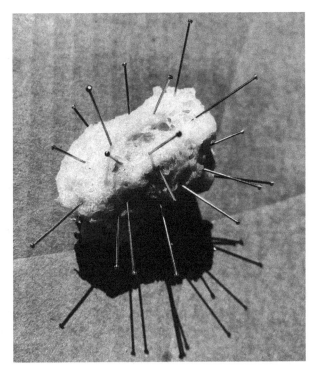

Pins in bread, south Italy

"What heals can harm, who heals can harm" is evident in the realm of illnesses and other misfortunes caused by **le maledizioni** which are all types of spells used for negative purposes against other people to cause harm.

Either of these paths, that of the healer and protector or that of the hexer, take both practice and a dedicated mindset in either direction. A healer inevitably learns the mechanics of what they are helping to heal, and therefore learns how the negative spells work, such as:

+ where the illness has taken hold and by what mechanism
+ where energy is stuck/has invaded
+ how to pull out what the spell invaded with before repairing the da
+ which supernatural power will heal which curse
+ what a spell can do and how far it can go

LE MALEDIZIONI

Le maledizioni (curses) are derived from cures, having taken curative formulas and rearranged the combinations of words, actions, and matter to harm life, rather than to improve it. These are copy cat formulas born out of human envy and synthetically derived from an original formula to get something someone else has or to jealously destroy the happiness and abundance of someone else. Whereas cures were born from human need to survive beyond harsh limitations of socio-economic conditions, handed down from the helping divinities who created the cures.

Le maledizioni often use the assistance of spirit attachments and other negative spirits. And so, the spirit world of higher helpers responded in kind by providing cures to counteract these harmful spells along with the cures gifted to rebalance health.

Is praticas, as they are called in Sardinia, are seers who can trace the lines of connection between curser and victim and undo these works. **Is praticas** also proactively protect others from these spells. These "fixers" exist throughout Italy. This divide between those who help and those who harm with magic is embedded in Italian consciousness around the idea of witches being those who do "bad" magic, while other people who do curative magic are considered just people, not necessarily healers nor witches. Generally speaking, in Italian style, this mindset depends on where the people live and how heavy-handed the church has affected their local culture. Some people, even of the oldest generations, have reclaimed the word **strega** (witch) as a name for themselves, however many people, even healers and witches, do differentiate between good and bad **streghe** (witches plural). The role of **is praticas** is a special one whose expertise is knowing how to stop negative works of magic from harming people and how to protect people from harm.

The realm of magic consisting only of harm done to others through spells blends curative tradition ingredients with a twisted effort to match with the contrast of poverty (both economic and also poverty of mind) which result in negative magic that harms life.

Of course not all magic is based on envy and lack. There are and have been many magical traditions that are used for positive and expansive actions based in daily sacred works, especially in regards to food (food production, transformation of ingredients, planting and harvesting), protection work, union magic (between lovers), astral flight, fertility, protection of house and household against theft, works to ensure health of farm animals, weather conditions, and more.

within the realm of **le maledizioni** that we find the most exact parallels in t·   cures (the foundation of traditions) and envious magic (synthetically and derived from curative traditions: a perversion upon original

Italian Magic: Secret Lives of Women

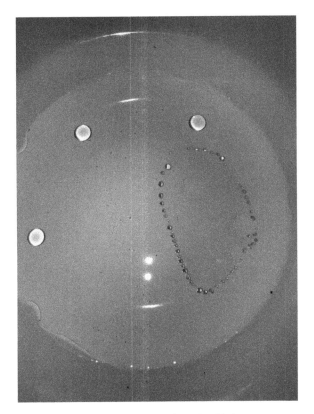

Photo: Oil and water, diagnosis of **il malocchio** by a woman

IL MALOCCHIO

The general name for the evil eye in Italian is **il malocchio,** which literally translates to: the bad eye, and culturally means the evil eye. **Il malocchio** is a psychic illness that is the result of envy. While it's name is "the bad eye", the illness itself refers to being fascinated, or rather being the object of fascination by someone with ill will.

Often, but not always, the terms used for those who make **il malocchio** (and **fatture**, and all **maledizioni**) are the same ones used for those who undo the negative works. So someone who throws the evil eye can be called **sfasciatrici** in Umbrian dialect, for example, and the one who cures the evil eye can also be called **sfasciatrici.**

While cures and defensive magic against **il malocchio** were already in use when the Romans began to document their world, and it has continued to be an important part of rural life, these are traditions which have bubbled over into contemporary Italian culture as well.

Other names for **il malocchio** from other regions and villages are:

- **la fascinazione** (literally translates to fascination)
- **l'invidia** (translates to envy, which is the vehicle or cause for **il malocchio**)

LE MALEDIZIONI

- **occhio** (Valnerina, Umbria)
- **occhiaticcio, occhiacciu** (Cerretano, Ponte Buggianino Umbria) [490]
- **ocru malu, ogru malu,** and other variations by village (Sardinia)
- **ocarinaticio** (Roccaporena, Umbria)
- **s'aghiadura** (Sardinia)
- **s'ogu liau** (Sardinia)
- **occhio della strega** (Umbria)
- **colpo d'occhio** (Bosa, Sardinia)

Names of the people who throw **il malocchio** at others (the operators) are:

- **iettatore / jettatore, iellatore**
- **s'oghiadori** (Sardinia dialect)

Names of healers / eve spell-breakers:

- **sfasciatrici, sfasciatrici d'occhio** (Umbria, means "eye markers")
- **guastatrici** (Umbria, means "eye markers")
- **segnatrici d'occhio**
- **lacanomante**
- **majarzas** (Sardinia)

The act of giving **il malocchio** is called:
-**occhiare** (Umbria) -**jettatura** (general)

The cures (which combine diagnosis and cure) are called:
-**mexina de s'ogu** (eye medicine, Sardinia) **sfarah lochia** (Meggiano,Umbria) [491]

- **lacanomanzia** (an anthropological term)
- **segna' l'occhio** (Sciedi, Umbria)
- **sfaciare l'icchio** (Umbria)
- **guasta' l'occhio** (Umbria)
- **occhi** (eyes, general, Campania ecc)
- **sfaciare l'occhio** (to smash the eye, Umbria)

To be someone who received it:
- **occhiata** (to be eyed)
- **invidiata** (to be envied)
- **con malocchio** (to be with il malocchio)
- **da malo occhio** (from bad eye)
- **aduggiare** or **l'uggiare**- outcome of the evil eye [490]

Italian Magic: Secret Lives of Women

ILLNESS ORIGINATING IN THE SPIRIT

What **il malocchio** is reveals a great deal about the Italian peoples' relationship with the spirit world and their pervasive beliefs about personal responsibility towards health. It considered a psychic illness that affects the spirit. And the Italian beliefs about the effects of the spirit on the body (and vice versa) run deep. In these beliefs we see commonalities with shamanism and other oral spiritual traditions. From these beliefs we find both secret and popular traditions revealing an acceptance of the existence of the world of spirits and their affects on health, positively and negatively, so much so that people outside of witchcraft, modern pagan or metaphysical practices live daily life with this awareness. Simply stated, the evil eye is a outflow of envious energy sent from one person to another. How it does it's thing is more complicated.

"Someone put the eyes on me," as it is phrased in Italy, is a way people announce their awareness that the evil eye is causing them physical or mental discomfort. Many people are very aware that a symptom like a headache, for example, that is not the result of an internal factor with a physiological root (such as a food allergy) nor other external factor, is likely caused by il malocchio, and they immediately seek out the cure from a relative or village healer when the eyes are on them.

PASSIVE ENVY + ACTIVE ENVY

Additionally there is a belief that envy can be both passive and active and both result in someone being the victim of **il malocchio**. Envy is always the cause, and the resulting **il malocchio** can hit people, animals, machines, and food production:

A person who passively affects someone with their envy is someone with a victim complex, the "why not me" person who looks at everyone else as being more fortunate than they are. These people are not intentionally creating a spell towards someone, but they are indeed creating a lot of focused negativity and projecting it towards someone else propelled by an envious desire to see the other person lose their health, prosperity, success, happiness, etc.

In American contemporary culture we call these personality types "energy vampires". Passive aggressive people are also those who may seem friendly enough but who harbor resentment and jealousy towards others they perceive are better off. They try to invade someone's personal space to achieve dominance in some way through, for example, fake friendliness and backhanded compliments, mostly to find out why someone else has something they don't. When a person compliments your new shirt but from the vibe of their voice you can tell they aren't really liking your new shirt at all and instead of checking you out in some way, you can feel it in their gaze. It's a common occurrence in Italy for people to not trust these types of backhanded compliments and what lies behind them.

While there are generations of loving, supportive mother-in-laws in Italy who are the keepers of the initiatic traditions of passing down Lineage knowledge to their daughter-in-laws, it is also common to find a jealous **suocera** passively throwing **il malocchio** at

LE MALEDIZIONI

her **nuora** who then suffers the physical effects, especially in contemporary culture where there is more independence in the community and a lack of coupling rituals that existed in the presence of the rural community. The additional danger of passive-aggressive personalities is that they are easy targets for spirit attachments to work through. Lower spirits (manipulators, thieves, jealous types) are often found influencing passive aggressive people, inflating their sense of envy and adding extra power to their negative energy output.

While in contemporary culture we may want to "call these people out" in the moment and "speak our truth," among Italians it's common to "keep things in their place", so instead of confrontation people immediately work to neutralize effects of **il malochio** by flashing the deflecting hand signs of the horns, by throwing salt after the person leaves, and then taking more powerful measures, such as seeking a healer.

Calling out a person who is projecting **il malocchio** would only worsen the situation, due to its passive-aggressive nature, and it's likely there is a spirit attachment involved, influencing the actions of the projector. The spirit attachment is the aspect who does the most damage and is much more difficult to appease than the human being harboring it. It is the spirit attachment who is moving negative energy through the vehicle of sight into the earthy world. And it will fight to maintain control.

Then, there are people who intentionally create a way to send **il malocchio** to someone else to purposely take away their success or joy or prosperity or relationship. An active envious person is one who spends time and effort sending spells to knock someone else off their path in whatever aspect they are experiencing positivity abundance, confidence, success or growth. In rural culture, the focus was: newborn babies, crops, food productions, farm animals, for example.

This can be done at a distance, through a visualization spell. This has also has been traditionally done by charging a simple object (stone, braid of victim's hair) with **il malocchio** and then throwing it into the intended victim's yard or secretly planting it in their home, sneaking it into their food. It is also accomplished with the help of negative spirits who transporting the objects without a physical person present into a hard-to-reach place in the home of the victim. So, a person may find a spell behind the walls of their home or under the floorboards or even inside a sealed couch cushion or pillow stuffing.

Whether active **jettatura** (the act of throwing of envy towards someone) or passive, the envy sends a psychic cord of connection between victim and operator. This is also a key to removing **il malocchio. This psychic cord goes into the heart of the victim.**

RECOGNIZING IL MALOCCHIO

In Italian agricultural communities, **il malocchio** has traditionally been focused on newborn babies and small children because they are a symbol of abundance and good fortune, and they are also vulnerable. This is why the majority of amulets, including the **cimaruta**, were created to protect them. Also farm animals, crops and food production (particularly cheese and bread preparations), and new mothers' milk production were the

Italian Magic: Secret Lives of Women

focus of attack, being fundamental aspects to rural life. In communities where people are entirely dependent upon nature's cycles to grow, harvest, and produce their own food and birth their own babies, **il malocchio** is serious business. It is believed that **il maocchio** can even cause cancer.

This is what il malocchio can look like in contemporary culture:

> For example, perhaps you write a book like this one, and announce it on social media. Then another author who likes to be seen as the authority on these matters starts to bully you by being territorial on social media where you announce a public lecture about your book in a shop where he usually gives workshops. Then the day of your event, despite your great mood, walking to your car you suddenly feel a pressing sense of anxiety that you know is unfounded and you stub your toe, and drop your car keys and start to feel a fog-like confusion. You realize that you are getting emotionally riled up even though these things are no big deal..and that it must be **il malocchio**, you calm down and clean and protect yourself and enjoy your drive to your event. But then there are problems: the competitive author's face keeps popping up in your mind and when you arrive at the location you feel noisy chaos in the air and have to center the energy of the room several times to quell the energy storm. Your usually sold-out events find many people canceling last minute due to strange traffic issues that won't allow them to arrive in time, so attendance is much smaller than the amount of tickets that were sold, though it nevertheless goes well. After, you eat some restaurant food that gives you a disproportionately severe allergic reaction, almost enough to go to the hospital, but instead you text your healer friends and get some benadryl and there's enough support and awareness within and around you to quell this **il malocchio**. Incidentally, while you are having the allergic reaction you see his face and so do your healer friends who have not been informed about the perpetrator. In the moment you recognize without a doubt who caused this, the negative energy speeds up to attempt to do all it can before you can clear it away. This is positive however, because mere recognition itself does loosen the effectiveness of "il malocchio." Just as an shadowy spirit attachment loses its power once it's recognized to be hiding itself behind a shadowed form.

This is an example of how **il malocchio** can attack you. The most important defense for a victim is to catch that something is happening and tell someone. This act of seeing or bearing witness immediately starts to release the grip of il malocchio.

The affects harm get much worse than this, especially for people who don't have psychic tools to use to help themselves. **Il malocchio** usually affects: something you are passionate about, it can affect travels and allergies and electronics, it affects emotions and mindset. Being a psychic illness, it affects the physical world by way of your thoughts, emotions, and energy body (your spirit) through the vehicle of your physical body and its interaction with these energies in your environment. The negative energy derails your normal interactions and makes them feel uneasy, in disease. This envious energy that attempts to get you "off track" in basic ways through a visualization spell that connects person to person energetically.

FASCINATION

Because **jettatura** (throwing the evil eye at someone) is an energetic transference, it can be said this occurs spirit to spirit. After all, your spirit is the energetic embodiment of your consciousness, emotions, and thoughts. It is your physical body which processes energies into symptomatic physical form; it's the embodied meeting point between the spirit world and the physical world. Physical matter is the end result of unseen energies in motion. Your physical body has physical senses which gather information from your physical world, and yet it is your spirit body which gathers and sends all the unseen information such as "vibes, love, warnings, and other sensations that have emotional qualities and combinations thereof. There is a reason these are called "extrasensory" sensations: It's not possible for your eyes to physically transfer something to someone else other than visual information available to the "naked" eye, but energy can be sent and focused through the eyes along energetic (psychic) unseen-to-the-physical-eye currents.

Psychic illnesses that are cured in Italian rural traditions are caused by negative spirits either:

+ Influencing others they work through, using them as tools and as...
+ spirits invited intentionally by sorcerers to help them carry out their spells.

The spirits and their ability to weaken the iron content (and therefore oxygen content in turn, vitality) of the blood of victims, results in the "withering away" of the victims beyond the reach of conventional doctors. Fascination, after all, means the victim is fascinated by the spell and fascinated (unable to turn away) by their own suffering not only because of the malocchio spell, but because of the psychic link between the sender and the victim.

BLOOD

The fascination, or inability to look away from the condition, has to do with quality of blood, it is believed in rural Italy. The person with stronger blood will fascinate the other, or psychically overpower the other. Having stronger blood that is fortified with more iron and inflated by anger, forcefulness, and rage, is seen as the blood most capable of exerting power over another. This is done through the gaze. Another way to describe this is to call to mind being in a public place where a stranger becomes aggressive and confrontational and you experience that sensation of cold fear where you freeze or shrink into yourself. This is a case of the "stronger blood" overpowering the weaker, in the sense that one expands (the aggressor) and one retracts (the fearful person). Fear is something that shrinks the energy of a person. This is also why il malocchio cures are in fact exorcisms.

Italian Magic: Secret Lives of Women

"[...]the idea that blood is the privileged vehicle of the force that produces the fascination"[491] is an ancient belief, and is a common one among farmers in rural Italy. This belief is consistent with the entire span of inherited cures passed down through initiation in Italy that in regards to illness having causation by spirits (the spirit of the victim and the negative spirits who assist the sorceress) and spells, the force of a spell's success has to do with the strength and force of the blood. The person with stronger blood (which has more iron) has the stronger gaze than a person with weaker blood, and that's where the true power (or over-powerment) lies. The blood is intimately linked with bodily fluids and the fluid of the eyes.

This knowledge, that fluids are conduits, was prevalent in pre-pagan Goddess culture of old Europe, and the symbolic language expressing this belief can be found on countless statues marking the places on the female body which produced these fluids. Further, in the way rural cures are tied together through sympathetic magic and homeopathy, the curse (being sent through conduit of fluids) is also the cure:

> *"the therapeutic technique of the imposition of hands, which is a very widespread practice reserved especially for healers who they have a particular magnetic charm, called* **umbra de caoru**,* *which could be translated with 'snake charm'".* [492]

Both the belief and technique of sending a magnetic energetic healing fluid from spirits to a patient (who also has a spirit) through the medium of a healer's hands is also shared by Spiritualism and its method of spirit healings and a German doctor named Franz Mesmer who coined the phrase "animal magnetism" in reference to the healing method he promoted called Magnetism where he explained an "energetic fluid moved into and healed his patients." through the use of polarity of hands.

* In Umbria this fluid is called **iella.**

Photo above: The author giving a channeled healing like the Sardinian healer to the right.

LE MALEDIZIONI

TOXINS, VIRUSES, PARASITES

It is believed that negative energy can be sent out like a toxin which behaves like a virus, affecting the health of the target. The transference is psychic, or energetic, from one person's spirit to another's.

> *The psychiatrist Arthur Ghuirham states that hatred and violence release toxins, which cause organic diseases usually attributed to viruses [and...] points out the similarities between viral infections and the evil eye [...] : "In the current era, perhaps the most common physical disorder caused by contact with the energy of evil is virus infection in any of its various forms. In reality, many symptoms of such infections are caused not so much by viruses that can be isolated in the laboratory but by the effects of the toxins of hatred, violence and evil in general." The evil influence, often, originates from malevolent and envious people. Dr. Ghuirham, who has made in-depth studies on the subject, notes that: "One cannot fail to be struck by the contact points between the viral diseases of modern Western Europe and the effects caused by the bad eye - in tribal communities.* [493]

Technically, all **maledizioni** behave like viruses in the body. Viruses affect the body by attacking its cells as perfect parasites, where the body becomes the host, which is essential for the virus, just as it is for the spirit attachment:

> *[...] another living organism gives them everything they need to work. They get inside the host's cells and take it over. Viruses use the host cell's machinery to make lots of copies, so many that the cell bursts and infects other cells around it.* [494]
>
> *"Once a virus gets inside a cell, it hijacks the cellular processes to produce virally encoded protein that will replicate the virus's genetic material. Viral mechanisms are capable of translocating proteins and genetic material from the cell and assembling them into new virus particles. In either case, the genetic material of the virus has invaded the cell through the barrier of its membrane, and infection will inevitably follow."* [495]

In fact, it's not uncommon to find words sympathetic to this science within the curative prayers against **il malocchio**, for example:

> *"... pozza crepa"* [puddle crack]- used in a prayer from Umbria

and

> *"scoppi, scoppi, e crepi"* [bursts, bursts and cracks]- used in a prayer from Campania.

Italian Magic: Secret Lives of Women

Both prayers, among their rhyming phrases, describe bursting and cracking the evil eye (and its sympathetic representation as an oil eye drop) in a manner that is in keeping with its concept. Previously noted were the cord-cutting cures for spirit attachments who manifest illnesses in the intestines for which the sympathetic cure is to cut the strings symbolizing both the intestines and the energetic cords of connection. This is another version of the "melting of the knots" rituals that "undo" what has been done.

MAGNETISM

The dangerous hunger of desire when it turns to "wanting to own in some way" rather than to just admire is where the spirit influence finds a way in. The Italian philosophy on health that spirits abound, and that spirit attachments are a natural, although negative, occurrence. Envy is an energy (or in the positive, love and desire to help) that magnetizes similar energy towards whomever is generating it, summoning a greater supply of energy to work with. This belief is in line with the ever re-presented Law of Attraction that states everything is a vibration and is not only sending out signals of whatever energy is being generated, but that same energy is also magnetizing back to it a matching frequency.

Without disabling the spirit who sent the evil eye, or without cutting off the spirit attachment who is sending the evil eye through a human being, the evil eye cannot be remedied. This is where the effectiveness of the Lineage cures versus the popular traditions (or magically- tooled ones) differ dramatically. In the Lineage remedies, as mentioned before, there are spirit people (the higher conscious ones, the Divine Feminine ones), severing the connection to negativity, and who better to exorcise or "chase away" negative spirits than powerful spirits themselves?

Most Apotropaic Masks look like the early goddess carved faces with wide open eyes and mouths, even if they have been reinvented as other characters. "Italy's Witches and Medicine Women Vol 1" speaks of the Italian belief in the power of the eyes to channel energy. Photo: Davide Tiso 2020. Author's collection of amulets.

LE MALEDIZIONI

EYES

There is more to the concept "the eyes are the windows to the soul" than a poetic idea. The eyes give us the opportunity to see the world around us, but also for our souls (our spirit selves) to see the world...which means that as channelers we can learn to see the world through the eyes of spirit guides and helpers in a bigger picture way, to see and to have access to more information than we normally have access to. And also in the opposite direction, we can be the tool for negative spirits to view and attack potential victims. The eyes are doorways, and through these doorways energy can be summoned and transferred, positive and negative.

Envy is incited through the eyes, and envious spells are sent in a visionary way also, which is why there is a common belief about being careful to not cause envy from your neighbors by being "showy"; not bragging about fortune nor anything that differentiates yourself from someone else in a special, non-ordinary way. Deeper than this "idea" is the belief that the eyes can actually summon energy and send it out, casting spells on their own whose powers and effectiveness are increased due to the strength of the blood. So, the more a person is negatively focused, the stronger their **il malocchio**.

To illustrate the power of the eyes I'll share a quote by Tommaso Campanella that is also shared in "Italy's Witches and Medicine Women Vol 1" and was sourced from a book called "Sud e magia" by Ernesto De Martino about the rural poverty magic of Calabria:

> "The eye manifests a lot of magic things. When a man meets with another man, pupil-to-pupil, the light most bright of one blinds and destroys the man who cannot bear with it...and often brings to the surface passion of the lover, anger of the irate person...They say the Basilisk kills with the eyes, because poisonous spirits come out from them. Whomever likes something opens his eyes to a point where it seems that he wants to put that thing in his own eyes...To know it more and appreciate it more. And while he's opening them, often escaping out of his eyes are spirits that are eager to get that desired thing too." 496

The fascination is accomplished with the power of the psychic gaze, whether unintentionally or intentionally. In the case of the many cures for **il malocchio**'s psychic infliction, the poison is also the cure. The eyes have the power to emanate psychic fluid to harm and also to help. This belief has been wonderfully etched into ancient pottery, sculptures, protection masks and even Roman armor, beginning with the tradition of pre-pagan Goddess sculptures emphasizing the eyes and its fluids and from here developing into apotropaic masks and sculptures for defense and protection, such as the Medusa effigy.

The lacanomanzia traditions of curing with oil and water also engage with psychic sight and the sympathetic use of oil drops taking shapes like eyes, and this sympathetic parallel can be found in the many natural amulets used against **il malocchio**.

Italian Magic: Secret Lives of Women

SYMPTOMS OF IL MALOCCHIO

- Brain fog - a sense of losing time - listlessness - lack of energy - trouble focusing on things you love to do - a cloudy depression that comes from nowhere or as a creeping heaviness - seeing an impression of the person who sent it to you - an obsession with the sender (as in a love spell malocchio) - dizziness fever of unknown origin, other illness that has no explainable origin ("taking psychic hits"), quickness to irritability and frustration, clumsiness feeling stuck, headaches, kaposi sarcoma, loss of breast milk, vomiting, temporary paralysis, memory loss, generally.

In rural Italy this can also affect farm animals through paralysis, where an animal suddenly stiffens and falls over and cannot return to itself. It also causes sudden irritability and violent actions of farm animals, for example after a neighbor walks by and speaks aloud a backhanded comment loaded with envy. There are many documentations and testimonies of farm animals falling over with loads of wood on their backs and being frozen in a stiffened position, nothing being able to help the animals (even the rare veterinary visit) except for a remedy against **il malocchio**, after which they suddenly come to their selves again, back to their feet.

TRADITIONAL DIAGNOSIS FOR IL MALOCCHIO

+ looking inside pillows and couch cushions to see if braids or knots have formed there
+ seeing/sensing repeated impressions or thoughts of the sender (their face, name, etc).
+ feeling a sense of fear or alarm repeatedly
+ finding an out-of-place object in your home or yard area
+ receiving an email or letter or even a photo that is charged with energy such as anger or stalker-ish or creepy vibes from the sender that makes you feel very scared.
+ lacanomanzia diagnosis (using water with secret prayers and a combination of one or more of the following: oil, wheat grains, salt, gold rings, scissors charcoal, matches or twigs, spoons/forks/knives, hair, etc depending on the village tradition) to both diagnose and cure.

JETTATURA + THROWING THE GAZE

Traditional **jettature**:

+ naturally: in a naturally jealous, envious, narcissistic person, by summoning envy and focusing it onto a victim intensely, or unintentionally (subconsciously) focusing on someone else's fortune in a jealous.

+ naturally: passive-aggressive "smother mothers", jealous in-laws, usually with the help of spirit attachments drawn to the envious individual.

+ intentionally: by a magically practiced person, by focusing envy and other negative desires into an object and then throwing that spell in the intended victim's yard or garden; mailing a spell to their home; planting a spell in their house; etc. or on/near/

in the body of the target (physically); employing a spirit attachment's help to transfer the envy and destructive desires to a victim.

+ intentionally: putting a spell in the target's food or drink. The spell is simple: an object (stone, braid of victim's hair, knots, anything full of envious energy with intent to take away the target's success, abundance, happiness or health).

+ intentionally: using the eyes to summon negativity as an energy and sending it towards a visualized target.

Photo: Ottorino's diagnosis of the author's **il malocchio** (it was not present).

RIMEDI CONTRO IL MALOCCHIO
Remedies Against il Malocchio

As can be seen in the various names of il malocchio and its healers, the prevalent word used is "eyes". Il malocchio works its influence and vibration through sight, both physical vision and psychic vision. It can be sent directly (face-to-face with a person) or at a distance (through psychic visualization). Wherever your weaknesses are it will find its way in. So, if you are aware of your weaknesses, you already have an upper hand. Being aware of changes in your energy helps shift your energy already, and changing your vibration is also an antidote. For those who don't have the psychic know-how to do this, amulets (as prevention) and cures (as a solution) are available.

WATER + OIL

The cures use physical matter, psychic vision, channeled spirit energy, and secret

Italian Magic: Secret Lives of Women

words. Perhaps the most well-known cure is the use of olive oil and water. This method was already in use when the Romans began documenting the world around them.

The general method uses water as the conduit to receive psychic information about both the victim and the sorcerer of il **malocchio**. It is a diagnostic method and it is a cure at the same time. Oil is dropped into the plate of water in sympathetic connection to the shape of an eye. If il malocchio is present, the oil drops will shift into different shapes which give the healer information about who sent **il malocchio**, how many people sent it, the gender(s) of the **jettatura(e)**, and what aspects of the victim's life **il malocchio** is affecting. This procedure is repeated 3 times if **il malocchio** is present. The healer activates the procedure while quietly speaking the secret inherited prayer that activates the channeled energy that cures the condition and restores the victim's energy.

The cures for **il malocchio** are referred to as formulas like many inherited cures. These formulas, a combination of matter, actions and secret words that activate the curative energy being channeled, are inherited on a solstice or equinox in a ritualistic manner.

FORMULAS

+ A healer takes a plate, soup bowl, or cup and adds water. Some healers will move this plate across the head of the victim. Some healers will place it on the table in front of the victim, requiring the victim to watch the plate for the duration of the ritual.

+ Then, there are various preparations: some healers will mark the forehead of the victim with an equilateral cross (and/or also the ears, shoulders, sides of the face and chest). Some healers will mark the plate while saying the secret prayer while tapping the 3 corners of the plate (using a hand to mark an equilateral cross over the plate, touching down 4 points) and never touch the victim, using the plate as a simulacrum. Some healers first hold their hand over the plate of water while saying the secret prayer. The details vary from healer to healers.

+ Next, the healer will drop oil into the water. Some healers dip their finger into a cup of oil an drop one drop at a time. Some healers will pour in the oil from a jug. Some healers will pour spoonfuls of oil into the water.

+ The quantity of drops are made in odd numbers : 3 or 7, sometimes 9.

+ Then, the healer observes the drops to see if they spread wider in the water or begin to break up and reform or make other shapes and movements. If the drops remain the same size as they were when added to the water, **il malocchio** is not present. If they move, then the healer must repeat this process 2 more times for a total of 3 times, continuing to gather information as well as release the psychic connection between victim and **jettatura**.

+ An additional note: the inherited prayers that are whispered during the ritual are also repeated in repetitions of 3, 7 or 9. It's not uncommon to find a formula that consists of

LE MALEDIZIONI

more than one prayer, each repeated differently (one said 3 times, the other 7 times). Some prayers are like fragments of symbolic language, others are quite direct.

TREATMENTS

These formulas can release il malocchio from past lives that have carried into the present, they can work on headaches of the present moment, and they can find and release an il malocchio that is part of a family curse. Each healer has a formula for a specific il malocchio, and not all formulas work for all malocchi. Sometimes a healer may diagnose a victim and then send them to another healer based on what is found.

The signature of the occhi cures, and all inherited cures, is that they begin to release pain and suffering immediately. In most cases, one visit to a healer is enough, but in more severe cases, victims may need to return to the healer to receive the formula again. The formulas may repeated on the same day, or be spread out over a specific number of days decided by the healer.

FINISHING TECHNIQUES

Once a formula's repetitions are completed, the 3 rounds are finished off with a ritualistic action that cauterizes the psychic cut, ending the **occhi**'s effect. Some healers may:

+ place a hot ember from the fireplace into the water
+ stab the water with scissors
+ place scissors into the water while saying another secret prayer
+ make the hand gesture of the horns towards the water

...while some do nothing at the end.

CLOSURE

Once making **occhi** is completed, the water and oil must be disposed of. Traditionally the water and its contents are disposed of in an area where no one else can accidentally walk "step into" the negativity that has been released, such as down the kitchen sink, outside in an area where people do not walk, into or buried near a body of running water like a river, etc, with the exception of one commonly used location: a crossroads.

In contrast to the concept of preventing others from stepping in the negativity, in many villages throughout Umbria for example, a crossroads has been traditionally used to deposit the water and its contents. In rural Italy a crossroads consists of 3 singular paths or roads converging (and not 2 roads dissecting to make a 4-armed cross), which is a common formation in many other villages too. The crossroads was a place used for protection, for asking requests of different feminine divinities, but this was not the only reason a crossroads or public place was used: often water was disposed of here so that when the **jettatura** traversed this place, she would have to re-absorb the negativity she sent

Italian Magic: Secret Lives of Women

out (sending energy back to the sender).

SYMBOLIC LANGUAGE OF DIAGNOSIS

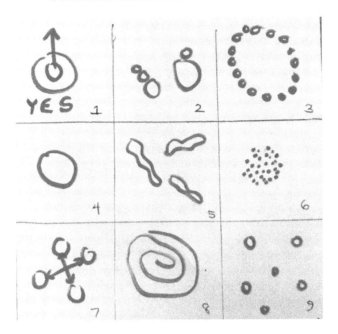

CHART KEY

1. If each drop spreads but remains in a circular shape, this means il malocchio is present.
2. If the drops break up and reconnect with smaller and smaller circles resembling an earring jewel, a woman and send the evil eye.
3. a necklace shape indicates a female jettatura.
4. oil drops that don't spread mean no evil eye is present.
5. serpent shapes indicate the intensity of the envy.
6. a cloudy mist of many tiny drops indicate the fractured mental state of the person who sent the evil eye.
7. drops that spread out and reconnect along straight paths indicate a group of people is gossiping about the victim.
8. a large serpent coil is similar to 5 and more info is needed.
9. Of course, each healer is able to read much more detailed information about the drops of oil with their particular skills, such as which aspect of your life the evil eye is trying to disrupt or destroy.

Among **segnatrici d'occhio** there is a common diagnostic language that may vary in its details but which generally finds the same encoded information. The most basic indicator of the presence of **il malocchio** is an oil drop(s) that spreads out into the water. From here, how it spreads, divides, reconfigures tells a healer more about who sent it and how long ago, how many people were involved, which lifetime, the gender(s) of the sender(s), and what aspect of a person's life is being targeted.

Some healers can discern if a past life was the beginning of an **il malocchio** and if it was sent by men, women, or a singular person. Some healers can discern if the victim's job or marriage is the focus of the envy. Healers can also discern the level of severity.

The basic shapes are: A circle represents a man. A circle that has divide and reconnected as 3 small circles of decreasing size is a woman. Circles that morph in some way (either a singular small circle that broke away and re-attached) or blob, either of which make it look like the oil drop is wearing a "hat" is considered masculine characteristic. Generally speaking, the shapes that are read are considered masculine or feminine based on the sympathetic parallel between masculine and feminine accessories found in rural Italy: necklaces, hats, watches, etc. They are the same shapes used in the divinatory traditions to determine the sex of the coming child (with spit and reading the shape of a pregnant woman's belly, breasts and buttocks).

The shapes that refer to an extreme danger are shapes that resemble serpents and skulls and also drops that have divided into an extremely large quantity of tiny drops, were almost the entire plate is covered by a fog film comprised of tiny oil drops.

WATER + WHEAT

Water and wheat are used in a similar manner to water and olive oil across Italy's mainland and the island of Sardinia. Similar preparations are made, with varying specifics: whether or not a healer will touch the victim and make marks on their head, forehead, neck, side of face, shoulders or chest. Some healers will use their thumb, some will make the sign of the horns, all before diagnosis.

SYMBOLIC LANGUAGE OF DIAGNOSIS

Generally, throughout the region of Umbria, when a grain or grains of wheat are placed into the water and remain vertical in the water, this means a male sent il malocchio. If the grain(s) of wheat lay horizontal in the water, then **il malocchio** is not present.

The quantity of grains used are from 1-11, always in odd numbers.

For some healers, *it is necessary that the seven grains of wheat have passed previously on the patient's body, an important detail, that shows how, in order to function, the grain or oil must be " loaded "with the energy of the person."* [497]

Italian Magic: Secret Lives of Women

Photo credit: Davide Tiso, 2020

CHART KEY [498]

Sex of the evil eye sender is determined by how the grains lay in the water. Vertical grain is a man, lying down in the water, a woman. For some readers, horizontal grains mean no evil eye is present, and vertical grains mean it is. Likewise if the tip of a grain has an air bubble, its considered an earring shape and therefore reveals a woman has sent the evil eye. If grains stay straight in the water like heads of snakes escaping the top of the water, then it means men were the senders of the evil eye.

CLOSURE

In Umbria, once the formula is completed, the water and its contents are disposed of in several ways: '*to be thrown into the street, part in the fire of the hearth, or [...] thrown part by road[...] or into the stove.* [499]

WATER + ANIMAL HORNS

Sardinian variations of **colpo d'occhio** cure by **majarzas**, special healers who also do works of magic, include a muflone horn, a young goat horn, and salt instead of oil in water. The diagnosis and curing procedures are similar to oil, water and wheat methods:

FORMULAS

Preparations are made, as with other **occhi** cures, varying from **majarzas** to **majarzas**. A piece of wild sheep horn or young goat horn and/or grains of salt are placed into a glass of water that is 3/4 full of water. Bubbles form around the horn and are read for information by the **majarzas**. Based on what she discerns from the bubbles, the **majarzas** quietly says secret prayers and/or makes marks on the victim's forehead face, etc. After saying the secret prayers, **is brebus**, the **majarzas** watches the bubbles to see if they lift off the bone and which patterns they make on the surface of the water. Their movement reveals whether or not the **colpo d'occhio** has been released, or if more formulas are needed.

LE MALEDIZIONI

SYMBOLIC LANGUAGE OF DIAGNOSIS

The part of the horn used had to be obtained from the middle area of the same, never from the tip, because this concave part could host **sa mala cosa** (the bad thing) which was instead what was wanted to be removed. 500 Bubbles moving away from the horn piece during recitation of the secret prayers indicated that **colpo d'aocchio** is being dissolved. Some **majarzas** also add grains of coarse salt to the water and discern information from their movements.

CLOSURE

There are varying closure rites for the formulas: some **majarzas** throw out the water. Others have the victim drink sips of the water containing the bone, similar to what is done in some psychic fear cures. Others **majarzas** have the victim face the sun *with its vivifying warmth, would have "dried up" the power of the curse.* 501 In Sardinian **sa mexina**, directions (facing east, facing towards or away from the sun, moon phases, times of day) are essential parts of cures.

L'ACQUA MEDAGLIA
Medallion Water

Photo: Davide Tiso, 2020

Medallion water is a cure found in Sardinia, Emilia Romagna, the Veneto, Tuscany and many other places. It uses water, coarse salt, wheat grains, **segnare** scoring and inherited secret words and an inherited medallion with a saint or Madonna on it. In the rural world of inherited cures, specific formulas exist for specific versions of illness, so **l'acqua medaglia** is unusual in that it's considered universal medicine. It can be used on various illnesses that affect farm animals, crop germination problems, car troubles, and it

Italian Magic: Secret Lives of Women

is also used against **il malocchio.** In regards to **il malocchio** it is both a diagnostic tool and a cure. It is considered a **terapia magica** magic therapy.

FORMULA

The healer takes a glass of water and places it in front of the victim. Next to the glass: 3 piles of salt and 3 piles of wheat: *"salt represents the sea, and the wheat represents the earth."*502 The healer makes the sign of the cross over the water (scoring it/marking it) and says the inherited words or religious phrases, asks the name of the victim, then throws 3 heaps of salt into the water. *

SYMBOLIC LANGUAGE OF DIAGNOSIS

If the salt makes a specific sound when it's dropped into the water, this means **il malocchio** is not present and the victim needs to see a doctor. Based on the way the salt moves in the water, the healer can still "read" details about the illness, pregnancy, or whatever is affecting the health. * If the salt makes no sound as it falls in the water, **il malocchio** is present. Then the healer will throw into the water the 3 heaps of wheat. And, based on bubbles around the salt and wheat and how they moves in the water, the healer can "read" details about **il malocchio.** Victims will begin to stretch their arms and legs while the cure it taking place* paraphrased from "I Guaritori di Campania" by Paola Giovetti.

THE KEY TO THE CURE

If **il malocchio** is present, the healer will score/mark the victim with secret words, in particular numerical repetitions. It's words which open up diagnosis for **il malocchio** and it's words which release **il malocchio.** The scoring is done with words whispered in odd numerical repetitions.

CLOSURE

Some healers may hold the glass of water over the victim's head while scoring them.

AT A DISTANCE

If the formula has been done for an animal or person who is not physically present, then the healer will say the secret words, then give some part of the ingredients to a stand-in person to transport back to the victim. If a farmer has come to get help for an animal who has il malocchio, the healer may give the farmer the medallion water to sprinkle onto the animal.

If a relative has come from someone in their family, the healer will perform the ritual and then take the grains of wheat and give them to the relative who must *put it on him, for example in his pocket. So he heals.* 503 In other words, this is a curative action sympathetic to how **il malocchio** is thrown at some people: energy must be transferred and then given to the victim secretly to cure. The **jettatura** changes something with envy and then sneaks it into the home or body of a victim. *

WATER + WHEAT + SALT

I am looking at where they go to put the salt and the wheat: if they put themselves up, on the long arm of the cross , it means that the person has a mask on his head and chest, if they go on the short arms of the cross, it means that the evil eye is on the arms, if they go down it is from the waist down.

For his formula, a healer uses a glass half-full with water, three grains of salt, and three grains of wheat. The healer will throw the salt and the wheat into the water, making a cross across the water with his hand with each toss, saying the inherited words. The healer watches where the grains go and can determine, from these movements, where on the body **il malocchio** has attached. Then, the healer can say secret words to release it. *

KEY: Above photo: grains indicate il malocchio is present on head and chest of victim.
Right top: grains indicate il malocchio is present on arms of victim.
Right bottom grains indicate il malocchio is present on legs or somewhere below the waist.
*paraphrased from "I Guaritori di Campania" by Paola Giovetti.

BRIEF LIST OF OCCHI VARIANTS

SARDINIA : appealing to the spirit world of saints believed in by the victim, using polarity of hands, aka "laying of hands" while saying secret words.

EMILIA ROMAGNA: water, match sticks, thread, secret words.

EMILIA ROMAGNA, LIGURIA : copper pot, secret words, pins in lamb heart.

SICILY: gold ring, olive oil, marks made with hands, secret words.

SICILY: terra cotta tile suffumugio with plants, secret words.

TUSCANY: use sprigs of heather (calluna vulgaris) to mark victim's body, then bathe in water. The ritual is repeated 3 times on the first night, 6 on the second, using 18 different branches, after which they are burned and with a broom sweeping the doorstep: *"With the broom sweeping away the evil, with the fire it burns out another fire."* [504]

CAMPANIA: olive oil, water, secret prayer, hold plate over head of victim.

CAMPANIA: The healer uses a kitchen butter knife and marks it with crosses and secret words. The healer then throws the knife on the ground in front of the victim and then moves it 3 times making the sign of the cross. Finally he takes the knife and, once again 3 times, passes it on the head of the person with headache, without touching it and making other crosses. [505]

AT A DISTANCE

This medicine can also be done at a distance: The healer does the formula on the knife and wraps it well in a cloth or a piece of paper, and gives it to the person who has need. They will then take care of making the crosses and the various words. No one else should touch the knife, under penalty of the disappearance of all virtues. [506]

And there are many more variants and formulas than have been documented. These traditions are not written down and they are generally not advertised.

PRAYERS

Some prayers against **il malocchio** can be found in print. In the case of the 2 included here, they are prayers that are retired, meaning that the healers allowed their interviewers to know them because they were the last healers in their line, they did not pass on their borrowed power to anyone in ritual transmission, so the prayers are no longer charged nor used.

PRAYER FROM: Castelluccio di Norcia, Umbria *
This prayer is a ritual closing formula, recited aloud, folding the fingers of both hands to form the "horns" and directing them towards the plate containing water and oil:

> "S'e de bene,
> pozza dura',
> s'e de male,
> pozza crepa."
> [507]

*Collected by Fabiola Chavez Hualpa in her book "Le Donne nel mondo rurale della Valnerina"

PRAYER FROM: Guardia Sanframondi, Campania *

"Fuggi, fuggi, "occhio" funesto, che or passa Gesu Cristo!
Gesu Cristo e passato, gli "occhi" malvagi sono scoppiati!

occhio, malocchio! scoppi, scoppi, e crepi, scoppi e crepi l'invidia e il malocchio,

Fuggi fuggi "occhio" funesto, che in tre ti hanno visto,
e in tre ti hanno guardato, scoppi adesso questo malocchio."

"Flee, flee, fatal "eye" which now passes Jesus Christ!
Jesus Christ is past, the evil "eyes" have burst!

LE MALEDIZIONI

"Eye," evil eye! bursts, bursts, and cracks, bursts and cracks envy and the evil eye
Flee flee fatal "eye", which in three have seen you, and in three have looked at you,
now this evil eye breaks out."

**Collected by Silvio Falato in his book "Ce steva 'na vota...Janare-lupi mannari- filastrocche-indovinelli"

DIFESE CONTRO IL MALOCCHIO
Defenses Against The Evil Eye

Defensive actions taken against il malocchio fall into a few categories: protection of the home using nature and iron; protection of the body using amulets and breve or punga; and using salt to neutralize the fascinator / jettatura.

Coarse salt is an important ingredient used to prevent **il malocchio** and it is commonly kept in a bowl on the windowsill, to prevent, or to filter out, envy. It's common to throw salt into the street where a **jettatura** is walking, if it is suspected she just threw the **il malocchio** at someone. Some people even throw a small amount of salt onto animals they fear are experiencing **il malocchio.**

Dog skulls filled with oil were also kept on the windowsills in some villages of Umbria.

There are natural amulets, jewelry amulets, and protective pouches that are included in he AMULETS chapter, so they will not be included here.

LA FATTURA

La Fattura (singular) literally means invoice or bill. **La fattura** is a spell made using a simulacrum: a sympathetic double / substitute for someone else's body combined with destructive words and intentions often carried out with the help of malignant spirits.

Generally, healers in rural Italy undo **le fatture**, but also, as with the **majarzas** of Sardinia, the **majare** of Sicily, the **janare** of Campania for example, most know the art of making them as well as undoing them. Other names for **le fatture** used in Sardinian dialect are: **mazzinas**. Fattura-breakers share the same names with fattura-makers, in the same way healers and those who throw sickness at others do.

Like an invoice or bill, the **fattura** wants to be paid: its energy invades the victim through the heart center and anchors there as well as in the knees and ankles and drains the energies of the body rapidly. The foci of **le fatture** tend to be: money, bodily organs, eroticism of a love target, and death, and they are feared for their power to do so. It is believed **fatture** are much more difficult to undo, because: the sender must be discovered, the malignant spirit(s) must also be exorcised, and the simulacrum must be found and undone within 7 days. Healers who make **controfatture** (marks/scores/signs against
274

Italian Magic: Secret Lives of Women

fatture) are found in communities less and less as time moves on.

While **il malocchio** affects mostly the emotional, spiritual, and mental realms, **le fatture** aim to bring immense and endless damage to the victim's physical body.

FORMULAS

The formula of a **fattura** is based on the reverse of a cure: instead of pulling out an illness, it puts in energy that will cause illness and decay. The formula of **la fattura** is to put something inside of; to invade and to anchor negative, destructive energy inside of another person's body that will continue to deteriorate the victim to the point of death. **Le fatture** work through psychic vibration to affect physical matter, mostly of the body.

The formula uses ingredients that create a body-like form: a double sympathetic version of the victim on which to inflict damage (inserting pins, stuffing with hair, tying off vital energy, etc.). It is then charged with destructive action words that are energetically infused into the mental aspect of the spells (i **scongiuri**) and often also physically written down and inserted into the puppet, (**puppia**) creating a psychic cord of connection.

Then the poppet is placed into the vicinity of the victim: either thrown into yard of victim, or a **fattucchiera** will visit the victim under false pretenses of a friendly visit with the secret purpose of hiding the poppet somewhere inside the victim's house or balcony or yard. In the case of an edible **fattura** or **filtre** the **fattucchiera** will try to get themselves invited for a meal and slip the **fattura** into the food or drink of the victim.

If the **fattucchiera** cannot get close to the victim, malignant spirits can be worked with to transport the **puppia** into the victim's home, usually in a place humans can't reach such as inside a sealed wall or inside a sealed couch or bed cushion.

The ingredients depend on the surroundings and whatever grows there and can include fabric and wool or stuffing, cork, plant stems with spikes to form a cross of the body, plant leaves to be sewn in lieu of fabric, pins or thorns or nails, hair of the victim, live toads, lemons, clay pots with lids, wax, photographs instead of poppet, clothing from the victim, food scraps with the saliva of the victim, liquid filters or ash.

Some fatture are not even brought into the vicinity of the victim and are instead secretly put in a public place where nature can act as the means to carry out the spell.

SYMBOLIC LANGUAGE OF FATTURA CURSES:

The desired result of a **fattura** is enacted on a simulacrum (double of the victim's body) in sympathetic parallel: If the goal is to kill a victim through choking or emaciation, an act will be done to the throat of the poppet, such as stuffing a frog with a big wad of the victim's hair so it can't eat and will starve. If **la fattura** aims to harm a bodily organ, that intent is pinned into the **puppia**. If the simulacrum is a death candle, **la fattura**'s effects will take place as the candle is melting and its effects will be completed when the candle has burned itself out, with physical death soon to follow. If an item of clothing is being used, as it rots buried under soil, so will the victim's body rot in parallel. If **la fattura** is made to obsess a desired lover or get rid of one, it will have that intended result.

Notice that all these actions: using a double, infusing it with energy, commanding energy with words that describe actions...are all the basic formulas of cures, just perverted to harm instead of heal.

PRAYERS

Prayers of **le fatture**, or charged spell words (**i scongiuri**), interestingly are built on top of curative prayers. Some are built with exact prayer structures, just with words altered to negative intentions. For a Sicilian example, please see Love Magic page.

AT A DISTANCE

Malignant spirits are always involved in **le fatture** (in the opposite way helpful spirits are invoked to cure) to transfer negative energy to victim, and sometimes the malignant spirits actually transport **la fattura** behind the walls of a home or inside some structure or pillow or mattress, usually in a place a human being can't get to (because it's sealed etc). In the cases of using live toads or lizards and simulacrum they are placed into terracotta bowls with lids and left to die there, having been psychically tied to the human victim who is also withering away during this time. Also, sometimes sympathetic spells are created out in a public space so they can use the flow of nature to harm and kill.

CLOSURE

While beliefs vary, it is generally agreed that there is a 7 day window from the time **la fattura** is set into motion during which a victim can discover this, locate it or reveal **la fattucchiera**, and find someone to undo the curse.

Italian Magic: Secret Lives of Women

The name **fattucchiera** means a person who makes the **fattura** (curse). Other Sardinian names are **bruxas** and **coga**, keeping in mind that the same names are often used for people who practice the art of undoing spells and curses. Other Sardinian names for **puppia** are: **pippia, buatedda, maghia, mazzina** and in Umbria's Valnerina **lu pupazzu.** [508]

A particularly feared bill used the victim's hair and a toad. The hair was inserted into the toad's throat which, being unable to eat, gradually deteriorated to death. The victim of the bill followed the fate of the toad. The bill with the toad expected the unfortunate batrachian to be closed in a crock-like pinecone pot which was buried in a secret place. As the toad decayed, the victim showed a clear, parallel deterioration. The death of the invoice victim coincided with that of the toad. [509]

In Paterno (Vallo di Nera) to make an invoice to death, a toad was placed in a crock pot together with the victim's personal effects and a photo of himself. The toad died of starvation and, with him, the victim of the bill. Or, a used garment belonging to the victim was put to rot somewhere causing death. [510]

On the Leonessian plateau, we documented an invoice case in which a toad was used. The victim of the crime was a boy. The toad was locked inside a little box that was heavy on the rope to hang the laundry. The victim remained motionless most of the time doing only small movements, corresponding to those made by the toad forced into the jar. If the toad died, the boy would also have died. [511]

In Monteleone, a woman victim of invoice [...]-she vomited her hair. It was cured by the parish priest in the church of St. Nicholas through an exorcism. [512]

A woman who was struck was healed thanks to the intervention of a specialist **sdregone** *and, at the same time in which was marked to be freed, vomited some oranges: the vehicle through which she had ingested the bill.* [513]

Examples above published in 2009 by Mario Polia dated from the 1950s. *The sorceresses made rag dolls with words written on and with or threw them into the garden of those they wanted to hurt.* [514]

A lady named Maria Grazie had her friend tried to find a "doll" in all the corners of her house. [and he saw...] at the bottom, well hidden, a rag doll completely covered with pins, a sign that this bill had been made with great hatred, precisely to cause death. So her friend had spread the doll representing her and, kneeling, he had begun to make signs in the air by reciting prayers, prayers and certain responses that only she knew, occasionally tearing a pin from the doll's body, and in less than half an hour [...] once the bill was paid [undone], Maria Grazia could have sat down without feeling any pain [that she had felt due to the doll]. 515

Sometimes a death bill used a specially prepared and ritually lit candle: as it burnt out, the candle would transmit the consensus to the victim.

LOVE MAGIC
LA MAGIA AMOROSA

Love magic is comprised of a combination of courtship rituals, divinations, and food magic along with some unpleasant magic, such as **legature** bindings and **fatture** poppets here called **lu pupazza** which don't end well for the targets.

In these communities where women could expect to marry one person for life, there was a lot of pressure on finding or choosing the right man. Compatible marriages are serious business in this type of community. The eyes of the community were also watching the women especially, so it was in her best interest to have the man she desired and to deter anyone in pursuit of her she does not want. Supernatural forces were often looked to for assistance in these matters. Plants and egg yolks were consulted for divination purposes and Madonnas and saints were asked to bring about compatible partnerships.

As with curative traditions that look magical, magic for partnerships uses the same set of procedures found in the curative rituals and similar ingredients: words as prayers, rhymes and invocations, knotted string, doubles, plants, objects to transfer or transform energy, bodily fluids, and **scongiuri**.

Community rituals, which won't be examined here in detail, revolve around declarations of love, food magic, courtship rituals, amulet presentation, dances, dowry transfers, and other community announcement type traditions. The two that bear mentioning in this collection due to their connections to the other rituals included in this book are: Courtship Food Magic, the Broom Dance, and the Mirror Dance. Community dances in general were very important for these communities as ritualistic celebrations.

The Broom Dance itself called **il ballo della scopa** on the central mainland, and generally the dance is a ritual for partner-picking: *a boy, holding a broom, addressed the girl he wanted to dance with by reciting an invitation rhyme: "Questo e' 'l ballo de la sala, non so se ballo bene, se (nome della ragazza) non ce vene, que sto ballo 'n se po fa". If the girl accepted, she passed the broom to another boy who, in the same way, repeated the invitation by addressing another girl,* 516 although in some villages it was the girls who invited the boys. The dance choices were not necessarily courtship choices.

The Mirror Dance itself is called **il ballo dello specchio.** In the Mirror Dance, the girl sat holding a mirror in her hand. The boy who invited her to dance stood behind her so

Italian Magic: Secret Lives of Women

he could be seen in the mirror. If the girl liked the invitation, she placed the mirror and got up to dance; otherwise, she made the gesture of erasing the image with her hand as you do on the blackboard, turned the mirror and remained seated. 517

The Dance of the Sigh, **il ballo del sospiro** was one where the girl asked her ancestors to pronounce the name of her choice of boy along with a rhyming request that if her choice did not then come invite her, that the dance would stop. 518

The Food Magic courtship ritual is one of transformation of natural items, which is also a process used in other food magic. **L'ammorda** ritual "the bundle" is one where a young man presents a young woman he's romantically interested in marrying with "the bundle"; a gift to her consisting of a handkerchief full of pears with the 4 corners tied in knots[...] *if the young woman accepted the gift, the following Sunday she prepared a sweet cake and, together with the young man who presented it to her, attended a dance party which, in this way, sanctioned the engagement.* 519

Food is used in many transformative ways for love magic: as a transformation representing union, in transformations requesting fertility, and as a secret way to control someone else's desires. Generally Love Magic consists of **scongiuri**, **legature** and **filtri:** word spells, bindings of one person to another in various ways and liquids.

INTENTIONAL DREAMING

Madonna de la Stella, a Madonna invoked for safe travels during journeys with poor visibility due to weather conditions, is also prayed to for divination assistance. Regarding desired love, she was loved as "the polar star", a guiding light from above. For example, *the girls of Scheggino (Perugia, Umbria) asked the polar star to make sure that they dreamed of the future husband. To this end, for 13 evenings in a row, they left the house and, looking up at the star, said: "Stella bella, polar star in 13 nights let me dream of the first love I have to marry".* 520

Other dream rituals used by young women were to place the confetti (sugar covered almonds) *under the pillow, convinced that her future husband would be presented to her in a dream.* 521

I SCONGIURI

I Scongiuri are spells with words and while they can be spells for protection against thieves from coming in your home, protection from illness, spells for fortune or healing or exorcism, there are soncgiuri used to harm someone else, such as a scongiuroiused with a fattura or for love bindings. They tend to be built upon the exact same structure as curative prayers and spells, but twisted into a negative.

LE LEGATURE

Le legature means "the ligatures", as in something to tie or bind; bindings. Knots are used to bind in both cures and in magic. The method of magical bindings used in love magic is based on the knots used in cures for twisted muscles, sprains, etc. Whereas in cures knots tie up the illness to stop it from continuing, knots have been perverted into negative magic to either tie someone to a lover or to tie them apart.

LE MALEDIZIONI

I FILTRI

Filtres are liquid spells: filtri d'amore, often made with menstrual blood. They can also contain burned and liquified items slipped into the drink or food of an intended victim. Some examples:

+ In some places in central Italy, for example, it was common for a young woman to use menstrual blood in food for casting a love spell on a desired target and binding them to her. In the way the courtship pears tradition of transforming food was done in Umbrian villages, menstrual blood was used to transform food into something extra, adding it along with spell words and baking it into something edible like a desert that would then be gifted to the targeted lover of the spell who would consume its energy and then turn towards her with attraction.

+ For this same reason, menstrual blood was also used in coffee and then given to the target of affections.

+ Binding a person to oneself was done using a string or cord into which words are spoken and intention to bind the lover to a person is represented by each knot. A prayer is used describing the action, such as this published one from Sicily presented earlier: *"Cristo e'nato, Cristo e'morto, Cristo e'resuscitato, protami il tizio, che lo ho legato"*.

    This **scongiuro** uses similar ideas to curative prayers including numerology, description of action, and structure and translates to: *"Christ was born, Christ died, Christ rose again, bring me the guy that I bound/ tied up"*.

+ **Le legature** were also created in reverse, so as to break up couples or turn spouses against each other.

+ When a young woman rejected one man for another whom she decided to wed, the community made a poppet, in this case called **lu pupazzu** and hung it on the door or window of the rejected young man for all to see. This has been documented by Mario Polia in Umbrian villages such as Avendita, Leonssa, Valnerina, and others. **Lu pupazzu** was made out of clothes that belonged to the scorned man, and lu pupazzu was also arranged in a way that signaled the end of his relationship often with the poppet holding a bent sickle *that is, bent to suggest the cut of the neck.* 522 It was a type of community mocking that also protected the newly aligned couple, showing the rejected man that everyone knew about the change of events.

+ Another community ritual done to rejected lovers *the night before the wedding, the young villagers scattered a long trail made up of straw, ash, lime and sulfur that united the door of the house of the scorned [...] to the door of the new bridegroom* as well as hanging garlic *to neutralize the effects of envy towards those who had the chance to crown their dream of love on the altar* [the new couple about to wed]. 523

And then, we have the hair **legatura,** one greatly feared in the rural community. So great care was taken to gather all shed hair so no one else could use it in a spell.

HAIR

Hair has significance in rural Italy. It has its place among protective beliefs, it's used in black magic, and it's used to send messages. It even takes up prominent space in so-called folk tales, whose reality is often manifested in rural life and not merely mitigated to the pages of stories in books.

Community beliefs about moon phases documented in Umbrian territories are that:

-luna crescente*, or growing moon, favors the growth of plants, hair, fleece; promotes the concentration of sap in plants, trees and fruits*
...and the...
-luna calante *or waning moon delays and decreases* these same things. 524

These beliefs are followed when cutting hair of people and sheep (along with wood and plants as well):

The general rule was the following: by cutting the hair in the waning phase, they would slowly grow back; by cutting them in the growing phase, the moon would have propitiated their growth with their own power. 525

Natural caretaking of hair included using egg yolks, castor oil, bone marrow of a calf (which is also used to cure skin burns), massaged into the hair and scalp, and washed with wine and nettle-infused water. 526

HAIR

A curious tradition of eliminating lice from San Felice *was to sprinkle warm olive oil on the scalp. The empirical method (also used to free pets from ticks) was based on the fact that the oil prevented the parasites from changing the air: so that animals died.* [527]

Oil and hair find their way into other curious supernatural stories of Janare witches, horses and night flights. A common story regarding hair in Campania is about the Janare witches: *the Janare witches were known to take peoples' horses at night to ride to the* **Sabba**.[528] In Patrizia's testimony from 2015 in Guardia Sanframondi, *she said that while this is a folk tale, it happened to her family:*

> *"Every night that the witches would meet, they would take my grandfather's horse. He was convinced they took the horse to reach Sabba (witches' sabbath). He noticed it because every night when they returned his horse it had a braided tail. He tried almost his whole life to capture the Janare who were braiding his horse's hair, but he never did. My mother (who is now 70 years old) remembers this because she was the youngest child in the family and her duty was to unbraid the horse tail, because it was considered a shame if you put out your horse with a braided tail. So every morning she had to unbraid the horse's tail. My grandfather solved the problem by selling his horse.".* [529]

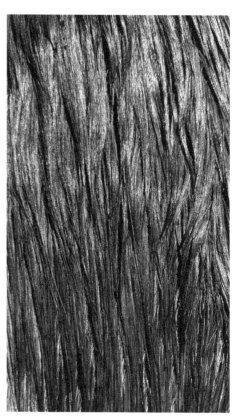

It was also common to find the horses oiled and sweating, sometimes frightened along with the braids. What's interesting about the oiling is that in Umbria oil has traditionally been used to kill fleas on animals, so the oil is used as a helpful, curative tool. It's therefore possible the oil was put on horses to help them during the night, and not to harm them. This possibility comes from a comparison with "night time braid" history in Sicily:

Braids, or rather tangled dreads called **trizzi** in Italy appear on horses and children, having suddenly appeared during the night. The common fear-inducing folk tales also exist here, with some stories claiming it's the **Majare**, the Sicilian version of **Janare**, at night accused of being shape-shifting malevolent witches whose spirits fly into homes to harm children. Yet there are equally as many sotries, if not more, about the **trizzi** being a gift from benevolent female spirits who also make the babies laugh and

282

protect their health (and that of horses too) with these gifted tangled **trizzi.** While trizzi are dreads, the braids are more like a fishtail knotted braid than a cleanly plaited braid.

> *"The **trizzi di donna** were a manifestation of the benevolence of the home Patruneddi."* 530
>
> (from Castelvetrano, province of Trapani).

> *"They made **trizzi di donna** to children; it was like a gift, to embellish them, to make them similar to themselves[...]. If cut, the children die; you have to wait for them to fall on their own* [the trizzi knots]." 531

Traveling a bit deeper into the Sicilian stories, we find groups of night time feminine spirits who've all been woven into the "night-time witch myth" and yet have specific and different roles from each other.

Most notably related to hair are the **Patruneddi**, the name given housewives in spirit form who bear some similarities with the **Donne di Fuora**, (a group of spirit-helper type guides who give abundance to mothers such as: divination methods, curative methods, and other knowledge that can improve daily life) but the comparison is only a distant one.

The **Donne** are respected as supernatural goddess provider figures in the way **La Signora del Gioco** is on the mainland (and the way the queen of the Faeries is on the island of Sardinia) which is still far different from the Romanized Goddesses who are part of binary marriages, demoted to wives of gods, and who were remodeled into war supporters and diviners for warring conquests. The **Patruneddi**, **Donne di Fuora** and **La Signora del Gioco** assist and teach women outside of temples in daily life settings.

The Patruneddi are considered by many to be the spirits of housewives who previously lived in the houses they now haunt, and that they mean no harm to the children and in fact often entertain them:

Translation of a **filastrocche** nursery rhyme in dialect:

> *"When you slept, I love you more, this sleep to my daughter comes and goes; and in their sleep they make her laugh certain ladies, whom I cannot name."*

HAIR

Photos: @Benedicaria facebook. Trizzi on Sicilians. Photo right: shot bt Andre Martin and published in the essay "Spreco" by Danilo Dolci, published by Einaudo in 1960.

> *In most cases **li donni** just wanted to play with the children, and to leave a mark of their presence at night they stroked them on the head. These fairy caresses left on the heads of the children one or more braids that in the morning could no longer be untangled in any way. Wise mothers knew that this was a sign of protection and never cut them for any reason! They waited for the tangled hair to fall on their own, which is why it was normal to see adults with these **trizzi*** 532 *mostly in Sicily.*

As with all rural folk tale sounding supernatural illness or occurrences, there exist also the people who cure or undo these things. And so there are women called to whisper their secret prayers and quickly undo the braids. But many people leave them in, fearing revenge from the spirits:

> *It is said that children whose mothers cut the braid grew out of grace, sickly, unlucky, or even died ...[ ] There are tales of horses that lived up to later age precisely because of these braids left intact (Sambuca, province of Agrigento).* 533

Lest anyone try to relegate these experiences to the past, here is a recent testimony:

> *We are in 2019 [and] some skeptics will think [...]surely these stories will seem bizarre or ignorant[...]I confide that my brother*

Italian Magic: Secret Lives of Women

also woke up one morning with his hair knotted and braided in a
way that human hands could not have done. At the time (he was
about 3 years old) he had beautiful long hair that came down from
the nape. Well, all the back locks were knotted and collected [...]
To untie him, a "night woman" from Belpasso had to operate, who
picked up my brother and recited some magic words, untangled his
hair in an instant." 534

FEAR OF FATTURE BY THE HAIR

The knotted hair used by **Patrenuddi** to protect health is a type of spell, a helpful one. In general however, women in rural areas kept an eye on their fallen hairs due to beliefs that they could be used by enemies in **fatture** and **mazzine** binding spells which sought to kill, break apart marriages, and more. Touching children on the head was also seen as suspect and was avoided. In direct hair envy,

The fascination could directly affect an abundant and lustrous hair
so that, amo ng women who knew they could boast such a privilege,
*the use of red laces was not infrequent.*535 Red laces and string have
a protective function.

Love binding spells and **fatture** in general often used stolen hairs of the targeted victims as a powerful force in these spells that was already linked to the person who was targeted by the spell. Knotted hair was not only used to tie a desired lover to a person, but to also "tie apart" a married or dating couple and causing enough emotional inner turmoil to break them up. In love pells of a revenge nature, a knotted hair **fattura** could kill a person unless the right sorceress or sorcerer could find and undo the *fattura*: *The bill* **[fattura]** *was particularly striking for the girl who left her boyfriend.* 536 Other spells intended to kill a lover who scorned the one who desired him used stolen items of clothing from the scorner and combined with **socngiuri**, were left to rot somewhere, tied to the energy of the scorner and as they rotted, the target of the spell would also deteriorate and die a physical death. This was also done with candles, using the action of melting away to take away the relationship/the love/the life. In the case of relationships, melted wax was used to seal the material items used intentionally with the **socngiuri** and names of targets.

+   To make someone fall in love: Menstrual blood was slipped into the desired target's coffee or food having prepared the spell using a **scongiuri** formula such as *"You will be mine, I am crazy [in love] about you, and you are crazy [in love] about me"*. Or these similar words were used while secretly burning stolen hair of the targeto r combing/ scraping through their hair, which is equivalent to burning, secretly saying words such as *"stay in love, crazy thing"*. 537

+   To turn someone's affections away: Hair is secretly stolen from the person and then burned while saying a formula like this one from Umbria *"You will no longer love me, you will no longer love me for a lifetime"*538 **Tu non mi amerai piu, to non mi amerai piu per tutta la vita***.* Then the ashes of the burned hair must secretly be

285

dropped on the head of target while reciting another prayer about the act of forgetting. 539

+ Breaking of Fatture: It's not uncommon for people to vomit hair and the food it was consumed with after a fatture is broken by a sorcerer. But if that fatture is not broken, it's also common to remain ill or die.

+ Wearing a fatture: Some love spells were created and then worn daily like a piece of jewelery by the person who created it, ensuring no one could break it and keeping its energy circulating in the village.

+ When someone asked a sorceress to cast a love spell to bind their desired man to them, and personal items such as clothing could not be stolen, it was enough to gather soil or earth that they'd walked upon to have a personal link to their energy to use in the spell.

+ Tangles. In the same way knots and tangles were avoided during pregnancy to keep any harm from the baby through a similar action with the umbilical cord, women also avoided making unintended knots or tangles while doing a spell to bind someone else to a person *"in order not to 'tie' (kneading, making impotent) their own man, or other family man."*

+ For some love spells the method used was to take a blessing or love decoration and, while focusing on the couple the sorceress intended to break-up, used them in reverse: so reciting the words in reverse or undoing the decoration.

+ Photographs of a desired love or targeted scorn revenge or targeted couple to break-up were also used in love spells.

+ *To verify the presence of the evil eye, it was used to pull out the wool of the cushions (or the hen feathers of the filling) and examine if there were any braids.* 540

> *The women of the past avoided leaving their hair fallen or lying on the comb around: they threw it on fire for fear that someone would use them to their detriment.* 541

And, ghosts were also appealed to for assistance with black magic against the will of someone else, as with a love spell. Among the different types of souls that were believed to exist in the astral realm the "addicted souls" of the deceased were called upon of-ten *accompanied by the sacrifice of an animal performed near a cemetery.* 542 The name for these types of sorceresses or sorcerers is **sdregoni** which translates to both witches and "scoundrels." 543

In Valnerina [Umbria], moreover, the women also took care not to abandon their hair in the water because they believed they would turn into snakes, which is similarly found *in Peru, the women of the Andean communities, after having washed their hair in the water of the stream, carefully collect the fallen ones because they are firmly convinced*

Italian Magic: Secret Lives of Women

that, if left in the water, they would transform in serpentines. 544

Braids and **trizzi** are not far from the idea of **legatura** binding which can be used both positively and negatively. Knots and braids can hold an intentional charge, and this is a consistent idea found throughout rural beliefs from birth traditions to spirit world interactions, in spells and bread magic.

> *Favorable terrain for the proliferation of magical practices was the persistence, in the rural class, of an ancestral culture still deeply imbued with faith in magic, in addition to the competitiveness that of necessity is triggered in small groups exposed to precariousness and poverty in which individuals are forced to make limited choices mainly within the group they belong to, as often happened in love relationships. In any case, magic offered an indirect and secret method of intervention - but not considered less effective for this - in cases where direct intervention was impossible, problematic, or dangerous.* 545

Historically speaking, the noctural occurrence of horses manes being braided has also been documented in other parts of Italy (north) and other European countries near north Italy where **La Signora del Gioco**, Diana as a fairy, **Matronae** and other feminine abundance figures such as Abundia were known to visit mountaintop villagers.

It's important to note that these female divinities were considered gracious, loving, and mostly providers of abundance to poor people as well as protectresses of the weak. They were known for their blessings bestowed, not for evil acts of terror. These divinities had strong reputations before Romanization and have no connection to the Romanized Diana as a huntress of animals and war supporter. Specifically, they were helpers, high quality miracle-worker helpers.

They were repoted as appearing as white vespers, sometimes young and in groups of 3 beings, sometimes alone. Often they were carrying white candles whose flames could be seen, and they allowed the wax from their candles to drip onto horse manes. They then braided the horse hair. From this perspective, it can be made more clear that the appearance of braids and **trizzi** were knotted/woven/bindings of good fortune.

DIVINATION

Types of DIVINATIONS in rural Italy:

Naturally, the subjects of query that rural divinations are used for have to do with rural life concerns, just as our various contemporary divination modalities do the same for us.

- to find lost or stolen items
- to find out a love match or willing husband or an unfaithful lover
- to know coming year's details for family and farm
- to know the sex of a to-be-born baby
- to determine health or outcome of illness
- to determine abundance or lack of the coming year's crops
- to diagnose **il malocchio** and reveal the sender

IRON KEY DIVINATION / MANTIC RITUAL WITH THE DEAD

Photo: Davide Tiso, 2020.

Iron Key Divination: Ferentillo, Umbria
Purpose: To discover who was responsible for a betrayal of love or a theft.
Tools: + iron key + church book (such as a brevial or missal) + spirits of the dead
Procedure: An old iron key was inserted between the pages of a church book so that the buttonhole was peeking out. Clenching the book between the indexes of the hands, the person doing the ritual called the souls asking for help in revealing the responsible [for theft or betrayal] and said aloud the names of the suspects: if the book began to twist [after a name was said aloud] this [movement] would thus reveal the identity of the guilty. [If the book remained still, the named person was innocent.] After the ritual, the [spirits were reeased while] saying to them: "Go in peace".

Italian Magic: Secret Lives of Women

Photo: Davide Tiso, 2020. **Setaccio** is from the author's collection.

SETACCIO / LU SUTAZZU DIVINATION

The **setaccio** is a tool used to sift flour. It's made of a very thin and flexible metal wire mesh suspended in a wooden circular frame. For divination, a person who has inherited this method and the secret words used to activate it, must also take a pair of scissors and stab one point into the wooden circular frame. Then, the diviner and the person with the question will each balance once of the scissor loops on their index fingers so that the **setaccio** is suspended gently by the scissors and fingers. For comparison, the setaccio and the scissors are comparable to a planchette, along with the lightly touching the fingers to the top of the planchette, so it can be moved by the spirits. Other names for setaccio are **lu sutazzu** and in Sardinian **su sedazzu.**

The diviner then instructs the querent to think of their question in a "yes" or "no" format. Then the diviner instructs the querent of specific words she must say during a "call and response" that is initiated by the diviner. The words are said, and then the **setaccio** moves in response to the question.

If the **setaccio** twists from, say, a horizontal direction to a vertical direction, this twist indicates a clear "yes" in response to the question. The **setaccio** will remain motionless when the answer is "no".

The diviner shown here is: Gabriella Lorusso, from Sava, Pulgia, Italy. She inherited this from her mother.
Photos show: balance scissor loops on finger tips. slight or great rotation depending on answer channeled yes or no...

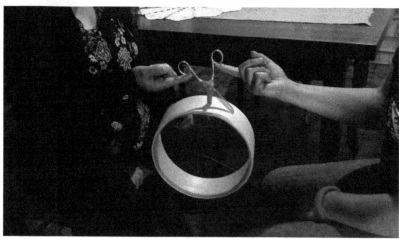

Italian Magic: Secret Lives of Women

DIVINATION

OLIVE LEAF DIVINATION

Olive leaves, and sometimes full branches, are used in rural Italy to divine answers to a variety of questions. They are used in combination with word formulas: rhyming symbolic phrases that activate the divination ritual. An indirect source of heat is used to activate the leaves into movements that are then analyzed. Sometimes saliva is also used to personalized the ritual.

Perhaps the most popular answers sought were for outcomes of romances and marriages, but other answers were sought, including asking the fate of an ill relative or when someone would die.

Olive Leaf Divination: Leonessano, Umbria
Ingredients: + olive branch + hearth with fire + formula
Procedure: Reciting aloud a formula requesting when a marriage would occur, the olive branch was placed on the hearth.
Diagnosis: + if it twisted, the marriage would take place within one year. 547

Olive Leaf Divination: Ascoli, Umbria
Ingredients: + olive leaves + warm floor by the hearth + formula
Procedure: Reciting aloud a formula requesting to know the outcome of a olive harvest, or other enterprise, leaves are placed on the warm floor.
Diagnosis: + if the leaves hopped, or twisted due to the heat, the olive harvest would be abundant + if instead they had ignited or blackened without moving, the omen would surely have been negative. 548

Olive Leaf Divination: Campania
Ingredients: + olive branches + fireplace + New Year's Eve
Procedure: burning some olive branches in the fireplace
Diagnosis: + the fate of a young couple is read based on the twisting of leaves. 549

Olive Leaf Divination: region of Marche
Ingredients: + olive leaves + warm floor of hearth + saliva + formula
Procedure: For amorous matters, wet 2 leaves with saliva and arrange them in a cross shape on the warm hearth, reciting a special formula, asking the leaves to unveil the future.
Diagnosis: + If they skipped wildly, they predicted true deep love + if they moved barely, it was a sign of lukewarmness + if they were still, they declared to the lover that the boy she had fallen in love with did not return her love at all.

The use of saliva magically polarized the response making it valid only for the person who had moistened the leaves: saliva, the vehicle of the word, contains, as the name, the specific energy of the person to whom it belongs, and is ancient in its divinatory usage. 550

Italian Magic: Secret Lives of Women

In Civita, Cascia, Ruscio and Trognano, Ospedalettto, Campi, Todiano, Sheggino, Bursino, Namigi, San Pellegrino di Norcia (villages in the region of Umbria), in the region of Trieste, and in many other rural areas, egg alumen was used to divine the fate of boyfriends, details about potential husbands, to know how soon a wedding might occur, and other aspects of romantic partnership.

Unmarried women drop egg albumen into a glass container holding water and leave it to unfurl overnight. The next morning, the shapes left in the water by the egg whites were very seriously studied.

Egg Divination: various villages in the region Umbria, done on the evening before and morning of Ascension (in May), a time it was believed the egg was to have *been blessed by the Madonna.* 551

DIVINATION

Procedure: Unmarried women drop egg albumen into a glass container holding water and leave the egg to unfurl overnight. The next morning, the shapes left in the water by the egg whites are very seriously studied.

Types of Queries: jobs of future husbands, whether a bride would travel away from her home after marriage, what type of home the bride would live in, what kind of financial abundance she might marry into.

Diagnostic symbolism of egg albumen:

+ plows, machines and ship sails, oxen, hammers, cows, wire-filaments (telegraph lines), shoes: predict careers held by future husbands or next jobs for boyfriends.
+ flowers meant a wedding ceremony
+ house shapes predicted bride's next residence with husband, castles and slippers alluded to a rich residence.
+ other shapes divined often gave hints as to habits of future husbands, such as how much firewood he'd keep on the porch, or what type of animals might be on a farm, etc. The details proved evidential for the women who later partnered with men who had the same careers predicted, etc. 552

DIVINATION FOR LOST OBJECTS

Some of the methods for divining the location of a lost item require community participation. In these cases, a seer also called a woman medium (**veggente, spiridada**) is the main operator of the rituals, and is joined by participants, such as neighbors and family members.

Due the community participation, there is a vulnerability involved. In the case of locating lost items, neighbors agree to sit around a table with a **veggente** who is trying to locate the lost item from a person who, consciously or subconsciously, may have it in their possession, whether they stole it or borrowed it and forgot or whether the user left it near a neighbor's field, for example. So *it's obvious add that to this sort of ordeal, any thief will be careful not to participate, therefore unjustified defection is itself a strong indication of guilt.* 553

These methods also give insight into the closeness of people in a community and the magic used certainly reveals the quality of relationships. This closeness, or transparency in some ways, requires also secrecy to protect magical traditions, either the helpful or harmful ones, and living in the watchful eyes also shows how a community can easily be divided amongst itself when an outside pressure, such as the church and its witch hunts fabricated fear-based stories whose purpose was to uncover less cooperative people in their war for masculine religious dominance.

13 Lamps Divination: to find lost objects, Sardinia
Ingredients: + veggente + prayer to St Anthony of the fire + midnight + 13 lamps
Procedure: At midnight, in an enclosed space lit only by the lamps, the **veggente** tunes in to the person who's been victim of a theft of an object or an animal to feel her loss. Then

the **veggente** concentrates on the thief, psychically imposing on them to feel an urgency to return the stolen item or animal. 555

Key Divination: to find lost objects, Sardinia
Ingredients: + veggente (seer), + person seeking an item + neighbors + key + table
Procedure: The **veggente**, the person seeking a lost item, and the person's neighbors and/ or family sit around a table. The **veggente** holds the key in a gentle way so that it is able to pivot and turn its serrated side towards to person who has the lost object themselves or somewhere on their property. This is like the **setaccio** method of divining answers and also similar to using a planchette. Spirit helpers are involved. If a person is indicated and is unaware they have the lost object, the **veggente** can help guide them to make a more precise search of their property to find it. 554

CANDLE FLAME DIVINATION

Candle flame divination is used to receive answers about a variety of questions, and it was already mentioned in the BIRTH chapter. Below is a divination method from villages in Abruzzo that is more complex involving the use of prayer power from virgin women. It's a form of ancient pyromancy.

Candle Divination: to determine the health outcome of someone prayed over, Abruzzo.
Ingredients: + 7 virgin girls + candle flame
Procedure: The power of virgin prayers was used to accompany a woman asked to go to church to pray for a sick person and ask Our Lady for responses through the flickering shapes of the candle flames.

+ favorable forecasts if it burned quietly,
+ if the flame is uniform, regular, without jolts, things will get well,
+ if the flame is agitated or twisted there is a danger of death 556

Additionally, signs and portents were observed during the procession to the church:

+ if, on the way to the church, the girls saw an ox, the patient would recover their health;
+ If they saw a priest, the ill person would be dead. 557

FAVA BEAN DIVINATION

The fava bean was used in a form of divination where it represented semen. The divination was for young women to know who their future husbands would be based on career: *3 beans were used: one complete with peel; one divided in half but provided with peel; a seed divided in half without peel.* Each been was placed into a corner of the handkerchief with one corner remaining empty. In the morning, *if the girl accidentally touched one of the corners containing the seed she would know by it's shape the social condition of her future husband: respectably, an excellent party; honest craftsman; poor laborer. The semen-free corner presaged the failure to marry.* 558 This method was used in central Italy and also in the deep south and in-between.

DIVINATION

BOXWOOD LEAVES were used in the same way olive leaves were used in divination: *girls of marriageable age rested on the red-hot surface of the fireplace, or on the stove, some boxwood leaves taken from the hedges of the cemeteries: if the leaves twisted, the wedding was near.* 559

ROSEMARY SPRIGS were used in plant divinations: girls put behind their ears a flowery sprig of rosemary so they would be able to see their future husband in a dream. 560

SCAPULA DIVINATION

In many areas across the island of Sardinia there is a tradition of divining with the scapula of a lamb. It's possible this tradition exists in other villages on the mainland where sheep are tended to by shepherds. In Sardinia the scapula is called **pala**. While the **pala** is used in divination, it is also used for protection, and it is acquired through ritual as well.

The **pala** is taken from the shoulder of a *"marked lamb" that is designated since birth for this divinatory rite.{m}* This bone is used to determine specific answers in regards to the health, crop harvest, and life length of family members and farm animals. *The oldest woman in the family does it, immediately after Sunday lunch, with all the kinship gathered.* 561 So the entire family is present to receive the reading from their elder.

The **pala** is examined for marks in specific areas of the bone, for bone thickness or thinness of structure in specific areas of the bone. These natural formations are read as indicators. Once the bone is used in the reading, the elder woman gives it to a family member to bury in a chosen area of the crop field *because it is believed that it protected the land used for grazing from fire and prolonged drought.* 562

Italian Magic: Secret Lives of Women

Pala divination is similar to the divination of haruspicy and heptomancy where the livers of sheep are examined in specific sections of the organ for specific markings to psychically read answers for specific questions. While haruspicy and heptomancy are ancient Roman, Etruscan and Greek modalities, the Sardinian **pala** bears more direct connection to divination with sheep shoulder bone used extensively among the Kalmyk, the Kirgiz, the Mongols and the Buryat of Siberia. 563 *For the Buryat of Siberia, there is an initiation and purification ceremony done 3 to 9 times using wild thyme, juniper and pine bark gathered in pot of boiling water along with a few hairs of the goat sacrificed. Then a divination was performed with the sheep's shoulder bone.* 564

The Sardinian divination and the Siberian one share another tradition, that of "resurrecting the bones". The Sardinian **pala** divination is *linked to the most ancient customs of Easter* 565 a regenerational celebration (originally founded upon veneration of a divinely feminine universe and the parallel of menstrual blood as regenerational, later stolen and masculinized by the concept of the Jesus resurrection myth), and despite its masculinization has been perpetuated as the abundance of the divine feminine through rare but existing rural stories of the **Signora del Gioco/Madonna Oriente/Abundia** reports. This version of Easter and its regenerational stories of abundance connected to a demonstration of resurrection of the bones also finds these stories in Siberia.

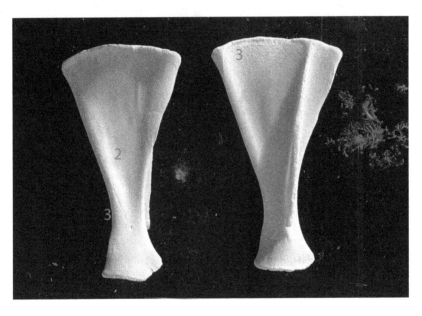

CHART KEY

Indications of the marks on the bone foretold: trends of the agro-pastoral year (abundant harvests of wheat, barley and oats); growth of the vegetable gardens; orchards and vineyards health of family members; whether deaths would occur that year or not; the number of illnesses and deaths and on which side of the family they would occur; and the health of the flock of animals, for example. *translated and paraphrased from Miranda Niedda Giagoni's "Majarzas e sanadoras: Tradizioni, racconti e usanze popolari in Sardegna."

RESURRECTION OF THE BONES

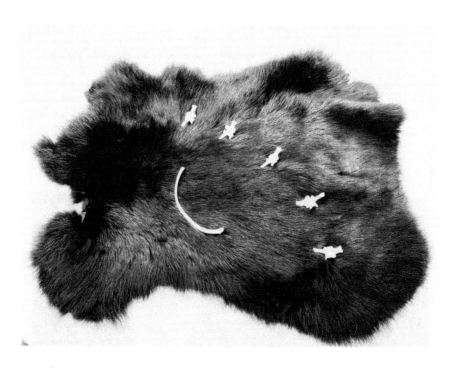

The most exciting things about rural testimonies, whether from extended relatives in whatever remnants they hold, personal story shares, or the rarer documented ones, is that we find here the "real" deal behind so-called folk stories.

If you're someone who loves real life in its non-glamorous expression and humble looking magic, you will naturally find some offense to the term "folk story," because this phrase, along with many other anthropological terms is a denigration. It's a way to say "oh, those country folk believe in fantasy and superstition, but let's enjoy it as a fairytale story." In truth, these stories are about actual experiences, usually as some meeting between the spirit world and the earthly one and between earthly people and spirit beings. Sometimes these stories have been changed over time to read more stylishly, and sometimes they've been changed in other ways, all expressions altered by outsiders, originally told in the psychic language of the time of locals. So it can be more difficult to discern the truth of the story as well as the deeper spiritual teaching within. Psychic and spiritual experiences are difficult to put into words even in contemporary times, so misunderstandings are common.

Italian Magic: Secret Lives of Women

It is the author's experience that for each of the folk stories she's been presented with by Italians who document their own village and/or regional culture, she's met half a dozen human beings who experienced the things and the spirit beings written about in these folk stories, as have their families.

Il rituale delle ossa is one such folk tale practiced in daily rural life. "The ritual of the bones" also often called "the resurrection of the bones" is expressed around the theme of caring for the bones of a consumed animal in a specific way so that it continues to live on. On a larger theme is expressed to declare a continuity of abundance be kept in motion, and on a more specific theme, it is expressed to ensure fertility of a new bride and to keep a shepherd's flock in good numbers.

Beginning this thread of connection with Sardinian shepherds, we find folk stories around the theme where a shepherd finds himself visited by a lone traveler and who then slaughters one of their flock to feed the traveler. In some stories, the shepherd has only one animal, in others, more, still in others he's lost most of his flock to an intense storm. In each story, the traveler advises him to *"throw the bones of the animal into the enclosure where the flock was first."*[566] and in the morning, the shepherd wakes to find he has an entire flock of sheep resurrected in their pen. If he has not been careful to bury all the bones, then the animal(s) resurrect with a limp in the exact spot of the missing bone. In some stories the lone traveler was the Madonna.

> In yet another story, a *version of Cinderella, where to work for the good of the girl is a calf with golden horns that is cut into pieces and cooked by the envious stepmother. Before being killed (this is a typical dismemberment ritual), the calf advises the girl to take care of her bones, to reunite them together, ensuring that not even one is missing and to bury them in a cave. Following the advice of the calf, the girl finds every Sunday, on the place where she buried the bones, a beautiful dress with which to dress before going to mass in which the king's son also participates.* [567]

The themes always revolve around specific core actions: an animal being slaughtered and eaten; necessity of the bones to be buried right away wrapped in their fur; the animal being resurrected after this is done and resurrecting lame, because someone kept a bones from being buried. Other details vary, but there is always an interaction of some sort whereafter advice is given about burying the bones: either a lone traveler visits the home of a person who has the flock of animals, or the animal speaks to a person about their impending death and how they would like their bones to be arranged. The interaction truly is between human beings and a spirit person manifested in flesh to teach this spiritual lesson that is truly about the continuation of life after death of the physical body (the spirit is resurrected).

This same theme is found in legends of Thor, where there is a parallel story to the Italian shepherds, but in the case of Thor the conditions are reversed: he is the lone traveler with the flock who visits the home of someone who takes him in. He slaughters 2 of his goats and offers it to the host family as a gratitude for shelter. He advises the family to *cast the bones on the goat hide.* 568 However, the son split the thigh bone of the goat and ate the marrow, so that the next day when Thor swung his hammer over the bones and fur; *straightaway the he-goats rose up and then one of them was lame in a hind leg."* 569

Thor would also place his hammer in the lap of a bride *to secure her numerous offspring. It is not excluded that in the Sardinian custom of burying the bones after the wedding banquet a desire for fertility for the bride was also implied.* 570 *In Sardinia [...] even in the early decades of the 20th century, it was customary to throw under the table, during wedding stalls, the bones of killed animals, and then bury them 9 days later.* 571

That the hunted or domesticated animal can be reborn from its bones is a belief also found in specific areas and among specific peoples of Sibera, America, Germany, South America, Africa, Bolivia, Italy, and beliefs against breaking bones in this case is also cited in tales of the Jews, Caucasus, Germans, in Romania's Transylvania, Austria, in Alpine countries France, Belgium England and Sweden. In these same places a missing bone was replaced for burial, if noticed in time, such as in this example: *In an Armenian tale [...] a similar banquet was observed by a hunter who abstained from eating but kept the ox rib he was served. Later, when the spirits gathered up all the animal's bones to bring it back to life, they had to replace the missing rib by a walnut tree branch.* 572

Among hunting peoples bones represent the final source of life, both human and animal, and the source from which the specifics is reconstituted at will. This is why the bones of game are not broken, but carefully gathered up and disposed of according to custom, that is, buried, placed on platforms or in trees, thrown into the sea, and so on. The "soul" is presumed to reside in the bones and hence the resurrection of the individual from its bones can be expected. 573 Not limited to hunters, these beliefs and rituals are also found in pastoral spiritual practices, shamanism, and the agricultural world.

Perhaps the most significant and overlooked part of these stories is the fact that they are teaching about the continued life after the spirit's separation from the physical body. Each component or character in the story is significant to illustrate this. First, we have the earthly folk-whether shepherds or host families. Then, we have the special guests: an anonymous woman who reveals herself later as a Madonna, a traveler who is the god Thor, and animals who are resurrected: mostly the animals are resurrected with a limp due to a missing bone. This is the sign that the animal is a threshold jumper: one who was living in the physical world and one who now inhabits the spirit world. This "lame" sign is also worn by gods in other stories such as the Roman and Greek gods who are wearing only one shoe, or who have a wooden leg (Saturn) or a limp (Vulcan) or an alluded missing half (Dionysis) . This idea is also found in shamanism:

> *the aspiring shaman, before reaching the celestial bride, that is, before passing into the realm of the dead, must cut a piece of meat from his thigh thus symbolizing a sort of ritual death, a price that must pay anyone who wants access knowledge that does not belong to this world. For this reason, the heroes who aspire to the supernatural undergo a mutilation that makes them "different"*

Italian Magic: Secret Lives of Women

from ordinary beings. They are generally lame or blind or have other physical defects, as if to demonstrate that the supernatural cannot be achieved by remaining unharmed. [574]

The other most significant and overlooked part of these stories is the fact that they illustrate interaction between spirit world people and earthly people. First, this is significant because rural Italian magic and lineage cures were learned this way, from the spirit world reaching into the earthly one and passing down wisdom. Secondly, it illustrates the parallel lives lived in the spirit world and their similarities to the earthly one. This is a didactic teaching tool of course: just as in rural life in Italy community meals and dances are important to make the mundane life more tolerable, also in these stories where spirit world helpers manifest in physical flesh there are banquets with food (physical food or spirit food) and some type of festivity or game where spiritual teaching takes place and secrets of the universe are taught, revealing the worldwide shamanic belief in continued life after separation in death from the physical body. We mostly see the celebration feasting the realm of the female abundance spirits. But food always seems to take a role in these symbolic stories, both in the physical earthly world scenes and in the parallel spirit world.

It's the spirit people who are really in charge of these experiences and teachings and the teachings can't happen without the experiences guided by them which are orderly and follow universal patterns and are not merely confused superstitions. This brings us to the most important factor swept under the rug: **La Signora del Gioco** and the other female spirit figures of these stories, the original Abundance divinities whose teachings these themes are based upon.

The masculine stories seem piecemeal and disconnected from a larger whole. The feminine stories, such as the Teachings of the Night School of La Signora del Gioco reveal a holistic connection between the Resurrection of the Bones and the other teachings as well as other traditions pre-dating the Great Pyramid era when animals, birth and death, spirit world travels and dream world experiences were all attributed to the Great Teacher who gives life to all: The Great Mother Goddess.

Keeping this in mind you might begin to view some of the pieces of this book in a different way: Thor's Hammer of resurrection and fertility might perhaps be taken from the female hammer of **s'accabbadora's** role as a human euthanizer and a threshold jumper, most likely these were once a singular role but separated by the masculine interference in spiritual storytelling as significant myths were re-written from a masculine framework. Even the deer god was originally female, and binary gender roles were not present in spiritual language in the way they have been for most of the world's memories. These masculine stories that seem to be broken off from some bigger picture that is never revealed are symptoms of their usurpation of what came before...and the masculine stories never reveal a bigger picture because they were synthesized upon what came before: a feminine cosmogony that made a parallel sense with the female body's birthing and feeding abilities.

THE LADIES OF THE NIGHT SOCIETY

Behind rural **filastrocche** nursery rhymes and folk stories which we can more respectfully refer to as village stories, behind the spiritual legends and strange sounding prayers are spiritual lessons about the Universe's energy, about spirits and life after death, of abundance and how it flows, of feminine autonomy and directions for Ascension.

The popular spiritual stories are usually remakes or ones that use symbols to hide the Goddess. The heroic central figures in the popular stories are usually male and the evil ones are female (often as witches or vampyric succubi, ghosts) and while they often seem incredulous or disconnected from a holistic viewpoint, this is only because they were rewritten from their original form into stories with masculine directives. Stories have survived, however, in testimonies from women, in more unadulterated versions, and they reveal the spirit beings behind these teachings, the spirit beings who the masculine stories of gods emulate. They are few but so important, because they tie together all the mysteries beyond even Italy's ancient history.

NAMES

Called by many names, the central role is the same: feminine spirits who teach human beings about the abundance of the Universe and how to access it. The many names of these specific spirit helpers are more like descriptions than first names that we find in the Greek and Roman Goddess pantheon. This is an important factor, because it's consistent with the naming of everything in the rural world where naming is not even necessary, but when it's used, it is used to describe people and things in a simple, evident way.

The names are also different due to logistical factors: these Abundance Goddess figures appear all across Italy and her islands, but sometimes they only appear as a singular being, and at other times they operate in specifically numbered groups. However they do manifest to earthly people, they do it consistently and always for the same purpose: to teach the mysteries of the Universe in a usable way for regular, daily life people outside of noble, elite temple culture, and they teach in a way similar to rural life's community gatherings such as group meetings, banquets, festivities and surrounded by nature.

La Signora del Gioco The Lady of the Games, **Abundia**, **Le Donni di Fuora** Ladies from Outside, The Good Lady, **Fata Maggiore** and **Mamma Maggiore** The Big/Greater Fairy and Great Mother, Lady Habonde, **Holda**, **Bensozia** Bona Socia; Good Partner [p91], **Madona Oriente**, **Horiente**, **Perchta**, **Richella** Mother of Riches, **Bona Domina**, Good Mistress, **savia Sibilla** wise Sibilla, **Donni di notti** Ladies of the nights, **Dee Madri** Mother Goddesses, **dette pure Donni di locu**, **Dunnuzzi di locu**, **Donni di casa** Ladies

Italian Magic: Secret Lives of Women

of the house, **Donni, Dunzeui, Signurij Belli Signuri** Beautiful Ladies, **Patruni di casa** Ladies of the House, **Signora Greca** Greek Lady, **La donna del bon Zogo, bonae res, bona domina** good mistress, the Teacher, and sometimes as Cibele, Rea, or Satia. Similar names are found also in France, Germany, and other European countries.

It is important to know the truth here: those involved in the inquisitions and documentations of the interrogations gave names to these Ladies as: Diana and Herodias, even though no rural women used these names.

> *At this point the attempts by priests, canonists and inquisitors to translate the multifarious names of the nocturnal goddess appear to us in a different light. Interpretative efforts and interpretative excesses were two sides of the same coin. Diana and Herodias offered the clerics a thread with which to trace their way through the labyrinth of local beliefs. As a result a feeble and modified echo of those women's voices has come down to us.* [575]

The names of the night school society by the people are all versions of this very simple and direct description such as: game of the good society **gioco della buona societa** (Italian) **Ludum bonae societatis** (Latin) [576] **Convito della Fata Maggiore** Banquet of the Great Fairy (Sicily specifically) society of the good mistress, the good game, and similar phrases to these. **Gioco (ludus** *in Latin,* **zogo** *in many dialects of northern Italy) is the oldest name of the Sabbath.* [577] These were the names used by the rural people. And, these people having personal spiritual ecstasies were mostly poor and mostly women. It was the church who gave the name **sabba** Sabbath to the society, just as the church implanted other Goddess names in the same way they implanted the devil.

There were also required greetings similar to the many call-and-responses found in rural Italy. The Ladies spoke versions of "**le benvente, figlie mie**" welcome my daughters, and the invited guests greeted her "be well, **Madona Horiente**".

"Italy's Witches and Medicine Women Vol 1" chapter 10 **Caccia alle Streghe** The Witch Hunts explains the way the church blended Roman spiritual pantheon names (that were popular during the Inquisition period) with christian ideas of the devil to create an evil Goddess idea, along with how and why they did it in great detail.

The Female Abundance spirits, these nocturnal goddesses are the figures central to rural Italian magic and cures because they created the Lineage of knowledge and even the tradition of handing it down. Created and passed down from Goddess to humans, the humans then learned how to initiate their own family members: from mother to daughter, from father to son, passing down the knowledge and rituals in the same manner.

These feminine spirit teachers of abundance are the figures that popular spiritual stories are based upon (whether stories of Jesus and his miracles, of Mithra and his regenerative power or Viracocha and his healings) only the female providers have either been changed into witches or replaced with male gods or male spiritual teacher/helper

THE LADIES OF THE NIGHT SOCIETY

figures in the stories, in any case, erased. This role of teacher, provider, healer was originally and naturally a feminine one, as also was the cosmogony of the universe acknowledged and celebrated.

While the presence of these Female Abundance figures and all the knowledge they disseminated was covered up and rewritten, remnants and untouched versions are everywhere, enough to show that they came before the masculine versions. And...

THEFT IS AN ADMISSION OF VALUE

In examining their stories, their presence and their root in our most ancient foundational times is where we can find a continuous line of connection of provision, knowledge, symbols, cults, universal laws that are consistent within the female lineage no matter how much time passes. While in the masculine mythology, we only find disconnected stories and symbols whose meanings people still search for...and that is because they were stolen and remodeled by masculine minds and are therefore synthetic and have no connection to a natural genesis on their own.

NUMBERS

Of the Abundance Goddess appearing as a singular wise woman in the northwest of Italy and north central Italy, **La Signora del Gioco** also referred to as the Good lady, The Lady of the Night Games, The lady of Good things and **Madona Oriente**, **Bensozia** and others, there are testimonies of rural women saying that she appeared at night, knowing their names and calling them to a circle in the forest, wearing a beautiful dress and being more beautiful than they, and that she flew them to the "society". **La Signora del Gioco** taught them secrets of the universe and other things about life on earth through divination that were indisputably true, so the women testified she was worthy of being trusted.

A woman named Sibilla Zanni who ended up being burned in 1390 first confessed in 1384 that *every week, on Thursday night, she had joined* **Oriente** *and her society. Oriente answered the questions of the society's members, predicting future and occult events...She* **[Oriente]** *had always spoken the truth and this in turn had enabled her to answer the quetsions of many people providing information and instruction.* 578

Essentially, **Oriente** functioned as a trance medium, providing both the energetic conditions for the society as well as the knowledge provided and channeled. A woman named Pierina Bugatis from the same area confessed the same details with added information that gave an even deeper look into the society.

Two old women from Val di Fassa *had simply spoken of a good mistress* **bona domina**. They also called her *in the Italian language Richella, that is, the mother of riches and good fortune'. They had said that the 'good mistress'. i.e., Richella, had come to them at night, on a cart. She had the appearance of a well-dressed woman but they had not seen her face. She had touched them [...]then they arrived at a place crowded with people who danced and made merry [...]They had gone to this place for several years, during the 4 Ember weeks[...]* 579 In the
304

Italian Magic: Secret Lives of Women

Canovese, in Val di Fiemme, in Ferrara and the out-skirts of Modena there were also reports of 'women of the good game' and 'wise Sibilla,' and in the area of Como 'the game of the good society'. And near Milan, from testimony "*Pierina thought that Oriente was the mistress of the "society" just as Christ is the master of the world.*' 580

And in Sicily, **bella Signora/ belli Signuri** Nice Lady/Good Ladies were the names given to nocturnal abundance goddesses like **La Signora del Gioco**. But in Sicily, more prominently than on the mainland, we find these Ladies also referred to as fairies and as different types of fairies, which is something also found on the island of Sardinia. For example, the many **belli Signuri** faeries went out to gather women from their dreams and invite them into the astral realm and into the society. Within the society, also referred to as the night school or school of games, the singular **La Signora** (called by other names) was in charge of the festivities and spiritual teachings: *none other than 33 powerful creatures, under the dependencies of a* **Fata Maggiore** *known as* **Mamma Maggiore***, Greek Lady and* **savia Sibilla**. 581 In other words, there was a main Goddess and many smaller Goddesses who did various works for the society.

So, among the festivities of the night society banquets where learning took place, many Ladies in spirit congregated with the earthly women and men whom they brought to this fairy place. The Fairies were often said to be in groups of **7**. And, some women did say that the Great Fairy was sometimes called a Queen and that she also was occasionally joined by her King. Whether the goddesses were seen singularly, or in groups of **3**s and **7**s, these are the same numerical groups used by Lineage healers.

All of these components, it should be said, are so very similar to what is found in Italian rural culture at times of the year, whether seasonal celebrations or wedding celebrations, the community has a gathering where food is shared, prepared according to traditional rituals, dances are made often enacting didactic spiritual teachings or reciting **filastrocche** nursery rhymes with the same intent. Community gatherings and food sharing are a huge component of rural life.

APPEARANCE

The Lady of the Game, La Signora del Gioco and the Great Fairy are all described in similar ways and while often said to be beautiful and well-dressed, there are some testimonies that she was scary looking, that her eyes and ears were covered, and that she could kill with her eyes alone, and that she sometimes had animal parts. Most often her face is not able to be seen fully, but rather details appear in profile. But mostly she looked like a woman, identifiable enough for the locals to know she was not of their town, even though she knew their names and how to find them. The locals saw her as a woman but more beautiful, more powerful and more knowledgeable. And, if they became too comfortable around her and behaved poorly, they would not be allowed to return to the society.

The Lady of the Game is described in Bergamo as being:

'*high and bent, with curled hair, dressed in long black skirts and a large fringed shawl [...] can be beautiful or repugnant. Sometimes she is accompanied by 40 white dogs or 7 cats, each with a rattle on his neck. [...] also as gorgeous, seductive in her lace dress and transparent veils. The unlucky, enchanted, ran to embrace her, but as soon as she approached her, the strange creature began to grow in abundance, stretching her legs up to the sky and dissolving in the wind.* 582

[...] a beautiful woman sitting on a throne. 583

Also described as wearing black dresses and obscuring her face, and frequently seen flying. And in many accounts, even in France and Germany, as being moved around on a throne-like cart by spirits in the high mountains. These cart accounts are especially numerous in the Alpine region.

And in Sicily:

In this courtyard, at the ancient monastery of S. Chiara, there were 7 Women of Fuora, one more beautiful than the other. 584

[...] they would have been beautiful women, of high stature, of opulent shapes and long and shiny hair. During the day they hid and went out only at night. They are supernatural beings, a bit 'witches a little fairy', without being able to discern how they differ from each other. 585

Returning to the central north of Italy's mainland:

In Val di Fiemme, another woman tried as a witch, Margherita [...] declared that the 'mistress of the good game' has 2 stones around her eyes, that is, one on each side, which open and close continually at her wish. She had a black band around her head with patches before her ears and eyes,' as was confirmed by another woman, Caterina della Libra. 586

She always journeys through the air and she has 2 patches around her eyes, one on each side, so she cannot see everything: and if she were able to see everything [explained Margherita] she would do great harm to the world." 587

In the middle of the 15th century, the 2 old women of Val di Fassa [...] had said that Richella hid her face: they had not been able to see her profile 'because of certain protuberances of a semicircular ornament attached to her ears.' 588

Italian Magic: Secret Lives of Women

WITH ANIMAL PARTS

Animals are also present at the night school: as mounts to fly on to the society, as combined with body parts of the Abundance goddess in the astral realm (partial shape-shifting) , and in resurrection demonstrations.

Animals are also present at the night school: as mounts to fly on to the society, as combined with body parts of the Abundance goddess in the astral realm (partial shape-shifting) , and in resurrection demonstrations.

In the case of Richella or the 'women from outside,' a semi-bestial nature, revealed by hirsute limbs, equine hooves, feline paws. 589

The 2 old women from Val di Fassa. They had made offerings to Richella [...] they had touched her hand, as if sealing a contract. They say her hand is hairy. She had stroked their cheeks with hairy hands. 590

MEETING METHODS

In many different areas, from Liguria to Val di Fiemme the Lady was reported as seen flying through the sky. She was also known to be part of the night processions, where she gathered spirits of people and animals and returned them to the moon, while she was in the form or partial form of a wolf. The night processions wandered through the forest, they crossed the plains in flight, and this was so well known in mountainous areas that people were afraid to see her because they believed it meant they could die next and become part of the night procession: As one mother-in-law exclaimed out at night seeing her *"escape, this is the fire of the lady of the game!"* 591

In many regions there are village stories about the women who fly to the walnut trees or to the moon as a meeting point, and then onward to the night school by departing on horses, pigs, castrated goats, on foxes and cats. So there are those who go to sleep at night and fly to a meeting point fountain or tree and wait to be taken to the nocturnal school. To remind us of the Sardinian flight traditions of rural Italy here is another version of a prayer asking to be specifically flown to the moon on their horses:

"Luna luna, para luna, Paristella, luna bella. Uve ses? In muntanna. Sennor' Anna, s'ebba mia, mi che jucat. 592

Also in Sicily, the groups of fairies were seen flying as were the women they gathered to take to the night society: *"these ladies leave the house at night, not with the body and the spirit, but only with the spirit. They go to find the spirits [...] for advice, answers and questions about future things."* 593

The people who were taught how to fly, or whose spirits were taken to go to the society once they entered the dream state, did so several ways. Some were taught how to use **unguenti** ointments that would allow their bodies to go into sleep paralysis so the soul could fly, others were taught to burn specific **suffumigi** fumigations (loose incense) to call the Fairies to them who would then take their souls to fly, and other used only their minds to achieve astral flight on their own and then be taken by the Spirits to the society.

> *Those who wanted a "nice lady" at home had to before midnight, burn incense, bay leaves and rosemary and make sure the house was perfectly clean and tidy.* 572 *Everything must be done before midnight.* 594

> *Before midnight, holding a lit* **cufuni** *brazier, she will burn pure incense, bay leaves, rosemary (and another herb called* **mancivi - mancavi**). *The perfume will call the "Beautiful Ladies" to come. Entering through the cracks or through the keyhole, as they are spirit. The herbs to call on the "Women of Outside" must be burned first in the middle of the room, and then in the four corners of the room.* 595

> *Before leaving home [for astral flight], these women warned their husbands of their departure by forbidding them to touch their body in their absence.* 596 *They went out through closed doors in the silence of the night, leaving their sleeping husbands behind."* 597

> *Others said they went out through closed doors in the silence of the night, leaving their sleeping husbands behind.* 598

There are testimonies regarding the pain the women would feel in their bodies once their spirits returned from traveling if, while they were gone, their bodies were moved, and a common fears of astral travelers was that their soul would not be able to return to their bodies if their bodies were moved while they "were out".

> *[...] of witches and benandanti [...] both groups claimed that, before setting out for their meetings, they fell into states of profound prostration, or catalepsy [...].* 599

This is how **benandanti** of Friuli were active in the astral realm: they didn't and currently don't rely on **unguenti** to fly but instead were taken in-spirit by angels who instructed them, called out of their sleeping bodies by spirit drums, or knew how to use their minds at any time to fly. Benandanti were people who only lived in the area of Friuli and they still do. These spirit-chosen people, for whom shamanistic flight is a natural part of life and an inescapable dut,y only exist in this north eastern part of Italy. To read a rare interview in their own words see the book "Italy's Witches And Medicine Women Vol 1", chapter 18: **Benandanti: Guardians of the Threshold.**

MEETING PLACES

The people who were taken on flights with the Good Ladies were also taken to

Italian Magic: Secret Lives of Women

destination points: trees (oak, walnut, lime), the moon, the woods, castles, meadows and grassy plains high up on mountaintops and other places lit with dim, blue light that were in the realm of the faeries and was a more full version of rural community celebrations with banquets of food and the presences of all the helper fairies as well as the Great Fairy and sometimes her King: *they met with many other Companies of various other places in a wood full of trees, and the their Prince did not want them to do wicked things, but to cure.*
600

MEETING DAYS

Tuesday, Thursday and Saturday nights were the nights that the Good Ladies would invite earthly people to fly with them to the nocturnal society. In Sicily, some women would go out flying 3 days a week, while in other places on the mainland, women would fly only on Thursdays and far less frequently (a few times a year). Fridays were days for making black magic and were not days associate with the Good Ladies nor the Fairies.

DATES OF TESTIMONIES

Dates of testimonies describing astral spirit flights with nocturnal Goddesses should not be considered the only times these flights took place, but rather the only times they were documented *by the church*. Because of the conditions of the documentation, the trials for heresy and the witch hunts, their language is of course corrupted. We find perfect consistencies in the ingredients of the nocturnal societies but then, depending on the time frame they were documented, trends of the time were inserted to turn the stories into the desired heresy the church was searching for (and in fact) created: the devil and devil types such **Lucifello**, and Goddesses of other names like Diana and Herodias. Still, it's wonderful to see these testimonies marked in a time and place and to keep in mind that they mark experiences outside temples and within the countryside among ordinary people. Nobility wasn't needed for these spiritual experiences to occur, just an invitation from the spirit world.

The dates listed here are absolutely not exhaustive, just a small sampling. Consider, while reading these dates, that in the 1980s there were still places in Italy without hospitals and who used midwives, and that until the 1950s-1970s there still existed many insular rural places who didn't document their own rituals nor traditions and who lived according to the ways in this book, growing and harvesting their own food, producing their own bread and cheese and taking care of their own magic. And, these are experiences which surely happened before these days (there was no reason to document them before the witch trials) and after. Here are a few dates of documentation of the Ladies: 1200; 1280; 1310; 1319; 1384; 1390; 1428; 1586-1588; 1500; 1505 -1506; 1640; 1782...

TEACHINGS

The teachings of the Ladies are similar to what many of us seek in contemporary spiritual practices: divination methods, curative methods, herbal knowledge, spiritual truths, principles of abundance, sexual restoration, sensual pleasure (tantra), autonomy, that life continues on after death of the physical body, spell-breaking, spiritual protection, order and cleanliness and respect in both the physical realm and spiritual realm, spiritual up-keeping and psychic protection and channeling. The Ladies themselves demonstrated the Universal Laws of Energy such as the law of Attraction Law of Thought, the Law of Will (right to protect) and the Law of Balances. These laws are the same ones the rural magic and cures are based upon, and naturally they come from the same Divinely Feminine source.

While Lineage healers passed down their energy and knowledge to someone in their family, as guided by Spirit, the Ladies chose people outside of Lineage lines who needed this knowledge and passed it down through the night school. An interesting contrast between the Lineage inheritances and the nocturnal school is that in the school, these Laws are taught and demonstrated. Astral travel is taught and procedures are taught, questions are answered like Readings. In the Lineage traditions, the inheritances are followed without fail , but there are no teachings of psychic skills. The channeling is essential, but it is activated when the Lineage healer uses the inherited prayers and actions, while the Spirits who channel the healing do everything else.

In contemporary psychic and mediumistic modalities (from channeling to healing to magic, etc) basic principles are taught for setting proper boundaries that help create an order and intent for a desired experience with the spirit world, utilizing vibrational qualities and focusing tools of the mind and often with the use of physical items room arrangement, atmosphere, charged items.

The Ladies taught whom they invited to the nocturnal schools the same principles to ensure a specific experience. **Preparations** for the Ladies or Fairies to come invite you into the school while you sleep:

- In all villages where the Ladies visited, people were instructed to keep their home clean, fresh and in good and proper order, including polished pans and pots and fluffed pillows, clean sheets and swept floors.
- In some villages (mainly throughout Sicily) women were instructed to burn a **suffumigi** fumigation of: rosemary, bay laurel and **mancivi** herb.
- Some women were instructed to prepare and leave a simple meal of fried fish out for the Ladies/**La Signora del Gioco**/the Faeiries.
- Some were instructed to cleanse the 4 corners of their home with water.
- Some were instructed to take off all their clothes, get into bed, and to use secret potions that would force their bodies into a 24 hour sleep during which is was their duty to find the Great Fairy and introduce themselves.
- Women told their husbands to not move their bodies while their spirits were out flying as they knew their spirit would be absent and any touch or movement would cause pain upon return.

> *as in the case of Oriente [...] they do not like to enter sordid places*
> *or filthy houses"* [601]

Italian Magic: Secret Lives of Women

*Asked if the Sibillia has returned to the game since then, she said
"I had gone twice, Not anymore, because the second time I realized
that I threw a stone," and after that she was not allowed to go back
to the game.* 602

Greetings: When the Ladies gathered their students, there were proper greetings exchanged in the typical call-and-response style. No matter what other festivities took place, the greetings and parting phrases were spoken. In addition, the invited people bowed their heads to **la Signora del Gioco**. In doing so, no one ever forgot who was in charge of allowing these incredible experiences to occur. The students were always aware the Ladies were the ones who had the knowledge, who held the secrets, and who had the power to gather all the spirit beings and spirits of physical people into the society.

Order and respect: If you behaved out of order in the society, you weren't allowed back.
- Some groups were invited into the forest, astrally, to sit in circles and receive answers to their questions. Others were taken to a fairy realm on plains or near other natural landmarks. Others still were in darkened areas with a blue light. Before the banquet was partaken in, a demonstration of the Resurrection of the Bones was given. Dancing and music and sensual pleasures began when it was time, always after the didactic teachings and according to the schedule of the Ladies. Order, respect and organization are all aspects of boundary-setting. In mediumship training, practicing these attributes ensures quality experiences with spirit world and not a porous scenario where all types of spirits are allowed in. The society of the Ladies has a specific aim, which is to teach knowledge to be used in daily life to improve the quality of life, and that aim cannot be achieved with chaos and, the realm of the Ladies, is in the spirit world.

Balance: Balance was demonstrated in the form of animals and people exchanges.

In the case of animals:
- animals killed for food during society banquets were also resurrected (in spirit) as part of the teaching that life continues on after death of the physical body. It also teaches responsibility: since the Ladies are psychopomps, through this action they teach the connection to spirits and the continuity of life that should be respected, that every action has a consequence.

In the case of people:
- Pierina Bugatis, who was burned as a witch for her participation in the night games, testified that *at the time, she replied that she was thirty years old but she had started to go when she was sixteen years old when her aunt Agnesina sent her in her place, otherwise she could not/was not able to die,* 603 meaning that her aunt used to go to the night games and, when it was time for her to die, she had to replace her presence with another to keep the balance and Pierina was this chosen to take her place at the night games. This is similar to Lineage healers in some villages needing to pass on their healing power in order to die. While not all Lineage healers pass on their knowledge and not all need to in order to pass on, the tradition is in fact based on this: continuity of life...the lives of people and animals, the effort to keep the knowledge, traditions,

311

and systems (society, healing) alive.

This balance between enfleshed souls on earth and souls living fully in the spirit world is something also taken care of by shaman elsewhere. In Siberia and the Amazon, for example, it is known that some shaman do devour the souls of people living on earth to bring about their deaths so as to keep a balance of souls on earth with that in the spirit world. Sometimes this is done for propitiatory reasons. Regardless, it is the shaman who received instructions to do this: they don't decide themselves. The victims who will be sent to the spirit world (through death) from the earthly world are chosen in different ways. What has been called "cannibalistic shamanism" refers to the shaman's ability to suck the soul energy out of a body thus ensuring it's death, similar to the effect of energy withering that can bring about death through the Italian **fattura** and **il malocchio**.

Friuli, Italy's **benandanti** who also partake in many of the night school experiences are also fighters whose purpose is to keep the balance between light and dark, albeit in a completely different way. They do not fight for one side to win, but they fight for balance. This subject is beyond the scope of this book. It is important to mention, however, that balance finds different definitions in the universe than in our physical world.

Abundance:
The main premise that The Ladies taught in the society, other than the demonstrated truth that conscious life continues after death of the physical body, is that abundance is available for all and that it starts with a state of mind. They did this in several ways:

- They took groups on astral flight journeys into the houses of wealthy people who lived nearby. In the homes, often in the cellars, the group enjoyed drinking the wine stores. If the house was clean and tidy, the Ladies also left a blessing for them. From Pierina's testimony in 1384:

> You also said that the Lady and her company go to various houses of different people, and here they eat and drink and are very happy if they find clean and tidy houses; then the Lady gives her blessing to the house. 604

And from a testimony in 1319:

> The wine does not diminish or grow less because it is the dead who drink it. 605

And another about the wine:

> the supply of which is never affected no matter how much is drunk.
> 606

Incidentally, **benandanti** of the past also were taken to houses to drink wine and experience these teachings of abundance.

Italian Magic: Secret Lives of Women

And in Sicilian tradition, a small banquet of food and drink are left out overnight in hopes that the Ladies of Outside and the Great Fairy come to partake in the spiritual energies of the food, leaving the energies abundance embedded within them. So that when the person who offered the food wakes in the morning, they can consume the abundance infused food.

The other gifts given: herbal knowledge, curing traditions, divination methods, protection methods, are other such tools of abundance for the students of the society.

An expanded view of the teachings here reveal the same Laws of the Universe that are presented in a slightly updated contemporary way with each generation, such as: thoughts are things, meaning that the brain doesn't know the difference between the thoughts you think and the touchable/tangible things in the physical world. For the brain, it is all real. This is demonstrated in the visits to wealthy homes. Though no one was physically drinking wine, the imagined experience was real enough for the entire group to say they drunk wine and yet the wine stores did not decrease. Pleasure was experienced by the group in the astral realm, the same was it would be in the physical realm. The banquets with the Fairies were the same: feasting, dancing, and music. Although none of the visitors could actually eat the spirit food because it was energy, and the people were there as spirits and not as physical beings, the food was eaten and sensual pleasures were experienced between spirits (some women testified they had sex with spirits and didn't feel it was a sin) and knowledge was given and received and lives were changed through these experiences.

For the 2 old women [...] to her they had made offerings; from her [Richella] they had received affectionate caresses and promises of wealth; with her, over many years, they had periodically forgotten the toil and the monotony of everyday life. [607]

Silence: There are testimonies from some of the people who were taken to the society who said they were all told to keep secret these things they were learning and the society itself.

So you believed that the East Orient educates its company members on any problems it poses [giving spiritual advice], and that she predicts future and hidden things; And that she has always told you the truth and all that in [your] turn you informed many people, that she instructed you and answered problems that you were facing and that you sought her instruction. [608]

You [Sibillia] also believed that in the same company there are two or two animals of every species except the donkeys because they carry the cross, and that if one were only missing, the whole world would be destroyed. [609]

The 'women outside' loved being treated kindly and surrounded with respect. If they were welcomed with the offer of delicious foods (jams, confetti, but more often honey), music and dancing, they returned their guests with good health and fortune. 610

To find everything in good order, the bed well made, the sheets white and fragrant, the pillows are fluffed, the copper in the kitchen is splendid, you sweep the rooms very well. The Ladies apparently didn't go into unkempt houses, and she imparts blessings upon those in good order and those "in which she has banqueted with her invisible retinue". 611

To the Lady, you always made her reverence by bowing your head and saluting her with these words:"Health to you, Lady of the East **Salute a te, signora Oriente**"; *And she replied,* "**State Bene, brava genter"** *All is well , good people.* 612

From April 12, 1384:

You would also like to say furthermore that the Lady's company is traveling, going in to different homes of different people, and here they eat and drink and they rejoice greatly if they find clean and orderly homes; Then the Lady gives her blessing on the home. You would say that the Lady does not want you to know anything about these things in the day. 613

Herbs, Cures, Spells:

the queen had given her medicine to treat the sick, so that she could earn money and alleviate her poverty. 614

You said that the Lady teaches you about the company the powers of herbs and that [...] she shows you all the things you ask her about diseases, theft and evil. And so she teaches you to do, and you find that everything she shows is the truth. 615

To the members of the society Oriente teaches the virtues of herbs, remedies to cure diseases, how to find things that have been stolen, and how to dissolve spells. But all of these things must be kept secret. 616

They [Ladies of Outside] even took them to the sea, far away, and made them walk on the water without getting wet. Every night they repeated it, and in the morning they disappeared without leaving a trace of themselves. 617

Three times a week, the nights of Tuesday, Thursday and Saturday went out in spirit [...] in Ventotene, to deliberate on the bills **fatture** *to be broken, the bonds to be dissolved.* 618

Resurrection of the Bones:
An integral part of the night school's teachings was the resurrection of the bones, which demonstrated to students of the night school that life of the consciousness continues on after death of the physical body:

> *You still say that in the company they kill animals and they eat the meat, the bones are laid in all skin and the lady with a wand holding it with a knob, strikes skin of the animals killed, and these immediately resuscitate and rise, but they are no longer able to work.* 619

The school itself exists in the spirit realm, and this demonstration showed in real time how the transition occurs. So the Ladies were demonstrating that they had the power of not only a psychopomp (one who gathers and guides spirits after their separation from the physical body and into their afterlife) but as spirit beings whose role is to literally aid in the transition of the spirit's life from one realm to another with her actions: Goddess power. This is in contrast to Christianity which says only their male god can do this.

This female demonstration of the resurrection of the bones is part of a set of greater teachings, unlike in the masculine stories of the Resurrection Of the Bones that are isolated events. The female story also makes sense and has a continuity looking far, far back in time where the Goddess was the only life force venerated as the essence of the Universe and her connection to animals and nature was also inseparable and lent themselves to finding the Goddess throughout history being called "Mistress of the Animals" and other such names.

LIMITLESSNESS

This. This is how Lineage cures, herbal knowledge and rural magic was spread all across Italy and her islands and NOT by a physical witch walking across Italy as it has been claimed. Further, these traditions are much older than middle period documentation and were NOT isolated as having generated during this time period, as also is claimed in the story of Aradia. Just as in shamanism of Siberia or Central Asia or South America or the many other places where it exists, it's the spirits who hold the knowledge and who pass it down to chosen human beings. This is also why these traditions have consistency, only their style or land-scape differing because different neighborhoods in Italy have different resources and these resources can vary in small and large ways over short and long distances. Higher spirits, meaning non-ghosts, have no limitations through time nor space nor geographic terrain.

THE LADIES OF THE NIGHT SOCIETY

Photo top: Tuscany. Photo bottom: Liguria

AMULETI

AMULETS and PROTECTIONS

Rural Italian amulets reveal a deep and ancient connection to nature's psychic language through their simple forms. Generally, the more decorative and designed an amulet, the more its meaning have been contrived by human beings, while in contrast, nature has its own meanings as explained to human beings in our most ancient origins. Inevitably amulets are connected to the powers of the Great Goddess Mother: psychic discernment, protection, deflection of negativity, repair from energy attacks, regeneration, empowerment and abundance, which are attributes sought and celebrated in our earliest days on earth.

These amulets display their innate qualities and their direct functions gifted from nature and they reflect the source they came from: amulets from trees look like trees. A stone with regenerative energy is red like womb blood (containing stem cells) of the Great Mother. Round black stones like eyes are the eyes of the Great Mother discerning psychic attack. Broom shapes filter out negativity. They are not flashy and overly decorative but express nature's apotropaic traits. Typically rural, nothing is superfluous. This is the true magic: born out of need, with solutions created by spirit helpers and instructed to earthly people, almost exclusively feminine, using what is accessible from the earth as supply.

The rural purpose of amulets is to protect daily life valuables, most essentially life itself: babies, breast-feeding mothers, pregnant women, farm animals, family members, crops, and then the home, the homes of animals such as the chicken coop, the borders of one's land, and all the food made from growing one's own crops. Natural rural amulets used in the perseverance and preservation of daily sacred life were naturally from nature and reflect an innate apotropaic source, which is appropriate for people living in cooperation with nature. Whether protective or reflective amulets, for magico-medical cures or banishing spirits and breaking spells...the ingredients used in amulets are found in other rituals consistently expressing the same meaning: iron, salt, trees, branches, flowers, herbs, stones, corals, and animal parts of specific animals whose forms are shape-shifted into during astral flights such as dogs, wolves, badgers, owls.

As with all rural traditions actions made in the physical world have their counterpart in the spirit world. Amulets for protection, while grounded in the earth and with the power to keep physical body safe, also have the power to set boundaries against negative spirits while protecting the spirit body.

In contrast, a popular Roman amulet was the phallus, a symbol distinctly separate from the natural elemental world. While there was also the hand "fig", the female counterpart of this, the phallus itself has an entirely conceptual protective meaning which is separate from nature and is also without a psychic meaning. The natural act of the phallus is penetration, invasion. The natural act of the hand "fig", in contrast, is to cut the psychic circuit from outside invasion; in other words, setting a boundary preventing penetration.

The natural amulets derive from natural protective forces and not from conceptually created ideas. The powers of nature are generally agreed upon worldwide, whereas conceptually created ideas vary. In indigenous traditions for example, trees are often personified and communicated with as one would pray to a divinity. The trees also offer specific protective energies and fertility energies based on the ancient knowledge of these trees whether the rue branch as a **cima di ruta** with domestic symbols of protection hung upon it like a Christmas tree whose meanings are all connected to the Goddesses powers granted to mothers, or dogwood stakes and **legnu stregoniu** pieces who grow protected by larger trees due to efforts of birds, or as the oaks who hid local people from thieves and soldiers during wartime or the oak trees who provided spirits of babies to women and protected them when they returned to these trees to give birth under their boughs. The nature itself taught some people its purpose, while the spirit world of feminine divinities taught others through direct interaction. This is in contrast to other spiritual practices who have synthesized mentally and created, with artistic freedom, the magical attributes of trees, and therefore different ideas are found in the different belief systems.

Depending on the village and its region's natural resources, the ingredients of amulets can be different although nature's psychic language is still consistently present. In Sardinia for example, early amulets were comprised of animal teeth and bones and then became traditionally more ornate and designed with hand wound silver resembling flowers and nipples, set around black stones and corals, with **cima di ruta** type amulets made from naturally bifurcated coral and fixed with tiny bells and even crosses with Madonnas painted on them.

In central Italy, animal teeth, badger fur, dog hair, **cornetti** made of naturally bifurcated tree branches along with iron pieces were more common. Many of these natural amulets were shaped to look like broom filters or simply the item itself. Further south in Napoli natural amulets existed alongside ones in a designed style, made of silver and sometimes gold, and with the presence of red and white corals, but often carved into shapes such as owls rather than retaining their original form. In the northwest of Italy, near the sea, amulets reflected the sea as a source. Many more amulets have been perpetuated based on rural ideas as a base and yet evolved with artistic liberty to beautify it or contemporize it. Inevitably the more designed an amulet becomes, the more likely its connection to its original purpose is lost along with the natural meaning of its symbolism. To keep some meaning alive, a conceptual one is created and perpetuated. This is how design evolves. The **cimaruta** is a perfect example of this being that there are no historical examples of it predating middle period cultivation. It's been suggested perhaps it was based upon a simpler Etruscan version, the only one that exists in a museum in Bologna, but still the divide between the Etruscan version and the highly designed and decorated "witch" version is great.

Amulets, just like cures, were adapted by outsiders wanting to grasp their

Italian Magic: Secret Lives of Women

magic such as happened in the middle period, and were remodeled and taken into a more commercially minded direction and were documented by the outsider culture in ways that reflected their conceptualized usage. Such as: escaping social pressures like arranged marriages, economic issues, job positions, revenge.

Photo: Davide Tiso, 2020

THE HOME

The home is a significant place in rural Italy's culture, with room placements and layouts carefully considered. Many women gave birth in front of the hearth. Rooms were used for specific tasks that were considered daily sacred rituals, such as in the transformation of ingredients into food. These daily sacred rituals and their results (bread, cheese)were often the focus of envy of others in rural stories, and the lives lived within the home could also be attacked by envy from others. A woman's magic was in her home, as well as her loved ones, which she also worked to protect and cure.

It's not a coincidence then, that many stories called "folk stories" about rural life are about negative spirits shape-shifted from their human form trying to get into the home to drain energy or blood from people inside it, or to plant **fatture** curses within the home's walls or inside cushions. The home is an intimate space, both physically and energetically, and therefore spells, curses and ghost stories often involve the home being broken into through cracks in doors, windows and through the spaces of keyholes, crept through by shadow cats and serpents and the true forms of the shape-shifters knocking on the front door revealing their identities.

The protective measures of the home, along with the protective measures of amulets worn on the body, are types of agreements, laws of the threshold between humans and spirits.

AMULETS AND PROTECTIONS

NATURAL AMULETS / APOTROPAIC PLANTS

Amulets in rural Italy are comprised of several general categories:

+ natural plants/woods/seeds/herbs/flowers
+ natural animal parts: badger hair, wolf teeth, dog skull, deer horn, serpent head, mummified parts of poisonous animals like scorpions
+ natural jewels: red coral, onyx, seashell spiral
+ designed jewels which are a combination of these items along with silver or gold and...
+ a combination of these items in a leather or fabric pouch worn close to the skin
+ and for a special few people, their own placenta...

LEGNU STREGONIU / WITCH WOOD

Witch wood is born through a natural phenomenon that often occurs in willow trees specifically. It's the result of a natural cavity opening in the trunk of the tree which is then made fertile by birds who nest in these cavities dropping seeds of berries and leaves. From this natural and incidental fertilization, elder trees are sometimes born in the cavity. Due to the symbolism and parallel to the uterus, the elder plants which grow in this way are considered to have potent fertility magic, so rural women take a piece of this wood and wear it on their bodies during pregnancy as protection against envy that could cause abortion. It is even used for farm animals. Considering that women would also go to the trees to take the spirits of their babies from the hollowed parts of special fertility trees, it's consistent that hollowed trees that have growth occurring would be related to as supportive of fertility, not to mention the symbolism of birds planting seeds there and their connection to bird goddesses.

There are 2 types of **legno stregone** witch wood, one born from willow trees, and another one from the holly plant:

> *"in the case of holly,* **stregoniu** *refers to the use made of this plant with coriaceous and thorny leaves used to defend witches; in the case of the elderberry seedling born in the cavity of a tree, the adjective means 'bewitched* **stregato**,*' in the sense of 'enchanted* **incantato**,*' endowed with power and not in the negative sense to which the reference to witches would lead one to think."* [620]

IL CORNIOLO / DOGWOOD

Dogwood's natural hardness made it a desirable amulet, along with it's very natural bifurcation that reminds one of hand -horns, which deflect negative energy. It's name is similar to the word spear, and it's used to defend against the evil eye and envy.

Italian Magic: Secret Lives of Women

APOTROPAIC FILTERS
BROOMS + BROOM - LIKE PLANTS, PREVENTATIVE

Handmade brooms and plants that grow in a broom-like formation have a traditional use in rural Italy, which is one of a filter. Brooms and plant bundles made of plants with inherent powers to filter out negativity have been used at points of entry to a home: at the front door, hanging in windows, and tied to balconies.

Negative energy is not some free-flying force in these beliefs, but rather it is sent by negative spirits (either the spirit of an envious person still in-the-flesh, or a disembodied spirit), and so the practice of using brooms to protect against witches is a longstanding one. To Americans it may sound strange-that a tool of a witch is being used to protect against a witch, but remember in rural Italy that magic is everywhere and commonly used, and the name "witch" refers to someone who does black magic to harm others. It is of course also mixed up in the church's anti-healer propaganda.

Psychic illnesses such as **sugatura** are believed to be caused by this type of witch who harms babies during the night while astral traveling (passing through the keyhole of doors, disembodied for the night, and having to return to their bodies by sunrise).

The protective procedure therefore is to use specific broom-like plants that have lots of tiny little pieces that act as a negative energy filter (salt is used in the same way) so that the disembodied witch will be stuck trying to count her way through the broom fibers or grains of salt (as per a type of agreement) and get lost in the count (due to her lack of education) and have to flee before the sun comes up.

While there is the typical vampire theme woven into these stories, it's not unfounded considering the resulting psychic illnesses, such as **sugatura** are ones where the blood is affected to the point of anemia. When present in children, there often remain bruise marks

321

on the neck or body where the "vampire witch" allegedly drained some blood. Further, there are so many personal stories about types of disembodied spirits helping women or haunting children, that it is possible to see threads connecting the illnesses, the hauntings, the cures, and the protective and preventative plants and amulets together in a holistic, comprehensive way.

Nevertheless, regardless of the cultural expression, the plants used as brooms (filters) are apotropaic ones, and their natural powers are agreed upon no matter where in Italy a person is and also throughout the Mediterranean. The powers of the plants are agreed upon and this is possibly one of the only unified curative and magical bodies of knowledge that spans the entire planet and all its various magical practices.

In rural Italy, many of these protective and negative filter plants have earned the nickname **scacciadiavoli** or **cacciadiavoli** meaning "chasing devils" or catching devils" in reference to their banishing abilities. Some of these plants are used in exorcisms which, in rural Italy, are the result of psychic illness that are caused by negative spirits (what contemporary people often call spirit attachments).

The broom-like plants in this category share common traits:

+ Lots of little pieces, whether tiny branch stems or lots of little leaves, spiky shapes.

+ On a physical level they repair a part of the body magically connected to boundary breaches.

Iperico (hypericum) is used on the skin, infused in oil, for healing bug bites and internally for lifting the moods lowered due to depression. Magically **iperico** is burned to exorcise negative spirits who attack a person's spiritual energy. Dried bundles are kept outside the

Italian Magic: Secret Lives of Women

door or hanging from windows to prevent night-time astral visits from disembodied spirits and they are left on the roof to prevent lightning fire.

Timo serpillo's (serpent thyme) iron content has made it an excellent plant to re-invigorate the body, in fact historically it's been used to replenish soldiers. In rural Italy it's been burned to repel serpents and scorpions. Magically it's used to restore someone's spirit after an attack by a negative spirit. Due to the belief it's believed to have be a strong repellent to negative energy and its physical feature of lots of spiky, tiny little leaves, it's hung in bundles outside the door to protect the home and under beds of infants to protect them from night-flying witches.

Brooms: above: public fountain, Triora
Below: inside the author's favorite BnB
La Tana delle Volpi, Triora.

AMULETS AND PROTECTIONS

 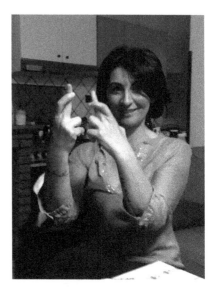

Photos: Silvia Pigna from Guardia Sanframondi, demonstrating "closing the circuit" against negative energy by crossing fingers and ankles.

The common theme here is that there is a sort of universal agreement between the negative spirits and the people the spirits want to harm: if there is some item left at the door that has many little pieces, the negative spirits must stop and attempt to get an accurate count of the little pieces. The deeper belief is that these negative spirits are shape-shifted witches from the countryside who make black magic and, since they are uneducated, they will not be successful in keeping count but will lose their count and have to start over and again. If the sun comes up as they are counting they must flee and hide so their identity remains secret. This, losing count thwarts the harmful efforts of negative spirits entering homes.

Other items used as filters to force a disembodied spirit to stop and count the tiny pieces of before preventing them from entering in the home:

+ bowls of salt, sand, or grains left on windowsills, *sometimes sacks of salt or grains or alfalfa seeds were used on the windowsills accompanied by bowls of fine salt.* 621
+ **setaccio** (grain sifter) used by doors or windows,
+ wild asparagus sprigs on the ditches of windows and walls 622
+ skeins of hemp or wool hanging on the door 623
+ brooms were also left behind the bedroom door as were rosemary sprigs
+ branches of holly hung on the door
+ horseshoe, splinter from the mill, trowel.
+ twigs and branches of juniper on the door

> *The objects horseshoe, mill, trowel-work as talismans because of the innumerable movements (beats, revolutions, rotations) performed by them. In order to carry out malfeasances, [to cross] the threshold*

of the house or room, the witch must know the exact number of those movements. The figure will work as a password. Otherwise, it will not be able to harm. To the series of amulets that draw their power from the difficulty of knowing the number, belongs the broomstick, or straw, used everywhere as a deterrent. 624

Ginepro Juniper: In addition to Juniper branches being used as filter protection against negative spirits, *in Castelluccio di Norcia* [Umbria] *the juniper wood carvings* [also called magic rods and apotropaic cornets] *were carved to protect from the evil eye and from the vagaries, especially if combined with a tuft of badger fur.* 625

Other protective features of juniper leaves, besides having lots of tiny little leaves, is that its wood burns as a bright white flame, and so is also used to purify homes, and juniper **suffumigi** fumigations were widely used at the turn of the new year, to burn away any energy preventing prosperity for the new year.

Perhaps most significant attribute of juniper is the *virtue of driving from the house the malefics and the evil entities that, especially at night, acted to harm the sleepers* 626 which reinforces the relationship in rural life between the spirit world and the earthly one. These ghost stories have a reality that plays out and is grounded in the domestic rural world where "myth" meets manifestation.

Shepherds also lit juniper branches on fire to set a barrier of protection for themselves and their flocks *against elves and witches who, otherwise, could harm livestock and damage milk production.* 627 For rural life, the world invisible to many people was part of their daily lives, their nighttime lives, and also during doorways in the year's passage of time such as solstices and equinoxes.

FLOWERS

Flowers of apotropaic plants, similar to leaves, reveal magically protective properties. Many of the plants listed thus far which protect against negative spirits have yellow 5 petaled flowers, such as "rue" ruta graveolens which is honored in **cimaruta** charms. Some of these flowers turn red when crinkled or infused in oil or even once they are dried, such as **iperico** hypericum. There are of course plants with special flowers whose parts arc used in flying ointments such as **stramonium** datura stramonium/jimsonweed and bella-donna.

In Taggia, a comune in the region of Liguria, there is a regenerative ritual celebrated on the 22nd of July. It's the anniversary of **santa Maria Maddalena** St. Mary Magdalene and **del Ballo della Morte**, the dance of death. There is a procession and extended celebration, but in this focused ritual, 2 men enact a scene for onlookers. One pretends to be **santa Maria** and the other is himself. The two enjoy a wild dance, enacting scenes of love and playfulness, accompanied by joyful music, when suddenly **Lena** (Maddalena as she is also known) falls to the ground in death.

AMULETS AND PROTECTIONS

During the procession, bundles of **lavanda** lavender are handed out for this moment of death when the man who was dancing with Lena must try to revive her. He does so by either hitting or brushing her belly with the lavender bundles, or in some versions he will cover her in many lavender bundles. Here, the significance is the plant lavender, associated since most ancient times with fertility and as having apotropaic protective powers gains negativity. Further, the brushing or hitting of Lena's belly, place of regeneration and birth, is evidence of the heart of this ritual and its seasonal connection. Villagers consider this a shamanic rite into the land of the dead to bring back her life, resembling the later story of **Persefone** Persephone and also resembling the story of **santa Anna** Saint Anne which is incidentally celebrated just a few days later. A funeral song at the end of this rite opens the enactment of Lena's resurrection, and then the dance begins again, honoring the cyclical powers of life and plants and light.

On the island of Sardinia flowers make suggestive appearances in traditional outfits and ornate breads which honoring the unfolding beauty of the goddess through her parallel: women and their ability to give birth to children. Flowers, amulets shaped like milk ducts of the breast (which look like flowers), nipples (life-giving milk and vaginal and labial suggestive costumes express all these ideas of the Great Goddess Mother and her do-main of life over which she protects and heals and watches.

BERRIES
Another distinctive feature of apotropaic plants also have red berries, sometimes black berries like Juniper berries psychic eye regeneration protection against negative spirit Juniper berries..which "see" like black stone eyes and "push out" negative energy.

ANIMAL PARTS

In rural places we find a connection between spiritual beliefs about animals in the usage of their parts for protection that also have a sympathetic link.

With the psychic illness **straidura,** caused by night-flying witches (in truth, astrally traveling spirits with harmful intentions, owl feathers (night flying bird) used in the cure. In some rural villages the barn was protected by the carcass of an owl nailed to the door, a practice banned by the church towards communities accused of being "syncretic". Owl statues are still used in many places, even contemporary businesses, to protect a home or business and in the visiting rooms of healers. The owls are stationed near the entry door, facing it, to ward off negative energy.

DOG BODIES

Dogs also are believed to be natural enemies of the witch, here defined as a person who does "black magic" to others. Dogs are attributed with having protective instincts against many of the animals used as doubles by shape-shifting witches who use "night flights" or astral travel to specifically: carry out **fatture** against people, who employ negative spirits to harm others, who shape-shift into cats to carry out curses. For this reason, dog skulls, hair and full bodies buried alive have been used to protect the home and people, acting as a filter whose energy prevents the embodied person with negative intentions from approaching or entering the home of someone they have targeted.

> A rather brutal filter method to protect a growing child was that of burying *alive under the bricks of the floor, just behind the threshold of the front door, because the witch, until she had counted all the hair of the dog, did not enter and meanwhile a child grew up"*. 628

This is a documented ritual in Rescia, Sciedi, Avendita and Valnerina [in the region of Umbria] In the region of *Abruzzo:*

> *after killing a dog, it was customary to place his body behind the front door. Another custom consisted of burying the dog under the floor of a room on the ground floor. In Ascolano, a similar custom: to keep the* **striadura** *from entering the house, especially if there were babies, 3 live puppies were buried at the door. The witches, who hate dogs, could not even have approached the door*. 629

In other words, the entire body of a dog, with its skull, teeth and hair would act as a longstanding filter due to an almost endless amount of hairs to be counted along with the protective teeth and skull.

DOG HAIR

The custom of wearing a tuft of dog hair to protect against witches was widespread in all the Marches [i.e. in all the provinces of the region of Marche] 630 similar to the way badger hair is worn, in a square patch shape that resembles broom bristles.

DOG BONES

It was customary to carry a tuft of dog hair or to fasten shoes using strings of dog skin 631 in Abruzzo as well.

Located on the right bank of the river Nera, near the Black Valley of the Witches, we find dog bones used as protective amulets. In various parts of Umbria dog bones were kept near the bedroom at night to prevent visits from night flying witches.

Some people also used dog skulls and dog skulls filled with a bit of olive oil, either on the windowsill or at their doors. During nights where shouts were heard from neighbors experiencing night flying witches, a community tradition in San Martino, for example was to say a magic phrase (equivalent of "beware the witches, beware their scorn") *and hurriedly put the bone, or the skull of the dog, on the windowsill.* 633 to extend the protection to a further barrier. Dog skulls were also kept as hidden fetishes as in the case of a personal testimony from Castel San Felice in Val di Narco, where a woman's mother secretly had one for decades *kept in a special niche in the fireplace.* 634

Dog bones and skulls protected bedroom doors, chimneys and window entry points as well as thresholds: **thresholds here meaning physical points of crossing into or out of a place**; whereas brooms and plants protected door keyholes and windows: **thresholds accessible through astral flight and shape-shifting only.**

While people using these filters were aware that the spirits aren't stopped by doors and walls, there is a sort of agreement between the enfleshed and the maleficent spirits that requires a password to be correctly given in a counting ritual, in order to gain entry into homes that are in fact protected by these countable fetishes. Because negative spirits can be disembodied or embodied, and thresholds can be physical or energetic, magical acts of protection (or cursing) exist in both the physical plane and in the realm of spirit. So, filters are used for entryways such as doorways, but also symbolic entryways or places that are difficult to seal, such as that wind can enter through and therefore, spirits.

Because thresholds as physical doorways or crossings have their parallel in the spirit world as thresholds between the physical world and the world of spirits, they are literally connected to life and death. Therefore protections must be able to cross worlds. The dog is long believed to be a psychopomp who traverses these worlds. In this light, the place of burial for dogs as well as placenta of newborns being under the thresholds of houses would seem cohesive rituals enacting both on the physical and spiritual planes. Therefore, the filter amulets focus upon those points. As with all rural cures, there are physical actions which have a corresponding and parallel action int he energy world of spirits.

DOG SKIN SHOESTRINGS

Dog skin shoestrings were used by night travelers or anyone who had to travel on foot late at night. They created a psychic barrier of invisibility against witches: the witches could sense the traveler but the dog skin would prevent them from being able to reach the traveler and harm him, whether the witches were in physical form or in spirit form. There was a specific call-and-response used in this situation, as many filter protections require as part of the energy agreement.

There are no shortages of stories about spirit activity at night, whether attacks in the home, or processions of spirits being seen or interacted with outdoors. A common documented story (meaning there are likely many more occurrences among people who don't talk to anthropologists) from men walking at night over distances is that they have noticed women at wells or small rivers seeming to wash their laundry. An odd sight at night, the men knew to respond using words as filters in a typical rural "call and response" style of interaction with the spirits. In this case, the interaction goes something like this:

Man asking the woman spirit after greeting her: *"isn't the water cold as ice?"* Woman spirit replies: *"if you didn't have the dog with you, we'd make you find out"* in dialect, of course. Full testimonies can be found here (follow the footnote) : 635

The people who used dog skin as laces did so because they believe, through their experiences, that it was kept them from being drowned or attacked by the women, or the spirits of the women even as they were being threatened. And, the local stories all report

Italian Magic: Secret Lives of Women

that the women, after failing to attack the men with dog laces, vanished suddenly.

DOG MILK

In Ternano, three drops of bitch milk [...] were used to combat the witches' spells. 636

Considering some of these details in the battles of good witches versus evil witches which have been prevalent rural Italy, it's an important moment to pause and reflect. These battles and all their amulets, protections, and details (plant filters, magic word filters, night spirits, shape shifters...) are not part of the Roman cult world with its constructed temples and inner study chambers reserved for noble families and elite moneyed peoples with opulent tools. It's the rural world that has been the cosmos-meets-earthly world of sorcery, night flights and night school, apparitions, shape shifting, astral travel with faeries, mediumship and more. In this light, it's easier to see where some of the confusing pantheon of goddesses and female divinities really made their place: OUTSIDE the temple cultures and actively part of rural peoples' lives.

For example, in the rural world the dog is a protector against and an enemy of black magic and the witches who perform it. Cats are the animal most frequently chosen by shape-shifting sorceresses who enact curses and spells using negative spirits. So it's interesting to note the prevalence of **Ecate** Hecate in many rural places and her protection of mothers and their babies, teaching them how to break spells and protect people, how to meet with her at crossroads and ask for protection for their babies in this place where 3 streets meet. Ecate Hecate has long been imagined with a dog at her side, remembering that she is a spirit and so is the dog, that she breaks black magic spells, supporting its undoing, and that the dog opposes the black magic vehicle for curses: the cat, as a shape-shifted witch. While the Romans made Heate part of their world, she was a psychopomp and abundance Goddess for rural people who were vulnerable and for whom sacred magic was a daily affair.

BADGER HAIR

In traditions where animal parts are eaten to strengthen the vitality of the corresponding human part with its energy (such as eating liver and brains), using animal fur and bones to strengthen a person's powers against negative spirits applies the same sympathetic usage, whether to promote communication with spirits or to be protected by spirits against other spirits. This usage is found in rural Italy, with emphasis placed on the animals who populate the vicinity.

Badgers, like dogs, are admired for their ability to sense and escape danger. Also, their habit of being noctural, being efficient in solitude and their perceived shrewdness makes their hair symbolically desirable to use as a filter against **il malocchio** and maleficent night time spirits.

AMULETS AND PROTECTIONS

Photo: Davide Tiso, 2020

BADGER PROTECTION OF BARN ANIMALS

- Badger hair is hung on barn doors and stable doors *where rabbits are bred.* [637] (Rescia, Pergugia)

- Badger hair is tied to a *yoke at the neck of the pair of oxen.* [638] (Rescia, Perugina)

BADGER PROTECTION OF NURSING MOTHERS

In Abruzzo, a ritual was that the **comare** gifted to the **puerpera** new mother a tuft of badger hairs to defend her from the evil eye, specially active on the production of breast milk. To emphasize the value of the gift, among the people who live there, we used to put the talisman in a golden case. [639]

BADGER PROTECTION OF CHILDREN AND MEN

Even today, in San Giorgio, someone puts on badger-haired children.
In Val di Narco the old men of the past always wore badger fur. [640]

GENERAL AMULETS

Badger hair was also combined with juniper wood carved into a cornetto horned shape. This was a common amulet used in Castelluccio, Umbria [621] Whether patches of hair, or hair combined with badger leathered skin, or coupled with **il cornetto di ginepro**

Italian Magic: Secret Lives of Women

juniper wood horn, this was used in daily protection of a person or their possessions which might received envy, such as *house keys or front doors.* 641

DEER HORN AMULETS

Contramazzinas, counter-spells in Sardinia have been traditionally made with a *perforated disk obtained by cutting a deer horn, duly enchanted by a sorcerer through* **brebus** *ritual words,* 642 recited on a full moon night; often combined *with hard stones, especially obsidian, carnelian, amethyst.* 643 Although for some sorcerers, the appropriate moon phase, in line with healer beliefs, is when the moon is losing its power in the wane.

The purpose of **su pinnadeddu** is to take a psychic hit for the wearer. The slice of deer horn, cut across the horn looking *like a small wheel, is tied to the child's neck, and the evil eye is downloaded there* 644 empowered to do so by the charged words of the sorcerer. Sometimes **su pinadeddu** can break once it absorbs the psychic attack:

> *"My grandmother, who was near and had felt the crash, had run immediately to look at my* **pinnadeddu**. *It had split into two pieces: the evil fluid had dumped there and saved me."* 645

AMULETS FROM THE SEA AND EARTH

Occhio di Santa Lucia The eye of Saint Lucia. In nature, this "eye" is the protective shield of a mollusk called Astrea rugosa. In the way the **su pinnadeddu** takes a psychic hit for the wearer, the **occhio di santa Lucia** does a similar service by watching for the incoming evil eye and protecting the wearer by trapping it in its spiral before it hits the victim and spirals it out. Consider how psychics often use a spiral flow of energy to clean their spirit bodies of negative energy, especially from other spirits, this shell, this symbolic eye of the Divine Feminine works similarly.

The red color of this shell is another marker: the Goddess speaks through this color, calling our attention to its naturally apotropaic power to protect and to restore, representing the regenerative blood of the Great Mother Goddess.

Saint **Santa Lucia** is invoked for curative assistance with eye illnesses and their cures using fennel, and here she is also invoked for psychic eye clarity.

The author has one of these shells, but it disappeared every time she tried to photograph it.

Corallo rosso Red Coral has long been used as a protective amulet. It's red color is an indication of the nature of its use. The regenerative and protective aspects of the blood of the Goddess is expressed in red coral through a story about Medusa:

AMULETS AND PROTECTIONS

"When Perseus took off the head of the la Gorgone/Medusa, tells the myth, some drops of blood fell at sea and, solidified, they produced the coral, estimated in all times as a very effective antidote against fascination because it participates in the nature of the Gorgon." [646]

Here, the nature of the Gorgon is her eyes that have the power to paralyze their prey just like a serpent can. So this ability to summon and protect through the eyes in attributed to the Medusa, so therefore her blood (red coral) also contains this power against the evil eye: to stop it in its tracks.

While Medusa's power to summon energy through her eyes is well-known, this is also a magical operation performed in rural Italy: summoning and sending energy (healing, protection and also envy and negative spirits) through the eyes. The power of the eyes is a serious power and a dual one: it's not only a physical ability but it's also a spiritual one. While we see our physical world, our spirit also peers out from the invisible world of spirit from our eyes into the physical world. With the eyes, it's possible to send energy, such as the evil eye **il malocchio**, or to curse someone with a spirit attachment, and also to heal.

Red coral is coveted for its natural bifurcations (branch shapes), but is also used in circular forms (like eyes) and **cornetto** forms (natural horn points reminiscent of the goddess' moon crescent)) and also carved into **manofigas** (hand figs). Red coral itself is referred to by elderly locals as *"stones of the sea"* [647] and as a "blood tree." Red coral was inherited in many regions, even those inland such as Umbria.

View from the mountains of Rieti, Lazio.

Italian Magic: Secret Lives of Women

Second item from left is a version of **su coccu**, collection of the author. Photo: Davide Tiso, 2020.

CORAL FOR BRIDES

In some places where the **suocera** mother-in-law passed down curative and domestic magic to her new **nuora** daughter-in-law, the **suocera** also presented the red coral necklace to her, often made from little tiny pieces. Sometimes the necklaces were inherited directly from the mother.

> *The most coveted gift from the girls of the past, when they trusted it, was the coral necklace that they would wear on the day of the wedding and on every other festive occasion.* 648

This would protect them from various types of envy for the duration of their lives. In other places, it was the boyfriend who would present the necklace

> *The gift from the boyfriend of the traditional necklace of corals, even more than the ring, definitively signed the offer of love and the request for marriage.* 649

The necklace was given to the **suocera**, in Umbrian tradition, who presented it for her son and to the community and then delivered it to the neck of her **nuora** in a sort of ritual, where everyone became aware of the couple's promise of marriage to each other. In fact, the shape of the coral necklace has a presence in **rimedi contro il malocchio** remedies against the evil eye: when this oil drop pattern making a necklace shape as a circle with little bubbles of oil all connected, it's considered to be an omen of the coral necklace, revealing a female is the **jettatura**, the one who made and threw the evil eye at someone.

AMULETS AND PROTECTIONS

CORAL FOR MOTHERS AND CHILDREN

To protect themselves from **il malocchio**, *the mothers wore a coral horn, or the common tuft of badger hair, on their shirts.* 650

In some areas, as in Rescia, a coral racelet was placed around the wrists of the children. In Meggiano, to defend the children from the evil eye **occhiaticio** *it was used to tie a string of coral beads to their arm or, in the absence, red beads.* 651

This ritual, of making a bracelet for the child from the mother's necklace beads, is similar to the practice of the mother sewing a bit of her own clothing into the baby's first dress or baptism dress.

Generally it was the mother or grandmother who prepared the apotropaic bracelet for her child, or grandchild, using the grains of the bridal necklace [...] as well as protection or **il malocchio** *and envy, they considered the coral bracelet effective also against witches.* 652

At Fonte Vena, to be effective, the bracelet had to be given by a relative. At Castel San Felice the protective bracelets for (wealthy) children were of gold and, together with the corals, were adorned with three white beads. 653

Red coral in its many forms was devoutly used to protect against negative spirits of all kinds as well as sorceresses and nightmares and it was believed to both attract and promote love. It was used in its natural tree shape, or in little beads, or carved into mano figas and other shapes. But if it couldn't be required, it was such an important amulet that its red color was used in a sympathetic nod as red string.

RIBBONS

Ribbons of red or green are also used in the same way, when the red coral could not be acquired nor afforded. It was commonly pinned to children to protect them from the evil eye. Ribbons are often reused from older items by people who can't invest in coral or **su coccu** or any of the more designed amulets which can be a great financial investment for families. Whichever amulet is used, the visual vocabulary and sympathetic meanings are consistent: red, green or black, branch shapes or eye-shapes, worn near the heart, either combined with other symbols of the Goddess' gifts in nature or stripped to the simplest one of all: Her red blood of regeneration and protection.

Italian Magic: Secret Lives of Women

Red coral with bells in natural coral/tree shape. Apotropaic. From "Gioielli: storia, lin-guaggio, religiosita' dell'ornamento in Sardegna" a spectacular book of Sardinian amulets and sacred ornaments.

BLACK STONES

A Sardinian amulet used to protect from the evil eye is called **su coccu**, but something similar is also found in Gargano on the mainland's eastern coast. It can also be called **sabegia** or **pinnadellu**.

It has the same purpose as the Eye of Saint Lucia and the deer horn: to take a psychic hit for the wearer from **il malocchio** and absorb it, leaving the wearer unharmed. It may also break from catching negativity. It can be made of osbidian or onyx, generally black but also sometimes white, red, or another stone, depending on its natural color, set between 2 silver decorative cups that are shaped like flower petals and breast milk ducts.In this way it generally hangs by a chain attached to either side of the stone. It is sometimes combined with other stones or shells. In Gargano, women wear *a pebble that contains another smaller one. Its composition recalls the maternal belly that hosts the fetus.* 654

The **su coccu** is generally worn by mothers and pregnant women. More commonly the form called **pinnadellu** is worn by children. As with most jewelery amulets, they are worn around the neck hanging near the heart center (which is where negative spells aim and anchor in). Sometimes they are pinned to the heart area, and mostly they are worn under the clothes and against the skin.

LIGHTNING STONES

Le Pietre del fulmine or lightning stones are a type of iron-infused stone that fall from the sky during storms and are believed to have protective powers. They are considered even "bullets from lightning" due to their physical iron content and shapes (sometimes egg-like or potato like or smaller rough balls) and carry a supernatural weight. While rural people are aware this is an atmospheric phenomenon, lightning and lightning stones are seen as supernatural events also, due to their possibly negative affect upon the farms and, being part of the weather, open to being manipulated by black magic sorceress so forces that can be used negatively.

In a society that draws its livelihood from agriculture, atmospheric phenomena, such as hail and violent storms, are subject to special religious or magical precautions aimed at preventing the onset of such calamities. Thunderstorms especially the violent downpours that break out in late spring, or early summer, are often fatal for cereal crops. 655

AMULETS AND PROTECTIONS

The lightning stones themselves are considered amulets rather than an omen however, and they are valued for their protectiveness against black magic, *Those who owned one of these ferrous nuclei hung it around their neck in the certainty of remaining immune to lightning and from the evil.* [656] Perhaps because this iron fell from the sky, *it was also believed that the "lightning stone" lost its virtue once it came into contact with the vulgar iron, for this reason it was carefully kept aside.* [657] *In the Marches, the ancient lithic arrowheads were considered talismans to be very effective in defending themselves from lightning as they were believed to be petrified lightning.* [658]

Black meteorites have appeared throughout Italy's ancient history as important atmospheric phenomena connected to the arrival of and veneration of feminine Divinities. In Sicily's history, black river stones were found from the mid 5th millennium B.C. [659] with carved breasts and pubic triangles.* Then again with the black aerolite storm of 204 BCE that would coincide with the Roman veneration of the Phrygian goddess Cybele (also known as Mountain Mother among other names) who was represented with by black aniconic stone, just as Diana of Ephesus was.** Other documentations record a continuity of this connection even until the recent 1626 date of the witch hunts in Northwestern Italy, where a woman named Benedetta Carzolia of Finale Ligure was reported as being seen kissing her black stone with her back to the church before entering [660] and was reported as doing so because locals were well aware of the pagan usage of black stones in veneration of the Divine Feminine.

*For information about the Divine Feminine and water source connections see "IWAMW Vol 1" or the from the source, "Language of the Goddess" by Marija Gimbutas
** To read more about this see "Italy's Witches and Medicine Women Vol 1" by Karyn Crisis, chapter 13.

Italian Magic: Secret Lives of Women

Photo: Davide Tiso, 2020. Author's medallion collection used for healings.

Il breve or the short, as in a "little shirt" is an amulet pouch that can contain a variety of ingredients for protection such as wolf/dog/badger teeth, olive leaves, coarse salt , animal hair, bread crumbs, garlic cloves, medallions, coins, pieces of wood, etc.

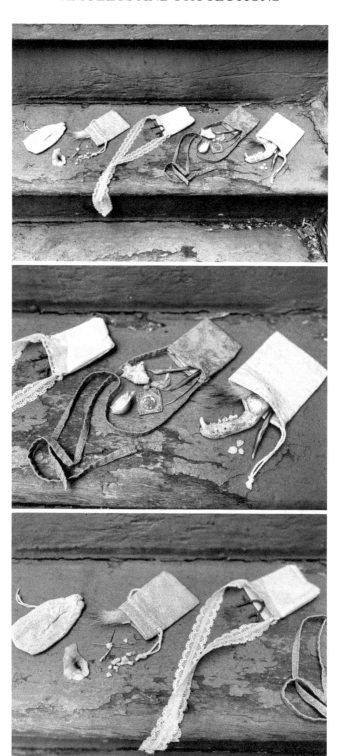

Italian Magic: Secret Lives of Women

TREES

Perhaps the most famous tree in Italy is the **Noce di Benenveto** the Walnut Tree of Benevento. This is partially due to its presence in Inquisition documents which made it visible in history. The popular stories around this tree, in a nutshell, say to the effect: the walnut of Benevento was a tree located in the **stretto di barba*** in the region of Camapnia. Witches from all across Italy and her islands would fly to this tree at night to receive potions and spells form the devil. The tree was a challenge to the church which was trying to stamp out paganism (and female rural healers) at the time. In the year 663 S. Barbato, Archbishop of Benevento, cut down the tree alleged to have a serpent living in its roots (the devil). This and the fact that this tree was present in maps also made its presence in history more crystallized than other local legends.

This is not the only magic tree connected to stories of witches taking flight and meeting the Goddess: there are many others from the island of Sicily, throughout the regions of Tuscany and Umbria other rural villages of Campania, and onward. There are oak trees and lime trees considered to be magical meeting places for night flights of witches too, not just walnut trees. At the same time, the legend of the walnut of Benevento was well known as far northwest as Badalucco in Liguria and also on in Sicily. And, we must correct the popular story to its original forms which state that women were invited to fly by **La Signora del Gioco** and the Fairies and that there was not talk of the devil at all.

Beyond this story, the tree represents a dual power. The walnut tree offered food, wood to burn, ointments, black dye and shelter under its boughs to poor rural people. At the same time it was feared due to the fact that often field workers left their babies under its shade that blocked the light so thoroughly that some babies developed jaundice from lack of sunlight, and this helped give the tree a nefarious reputation for causing illness. Similar to fountains, the tree was a place where women were gathered after reaching the dream state and moving into the astral realm. From here, the spirits who invited them to the night school would fly with them to their final meeting place...which sometimes was in fact a tree.

In Italian village stories and popular tales the woman has a dual power: the power to heal and the power to curse. It's a strong symbol of women having access to secrets that both the church and Roman nobles tried to keep control over as though they were a commodity. Generally speaking, in a broader sense it's a symbol of poor people having

---

*the Stretto di Barba is an area of Campania with a peculiar river and where the Goddess is alleged to have phsically manifested herself, among other wonderful magical happenings. Read more about it in "Italy's Witches And Medicine Women Vol 1" and Carlo Napolitano's "Il triangolo stregano" ..which inspired the author to visit Campania and ultimately to write "IWAMWV1".

Italian Magic: Secret Lives of Women

access to knowledge the wealthy seek to harness and often cannot even reach with their money nor power, which created frustration, competition and ultimately the witch hunts It's a symbol of people having access to the universe outside the glorious temples.

More importantly than these earthly ideas are the ideas of the spirit world embedded within their tales: ascension. In shamanism of Central Asia, Indonesia, Siberia, Iran, Hungary, South America, North America, Vanuatu, Indonesia, Australia, (and others, keeping in mind there are many different groups in these areas with their own slightly different styles yet all based on the same spiritual principles), in rural Italian shamanism and even in spiritualism we find : trees, ladders and tree-like columns and mountain tops used as points of focus for ascension into the spirit world and assisted by common animals such as horses and birds. So the tree is an actual conduit not just of Divine knowledge, but a conduit for astral travel itself.

> *...climbing birch trees,* [661] *...climbing of a tree-pole in ritual ascension* [662] *......they posses a sort of magical rope with which they can climb to the tops of trees* [663] *...go up to the sky by ladder* [664]*... birches are called "pillars"...*[665] *Among the Jakun is the "soul ladder"* [666] to cite just a small few examples from shamanic traditions around the world.

And in rural Italy, we find these ideas of ascension in one of the many prayers to the Madonna:

> *Madonna, Madonna,*
> *che del ciel siete colonna,*
> *che del paradiso siete la scala,*
> *soccorrete a chi vi chiama,*
> *Adesso che vi chiamo io,*
> *Soccorrete a li bisogni mia* [667]

> *Madonna, Madonna,*
> *that of heaven you are a column,*
> *that of paradise, you are the ladder,*
> *help those who call you,*
> *Now that I call you,*
> *help my needs.*

The tree in rural Italy also provides invisibility protection, it provides fertility and the spirits of babies for women ready to give birth, it provides food and wood to burn and build with and offers branches and oil for protection and psychic powers. As an axis mundi, the olive tree provided all these things and is associated with the Abundance of the Goddess as well as being a representation of her body coming down to earth. The statue of Diana of Ephesus, often wrongly described as having many breasts, is a representation of the Goddess as an Abundance provider in the form of a date tree with its many fruits. She is also is the shamanic figure "Mistress of the Animals" here, with animals and bees

341

TREES

surrounding her. The Lady of the Animals has presence in Italy and Europe that predates this statue and continues outside of its story in the spirit world of **La Signora del Gioco**.

The tree as a world pillar between the cosmic zones in shamanism is a common theme as *"sky, earth, underworld-connected by a central axis. This axis passes through an "opening" [...]that the gods descend to earth and [...]it is through this same hole that the soul of the shaman in ecstasy can fly up or down[...]"* 668

The symbol of flight in shamanism is not about the flight itself but rather what is achieved: an opportunity to know the universe and to receive knowledge unavailable to the daily life earthly mind, its cognitive abilities and logic alone. While this is achieved through consciousness, it is aided by spirit consciousness of all types (human, divinity, plants, animals, elements). People can learn to lucidly dream and participate in astral travel on their own abilities, but in shamanism the ability to achieve specific types of flight and to receive specific duties, are granted by the spirits who choose the human shaman and not the other way around.

In the Buryat shamanic initiation, a series of 9 ritual ascent trees are arranged and tied with horse hair and other horse-representative tools. Among other rituals, the initiates must climb trees representing ascent and at the top they *"...shout to invoke aid of the gods. As they climb, they all fall into ecstasy"*. 669 In some traditions, shaman wear costumes representing the animals whose voices they had to learn and which help them fly. Trees and horses are found in other shamanic initiations too, including Italy. In some villages of Italy women invoke the Goddesses or Madonnas of ascent, asking to be taken on flights to the moon with the spirit of their horses. Other women, it is said, fly up the trees on pigs, others as cats and even foxes.

And the trees also literally provided fertility in rural Italy, where women would go not only take the spirits of their babies-to-be from the cavity of the tree, but also to where they would return and give birth. The trees also provided invisibility in war times and psychic protection from its parts, such as with the oil used to break **il malocchio**. Brooms, as negative energy filters, come from trees, and as stated the trees served as gathering places on earth and in the astral realm to learn from the "body" of the Goddess.

> *"Since the ability to ascend (or to fly magically) is essential to the career of medicine men, shamanic initiation includes an ascensional rite."*670

SPELLS

There is a spell that has become part of the Inquisition testimonies and which still lives on the tongues of villages across Italy. The spell is similar to the Sardinian prayers that as the Goddess to be taken to the moon: but these spells ask to be taken to the Tree.

Italian Magic: Secret Lives of Women

"Unguento, unguento,
mandame alla Noce di Benevneto,
supra acqua et supra ad vento,
et supra ad omne maltempo" .

671

"Unguento, unguento,
portame al Noce di Benevento,
supra acqua e supra vento
e supra omne tormento".
672

"Sott'aqqwa,
sott'a vjente,
sott 'a la noce de Bbenevjente"
673

"Mi ungo e mi riungo "
e in un'ora ora vado e torno,
sotto acqua e sopra vento
vado alle noce di Buonconvento..oh"
(Pitigilano, Toscana)

"Sopr'acqua e sotta vento,
portame a la noce de bono vento".
674

"Sopr'acqua e sopra vento,
sopra la noce de Benevento."
(from Poggioprimocaso)
675

"Sopr'acqua e sotta vento,
portame a la noce de bono vento."
(from Villa San Silvestro)
656

" Ventu, forti ventu, portimi supra
a'nuggià di Spartiventu!"
677

"Ointment, ointment,
send me to the walnut of Benevneto,
above water and above wind,
and above all bad weather"

"Ointment, ointment,
take me to the Noce di Benevento,
supra water and supra wind
and supra omne torment ".

"Under water and under the wind,
uner the walnut tree of
Benevento! "

"I grease and rejoin
and in an hour I go
and come back,
under water and above wind,
I'm going to the nut of Buonconvento."

"Above water and under wind,
take me to the nut of good wind".

"Above water and wind,
above the walnut of Benevento."

"Above water and under wind,
take me to the walnut of the good wind."

"Wind, strong wind, take me above the
walnut of spartivento!"

WATER

"The water that is the fundamental substance of living matter, it is compared to the woman and the moon, both intense symbols of fecundity. In the popular imagination it can even heal." [678]

While the tree holds a special significance in the shamanic flight traditions of Italy, so do water sources such as wells, community fountains (often having basins where women can also do laundry, or stones with underground rivers), and rivers. Water sources are places where spirit women become visible: **pana,** witches looking to trap travelers, spirit teachers of knowledge, healing nymphs, and abundance goddesses. Water sources are literal conduits in rural communities, shamanic meeting places for mothers and maidens who had daily life needs where those needs were actively met, outside of the limited-access inner sanctums of many Roman temples.

In rural communities, fountains were also a meeting point for women who were destined to arrive at the night school through astral flight. The fountain in Pitigliano, Tuscany, is known to be a place where women met in spirit as a group before being taken

Italian Magic: Secret Lives of Women

together to the moon to learn from the spirit women teachers who found them by day during laundry washing and instructed them how to fly with the mind.

In healing methods, water is often an essential ingredient. Some regions such as Emilia Romagna have a majority of cures that use water and very little else: water and oil, water in copper pots with straw crosses, water poured over injuries and then collected and ritualistically discarded. Water pulls out, puts in, and water reveals. In the rural world:

- water makes spirits visible
- water makes causes and presences of spells visible
- water makes illness and its causes visible
- water makes the energetic presence of the Madonna/Goddess visible
- water is sometimes used as the ritual conduit for Lineage healers who will inherit their secret curative words. A testimony from Sardinia about inheriting curing words at the river:

> *"No, you can not unveil* **is brebus** [words] *, I learned them with a river in the middle, me on one side and she who taught them on the other. The water has taken away the words in the sea and nobody can know them."* [679]

It should be no surprise then that the washerwomen **lavatrice** and midwives **levatrice** (women who spent much time around water) were associated with its supernatural powers and secret knowledge, and they were also associated with the spirits who visited the waters and the magic they imparted. Even the Sicilian name **majare** (which refers to herbalists and sorceresses who have a dual power reputation like the **janare** on the mainland) is related to the term "shirt washers." That the prayers and rhymes speaking of the Goddess come down-to-earth as dew or mists or snow, were part of their ritual teachings and that water was thrown into the 4 corners of houses to prepare for the Ladies of the Night school make natural sense, each small parts of a larger whole.

WATER

100 HERBS WATER   L'ACQUA DELLE CENTO ERBE

A widespread ritual of **al paese** the country still practiced today is the "100 herbs water", or **l'acqua di san giovanni**. This is an infused water with curative and magical properties prepared on **la notte delle streghe** the night of the witches, which is the night between June 23rd and the morning of June 24th. This date has special characteristics:

- it's a night when the "veil between worlds" is thin.
- it's the night before the sun is at it's highest zenith, and therefore specific plants and herbs harvested then have maximum power.
- many of the plants coming to full potency at this time are either **scacciadiavoli** chasing devils plants or panacea "cure all" plants.
- the dew from this moonlit night is considered charged with extra curative properties.
- this is one of the 4 points of the feminine clock of solstices and equinoxes, a night where, in some places such as Sicily, new witches **majare** are made by their mothers from whom they inherit magic and curative secret knowledge.
- it's the night of and before special days where witches were known to be out gathering curative and magical herbs and also participating in astral flights where they were being taught by the feminine spirits (the Great Fairy, **la Signora del Gioco**, etc) this secret knowledge.

LA NOTTE DELLE STREHGE

The night of the 23rd is called **La notte delle streghe**, or "the night of the witches". The plants collected on this night are ones you'll recognize from both curative recipes and magical ones, most notably magical cures that banish negative energy and negative spirits. Many of these plants have a high iron content as well, which is restorative to the blood. And, the blood's iron content is affected by negative spirits who seek to weaken a person's spiritual defenses during a psychic attack. These magical plants are of course associated with witches and healers who use them and know their secrets.

June 24th day for herbalists in Italy is when the sun's zenith is at its highest point and therefore specific apotropaic plants are at their most potent condition, ready to be plucked from the earth. Herbalist or not, this night-before and day-of tradition is common knowledge for many people in Italy. Some people still tell stories in oral tradition about its connectedness to the walnut **noce** tree of Benevento. This ritual, born in the countryside where the herbs grow, is said to have originated in Arezzo, Tuscany.

The name **l'acqua di san giovanni** or san giovanni's water is a bit misleading, being that it references a male saint. The water's special calendrical date is one that was usurped by the church, as many have been, and therefore its connections to the many rituals of the goddess were changed. The church, emulating the curative power of the Divine Feminine, built a legend about this saint and the archangel Michael defeating evil with the hypericum **iperico** plant, with it's holey flowers (when crinkled) and blood red oil that results from its infusions having to do with a bit of blood lost in the battle (substituting this synthetic idea for the more natural menstrual blood and its scientifically proven

346

regenerative properties). These 2 days for making this water would be more appropriately named after witches and healers, because they are the ones who use these plants to cure and to exorcise psychic illnesses.

This Water is part of rural Italy's longstanding traditions of medico-magical rituals and is still made by in many areas of Italy. In natural Italian style, it gets its name due to the fact that is made from as many wildflowers, herbs and curative plants that a person can gather by hand. There are a variety of recipes based on availability of nearby plants which varies from village to village, region to region. While the recipes vary, the focus is the same: to gather as many of these apotropaic plants as possible leading up to the night of the 23rd, with a focus on a holistic way of rural life: making magic out of what's readily available growing on the side of roads, in nearby fields, on mountains.

The process of making the water is part effort, part magic, starting with gathering herbs, flower blooms, seed pods, leaves and plants. Then, they are put in buckets or containers full of water which will remain uncovered on the night of the 23rd so that they infuse the water under the moonlight and also acquire the special magical **guazza** dew of the early morning of the 24th. In the morning, the plant pieces are strained and everyone washes their faces and arms with this healing and purifying water. Babies first, if there are any in the home.

The water must be exposed to the night air, outdoors, an operation known as **serenata** *and the water itself is called* **serenata**. *The custom is still in force in some areas of Valnerina, Umbria.** 680

THE DEW

In the **comare** traditions, often described in **filastrocche** nursery rhyme type poems that are actually describing rituals and initiations in a didactic manner, this water's plants and magical dew are attributed to the Goddess' (as Madonnas) magical restorative energy come down to earth, embodied in nature as the plants, flowers and as one of her sacred water forms: dew. This magical water concept is found in many prayers and stories about the Madonnas, such as in the tales of **Madonna de la Stella** (of the stars). The dew is water from her spirit body, celestial moisture come down from heaven to earth.

This water is kept in use, depending on how much was made. Some people make just enough for the morning wash, others make large amounts to use to wash windows, floors, and themselves. The water transmits the healing properties of the plants and also has

---

*Note: Valnerina, the black valley, has a reputation as the "valley of the witches". Virtually inaccessible until 1998 (when the 4 kilometer Forca di Cerro Tunnel near Spoleto was completed). That said, its long history of geographic isolation means that this perfect day trip destination remains largely unknown to travelers. It is an area both stunningly beautiful and foreboding, where the weather can go from sunny skies to black clouds in a matter of minutes, where the isolated hamlets and claustrophobia-inducing sheer rock walls remind you that centuries ago the inhabitants of these impenetrable peaks held out against conversion to Christianity for long after the rest of the region, where dragons and witches lurked in caves, and where – just to make the area a bit more hostile – each tiny town was locked in perennial warfare with the next one over.

WATER

the dual magical power to chase away negative spirits, such any sent by envy, or negative spirits who cause illness.

THE PLANTS

Depending on the region or village, there are certain plants that "must" be included in the recipe according to beliefs there, and yet in other recipes they are not included due to the fact that those plants don't grow nearby. Two of the most common plants that fall into this category are Rue **ruta** and Hypericum **iperico** also known as "st john's wort" (by now you see this pattern of the church usurping feminine rituals, feminine cures and curative plants with masculine names.) Some people will say rue "must" be included, and others don't consider it essential at all, while others say mandrake is essential, but if you're fortunate enough to meet people who still make this water as an inherited family traditions, you'll find more common instead a consistency of plants that are used in exorcism cures (like **erba de la Madonna** and **iperico** and **gentian**) having perhaps less exciting folklore value but more real life spirit banishing usage. Something to keep in mind about many Italian traditions: the main concept remains consistent at the core, but the details found in ingredients vary.

VARIOUS RECIPES

hypericum, sage, mallow, broom, walnut leaves, honeysuckle, rosemary, lavender, basil, roses, thyme, Roman mint, chamomile, iris or gladiolus, **erba de la Madonna** or **erba de Maria** and **Erba de San Pietro**. 682

barberry, mint, carlina thistle (also a negative spirits filter plant), sage, black currant, rue, periwinkle major, hypericum, rosemary, helichrysum, rose, lavender, verbena, marjoram, honeysuckle, basil.

mugwort, lavender, verbena, hypericum, sage, mandrake, rosemary, garlic, mallow, fern (male), thyme, mullein

L'acqua di San Giovanno made by Doriana Fraschiroli, herbalist in Liguria.

Italian Magic: Secret Lives of Women

L'AMARO BITTERS

While 100 herb water is infused with medicinal and magical plants used to purify the health and repel negative spirits through washing the skin, floor, and windows, an **amaro** is an alcoholic drink infused with upwards of 40 medicinal and magical plants used to promote good digestion. The name, **amaro**, literally means "bitter" due to the many bitter herbs and spices used in its proprietary recipes.

In keeping with the Italian beliefs around health: that the spirit's ease is important for the body's ease and that a happy spirit equals a happy body and vice versa, digestion is essential to this balance. Many of the psychic ailments that are caused by negative spirits or spells trying to drain the energy and vitality of a person affect digestion. Naturally then, in the world of rural cures, it is believed the mouth of the stomach area is the mouth of the soul. And in fact, a spiritual idea that is present in our contemporary times (and gets re-introduced every generation as spiritual principles do) is that our gut is our second brain and in many ways our more powerful brain. Even science now admits the vagus nerve sends signals from our gut area UPWARDS towards our brains and that these signals are gathered from emotional sensations felt in this part of our body often called "intuition" or "gut feelings". In fact our gut area is more sensitive to this type of information and moves faster than our physical brain does to make protective decisions for our bodies.

Amaro drinks bought in shops or restaurants are not generally used to cure ailments, but rather they are taken after dinner as a digestion-promoting effort or as a preventative measure against digestive upset. Personal responsibility it part of the Italian philosophy on life. But, in rural areas, healers can be found who still make their own inherited recipes that are in fact used for curing digestion issues.* Ultimately, **amaro** bought in stores are an elegant industrialization of rural curing traditions. While most **amaro** are made from recipes once belonging to monks that go back 100-200 years, historically rural healers have family Lineages they can trace back 300-500 years. And we know the church stole many rural curing traditions (though they failed to cure anyone with them) and that herbal knowledge was stolen in far more ancient times from female healers who were thereafter forbidden to use it as men took credit for the discovery.

Though commercialized, many traditional rituals for making **amaro** are still respected, such as: harvesting plants grown near a sacred river, waiting for specific moonlight phases to begin and conclude production, and the plants and herbs and spices used. For example, in the making of **Liquore di Genziana**, made in Rieti and Sabina (central Italy), Northern Italy and some villages of Abruzzo, *the whole process, from harvesting grapes (for wine) to the mixture of the various ingredients, is made in the crescent moon. The final stages, however, are made on a waning moon because plants and aromas have given all their potential in infusion.*683 An amaro from Benevento, **Liquore Strega**, harvests their plants in the last days of rising moon and lets them dry separately in the waning moon. **Fernet Branca**, whose name means "clear iron" infuses aloe ferox (a bitter aloe with high

---

* "Italy's Witches And Medicine Women Vol 1" features an interview with Triora's **strega** Anotnietta and the author's experience being instantly cured by her home made **amaro**.

iron content) in an iron pot with very hot water. An iron ladle is used to stir the aloe ferox and water which causes a chemical reaction that turns the ladle very pale in color, thus earning the name "clear iron", in typical Italian fashion of simply naming things as they are.

Genziana is a typical digestive tract typical of the Apennines and the Italian Alps, but is also widespread in the mountain regions of France in particular and in Southern Europe in General. In the Italian Appennino you will find different recipes, depending on the tradition, the uses and the costumes that go back far back in time.

There are a lot of recipes to get the famous Gentian of **Genziana***.* **Liquore di Genziana***. These are recipes often used in the areas of Northern Italy and in some Abruzzo villages in the center of Italy:*

+ *Put a dried root of* **Genziana Lutea** *(about 100g) in a liter of Grappa and leave it infused for a period ranging from 30 to 40 days in a cool, light-free place. Alcohol content ranges around 40 ° to 45 ° degrees.*

+ *Put a dried root of* **Genziana Lutea** *(about 100g) in a liter of pure alcohol (96 °) and leave it infused for about 30/40 days (also in a cool, light-free place); then Sugar Water is added to a 1/1 ratio. The alcohol content is around 50 ° to 55 ° degrees.*

In the Italian Appennino you will find different recipes, depending on the tradition, the uses and the costumes that go back far back in time. This is one of the recipes made according to the tradition typical of my areas (Rieti and Sabina):

An eno-alcoholic solution (2/3 of dry wines in Sabina's areas + 1/3 Alcohol at 96 °) is added, 200g sugar, Cinnamon, **Iperico***, Carnation and 100g of* **Genziana Lutea L.** *are added. Leave in infusion for 40 days in a cool and dark place. According to the tradition of my areas, the infusion should be made at the early dawn lights on a crescent moon day (this, as you will know, in order to maximize the properties of individual plants/aromas). The moon is of great importance because the whole preparation of the* **Genziana** *liqueur is marked by the moon phases. There are many variants of the recipe that I've written above but this is typical of my area handed down from generation to generation (and that's what we still use to make the liqueur you've got to taste). Everything has to be done at certain times of the months, also the collection of the Gentian roots we make must be done after 7/10 years after the birth of the plant. There are many types of Gentian plants: the Lutea (or Regia, because it is yellow like gold) is the most suitable one according to our ancient tradition. **

Italian Magic: Secret Lives of Women

While the details of recipes are guarded secrets, you find the same types of plants used to repel negative energy and the evil eye, such as: herbs loaded with iron, plants and spices that prevent and cure intestinal cancer, plants that set boundaries and "chase" away spirit attachments. All the ingredients offer medicinal value and, in parallel, a protective and cleansing value for the spirit. Gentian Lutea is said to cure cancer and its harvest is protected by law.

Of course the alcoholic version of the rural tonic is available year round, whereas the homemade **amaro** is based on supply of herbal availability around the home of the healer.

TYPES OF HERBS, FLOWERS and SPICES found in Amaro:

orange peel, peppermint, fennel, gentian lutea flowers and root, sage, angelica, asparagus, angelica, aloe ferox, mint, rosemary, juniper, calendula, hypericum, myrtle leaves, birch, hawthorn flowers, coriander, cumin, clove, mallow, red pepper, cardamom, ivy, licorice, hyssop, melissa, chincona bark, rhubarb root, saffron, chicory, laurel, lemon, tarragon, chamomile, olive leaf, basil, florentine iris, Samnite mint, marjoram, oregano, burdock, barberry leaves, artemisia comune, pumpkin leaves, Roman artichoke, field horsetail, dill, aquatic hemp, ash tree, green anise, caraway, back walnut husk, ginger, achillea, hops, wild rose, white willow, black elderberry, milk thistle, betony, dandelion, thyme, currant, blueberrry, valerian, strawberry leaves, raspberry leaves, nettle, beragmot, mustard, prune, corn and more!

Photos: l-r: Gentian root harvested, Gentian plant, Cross-shaped leaves of Gentian plant

*Transcript from author's interview with Mauro Spadoni of Liquore di Genziana, 2016

MAIDEN, MOTHER FLUIDS

Every body has water in its cells and most of the human body's composition is indeed water, making every body a conduit. Within the female body her fluids of: water, menstrual blood, vaginal fluids, milk, even her tears and spit were all revered as an embodied parallel on earth to the Goddess' fluids necessary for life, which then also connected earthly women to the natural sources of fluid on the earth's body such as rivers, lakes, oceans and even the gathered sources such as wells.

> *The most important element of the cult becomes thus the water and the springs, the liquid mystic that microcosmically reminds us the mysterious humidity of the female sex and natural liquids secreted by the woman, which envelops the infant right in the moment of his birth.* [684]

Historically, water was one of the most widely used substances for physical cures and psychic ones as well, in addition to purification rites and magic. Water finds important roles in rural cures, but so do the female fluids of milk, urine, and blood. Briefly:

BREAST MILK

Cures for otitis and other ear inflammations were regularly cured with breast milk: *In various places in Valnerina it was used to pour into the ear canal a still lukewarm woman's milk.7 [...]to treat the earache it was used to ask the milk to be dripped in the ear canal by a mother of twins, as it has a special therapeutic power.* [685]

Breast milk was also dropped directly from the breast on the eye for pains and was also used to cure: *treatment of chronic fevers and certain gastric diseases, the celiac disease; for the gastric atony; for fevers; for heartburn; mixed incense for the treatment of mastitis; in ocular transfers of blood of traumatic origin;* [686] and lung diseases.

In each case and in each place, there were preferences: sometimes the mother of a male child was sought for her breast milk and sometimes it was a mother who had just weaned her baby, and in other cases the mother of twins was believed to have the most powerful milk.

URINE

In the same locality, the memory of an ancient therapeutic use of the virgin girl's urine persists also combined with breast milk. That of mothers of male twins, mixed with oil, or with goose fat, or with honey, was used for the treatment of otitis and other ear affections; considered especially active to neutralize the poisons and even against the madness produced by the administration of giusquiamo henbane, was used for the treatment of gout and to stop diarrhea. [687]

SPIT

Water from the body, spit, is also used in many rural cures directly, to protect

Italian Magic: Secret Lives of Women

against the evil eye, and as a way to mark the location where curative magic will be made.

Antonietta's herbs harvest. hypericum, lime tree, ferns, strigonella, walnuts, large snails, walnuts, nettles, mallow.

WEDDED TO THE MADONNA:
RURAL PRIESTESSHIP

Hidden in plain sight, woven into simple words, practiced in daily life...these are the rural traditions of living in spiritual marriage to the Divine Feminine. The results are what is called "the Secret" in Val D'Aosta for example, rather than priestesship. Regardless of a reference name or not this is a foundational shamanic dynamic, and its power has been envied by the church who was frustrated at uneducated people having a god-force power and so they created a heresy campaign that became the witch hunts and ultimately and erroneously clumped these traditions with those of black magic.

Many of us in contemporary times look away from the ordinary and away from the mundane to seek to the supernatural. And, if we find it, then we understand it's purpose is to be expressed in the ordinary and mundane daily life and not hidden away or reserved for special rituals. The Secret isn't a tool kept on the shelf. For rural Italian people living in a fully agricultural community, ordinary mundane life is lived in partnership with nature, not in control over it. So there can be little escape from the powerful presence of nature's cycles and its natural purpose of offering a conduit for Source/Goddess/Universe's knowledge. Nature is the expression of the Source of life embodied on earth and it speaks to us as a conduit for the Divine Feminine. Italy's lineage healers are also an embodiment of the Divine Feminine's love and healing power expressed on earth.

The advent of the patriarchy's synthesized conceptualization of nature, with its weaponry and industrialization of animals, people, and food sources and its usurpation of healing and magical practices that had been established long before men invaded and rearranged community life has resulted in what most people know as "magic"; an energetic form of supply and demand, essentially, based on the patriarchy as control over something or someone else. Their magic was created to defend their type of society. In contrast, rural magic is a co-creative partnership, created by the Divine and whose elected human healers freely give to those who need it, its powers coming from a much higher source than humanity, so it's not of humanity and can't be owned by humanity. It can be channeled through humans, but not forcibly, only in partnership. In this magic, this higher consciousness is ultimately in charge of the experience. Will alone cannot create the channeled experiences for the healer nor for the patient. The human being must be humble enough to know they are not the Source; rather, they are only a channel for Source, and the key to this partnership is achieving Universal love which is far different from human love: it is unconditional. This is why these traditions exist in small, quiet, remote places where they are not in danger of being commercialized, and where people can hear the call, through nature, to become a priestess/ a devoted partner of the Divine Feminine Source) in the first place.

Italian Magic: Secret Lives of Women

Indigenous traditions such as we find in rural Italy's mainland and her islands are shamanism, based on a devoted partnership with the universe and a surrender to the plans of Spirit, over and above one's will. This magic, these cures, and this Secret can't be bought or sold: it is gifted. And, it's gifted from someone(s) who can't be forced or controlled: higher consciousness. There is no human hierarchy that can grant this partnership with power: doors can be opened, learning can take place, but ultimately the spirits are the consciousness at work here, and this is the Secret itself.

The Secret is ultimately a state of mind, of service, of love. There are initiations and rituals to mark someone receiving "the Secret", but it is not something talked about with outsiders. Not just because the insiders prefer to hide under religious language, which is in part true depending on their age and location, but because if you carry The Secret, you'll feel a natural inclination to never speak about it, or to deflect attention away from it, in part because you know it's not yours.

Ascension is not for rising up to the heavens/Source and remaining there...that's death. Ascension is a way to reach "upwards" to stretch our capacity for perceiving and allowing the higher, faster frequencies of the Divine to enter our bodies (physical mental and spirit) so we can develop a channel to bring it through ourselves and into the earthly experience. This is what our souls seek: to grow, and the human body is just a tool for this and often the human life looks so much different to our souls than it does to our human will. For the Divine to fully experience itself through our souls, we must be open to creating, which is a process of allowing connections to be made. Giving to another human being is one of the ways connections are made outside of ourselves. This is, in other words, "bringing heaven down to earth." In shamanism, the healer who ascends and returns is essential to the community and must remain in the community so those who need help can find it. This is also the role Italian Lineage healers are asked to step into.

The original function of a priestess is to be a devoted student of the Divine who, in return, grants the priestess the ability to perceive life and everyone and everything/ everyone in it through the perspective/the eyes/the heart of the Divine and to bring Divinity down to earth through: healing, divining (as a channeler, Medium, trance Medium), sexual and sensual exchange, teaching and protecting (spell-breaking).

A priestess in more contemporary terms reserves priestess roles for group rituals and ceremonies and designated moments. The original function is that a priestess has a daily life connection to the Divine and lives according to the instructions and connection they have with the Divine. In return, the Divine who, in return, lends the priestess Her eyes and ears and perspective in order to see other seekers with. A priestess is given the opportunity to borrow the Goddess' energy with which to heal health issues and psychic ailments and to see others through the eyes of higher perspective (universal love) and be able to read them psychically to help them return to balance (if needed) or to open doors for the seekers to walk through an empower themselves. It's wearing the eyes of the goddess, seeing her children (people) as she does, so as to love them where they "are", unconditionally. A priestess, and especially one in a daily life environment, must be open to giving the gifts of the universe to whomever is ready at whatever level they are ready to receive.

WEDDED TO THE MADONNA: RURAL PRIESTESSHIP

In rural Italy, these opportunities of connection present themselves as: relationships, families, community. The power of the Madonnas as the Divine Feminine Mother of God is the same power as Demeter who handed down her knowledge to her daughter Persefone, the same as the Goddesses of many names. In fact, all feminine Divinities before Romanization were autonomous: female beings with no "husband" whose role was to help other female beings become empowered through their relationship to the Divine and to thus receive abundance in whatever form it was needed. Abundance from the Divine is different from human ideas of abundance, of course, and is meant to improve daily life conditions. In rural life, this abundance is: plentiful harvest, safety from lightning and fires and bad weather, protection against negativity and the power to break spells, choose enduring love relationships, to have sufficient breast milk, to have the bread rise and cheese set, the power to restore health with plants and water, to divine futures and maintain fertility.

The sacred grains used since most ancient times in domestic Goddess culture as food and as veneration to the Goddess who provided them are the ones still honored and used in rural life. The plants used to cure since most ancient times are the ones still used to cure and still venerated as Divine Feminine energy gifted to the earth. The ancient veneration of fluids (water, milk, blood) as having a parallel between the Goddess and human women are still honored in rituals and in prayers to the Madonnas. The currencies of rural priestesship is nature and energy as cures, as food, as divination, as partnership. Rituals and their didactic nursery rhymes celebrate these secret powers in plain sight.

The rituals of initiation were performed sometimes in groups and sometimes as play reenactments on earth, and sometimes as groups in the dream world with the spirit of **La Signora del gioco** taking women astrally to the moon, to the walnut tree of Benevento, and to other trees and grassy plains. Some initiations in the astral realm required women to use **unguenti** ointment to keep their body in a deep sleep for 24 hours which also caused them to suffer. This ability to have one foot in the spirit realm and one foot on the earthly realm in partnership with the divine feminine is not a working relationship reserved for rituals alone, but rather it is a way of life; a sensation pervasive in all daily activities.

The spiritual marriage to the divine feminine is not complete without it's parallel on earth: the woman is married to the divine feminine as her spirit spouse, and she is guided to her earthly partner with whom she will have as an earthly spouse. Her spirit spouse, the divine feminine, is ever-present but is channeled specifically during the lineage traditions of curing and magic and ritual. This spirit spouse will be the assistant spirit to the healer throughout their lifetime, like a guardian guide in spirit, a co-creative, co-healer working partner.

The following prayer from Sicily is just one of the many prayers to many Madonnas that are devotional and which express a spirtual marriage to the Divine Feminine.

"Vi salutu, Bbedda Matri Maria/ spusa di l'arma mia/
e vogghiu-zzoccu m'aviti prumisu/ La santa gloria ru Pararisu"

Italian Magic: Secret Lives of Women

"I salute you beautiful Mother Mary/ wife of my soul/
and I want that promised me/ blessed glory in Heaven" [688]

The purpose of the spirit spouse and shamanism in general is for the Divine to have a channel through which to bring the universe down to earth. This is the essential relationship through which comes all the magic, cures, rituals and the traditions in shamanism. Nature is a conduit, and people are too. The spirit spouse is a personal guardian and guide, and in rural Italy we find Madonnas, female Saints and Goddess in this role. The connection between higher spirits and humanity is expressed in different ways, centered around the purpose of restoring balance. The tools of the shaman are to ascend to the world of spirits and with their permission, bring their energy down to earth AND to honor the Divine when the Divine manifests on earth (such as the Madonnas embodying their energy on earth as mists, dews, snow and guiding starlight.

This is why the prayers, the didactic rhymes and invocations use words about these ideas in very plain daily life language in the rural world. Whether Italian shamanism, shamanism from Central Asia, Indonesia, Siberia or even Spiritualism, the tools of ascension are similar and variations on a theme: ladders, columns, birds, horses, flying, climbing, going up, journeying into a realm that most human beings can't go while still in their bodies.

The symbolic meanings of the prayers and rhymes are embedded the same way the secret cures and magic are: among regular, daily life surroundings or in "plain sight". You'll find rhymes that seem so simple they are almost non-sensical if you don't understand what you're reading. So if you're looking for supernatural and grandiose ideas, you can look instead to Roman nobles and elite Greek philosophers. For real, hands-in-the-earth magic, hedgecrossing, astral travel, initiations trance channeling and miraculous cures done by regular people, the rural world is where these things were as plentiful as wildflowers, herbs, and grain.

For example, among prayers to Madonna de la Stella we find the Divine Feminine bringing her energy down to earth embodied as: guiding starlight, and as many forms of water: fog, dew and snow, all attributed to the Great Goddess Mother since before the Great Pyramids were built. In the local stories of Madonna de la Stella, the variations are all on the theme of traveling during dangerous conditions (difficulty in navigations). The Madonna manifests first as a woman with newborn child who asks sailors to take a ride on their boat wherever they are going. All but one sailor refuses because they are worried about the dangerous voyage. The one sailor allows her to stay in his cabin and offers her his scarf or a shirt as a garment for extra warmth while the sail in the heavy fog and rains and rocky waves. Suddenly, after his kindness, bright starlight comes through the bad weather and guides the men to the shore they seek. Upon landing, there are various stories about the ground being covered in snow (during the month of August) or a blanket of dew covering the ground...some type of water allowing small footprints to be found at the same time everyone is aware the lady has vanished. Upon following the footprints however they find a statue of the Madonna wrapped in the scarf or shirt that was lent to her, as a sign to the men that She was the one helping their passage. The overall message is one Abundance:

of guidance offered during troubling conditions. This is venerated in prayers in which you'll notice the acknowledgment ascension of the human to reach Her, and of Her coming down to earth :

Madonna de la Stella mia avvocata Madonna of the star my advocate
che in cielo e in terra ti vengo a vedene that I come to see you in heaven and on earth
in questo luogo dove sei posata in this place where you are laid
fate le grazie la notte e lo dine thank the night and the day
fate la grazia e chica ve la chiede do the grace and ask it
cosi' vi chiedo che la fate a mene so I ask you to make it
cosi ti prego, vergine Maria so please, Virgin Mary
io ti saluto e dico avemaria I greet you and say avemaria 689

In this next prayer, there is reference to the high energy of the Madonna coming down to earth so she can be received by human beings through the high vibration of love:

"Madonna mia bella Our beautiful Madonna
che dal cielo calasti in terra who from heaven you fell to earth
calasti in terra per amarci you fell to earth to love us
la Madonna che c'abbracci the Madonna who embraces us
che ci abbracci co' tanto amore who embraces us with so much love
la Madonna del mio cuore" the Madonna of my heart". 690

There are many more prayers to Madonne della Neve (of the snow) and Madonna of sacred water, many more prayers about columns, ladders, and flight. In this next didactic **filastrocca** nursery rhyme from Sicily we find the description of a ritual for **majare,** (or on the mainland counterparts **comare** and **janare**) for gathering the magic plants on the mountain (Great Mother's body on earth) with the magical Dew (the morning of June 24th). You'll recognize the list of magical plants called **scacciadiavoli** chasing devils or banishing plants:

"Andiamocene alla montagna, "Let's go to the mountain,
C'è Maria che ci accompagna: There is Mary who accompanies us:
Ci accompagna stamattina, She accompanies us this morning,
Per raccogliere la rugiada. To collect the dew.
La rugiada è una spugna; The Dew is a sponge;
Benediteci i pensieri; Bless us the thoughts;
La rugiada è nella menta The dew is in the mint
Benediteci i sentimenti: Bless us the feelings:
La rugiada è nelle viole, The dew is in the violets,
Benediteci le parole; Bless us the words;
La rugiada è nelle mele, The dew is in the apples,
Benediteci la persona, Bless us the person,
La rugiada è nel timo, The dew is in the thyme,
Benediteci, Bella Madre; Bless us, Beautiful Mother;
C'è Lucifero che ci tenta, There is Lucifer who tempts us,

Italian Magic: Secret Lives of Women

Benediteci Madre Santa." Bless us Holy Mother." [691]

This coded rhyme from Sicily describes the ritual of gathering magic plants on the mountain (a symbol of the Divine Feminine's body on earth) that have been descended upon by the Divine Feminine's (in symbolic form of Maria) sacred fluid come down to earth as dew, bestowing magical blessings through this conduit and marking all the magical plants that need to be gathered on this day, the morning of June 24th.

La Bella Lavanderina

La bella lavanderina The beautiful washerwoman
che lava i pannolini; who washes diapers;
fai un salto, jump in,
fanne un altro, do it again,
tira la coda al gatto, pull the tail of the cat,
tira le campanelle, pull the bells,
fai una giravolta, turn around,
fallo un'altra volta, do it again,
alza gli occhi al cielo, roll your eyes to heaven
abbassa gli occhi in giù: lower your eyes down,
dai un bacio a chi vuoi tu. give a kiss to whoever you want.

Many slightly different versions of the **filastrocca** nursery rhyme above can be found and are commonly known. Within its phrases is another ritual in plain sight. The **lavanderina / lavatrice** washerwoman was often also the midwife and thought of interchangeably with the witch. She was commonly known to be a woman who held secret knowledge. The actions in this rhyme speak a psychic language, tying together many of the rituals you already read about here, and at the same time seem to be describing mundane actions. So there is a double power of words:

+ The washerwoman does wash clothes, but she also purifies with water, knowing its secrets and using water for cures in other rituals.

+ She jumps "in", here referring to crossing the threshold. She must jump in to arrive there, and she must jump back to return (that's where the knowledge comes from).

+ The cat is an animal that witches shape-shift into; borrowing their form to psychically spy on their intended victims...so if a washerwoman sees the shadow of a cat near her, she must try to pull the tail of the cat to reveal the identity of the spy before harm is done before a spell is cast. This idea is also found in the eel-form of the Janare of Campania. It's a protective measure.

+ Pulling the bells clears negative energy and they are used often to do so.

+ "Turning around" here means making a magic circle and facing all the 4 corners in doing so, which is a common ritual found in **comare** traditions, whether used to invoke

WEDDED TO THE MADONNA: RURAL PRIESTESSHIP

La Signora del Gioco or the **Donne di Fuora**, to invoke **Santa Lucia**, etc.

+   Rolling the eyes up and down, the lavanderina acknowledges the realm of the Goddess in all her forms above, the ancestors below and the earth in between...

+   which is where a kiss is given to the next person, the next initiate acting out their psychic duties as a **comare**: keeper of magic and secrets of nature, purifier, fence crosser/astral traveler, catching psychic spies and clearning the air of spirits with bells, acknowledging the above, below and in-between.

THE WAY UP
ASCENSION

Up from the Earth's Magic Parallels to
the Goddess energy in nature

up

Through earthly/supernatural female figures

up

To the moon and through Goddess herself.

In rural life, this is the thread of conection to the mother magic:

the Great Mother Goddess in various forms,

channeling Divine Feminine energy through mothers, the commnity women.

Without this spirit world intecession, none of the magic nor cures would work These spirit partnerships are what differentiate rural magic from middle perdiod DIY and conceptual magic.

View from the top of Monte
Maggiore, Caserta, Campania.

FOOD MAGIC

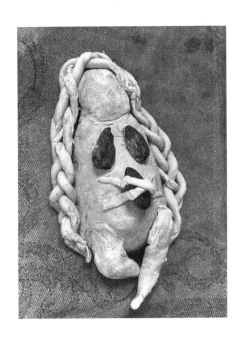

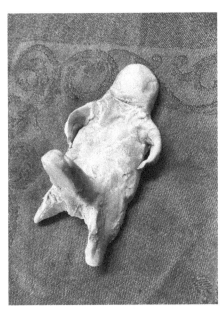

FOOD MAGIC FOOD MAGIC

Food magic in rural Italy revolves around daily sacred rituals: protection, fertility, veneration of the divine feminine, transformation of gifted foods in love rituals, and food production itself, which is believed to also suffer from the envy of others.

Food magic is about ritual actions of transformation and working with the natural flow of energy. The tools used are daily life ingredients: wheat, yeast and things made from wheat; milk and things made from milk; fruit of the seasons; nuts with magical meanings; sewing kit supplies, hands, and sometimes body parts or fluids such as menstrual blood, hair, fingernails or any other bits; animals, insects, reptiles and animal bones.

There is food magic that represents a desired outcome: ingredients combined to achieve fertility or a happy marriage as often seen in bread magic. Symbols of the Goddess are venerated through bread which can also be seen in breads with breast-shapes adorned with wheat patterns, along with breads which commemorate the dead.

Then, there is food magic done to harm others such as **fatture**, where body parts are stolen from an intended victim are embedded in something edible and then offered to the victim. If the victim can't be reached, a simulacrum double is used such as a live frog or reptile. Much of food magic isn't even action-oriented in the way we think it might should be and is instead diagonostic such as with remedies against **il malocchio**, and psychically discerning if conditions are favorable or not around food production: is the wind blowing from the wrong direction to make the cheese (east)? Has someone sent negative energy across the wind towards the bread dough? Has the meat absorbed the anger or terror of the death of the animal killed? And then..do spells need to be broken? Is abundance being asked for (babies, happy marriages, attention from desired lovers...

That food has divination power should be no surprise at this point: olive oil, wheat grains and salt are all used for psychic discernment against the evil eye and also for its cures, having their own connections to the Goddess' body on earth, considered an axis mundi tree of Abundance Goddess Diana. Wheat stalks are used to cure warts and muscle twists. And the wheat, one of the most important grains gifted from the Goddess Demeter used in those against **il malocchio** is also used in the making of community breads used in specific traditions and which hide symbolic imagery in plain sight. Herbs and flowers with symbolically protective colors are used to prevent black magic attacks and to filter out negative spirits and cure psychic illness. Fava beans, dedicated to the Goddess Carna, are also used in divination like olive leaves.

A few of the most magically attributed foods used in rural magic:

FAVA BEAN

Fava beans have an interesting history considering they were both feared and also used to attract abundance. The Goddess Carna, connected to them, was invoked while making propitiatory rites for growth and expansion. Also, due to the fact that they turn a blood red color if left soaking in water for more than a day, they are not only associated with the Goddess' regenerative power of life-after-death, but also of her protective power.

Italian Magic: Secret Lives of Women

And, the fava bean is the *first nourishing and fresh vegetable food offered by the Earth to its children after the long series of winter months. This legume, therefore, assumes the value of a sacred first fruit to the Great Mother.* At the same time, it represents the gift of the dead [Demeter and Persephone] 692. While some of the fear around fava beans is towards the human-flesh looking parts of the plant which appear at various stages of development, the larger fear is around the long straight stem *hollow and without knots along its length, acts as a vehicle for communication between the world of dead and the region of the living. Passing through that natural conduit, the souls of the transgressed [...] can can return to earth to re-enter the cycle of the birth of death.* 693 So it was believed someone could become possessed through this plant channel.

ALMOND

Associated with the White [Light] Goddess Cibele as Great Mother and her regenerative power, the almond is a double of her life-producing body, full of blood and breast-like milk. They are used to protect against il malocchio in some places, tied together with red string, and in other places they are used to manifest fertility for couples.

EGG

Used to represent a transformational vessel like the womb and placenta, the egg is most commonly seen in fertility magic and veneration of the Goddess in community rituals with breads wrapped around them in the shapes of birds and young women. Eggs are also used in **fatture** as a **puppia** simulacrum in the same way that lemons with pins are used. In fertility magic, the egg represents the desired outcome from union: a baby. In **fatture** curses, the egg or lemon act as a body absorbing focused points of harm.

WHEAT

The ultimate symbol of life-after-death, the *"wheat that undergoes a"Passion", tortured, beaten, put to death, is the first divinity that rises again"* 694, with its harvesting and processing efforts involving beating, boiling, and beating again. And yet, after all this it provides nourishment. It was first attributed to the Female Divinity, but as an image so strong, it was stolen by all the masculine gods in ensuring religions, as all symbols of regeneration (like blood) have been.

From growing and harvesting and processing the wheat by hand, to kneading the dough, forming the gnocchi and other pastas and celebrating or mourning with breads shared in the community, rural life finds this as womens' work, accompanying all the profound life moments in rural communities pasta magic aiding birth, restoration of the new mother after birth, breads for funerals and fertility magic, community breads for solstices, grains for holiday celebrations, the same grains that were the first ritual items used for domestic goddess veneration. The making of bread is quintessential transformational work, and womens' work since the ancient days of domestic Goddess worship where wheat, millet and lentils were honored as gifts of the Goddess and also used in magic for protecting babies and health, and work that emulates the rising and falling of a mother's belly.

PLANTS :
HERBS, BERRIES, WOODS, NUTS, LEAVES , SEAWEED

Perhaps the only body of knowledge agreed upon throughout Italy's various spiritual and historical practices throughout time is the curative and magical properties of plants. Usages vary, from practices of secret traditions to kitchens of grandmas to contemporary witches, with some verging on mythical and purely conceptual ideas and some usages offering miraculous cures orally transmitted through family lines who can trace their lineage back hundreds of years.

Italy has an incredible biodiversity *with over 7,672 species of plants recorded, as of 2019 [...] of which 7,031 are autochthonous.*[695] In the age where we rely on technology and printed information to tell us the details, Italy's nature still surprises: it's natural to find medicinal herbs growing in places where books and online resources say they do not grow.

For example, the elusive **erba della Madonna** grows on mountaintops that allegedly have an altitude working against that plant according to books, and yet, there it grows, while having disappeared from some longstanding habitats where it was commonly found in the wild. **Hypericum** also grows in unlikely places, seemingly in rebellion to what the plant finder books instruct as if to say "we are wild, we can't be put into a neat and tidy categorization".

As with most of Italy, you can find so much more than is written about in books if you venture into places the books don't mention. It's natural to see datura **stramonium** and **belladonna** growing wild in some places and in many unlikely ones. Dirt roads that seemingly offer no touristic sparkle and shine reveal potent and protective plants growing freely among ancient ruins that take a patient eye to discover, or simply an awareness that they are right in front of you. Many healers gather herbs they use from little patches of land on the side of the road near their homes, on a street, from a local mountain path, or from their own yard, growing out of the walls without even knowing their names. It's truly exciting that the land is a natural pharmacy if you know what to look for.

The amount of plants known and used by healers and locals constitutes a tremendous body of knowledge that is kept orally. Some areas, such as the mountains of Campania, are known for an abundance of poison plants, therefore flying ointments were more common in this region historically. Islands like Sardinia and Sicily and coastal mainland areas use plants that grow in the sea water which are only used here because they don't grow elsewhere. The province of Imperia in the region of Liguria is known historically for a vast array of medicinal plants and the knowledge of how to use them which is carried by lineage healers, many of who were raised by parents who

Italian Magic: Secret Lives of Women

couldn't read nor write.

Rural Italy has a deeper system of categorization of plants than contemporary usages. These plants systems were already in use by the time Romans and their predecessors began documenting natural healing, and they share many traditions with ancient Greece and from time periods vastly older. Rural Italy's agricultural traditions are based on first-hand knowledge of life lived in nature's cycles for survival. While contemporary magic tends to conceptualize a lot of nature such as using moon phases to charge spells for example, the source knowledge and proper usage of these natural energies comes from the people who live in companionship with the nature. And, the significance of moon phases, for example, can be fundamentally different between agricultural rituals and contemporary or even middle period magic, due to the rural practice of physically observing the affect of the moonlight on nature and on the body. What seems to make sense conceptually often is the reverse in nature. For example, the full moon isn't a desirable phase for many rural traditions like curing.

This Chapter very lightly touches on magical attributes of plants and a includes a very, very truncated list of plants. The list of plants used to exorcise **vermi** from Sicily alone is long enough that it deserves its own book. Keep in mind that herbal knowledge comes from **al paese** (the countryside) and the rural people and farmers who grow, harvest, and transform the plants. This knowledge has been received, maintained, and passed on orally by people who live in the very cycles of nature that contemporary magic claims to be connected to. These knowledge-keepers often can't read nor write, so they don't get any credit for holding this knowledge historically, but they live in nature and they know.

For example, herbal documentation from the middle ages and onward, and even before, was credited to men who were not farmers but rather philosophers or self-declared naturalists and the documentation omits the living legacies of the female-dominated rural world of healers as well as the male farmers working the land and working with the plants, learning from them. At the same time men documented plant properties, they weren't able to successfully cure like healers of rural traditions could, and even their medical establishment started in the 1300s failed so miserably to keep people alive in Italy (including newborns) and therefore need to use midwives and witches as scapegoats for their failures. They documented what they learned form the rural people and stole curative traditions, the ones they could, calming the knowledge for themselves. Male healing lineages in rural Italy, in contrast, are part of oral traditions that solve community health needs and are not claimed to be owned by anyone.

In rural Italy, plants have been traditionally categorized with their seasonal attributes first and their innate magical properties or sacred functions after (although interconnected) and not by their contemporary magical uses. It can be said also that while there are an incredible amount of natural items used in rural Italian daily sacred magic and cures, their uses are traditional and not DIY, so their uses are more limited than contemporary spellwork. For example, emphasis on sympathetic recognition of a plant's innate protective properties psychically and physically is part of the traditional

PLANTS

knowledge rather than a list of uses for what it can "get you" materially. There is less imagination employed and more handed-down ritual. Plant wisdom is kept in its place, with the exception of sorceresses, and honored as such. Usage knowledge and problem-solving (economic curative, divination) is received from the spirit world during astral travel, rather than being discovered using personal creative skills to craft plant recipes for magical spells.

This section will not list the many curative properties of plants. Each plant has many curative properties and magical uses, and it would be disservice to try and include pertinent information here. Rural healers don't document their knowledge anyway they are too busy using it, and while they use it, it's alive in their memory and activated through channeling: they learned HOW to use it and trust this and it does work. When the cures are not needed and the healers are not being asked to heal, the knowledge goes dormant. It's still alive, it still can be received from the world of spirit, but the knowledge will rest in dormancy until the keepers of this knowledge in the spirit realm decide to hand it down to other humans.

Instead of attempting to enter this world of knowledge you can find lists of important plants here, with just a few pertinent magico-medical uses that show a continuity among all the other rituals and traditions within this book which, keeping in mind, is also a very truncated collection.

It's our contemporary culture's need to "have and hold and own" to need to know everything we think we need to know before we make an action step. In the case of medicinal plants, serious training is required, but in the rural world this training happens person to person, healer-to-nature. For an interesting examination of plant knowledge of **Valle Argentina** the "Silver Valley", a mountainous area in the region of Liguria, see this book: "La medicina popolare nell'alta valle Argentina" by Sandro Oddo. However, this book only contains lists of plants and some of the ways they are used along with a strong warning to not experiment with plants outside of teaching guidance. There are no recipes within this book, but it will offer a look at a very specific area known for Lineage healers who use plants to cure physical and psychic illness, showing the quantity of how many plants are known by these healers, in detail.

Also, you'll notice many plants used to protect against lightning. The rural beliefs about lightning are that it is a celestial fire, and a part of the weather that can be manipulated by black magic. In keeping with traditions created by the spirit world, this usage naturally applies to agricultural communities or places where fire can damage homes and livelihoods that literally support daily life and whose loss is detrimental.

Generally, the apotropaic (protective) plants also reveal themselves through physical characteristics: bright red berries and flowers that turn red in oil denoting regenerative power of the Divine Feminine; little leaves and pieces that act as filters; spike and sword-shaped leaves which protect; magical woods that repel worms and lightning or offer magical fruit encased in shells that denote a supernatural power.

Italian Magic: Secret Lives of Women

Apotropaic plants, Banishing plants, Regenerative plants, Binding plants, Abortion plants, Divination plants, Astral flight plants, Solstice plants of summer, Solstice plants of winter, Witch grasses and plants, Panacea plants, plants of Love, Ritual Grains and Seeds, plants of the Eternal Return, plants of Divination, and plants of Dual Power....

...and all of them in singular or in combinations are curative plants for physical or psychic ailments.

APOTROPAIC (MAGICALLY PROTECTIVE) PLANTS

GARLIC l'aglio: Protective
Medico-magical uses:
- Used to cure bites from poisonous animals and insects and also effective against poisonous (negative) energies that behave like parasites and viruses (spirit attachments).
- Used in orally transmitted magical cures for ailments involving spirit attachments/ energy parasites that affect the digestive tract, intestines, and blood such as with the psychic ailments **vermi** worms and **anima caduta** lost soul, etc.
- Used frequently for babies and children in whole clove form (hung around the neck from red or green strings), and for adults macerated or in combinations with other herbs, oil and wine for various ailments stemming from these causes.
- Used in conjunction with secret prayers and invocations to cure the affects of energy vampires on digestion and vampiric effect on blood.
- Traditionally used in the **breve** and **punga** amulet medicine bags worn around the neck near the heart, or sewn/pinned into clothing for active protection against **il malocchio.**
- Commonly collected near the June solstice, when it is at its highest potency and used in the 100 herbs water **l'acqua di san giovanni** made on June 23rd and June 24th.
- Also burned in **suffumigi** fumigations to Ceres along with onion leaves and poppy flowers. Burned as an incense with salt, onions, poppies and dill in gratitude towards the goddesses.
- Associated with the goddess **Ecate, Demetra, Ceres, Cibele**, and other Goddesses whose efforts support mothers in magic and in health cures along with protection traditions against negative magic through passing down secret knowledge from the spirit world through astral travel (shamanic flights) and ecstatic experiences.
- As a gift from **Ecate**, and associated with her powers to pull out negativity and break spells and curses, rural mothers used it en force for their babies and children for protection against envy and maleficent spirits.

FENNEL il finocchio: Protective
Medico-magical uses:
- Used as a negative energy filter, its tiny leaves act like a broom, preventing negative energy from entering the home.
- Used as dried bundles hanging on doors and near or stuffed inside keyholes of doors

- Used in the same way as other broom-like magical filter plants.
- Used against black magic and spirits connected to it.
- Used to cure poisonous bites of scorpions and snakes and negative energy from spirits.
- Used as digestive bitters in **amari,** medical-magical digestive dirnks.
- Invoked along with Santa Lucia in a specific prayer asking that she bring it from its celestial source and create a white light circle around the home to protect the people in it.
- Connected to menstrual blood.

HOLLY l'agrifolio: Protective.
Medico-magical uses
- Used to protect against negative spells **fatture** and darker energies and spirits
- Used to counteract bites of poisonous animals.
- Hung in broom-like bundle on front door to filter out negative spirits and energies.
- As a **legnu stregoniu** its wood is used to prevent miscarriage resulting from envy.

ELDERBERRY WOOD il sambuco: Protective
Medico-magical use:
- Used as the magical **legnu stregoniu**, it is protective against miscarriage due to envy.

ROSEMARY il rosmarino: Protective
Medico-magical uses:
- Used to protect the home from lightning.
- Used at windows as filtering protection against negative energy due to its many little pieces.
- Used to keep poisonous animals like snakes and scorpions from the home and burned to push out snakes.
- Used under pillow and bed to prevent nightmares.
- Used in **suffumigi** fumigations to drive out evil energy and poisonous animals.

JUNIPER il ginepro: Protective. Wood and Berries and Greens
Medico-magical uses:
- Used to ward off snakes and push away negative energy.
- Used in **suffumigi** to purify the home, its tiny pieces filtering negative energy.
- Burns a bright white light believed to drive away black magic **fatture** and **il malocchio.**
- Used as a double to transfer illnesses into by Lineage healers.

PEAR TREE il pero: Protective
Medico-magical uses:
- Its wood is used for protection against lightning and fire by lightning.
- Used in love magic for suggestive food transformation rituals.

Italian Magic: Secret Lives of Women

SORGHUM la saggina: **Protective**
Medico-magical uses:
- Used as a magic filter plant in agreement with negative spirits: that they must be able to count the **saggina** fibers in entirety and accurately before entering the house to harm.
- Used to make actual brooms, and these brooks were kept at doors and entryways to protect the family from black magic energy and the sorceresses who make it.

DOGWOOD TREE il corniolo: **Protective**
Medico-magical uses:
- Used to protect against the evil eye: it's natural branch bifurcation splits the negative energy sympathetically. It's hard wood, suitable for war spears, earned its reputation for battling negative energy due to its superior strength.
- Its red berries refer to its apotropaic protection against negative spirits.
- Protective against the evil eye and envy.

FIELD MAPLE TREE acero campestre: Protective
Medico-magical uses:
- Used for protection against lightning.
- The tree can offer invisibility, cloaking, hidden protection; connected to the Divine Feminine through Madonnas.

BUTCHER'S BROOM il pungitopo: Protective
Medico-magical uses:
- With its red winter berries warning of its apotropaic power, and its pointy sharp leaves, it's used as a negative energy filter hung on doors in bundles like brooms.
- Used to protect against **fatture** spells.

SAGE salvia, salvia verbenaca and **salvia dei prati: Protective**
Medico-magical uses:
- Used to cure bites from poisonous animals like snakes and scorpions.
- Used to keep away negative spirits and energies.
- Used to promote to menstrual blood and fertility, connected to the regenerative power of the Divine Feminine
- Solstice plant, used in 100 Flowers Water.

BLESSED OLIVE TREE wood, leaves, oil: l'olivo benedetto: Protective
Medico-magical uses:
- Branches used to protect the house from evil energy and lightning for a year's span and then *burning the old frond in the home, reserved for all sacred things that have become obsolete or unusable.* 697
- Used in many recipes carried within **breve** *the canvas-bags to hang around the neck, along with ingredients such as badger hair, coarse salt, wolf's tooth, etc, protecting against the omnipresent snares of fascination: evil eye and envy.* 698
- *Used when visiting the deceased, by blessing the body with the olive tree branch, the   same custom was in force which aimed to protect the corpse from harmful*

influences of various kinds and also to protect the participants in the wake of possible negative energies coming from the corpse. [699]

- Used to protect against lightning due to atmosphere and also due to envy of neighbors.
- It's oil is used in lecanomanzia or **rimedi contro il malocchio**, in the method of making **occhi** eyes in a bowl of water to diagnose the evil eye, to identify the sender, and to release it.
- Used in other forms divination, such as with spit and fire.

SORGHUM **la saggina: Protective**
Medico-magical uses: the rustic brooms of the past were made which, in addition to sweeping the floors, constituted an effective defense against witches. These, in fact, in order to be able to enter the house and fulfill their evil, they would have had to count each of the countless stamens that made up the ramazza, but the operation would have taken them until sunrise, when they were forced to beat a retreat, or to be discovered. A filter plant, used to make the rustic brooms of the past

THYME **il timo serpillo: Protective**
Medico-magical uses:
- pushes out negative spirits and evil intent
- keeps away snakes and scorpions
- filter plant, used to protect home against black magic
- worn under clothes to protect against black magic

Protective grains , cereals, beans as wheat, lentils, millet, fava, beans, farro,
- used in il malocchio divination and cures
- used in veneration of Goddess
- used in community rituals of transformation

HAZELNUT: **il nocciolo: Protective**
Medico-magical uses:
"like all the fruits enclosed in peel, and therefore similar to the egg, the hazelnut together with the tree also became a symbol of Fertility and Regeneration". [700]
- has power to keep away negative energies, spirits and poisonous animals such as snakes and scorpions.
- can be used for invisibility
- used in water dowsing

ARTEMISIA **buumegu: Protective**
Medico-magical uses:
- Used carried on the body against the skin as protection during travels

LAVANDA **Protective and regeneration**
Medico-magical uses:
- gathered on **La Notte delle Streghe** the night of the witches
- used to protect against **il malocchio t**he evil eye
- used to attract abundance

Italian Magic: Secret Lives of Women

In Northwestern Italy, there is a legend that Mary Magdalene stopped and rested in a cave before moving onward to Provence, where she died. Near this cave of course a church was built, and this church celebrated its chestnut harvest and the presence of Mary Magdalene in a 2 day festival that is blended with local rituals and traditions every July near the 21st.

The central theme is performed, oddly by 2 men, after which the entire community takes part. As with many local community traditions, a procession is involved followed by a fest and festivities.

The second day of this reenactment, which falls on a Sunday, the celebration ends with the Dance of Death in which the central theme is enacted. 2 men are actors, and the community surrounds them holding lavender bundles. One of the men pantomimes an anonymous man which the other one pantomimes Lena (as Maddalena is also known). They dance to joyous music and enact scenes of love and happiness and then, suddenly, Lena falls dead. The anonymous man desperately tries to bring her to life again by beating her with lavender bundles while a funeral lament song is played. Lena does rise again, while the funeral song changes to one of resurrection, and the two begin their dance again.

Bunches of lavender are enjoyed by the community, having a meaning of regeneration of the Divine Feminine power (agriculturally of course) and also one of protection against negative energy and misfortunes and as a plant that promotes prosperity.

BASIL **il basilico: Protective**
Medico-magical uses:
- Used against depression caused by black magic
- Used for purification in infusion water
- Burned and boiled to keep out spirit attachments, scorpions, snakes.
- Protects against the il malocchio and envy in general
- Used as filter plant in bowls on windowsills
- Never cut it with an iron tool or it will lose its protective virtues

WALNUT **il noce: Protective**
IRIS **l'iride: Protective**
BEECH **la saggina: Protective**

PLANTS WITH DUAL POWERS:
Oak, Walnut, Hazelnut...and also the Moon

PLANTS OF THE ETERNAL RETURN:
Oak, Boxwood, Poplar, Cherry, Iris, Sorrel

PLANTS OF LOVE:
Pear, Ivy, Fig, Mandrake

MANDRAGORA: **Mandrake** also known as **La Magica Bamboilna** the magic doll

PLANTS

In certain villages of Umbria, Mandrake is hunted and its spirit is connected with through propitiatory offerings to increase abundance of both harvest and money wealth.

A natural dowsing-type tool is used to find the female root of mandrake. The tool used to "find the bone herb" as it's a also called, is made of Juniper wood and sometimes Hawthorn wood, in 2 pieces: one wrapped around the other like a serpent. A dog is brought as a scapegoat, to absorb and negative energies from the mandrake's spirit that may be released during harvest.

The female root, once harvested, is dressed in a red dress and called the little magic doll, referred to as la bambolina. Next to the la bambolina were placed 2 small bowls: one of wheat grains or local lentils, one of coin. On her dress were pinned some paper money. These offerings were propitiatory to the spirit of the mandrake, in hopes that she would be pleased with them and make both the food harvest and money supply increase in abundance.

*paraphrased from "Le piante e il sacro: La percezione della natura nel mondo rurale della Valnerina" by Mario Polia

FLOWERS and GODDESSES:
ACONITE, PEONY - Ecate
POPPY - Demetra
ALMOND FLOWER - Ceres, Cibele
MANDRAKE - Venere, Aphrodite

HERBS:
LAUREL, ROSEMARY- Donne di fuora, La Signora del Gioco

HAWTHORN: protect thresholds

Strigonella herb

FENNEL Prayer

In the region of Umbria, Santa Lucia is invoked for healing of the eye, but not simply in the manner of a medical cure. Firstly, she is believed to reside in a spiritual paradise where grows a spiritual counterpart to the earthly fennel plant. The invocations ask her to bring fennel from its source in paradise down to earth, and to first use it to create

Italian Magic: Secret Lives of Women

a protective barrier around the home of the patient, like a magic circle, and then to enter the home and heal the patient's eyes, spiritually. Part one is presented below:

> **"Santa Lucia, santa Lucia,**
> **passa 'ntorno a casa mia,**
> **co' 'n mazzu de finocchiu**
> **puliscime bene l'occhiu"** 701

ROSEMARY Prayer

In Sicily, while many healers spiritually wed themselves to the Madonna and her healing powers, there are also healers who invoke the healing powers of the rainbow and the healing power of rosemary: **"Ti scunciuru malu natu, ti nn'a-gghiri unni si natu: ca Ddiu nasciu, Ddiu arrivisciu, ppi sarvari a-nnui; rrosmarina, chi Ddiu ti binidici, dunami la virtu', chi Ddiu ti fici".** 702

PANACEA PLANTS
Panacea plants are ones used to cure almost anything physical and psychic.
The 3 most widely used panacea plants are: Rue and Mallow and Verbena,
also known as "the iron plant." They even have their own proverbs:

"la malva da tutti li mali salva" "Malva from all evils saves" 703

"la ruta ogni male stuta" "Rue heals every suffering"

TRADITIONAL PLANTS USED IN SICILY
to fight Vermi helminthiasis and its psychic illness affects

"Ogni erba havi a so' virtue". Every herb has its own virtue.

> *"Sometimes it is not God or a Saint whose help is*
> *asked to fight worms but a medicinal plant"*. 704

This is a list of plants (and additives) traditionally used in many or some parts of Sicily to cure **vermi**. Many of these plants have toxic parts, and these were the parts used with the specialized knowledge on how to do so, orally transmitted from one healer to the other.

- Garlic; cooked in milk, cooked in wine, rubbed on the body, infused in olive oil then rubbed on body, with spool of thread, cloves threaded by string and fabric and worn as necklace for 3 days.
- Lemon bitter drink

PLANTS

- Pomegranate bitter drink
- Coffee
- Spit
- Paraffin wax
- Marine absinthe (Artemisia cretacea)
- Parsley (Prezzemolo)
- Delphinium staphysagria (Stavescare)
- Corallina officinalis seaweed (Coral moss)
- Jania Rubens (Corallinaceae)
- Alsidium helminthochorton (Corsican moss)
- Sargassum vulgare (Sargassum seaweed)
- Digenea simplex e Ulva sp (seaweed)
- Simienza di viermi (aka cabbarasi)
- St johns wort (hypericum perforatum)
- The Tree of Heaven (Ailanthus altissimia)
- Spanish Origanum (coridothymus capitatus)
- Fern Athurium filix-foemina (lady fern)
- Green purslane (Portulaca oleracea)
- Wild carrot root (Daucus carota)
- Love in the Mist seeds (Nigella damascena)
- Corn cockle (Agrostemma githago)
- American wormseed (Chenopodium ambrosioides)
- Tansy Tanacetum (vulgare erva di vermi)
- Rosemary (Rosmarino)
- Rue (Ruta chalepensis)
- Mint (Menta)
- Snow Thistle (Sonchus oleraceus)
- Bay leaves (Laurus nobilis)
- Wild chamomile (Achillea ligustica)
- White Herb/Wormwood tree (Artemisia arborescens)
- Pitcher plant (Calamintha nepeta "nipitedda")
- Vine shoot (Vitis vinifera)
- Dog rose (Rosa Canina)
- Broadleaved pepperweed "sciatic herb" (Lepidium latifolium)
- Small flowered willow-weed (Epilobium parviflorum)
- Olive Tree
- Snow Thistle
- Mulberry
- Onion (Allium cepa)
- Sweet marjoram
- Savi
- Snakeroot eryngo (Eryngium campestre)
- stavescare (Delphinium staphysagria)
- Scurfy pea (Bituminaria bituminosa)
- Tree of Heaven (Ailanthus altissima)
- Swingle

Italian Magic: Secret Lives of Women

- American worm seed (Chenopodium ambrisioides)
- the Rainbow

705

The following list of herbs are used by healers in the Silver Valley of the region of Liguria and have been compiled by Sandro Oddo in his book "La medicina popolare nell'alta valle argentina" in their Italian names.

Abete Bianco	White Fir	Betonica	Betony
Abete Rosso	Spruce	Betulla	Birch
Acanto	Acanthus	Biancospino	Hawthorn
Acetosella	Shamrock	Bietola Selvatica	Wild chard
Agave	Agave	Bistorta	Bistort
Aglio	Garlic	Bocca di Leone	Lion's mouth
Agrimonia	Agrimony	Borragine	Borage
Alloro	Laurel (Bay)	Borsa Pastore	Shepherd's bag
Altea	Altea	Bosso	Boxwood
Angelica	Angelica	Brionia	Brionia
Anice	Anise	Brugo	Brugo
Aparine	Cleavers	Bugula	Bugula
Aquilegia	Granny's bonnet	Buon Enrico	Good Henry
Arnica	Arnica	Caglio	Rennet
Artemesia	Artemisa	Calamo Aromatico	Calamus
Assenzio	Absinthe	Calendula	Calendula
Avena	Oats	Camedrio	Germander
Barbabietola	Beet	Camedrio Alpino	Alpine germander
Barba di Becco	Beard of Beak	Camomilla	Chamomile
Bardana	Burdock	Camomilla Romana	Roman chamomile
Belladonna	Belladonna	Canfornia	Camphor
Canna	Cane	Equiseto	Horsetail
Capelvenere	Maidenhair fern	Erba Dorata	Golden grass
Carciofo	Artichoke	Erba Medica	Alfalfa
Cardo dei Lanaioli	Woolen thistle	Erba Pignola	Sedum acre L.
Carlina	Carlina thistle	Erba Rugginina	Rusty grass
Carota	Carrot	Erba Trinita'	Trinity grass
Castagno	Chestnut	Erisimo	Hedge mustard
Cavolo	Cabbage	Eucalipto	Eucalyptus
Cedronella	Cedronella	Euforbia	Euphorbia
Celidonia	Celandine	Farfaro	Coltsfoot
Centaurea Minore	Centaurea minor	Favagello	Ranunculus ficaria
Centinodia	Bindweed	Felce Dolce	Sweet fern
Centocchio	Chickweed	Felce Maschia	Male fern
Cicoria	Chicory	Fico	Fig
Ciliegio	Cherry tree	Finocchio Selvatico	Wild fennel

PLANTS

Cipolla	Onion	Fiordaliso	Cornflower
Crescione	Watercress	Fragola	Strawberry
Cuscuta	Cuscuta	Frassino Maggiore	Ash major
Digitale Gialla	Digitalis grandiflora	Fumaria Officinale	Fumaria Off.
Dulcamara	Bittersweet nightshade	Gelso Nero	Black mulberry
Edera	Ivy	Genepi	Genepi
Elleboro	Hellebore	Genziana Maggiore	Greater Gentian
Epilobio	Epilobium	Genzianella	Genzianella
Geranio	Geranium	Lino	Linen
Giglio	Lily	Luppolo	Hops
Ginepro	Juniper	Maggiociondolo	Laburnum
Ginestra	Broom	Maggiorana	Marjoram
Ginestra dei Carbonai	Scotch broom	Malva	Mallow
Ginestrino	Lotus corniculatus	Malvone	Malvone
Giusquiamo	Henbane	Margheritina	Daisy
Gramigna	Gramigna	Marrubio	Horehound
Grano	Wheat	Melissa	Melissa
Granturco	Maize	Melo	Apple tree
Iperico	Hypericum	Menta	Mint
Iperico Androsemo	Hypericus Androsemus	Mercorella	Dog's Mercury
Ippocastano	Horse chestnut	Millefoglio	Yarrow
Issopo	Hyssop	Mirtillo	Blueberry
Lamio Bianco	White lamio	Mirto	Myrtle
Lampone	Raspberry	Morella	Morella
Lanciola	Lanciola	Nepitella	Calamint
Larice	Larch	Nespolo	Loquat
Lattuga	Lettuce	Noce	Walnut
Lavanda	Lavender	Olivo	Olive
Lichene	Lichen	Ombelico di Venere	Navelwort
Limone	Lemon	Origano	Oregano
Lingua di Cane, Cinoglosso	Dog's Tongue	Ortica Maschia	Stinging nettle
Orzo	Barley	Quercia	Oak
Papavero	Poppy	Rapa	Turnip
Parietaria	Parietaria	Rapanello	Radish
Partenio	Feverfew	Rapontico	False rhubarb
Passiflora	Passionflower	Ribes	Currant
Pastinaca	Parsnip	Robinia	Black locust
Patata	Potato	Rododendro	Rhododendron
Pera	Pear	Romice	Yellow dock
Pervinca	Periwinkle	Rosa Canina	Dog rose
Piantaggine	Plantain	Rosa Rossa	Red rose
Pilosella	Mouse ear	Rosmarino	Rosemary
Pimpinella	Pimpinella	Rosolaccio	Wild poppy
Pino Silvestre	Scots pine	Rovo	Bramble

Italian Magic: Secret Lives of Women

Pino Marittimo	Maritime pine	Ruta	Rue
Poligala	Polygala	Salsapariglia	Sasparilla
Polipodio	Polypodium	Salvia	Sage
Polmonaria	Pulmonary	Salvia dei Prati	Meadow sage
Pomodoro	Tomato	Salvia Verbenaca	Wild sage
Prezzemolo	Parsley	Sambuco	Elder
Primula	Primrose	Sanguisorba	Burnet
Prugnolo	Blackthorn	Santolina	Santolina
Pungitopo	Butcher's broom	Santoreggia	Summer savory
Saponaria	Soapwort	Tasso Barbasso	Common mullein
Scabiosa	Scabious	Tiglio	Linden
Scrofolaria	Scrofularia	Timo	Thyme
Sedano	Celery	Tragoselino Becchino	Pimpinella major
Segale	Rye	Trifoglio	Clover
Semprevivo	Houseleek	Trigonella	Fenugreek
Senecio	Groundsel	Valeriana	Valerian
Senecione	Senecione aureono	Valeriana Rossa	Centranthus ruber
Serpillo	Serpent thyme	Vedovella	Scabiosa
Sigillo di Salomone	Seal of Solomon	Verbena	Verbena
Sorbo	Rowan	Veronica	Veronica
Stramonio	Starmonium	Viola del Pensiero	Wild pansy
Strigonella	Stachys recta	Viola Mammola	Sweet violet
Susino	Plum	Vitalba	Clematis
Tabacco	Tobacco	Vite	Vite
Tamaro	Tamaro	Zucca	Pumpkin
Tanaceto	Tansy		
Tarassaco	Dandelion		

PLANTS

Photos top row l-r: Nigella damascena, Carob pods.
Middle: Belladonna growing on Mt Taburno, Campania.
Bottom: Camedrio and seeds from the datura stramonium plant.

UNGUENTI: FLYING OINTMENTS

This is not a deep study of plants used in flying ointments, but it's necessary to mention their existence because they were used to achieve **il volo** astral flight. **Unguenti** flying ointments were made based on the availability of plants and were more common in the south of Italy and in Sicily where these plants grow more readily, naturally.

Flying ointments were not the most common way for people to fly in Italy's past, nor were they a widespread tradition: the most common way to fly was using just the mind, after being summoned by spirits of different types and taught how to do so, such as with students of **La Signora del Gioco**'s night school, Sicily's **Le Donne di fuora** and Friuli's **Benandanti**, as well as followers of Demeter, known as both a goddess of healing and as "goddess of ecstasy"[706] in the region of Puglia, although there are associations of ointments with **Le Donne di fuora** and Demeter. Sometimes these calls to flight were accompanied by frame drumming and sometimes through other rituals taught by the spirits which aided the process. Indigenous traditions in rural Italy, especially prior to the Roman entry and the middle period's focus on materialism, came from the spirits who taught Abundance, and therefore the means to achieve Abundance (in this case to achieve astral flight) were taught through available and accessible means.

The effects of ointments on the body were reportedly the same as mental induced flight: that the body was immobile for hours or even an entire day, and that the body was imperceptible to externally inflicted pain or movement during the time period that the spirit was in flight. Another common experience between **unguenti** ointment induced flight and mental induced flight was the observation of animal transfiguration, that is, people in flight either accompanied by animas or having transformed in part or in whole into animals. These animals are the same ones found in shamanism, and while in shamanism all shaman do not transform into animals, many do have an animal whose bird calls, for example, they must learn or other attributes they must emulate in order to achieve flight.

"Others said to go out of the closed doors in the silence of the night, leaving their sleeping husbands behind." [707]

In a testimony from the 1400s:

A priest of our order entered a village where he met a woman who was so insane that she believed she was flown overnight in the company of Diana and other women. When he tried to drive such heresies out of his mind with pious speeches, the woman remained perfectly convinced of her ideas. The priest then asked her: 'Let me assist you when you leave next time'.[...] On the scheduled day [..] the priest presented himself in the company of some trusted citizens in order to convince that fanatic of her madness. The woman, after placing a large bowl on the ground [....] Entered it and sat down. Then she anointed herself with an ointment accompanied with magic formulas and bowed her head falling immediately asleep[...] she dreamed of Venus and other superstitions so vividly that, launching loud cries and waving her arms, she knocked over the bowl and fell injuring her head. When, upon awakening, the priest revealed to her that she had never moved [...] 708

Testimonies of men in both Bergamo and Como during this time period say that each found their wife and female servant *lying on the floor, rigid as a corpse, unconscious, so that there was no way to awaken her.* 709 and *naked, in a corner, with her genitals on display, completely unconscious and covered by animal excrement.* 710 Upon awakening both women confessed to having been at the sabbath or other places. Animal excrement was used in curative traditions to heal skin ailments, so naturally it was used as a vehicle for flying ointments which were born naturally from the curative ones.

While the testimonies above are from the 1400s, *"Apuleius [...] in the "Metamorphosis" or "The Golden Donkey," gives us the most interesting testimony, speaking of the night conferences held by Diana*711 *in 170 AD.*

*As for witch ointments proper, they were known under different names such as: unguento delle streghe, unguenti del sabba, unguento populeo, unguento del pioppo, unguenti sonniferi, unguento per dormire, unguento per volare...*712 among others. [ointment of the witches, ointment of the sabbath, popular ointment, poplar ointment, dreaming ointments, sleeping ointment, flying ointment].

The ointment was almost always described as dark (mostly green) and with an unpleasant smell. 713

Of course there were many ointments used in healing. Naturally, ointments were applied with fingers or wooden sticks. This application was the same for flying ointments. Broom handles could have been used naturally used to put ointment into body cavities for those who wanted to experience a faster result, but fingers did the same. While brooms have been eroticized, the function is also practical. Brooms served other magical purposes such as protection through filtering. *Often the brooms were made with birch wood (Betula spp.) or broom (Cytisus scoparius). The second is a psychoactive plant, while the first is the shamanic tree of Northern Europe.* 714 At the same time, there was poisonous risk to taking these plants internally and *by spreading them on the skin and on the mucous membranes, in fact, side effects were avoided and the absorption of the active ingredients was maximized.* 715

The plants used are the typically known ones: belladonna, datura stramonium,

Italian Magic: Secret Lives of Women

mandragora mandrake, giusquiamo henbane, amanita muscaria mushroom   Artemisia absinthium, also papavero poppy and aconito aconite. Ointments were made thicker with the use of wax and animal fat, toad fat or bear fat, sometimes imbued with blood. Specifically as but not limited to: *seeds of black and white poppy, roots of mandragora, henbane juice, mastic resin, cinnamon, opium, saffron, clove flowers, tobacco, dandelion, carlina thistle, laurel, lettuce,* 716 enhanced with a diet of *with celery, chestnuts, beans, onions, cabbage and beans,* 717 which some people claimed consistently affected their dreams.

Generally, the rural ointments made by people with orally transmitted knowledge of the plants were rather simple, just as all cures and foods and preparations were, while middle period ointments made by practicing sorcerers and those "trying" to get the effects reflect a much more contemporary and complicated effort: it was as if people researched all the plants and substances they could that might affect dreams and clumped them together for potentials, and thus the ingredients were many.

As far as the common experiences people reported from the plant ointments, the reason for consistency is a natural one and common among ayahuasca users as well: the spirits of the plants in the astral realm are always the same ones: as each herb has its healing virtue, so does each one have its teacher spirit. So the experiences, under the influence, are guided by spirit teachers from the plants, often in the form of animals or hybrids and vivid colors, who are in charge of the astral flight and what is available there. For example, scientists who have tried ayahuasca have reported meeting the same sentient serpent in spirit who taught them technical information. Among flying ointment users are common sights of human-hybrid animals and a parallel world to the earthly one. The experiences are common because the intelligences involved are common to each other.

View from Mt. Taburno, Campania

THE MYTH OF SYNCRETISM

While technically syncretism means "a fusion of diverse religious beliefs and practices", in an over simplified definition, the popular definition tends to be one of "religious people grasping for magic to embed within their system," and not the other way around. As a result, people tend to dismiss rural traditions in Italy as a specific syncretic blend that is "just christian traditions with a little paganism embedded." Some people (Americans) even accuse rural magic as having "stolen" traditions from witches, and there are various other opinions.

The rural traditions, however, have been around since the beginnings and they are part of a holistic lifestyle rather than being piecemeal conception that other magical practices have been woven together with. Rural traditions come from the spirit world of teachings, as shamanism does, and this book gives just a little insight to a much more detailed world that has been stolen or re-customized by both DIY witches and the church. Rural fold don't write down their traditions, and therefore can't defend themselves among the all-important (socially deemed, anyway) written documents.

To accuse rural people of theft, people who largely live in areas that are have long been impenetrable by outsiders due to rough terrain, and who have been largely illiterate and survive with oral traditions, is absurd. Rural people, like poorer people around the world, are often accused of being dumb, superstitious, and other denigrating terms. But with some education, it's quite simple to notice that around the world, "rural" folk are practicing the oldest traditions that have ever been, and that these have been emulated, rebranded and modernized by people who gravitate towards terminology like "quantum," "metaphysical" "spiritual laws of abundance". The traditions may look weird, such as spitting on a wart and mumbling an invocation, but they are part of a greater whole in thought, word and deed. In Italy, because of the access to people that the church has had and the harmful power it has wielded, rural people have had religious rules oppressed onto their communities, and at times are watched by visiting clerics, and yet, they are capable of maintaining their own inner beliefs and traditions:

> *a craftsman from Riola [Sardinia] claims to be a free thinker, one who never goes to church. He says: "I already believe in God, I believe in it, and in the Saints too I believe...but if the pastor is waiting to see me in church, he will be waiting until my beard turns white."* [718]

Additionally, rural communities have their own meanings for the church statues and relics, and there are plenty of local stories of rural folk chasing away church clerics

Italian Magic: Secret Lives of Women

who try to mess with their traditions with their churches, in the way they have established them. And, it's difficult to dismiss rural magic as "just Christianity" when the church in fact has banned most of their practices, even cures that used prayers with Jesus' name or saints within them. The medicine bags used by rural healers have also been plagiarized by the church, who then turned around and banned rural people from using them.

Presented below is a truncated list of rural traditions banned by the church compiled from Ugo Dessy "Sa Mexina: La Medicina Is ominis de Nexina-I guaritori:

+ Cure with herbs, joining prayers or sacred verses;
+ treat the colic of oxen or horses by imposing the feet of two twin brothers on the belly of the sick animal;
+ plant a bucranium on top of a pole where livestock is housed to safeguard it from the evil eye;
+ use the egg to perform magical rituals, for therapeutic or aesthetic purposes (such as to rub the egg of freshly made hen on temples for migraine or cheek to make the skin soft and velvety);
+ use the chicken dung or other volatile still hot as an ointment to heal wounds;
+ facilitate in any way the transition to the dying (either placing a yoke from under the cervix oxen laying it on the bare earth or even removing a tile from the roof, to allow to the soul of the dying man to leave, to detach himself from the earthly environment to which he is "too much bound"
+ to close the door of the house when a funeral procession passes, to prevent death from entering and entering it no two ways
+ nail the striga or barn owl to the front door to preserve it from death or other fatal events of which the bird is a carrier;
+ to stir, or to mourn the dead with lamentations or dances or other funeral rites
+ to open locked doors without a key
+ to make it rain
+ to have abundance (it is still used in the Sartiglia - composite ceremony carnival oristanese - invoke a good harvest blessing the crowd with sa pippia de maju, la May pupa, consisting of a bunch of periwinkle)
+ to send the soul in Heaven, or to make it die without suffering
+ put a dead dog in a pool of water to make it rain or even bury it at the feet of one tree to make it fruitful
+ to use the imposition of sacred relics on sick parts of a person for healing purposes

Author Note

The material for this book, as with the material in "Italy's Witches And Medicine Women Vol 1", comes from interactions, experiences, training, initiations, and interviews with people in Italy.

How I met these people and how they welcomed me is an exciting story about the power of the spirit world, and it's the spirit world who guided me to include the documented reference notes to honor Italians who've lived this life, to honor Italians who've documented this lifestyle, and to expose Americans to Italian sources of research other than the Romans.

While this book barely scratches a dent into all the daily sacred rituals that do exist, its purpose is to serve as a connection point of hidden sources that demonstrate: holistic cohesion, natural structure, and a foundation of metaphysical principles such as "thoughts are things", all of which deflate the common anthropological stance that the rural world is based on "superstitions".

For those of you interested in tracing rituals in this book to regions your extended family is from and don't find your village or region listed within these pages, know that if they were from a rural location, it's likely this daily sacred lifestyle existed there. Cities, however, were places where contemporary patriarchal magic, DIY conceptualization and middle period masculine magic existed: these are derivative from the rural magic and not the other way around. The rural world is a shamanistic one: with rituals deeply in tune with nature, as are the people who worked the land, where supernatural powers to cure are inherited from the spirit world and continue to cure only with power granted from the spirits.

- You'll find Italian words in bold throughout this book followed or preceded by the English translation unbolded rather than in parentheses. Also, if there is a name of a deity that is spelled several ways, you will find those various spellings used rather than a singular one.

- You'll also find a strange philosophy to our contemporary world: magic against witches seemingly made by other witches. To be clear, in the rural world, people who do magic to help and return life to a positive balance have traditionally not been considered witches, even if they call their medico magical rituals "spells" (and some of them do). People who curse and kill with black magic are called witches. This distinction is important to accept in order to understand these stories in the words of Italians themselves and the way Italians name people, places and things. "Other people" break the spells of witches and restore health, using the curative magic that the cursing magic based itself upon.

- Finally, although this book is about the very real rural world where women were traditionally the sole operators of this particular magic in this lifestyle and who worked in partnership with specific spirits who aided women only, it is the author's request that this book not to be used to argue that only women are magical or that only women should practice magic as witches or under "other" titles. While everyone is entitled to their opinions and beliefs, it is the author's belief, based on direct experience, that all genders and all people are built with physical senses and spirit/psychic senses and therefore all people and all genders are potentially magical.

REFERENCES

1. Fabiola Chavez Hualpa , "Le donne nel mondo rurale della Valnerina" (Tipolito Federici, 2012), p.347
2. https://www.healthline.com/health/how-is-sperm-produced
3. Mellaart, James, "Catal Huyuk: A Neolithic Town in Anatolia" (McGraw-Hill, 1967) . p. 181.
4. https://en.wikipedia.org/wiki/Çatalhöyük#cite_note-mellart181-27
5. ibid.
6. ibid.
7. ibid.
8. ibid.
9. https://en.wikipedia.org/wiki/Cybele
10. Lynn E. Roller, "The Mother Goddess in Greece" citing Pindar, fragment 80 (Snell), Despoina Kubela Mātēr, (University of California Press, 1999), p.125
11. https://en.wikipedia.org/wiki/Cybele
12. http://www.ftnews.it/articolo.asp?cod=729
13. Eisler, Sacred Pleasure: Sex, Myth, and the Politics of theBody, (HarperOne; 1st Edition, 1996) p.61.
14. Marija Gimbutas, "The Language of the Goddess" (Harper & Row, 1989), p. xx
15. http://www.ftnews.it/articolo.asp?cod=729
16. https://www.bbc.co.uk/programmes/articles/1dRznJkKZ6DnG0fXMD2hxNP/catalhoyuk-an-example-of-true-gender-equality
17. ibid.
18. ibid.
19. Gimbutas, "The Language of the Goddess", (Harper & Row, 1989), p. xx
20. http://www.ftnews.it/articolo.asp?cod=729
21. Chavez Hualpa, "Le donne nel mondo rurale della Valnerina" (Tipolito Federici 2012), p.21
22. http://www.medasa.it/
23. Pasquali Coluzzi, Crescenzi, "La Nascita, Usi e riti in Campania e nel Salento" (Fridericiana Editrice Universitaria 2010), p.32
24. Hilary Marland, "The Art of Midwifery: Early Modern Midwives in Europe" (Routledge, 1994)
25. Antonella Caforio, "Figure femminili Protettrici della nascita: la baba, la femme-qui-aide, la levatrice nella cultura europa" (I.S.U Universitaria Cattolica 2002), p.18
26. Tullia Pasquali Coluzzi, Luisa Crescenzi, "La Nascita, Usi e riti in Campania e nel Salento" (Fridericiana Editrice Universitaria 2010), p.32
27. Caforio, Figure femminili Protettrici della nascita: la baba, la femme-qui-aide, la levatrice nella cultura europa EDUCatt Universita' Cattolica 2002) p.18
28. Coluzzi, Crescenzi, "La Nascita, Usi e riti in Campania e nel Salento" (Fridericiana Editrice Universitaria 2010), p. 4
29. ibid.
30. ibid, p.3
31. ibid., p.5
32. ibid., p.2
33. ibid.
34. Chavez Hualpa, "Le donne nel mondo rurale della Valnerina" (Tipolito Federici, 2012) p.352 (Zanetti 1892: 120)
35. https://superstizioni.blogspot.com/2012/02/la-nascita.html
36. https://www.contusu.it/la-nascita-in-sardegna/24
37. https://superstizioni.blogspot.com/2012/02/la-nascita.html
38. L. Manocchi, "Feste, costumanze, superstizioni popolari nel circondario di Fermo e nel Piceno" (Tipografia Economica, 1920)p.143

39. Hualpa, "Le donne nel mondo rurale della Valnerina" (Tipolitografia Federici, 2012), p.347
40. ibid., p.323-324
41. ibid., p.329
42. ibid.
43. ibid.
44. G. Finamore, "Tradizioni popolari Abruzzesi" (Aquila: Polia, 1997), p.81
45. https://superstizioni.blogspot.com/2012/02/la-nascita.html
46. Chavez Hualpa, "Le donne nel mondo rurale della Valnerina" (Tipolito Federici, 2012), p.331
47. ibid.
48. ibid., p.351
49. https://superstizioni.blogspot.com/2012/02/la-nascita.html
50. Chavez Hualpa, "Le donne nel mondo rurale della Valnerina" (Tipolito Federici, 2012) p.332
51. ibid., p.333
52. ibid.
53. https://superstizioni.blogspot.com/2012/02/la-nascita.html
54. https://superstizioni.blogspot.com/2012/02/la-nascita.html
55. Chavez Hualpa, "Le donne nel mondo rurale della Valnerina" (Tipolito Federici, 2012), p.347
56. ibid., p.336
57. ibid., p.334
58. http://www.americatholig.org/Features/Saints/saint.aspx?id=1391
59. Chavez Hualpa, "Le donne nel mondo rurale della Valnerina" (Tipolito Federici, 2012), p.346
60. ibid., p.334
61. Mircea Eliade, "Shamanism: Archaic Techniques of Ecstasy (Princeton/Bollingen Paperback Printing, 1974), p.508
62. ibid., p.5
63. Cf. Gustav Raenk, "Lapp Female Deities of the Madder-Akka Group." (SS,VI 1955) p.88
64. Mircea Eliade, "Shamanism: Archaic Techniques of Ecstasy (Princeton/Bollingen Paperback Printing, 1974), p.6
65. ibid., p.5
66. ibid.
67. ibid., p. 506
68. Chavez Hualpa, "Le donne nel mondo rurale della Valnerina" (Tipolito Federici, 2012), p.334
69. Mario Polia, "Cosi pregavano i nostri padri: Preghiere popolari della Valnerina" (Editrice Centro Italia, 2009), p. 203
70. ibid., p.867
71. Coluzzi, Crescenzi, "La Nascita, Usi e riti in Campania e nel Salento" (Fridericiana Editrice Universitaria 2010), p.18
72. ibid., p.21
73. Dolores Turchi, "Lo sciamanesimo in Sardegna: credenze, rituali, pratiche e aneddoti alla scoperta di uni isola piena di mistero." (Newton Compton Editori, 2017), p.131
74. Chavez Hualpa, "Le donne nel mondo rurale della Valnerina" (Tipolito Federici, 2012), p.349
75. ibid., p.334
76. Mario Polia "Tematiche del pensiero religioso e magico" (Editrice Centro Italia, 2009), p.673
77. Eliade, "Shamanism: Archaic Techniques of Ecstasy" (Princeton/Bollingen Paperback Printing, 1974), p. 53
78. Chavez Hualpa, "Le donne nel mondo rurale della Valnerina" (Tipolito Federici, 2012), p.352
79. Polia "Tematiche del pensiero religioso e magico" (Editrice Centro Italia , 2009), p.675

80. Chavez Hualpa, "Le donne nel mondo rurale della Valnerina" (Tipolito Federici, 2012), p.475
81. Mario Polia, " Tra cielo in terra. Religione e magia nel mondo rurale della Valnerina" (Editrice Centro Italian, 2009), pgs. 672-673
82. Chavez Hualpa, "Le donne nel mondo rurale della Valnerina" (Tipolito Federici, 2012), p. 474
83. ibid., p.475
84. Polia "Tematiche del pensiero religioso e magico" (Editrice Centro Italia , 2009), p.672
85. Turchi, "Lo sciamanesimo in Sardegna: credenze, rituali, pratiche e aneddoti alla scoperta di uni isola piena di mistero." (Newton Compton Editori,2017), p.187
86. ibid.
87. Chavez Hualpa, "Le donne nel mondo rurale della Valnerina" (Tipolito Federici, 2012), p. 321
88. ibid., p. 322
89. ibid.
90. Chavez Hualpa, "Le donne nel mondo rurale della Valnerina" (Tipolito Federici, 2012), p.328
91. ibid., p.330
92. https://www.ncbi.nlm.nih.gov/pubmed/535548
93. Coluzzi, Crescenzi, "La Nascita, Usi e riti in Campania e nel Salento" (Fridericiana Editrice Universitaria 2010), p.35
94. ibid., p.31
95. ibid., p.32
96. Chavez Hualpa, "Le donne nel mondo rurale della Valnerina" (Tipolitografia Federici, 2012), p. 359
97. ibid., p.357
98. ibid.
99. ibid.
100. Chavez Hualpa, "Le donne nel mondo rurale della Valnerina" (Tipolito Federici, 2012), p.359
101. Miranda Niedda Giagnoni "Majarzas e sanadoras: tradizioni, racconti e usanza popolari in Sardegna (Editrice Democratica Sarda, 2009), p. 28
102. ibid., p.28
103. Gimbutas, "The Language of the Goddess" (Harper & Row, 1989), p. 82
104. Carlo Ginzburg, "The Night Battles" (Johns Hopkins Paperbacks edition, 1992), p.61
105. ibid.
106. ibid.
107. Chavez Hualpa, "Le donne nel mondo rurale della Valnerina" (Tipolitografia Federici, 2012), p. 355
108. Polia, "Le piante e il sacro: Le percezione della natural nel mondo rurale della Valnerina" (Quater, 2010), p.115
109. Chavez Hualpa, "Le donne nel mondo rurale della Valnerina" (Tipolito Federici, 2012), p.355
110. http://www.tecalibri.info/C/CAMPORESI-P_latte.htm
111. ibid.
112. http://www.tecalibri.info/C/CAMPORESI-P_latte.htm
113. http://spazioinwind.libero.it/folkgrotte/lattaie.htm
114. http://www.valleylife.it/dettaglio_articolo2.html
115. http://www.istitutoeuroarabo.it/DM/ninfe-ed-acque-in-sicilia-una-relazione-sacra/
116. http://spazioinwind.libero.it/folkgrotte/lattaie.htm
117. Coluzzi, Crescenzi, "La Nascita, Usi e riti in Campania e nel Salento" (Fridericiana Editrice Universitaria 2010), p.60
118. ibid., p.61
119. ibid., p.62
120. ibid.
121. http://spazioinwind.libero.it/folkgrotte/lattaie.htm

122. https://osservatorioturistico.sicilia.it/geoportale/index.php/2017/10/04/ninfe-dee-sicilia-un-territorio-sacro/
123. ibid.
124. Coluzzi, Crescenzi, "La Nascita, Usi e riti in Campania e nel Salento" (Fridericiana Editrice Universitaria 2010), p. 60
125. Chavez Hualpa, "Le donne nel mondo rurale della Valnerina" (Tipolito Federici, 2012). p. 366
126. ibid.
127. ibid.
128. ibid.
129. ibid.
130. https://www.pianetamamma.it/il-bambino/allattamento-il-bambino/allattamento-un-aiuto-dalle-erbe-galattogene.html
131. Vanessa Maher, 1992 "Il latte materno. I condizionamenti culturali di un comportamento" (Torino Rosenberg & Sellier, 1992).
132. Chavez Hualpa, "Le donne nel mondo rurale della Valnerina" (Tipolito Federici, 2012), p.349
133. ibid., p.363
134. ibid., p.322
135. ibid., p.360
136. ibid., p.360
137. ibid.
138. ibid.
139. ibid.
140. ibid., p.361
141. ibid.
142. ibid., p.361
143. ibid
144. ibid.
145. G. Finamore, Tradizioni popolari Abruzzesi. (Aquila: Polia, 1997) p.97-98)
146. Chavez Hualpa, "Le donne nel mondo rurale della Valnerina" (Tipolito Federici, 2012), p.361
147. ibid., p.110
148. ibid., p.372
149. ibid
150. ibid., p.353
151. https://superstizioni.blogspot.com/2012/02/la-nascita.html
152. Gianfranca Ranisio, "Venire al mondo. Credenze, pratiche e rituali del parto" (Roma, Meltemi,1998).
153. Chavez Hualpa, "Le donne nel mondo rurale della Valnerina" (Tipolitografia Federici, 2012), p.353
154. ibid., p. 352
155. Zeno Zanetti, La Medicina delle nostre donne. Studio folk-lorico, (Citta' di Castello:Lapi, 1892), p.131
156. https://superstizioni.blogspot.com/2012/02/la-nascita.html
157. Zanetti, La Medicina delle nostre donne. Studio folk-lorico, (Citta' di Castello:Lapi, 1892), p.131
158. https://digilander.libero.it/aisea/atti_2006/saggio%20FRANCESE.pdf
159. Chavez Hualpa, "Le donne nel mondo rurale della Valnerina" (Tipolito Federici, 2012), p.380
160. https://superstizioni.blogspot.com/2012/02/la-nascita.html
161. Ernesto De Martino, "Sud e magia" (Milano, Feltrinelli,1959)
162. https://www.mondo-doula.it/articolo.aspx?articolo=148
163. De Martino, "Sud e magia" (Milano, Feltrinelli, 1959)
164. Chavez Hualpa, "Le donne nel mondo rurale della Valnerina" (Tipolitografia Federici, 2012), p.378

165. Mario Polia, "Le piante e il sacro; la perceione della natura nel mondo rurale della Valnerina (Editrice Centro Italia , 2010), p.190

166. Coluzzi, Crescenzi, "La Nascita, Usi e riti in Campania e nel Salento" (Fridericiana Editrice Universitaria 2010), p.26

167. Polia, "Le piante e il sacro; la percezione della natura nel mondo rurale della Valnerina" (Quater, 2010), p.190

168. Chavez Hualpa, "Le donne nel mondo rurale della Valnerina" (Tipolitografia Federici, 2012), p.362

169. ibid., p.325

170. ibid., p.326

171. G. Zanazzo, Tradizioni Popolari Romane. Usi, costumi e pregiudizi del popolo di Roma. (Bologna:Forni, 907), p.38

172. ibid., 22nd Inf. 23 in Sicily; Inf. 27-327

173. Z. Zanetti, " La Medicina delle nostre donne. Studio Folk-lorico. (Citta di Castello: Lap, 1892), p.111

174. Coluzzi, Crescenzi, "La Nascita, Usi e riti in Campania e nel Salento" (Fridericiana Editrice Universitaria 2010), p.50

175. Chavez Hualpa, "Le donne nel mondo rurale della Valnerina" (Tipolito Federici, 2012), p.110

176. Dessy "Sa mexina: Is ominis de mexina la medicina- I guaritori." (Alfa Editrice, 1989) , p.78

177. ibid.

178. Coluzzi, Crescenzi, "La Nascita, Usi e riti in Campania e nel Salento" (Fridericiana Editrice Universitaria 2010), p.51

179. Mario Polia "Tematiche del pensiero religioso e magico" (Editrice Centro Italia, 2009), p.411

180. Dolores Turchi, "Ho visto agire s'accabadora: la prima testimonianza oculare di una persona vivente sull'operato de s'accabadora" Edizioni IRIS, 20080, p.9

181. https://superstizioni.blogspot.com/2012/02/la-nascita.html

182. Coluzzi, Crescenzi, "La Nascita, Usi e riti in Campania e nel Salento" (Fridericiana Editrice Universitaria 2010), p.35

183. https://superstizioni.blogspot.com/2012/03/la-morte.html?view=classic

184. Turchi, "Ho visto agire s'accabadora: " Edizioni IRIS, 20080, p.12

185. http://himetop.wikidot.com/galluras-museum-sa-femmina-aggabbadora

186. http://www.lacanas.it/2016/05/20/sacabadora/

187. Turchi, "Ho visto agire s'accabadora: " Edizioni IRIS, 20080, p.11

188. ibid, p.13

189. ibid, p.14

190. ibid, p.18

191. http://www.luoghimisteriosi.it/sardegna_luras.html

192. Turchi, "Ho visto agire s'accabadora: " Edizioni IRIS, 20080, p.36

193. ibid., p.9

194. ibid., p.35

195. ibid., p.21

196. http://www.lacanas.it/2016/05/20/sacabadora/

197. ibid.

198. Gennaro Finamore, "Tradizioni popolari Abruzzesi" (Aquila:Polia,1997) p.108

199. Giovanni Crocioni, "La gente marchigiana nelle sue tradizioni" (Milano: Corticelli, 1951), p.54

200. http://www.lacanas.it/2016/05/20/sacabadora/

201. Turchi, "Ho visto agire s'accabadora: " Edizioni IRIS, 20080, p.69

202. ibid., p.65

203. ibid., p.65

204. ibid., p.68

205. ibid., p.67

206. ibid., p. 68

207. ibid., p.69
208. ibid., p.47
209. ibid., p.50
210. Turchi, "Ho visto agire s'accabadora:" (Edizioni IRIS, 2008), p.47-51
211. Polia, M., Chávez Hualpa, "Mio padre mi disse". (Rimini: Il Chercio, 2002) p. 74)
212. http://www.lacanas.it/2016/05/20/sacabadora/
213. Turchi, "Ho visto agire s'accabadora: " (Edizioni IRIS, 2008), p.25
214. ibid., p.31
215. ibid.
216. ibid., p.25
217. ibid., pgs. 24,5
218. https://superstizioni.blogspot.com/2012/03/la-morte.html?view=classic
219. Turchi, "Ho visto agire s'accabadora: " (Edizioni IRIS, 2008), p.55
220. ibid., p.79
221. ibid., p.67
222. ibid., p.79
223. ibid., p.54
224. ibid., p.55
225. ibid.
226. Mario Polia "Tematiche del pensiero religioso e magico" (Editrice Centro Italia, 2009), p.414
227. Turchi, "Ho visto agire s'accabadora:" (Edizioni IRIS, 2008), p.83
228. Gimbutas, "The Language of the Goddess", (Harper & Row, 1989), p.189
229. Turchi, "Ho visto agire s'accabadora: " Edizioni IRIS, 20080, p.83
230. ibid.
231. Gimbutas, "The Language of the Goddess", (Harper & Row, 1989) p.300
232. ibid.
233. Turchi, "Ho visto agire s'accabadora: " (Edizioni IRIS, 2008), p.83
234. http://www.luoghimisteriosi.it/sardegna_luras.html
235. ibid.
236. http://www.luoghimisteriosi.it/sardegna_luras.html
237. http://himetop.wikidot.com/galluras-museum-sa-femmina-aggabbadora
238. ibid.
239. Eliade, "Shamanism: Archaic Techniques of Ecstasy (Princeton/Bollingen Paperback Printing, 1974), p.237
240. ibid., p.182
241. Dessy "Sa mexina: Is ominis de mexina la medicina- I guaritori." (Alfa Editrice, 1989) , p.16
242. Eliade, "Shamanism: Archaic Techniques of Ecstasy (Princeton/Bollingen Paperback Printing, 1974), p.93
243. ibid., p.97
244. http://www.nurnet.net/blog/sa-morte-secada-avvoltoi-sciamani-e-circoli-megalitici/
245. Turchi, "Ho visto agire s'accabadora: " Edizioni IRIS, 20080, p.60
246. ibid., p.63
247. ibid., p.61
248. ibid., p.62
249. ibid., p.16
250. ibid., p.32
251. ibid., p.36
252. ibid., p. 32
253. Emanuela Tocci, "Tradizioni Rituralistiche e funerarie tra passato e presente nel territorio di Acri"
254. ibid.
255. Turchi, "Ho visto agire s'accabadora: " Edizioni IRIS, 20080, p.10
256. Polia "Tematiche del pensiero religioso e magico" (Editrice Centro Italia, 2009), p.448

257. ibid., p.436
258. ibid., p.420
259. ibid., p.437
256. ibid., p.448
257. ibid., p.436
258. ibid., p.420
259. ibid., p.448
260. ibid., p.437
261. Polia-Chávez, "Mio padre me disse" (Rimini: Il Cerchio, 2002), p.271
262. Turchi, "Ho visto agire s'accabadora: " (Edizioni IRIS, 2008), p.84
263. ibid.
264. ibid.
265. Polia "Tematiche del pensiero religioso e magico" (Editrice Centro Italia, 2009), p.420
266. Turchi, "Ho visto agire s'accabadora: " (Edizioni IRIS, 2008), p.108
267. https://superstizioni.blogspot.com/2012/03/la-morte.html?view=classic
268. Turchi, "Ho visto agire s'accabadora: " (Edizioni IRIS, 2008), p.106
269. Tocci, "Tradizioni Ritualistiche e funerarie tra passato e presente nel territorio di Acri"
270. https://superstizioni.blogspot.com/2012/03/la-morte.html?view=classic
271. Tocci, "Tradizioni Ritualistiche e funerarie tra passato e presente nel territorio di Acri"
272. ibid.
273. ibid.
274. ibid.
275. Turchi, "Lo sciamanesimo in Sardegna: credenze, rituali, pratiche e aneddoti alla scoperta di uni isola piena di mistero." (Newton Compton Editori, 2017), p.p.109
276. https://superstizioni.blogspot.com/2012/03/la-morte.html?view=classic
277. Tocci, "Tradizioni Ritualistiche e funerarie tra passato e presente nel territorio di Acri"
278. Polia "Tematiche del pensiero religioso e magico" (Editrice Centro Italia, 2009), p.443
279. Tocci, "Tradizioni Ritualistiche e funerarie tra passato e presente nel territorio di Acri"
280. ibid.
281. Polia "Tra sant'Emidio e la Sibilla. Forme del sacro e del magico nella religiosita' popolare ascolana" (Bologna: Forni, 2004) p. 137
282. Finamore, "Tradizioni popolari Abruzzesi" (Aquila: Polia, 1997), p13).
283. http://www.claudiazedda.it/sardegna-vendetta-attitadoras-e-rituali-funebri/
284. Polia "Tematiche del pensiero religioso e magico" (Editrice Centro Italia, 2009), p.443
285. Polia "Tematiche del pensiero religioso e magico" (Editrice Centro Italia, 2009), p.444
286. ibid.
287. Chavez Hualpa, "Le donne nel mondo rurale della Valnerina" (Tipolitografia Federici, 2012), p.56
288. ibid.
289. Tocci, "Tradizioni Ritualistiche e funerarie tra passato e presente nel territorio di Acri"
290. Polia "Tematiche del pensiero religioso e magico" (Editrice Centro Italia, 2009), p.437
291. ibid., p.447
292. Eliade, "Shamanism: Archaic Techniques of Ecstasy (Princeton/Bollingen Paperback Printing, 1974), p.363-366
293. Polia "Tematiche del pensiero religioso e magico" (Editrice Centro Italia, 2009 p.446
294. ibid.
295. Paolo Toschi, "Tradizioni popolari italiane. (Torino: RAI ERI Classe Unica, 1967) p.144-154.
296. Polia "Tematiche del pensiero religioso e magico" (Editrice Centro Italia, 2009), p. 445
297. ibid., p.445
298. ibid., p.446
299. ibid., p.444
300. ibid.
301. H. Ling Roth, "The Natives of Sarawak and British North Borneo" (London,1896)

302. Eliade, "Shamanism: Archaic Techniques of Ecstasy (Princeton/Bollingen Paperback Printing, 1974), p.359
303. Turchi, "Lo sciamanesimo in Sardegna" Newton Compton Editori, 2017), p.358]
304. http://www.claudiazedda.it/sardegna-vendetta-attitadoras-e-rituali-funebri/
305. ibid.
306. Tocci, "Tradizioni Ritualistiche e funerarie tra passato e presente nel territorio di Acri"
307. ibid.
308. ibid.
309. ibid.
310. Tocci, "Tradizioni Ritualistiche e funerarie tra passato e presente nel territorio di Acri"
311. Eliade, "Shamanism: Archaic Techniques of Ecstasy (Princeton/Bollingen Paperback Printing, 1974), p.356
312. ibid., p.358
313. Tocci, "Tradizioni Ritualistiche e funerarie tra passato e presente nel territorio di Acri"
314. https://superstizioni.blogspot.com/2012/03/la-morte.html?view=classic
315. ibid.
316. Polia "Tematiche del pensiero religioso e magico (Editrice Centro Italia, 2009), p.437
317. Eliade, "Shamanism: Archaic Techniques of Ecstasy (Princeton/Bollingen Paperback Printing, 1974), p.207
318. ibid., p.208:72
319. ibid., p.209: 77
320. https://superstizioni.blogspot.com/2012/02/la-nascita.html
321. Polia "Tematiche del pensiero religioso e magico" (Editrice Centro Italia, 2009), p.437
322. Eliade, "Shamanism: Archaic Techniques of Ecstasy (Princeton/Bollingen Paperback Printing, 1974), p.208
323. Polia "Tematiche del pensiero religioso e magico (Editrice Centro Italia, 2009), p.437
324. Simonetta Delussu, "Stregoneria in Sardegna" (2011)
325. Eliade, "Shamanism: Archaic Techniques of Ecstasy (Princeton/Bollingen Paperback Printing, 1974), p.206
326. Chavez Hualpa, "Le donne nel mondo rurale della Valnerina" (Tipolitografia Federici, 2012). p.513
327. ibid.
328. ibid.
329. https://italiaeoisagunt.blogspot.com/2010/04/la-festa-dei-serpari.html
330. Dessy, "Sa Mexina: La Medicina Is ominis de mexina – I guaritori" (Alfa Editrice, 1989) p.30
331. ibid., p.27
332. Eliade, "Shamanism: Archaic Techniques of Ecstasy (Princeton/Bollingen Paperback Printing, 1974), p.215
333. Finamore, "Tradizioni popolari Abruzzesi" (Aquila:Polia, 1997) p.91-92
334. Ginzburg, "The Night Battles" (Johns Hopkins Paperbacks edition, 1992), p.7
335. ibid., p5
336. Mariangela Napoli, "The plants, rituals, and spells that 'cured' helminthiasis in Sicily," (Journal of Ethnobiology and Ethnomedicine, 2008) p.5
337. ibid. p.7
338. ibid.
339. ibid. 6
340. ibid.
341. Paola Giovetti, "I guaritori di Campagna: viaggio attraverso la medicina poplare in Italia" (Edizioni Mediterranee, 2016), p.35
342. ibid., p.36
343. personal testimony from Sicilian friend speaking about majare.
344. ibid.

345. Giovetti, "I guaritori di Campagna: viaggio attraverso la medicina poplare in Italia" (Edizioni Mediterranee, 2016), p.57
346. Ginzburg, "The Night Battles" (Johns Hopkins Paperbacks edition, 1992), p.41]
347. ibid., p.42
348. Dessy, "Sa Mexina: La Medicina Is ominis de mexina – I guaritori" (Alfa Editrice, 1989) p.8
349. ibid., p. 45
350. ibid.
351. Polia, "Il ciclo dei mesi", (Editrice Centro Italia, 2009), p.171-177)
352. Karyn Crisis, "Italy's Witches and Medicine Women Vol. 1" (Golden Bough Books, 2017), p.220
353. Dessy, "Sa Mexina: La Medicina Is ominis de mexina – I guaritori" (Alfa Editrice, 1989), p.44
354. ibid.
355. ibid., p.44
356. ibid.
357. Giovetti, "I guaritori di Campagna: viaggio attraverso la medicina popolare in Italia" (Edizioni Mediterranee, 2016), p.49
358. Karyn Crisis' in person interview with Ottorino near San Giovanni Valdarno, Toscana, 2018
359. Napoli, "The plants, rituals, and spells that 'cured' helminthiasis in Sicily," (Journal of Ethnobiology and Ethnomedicine, 2008) p.16
360. ibid., p.13
361. ibid.
362. ibid., p.5
363. https://lagrandemadre.wordpress.com
364. Chavez Hualpa, "Le donne nel mondo rurale della Valnerina" (Tipolito Federici, 2012), p.495
365. ibid.
366. Sandro Oddo "La medicina popolare nell'alta valle Argentina" (Pro Triora Editore, 1997) p.57
367. ibid., p.57, 58
368. ibid.,
369. ibid., p.59
370. ibid., p. 58
371. Zanetti , "La Medicina della nostre donne", (Citta' di Castello: Lapi,1892), p.33
372. Polia "Tematiche del pensiero religioso e magico "(Editrice Centro Italia, 2009), p.670
373. Chavez Hualpa, "Le donne nel mondo rurale della Valnerina" (Tipolitografia Federici, 2012), p.401
374. Zanetti , "La Medicina della nostre donne", (Citta' di Castello: Lapi,1892), p.155
375. Chavez Hualpa, "Le donne nel mondo rurale della Valnerina" (Tipolitografia Federici, 2012), p.400
376. Napoli, "The plants, rituals, and spells that 'cured' helminthiasis in Sicily," (Journal of Ethnobiology and Ethnomedicine, 2008) p.9
377. ibid., p.5
378. Giovetti, "I guaritori di Campagna: viaggio attraverso la medicina popolare in Italia" (Edizioni Mediterranee, 2016), p.131
379. Giagnoni "Majarzas e sanadoras: tradizioni, racconti e usanza popolari in Sardegna (Editrice Democratica Sarda ,2009), p.48
380. De Martino , "Sud e magia" (Milano, Feltrinelli, 1996) p.33
381. Polia "Tematiche del pensiero religioso e magico "(Editrice Centro Italia, 2009), p.667
382. Giovetti, "I guaritori di Campagna: viaggio attraverso la medicina popolare in Italia" (Edizioni Mediterranee, 2016), p.94
383. Napoli, "The plants, rituals, and spells that 'cured' helminthiasis in Sicily," (Journal of Ethnobiology and Ethnomedicine, 2008) p.9,10
384. Oddo "La medicina popolare nell'alta valle Argentina" (Pro Triora Editore, 1997) p. 60

385. ibid., p. 58
386. Napoli, "The plants, rituals, and spells that 'cured' helminthiasis in Sicily," (Journal of Ethnobiology and Ethnomedicine, 2008) p.7
367. Polia "Tematiche del pensiero religioso e magico" (Editrice Centro Italia, 2009), p.670
388. Ugo Dessy, "Sa Mexina: La Medicina Is ominis de mexina – I guaritori" (Alfa Editrice, 1989) p. 98
389. ibid.
390. ibid.
391. ibid,
392. ibid.
393. ibid.
394. ibid.
395. ibid.
396. ibid.
397. Chavez Hualpa, "Le donne nel mondo rurale della Valnerina" (Tipolito Federici, 2012), p.403
398. ibid.
399. Polia "Tematiche del pensiero religioso e magico "(Editrice Centro Italia, 2009), p.649-650
400. ibid.
401. ibid.
402. Napoli, "The plants, rituals, and spells that 'cured' helminthiasis in Sicily," (Journal of Ethnobiology and Ethnomedicine, 2008) p.9
403. Oddo "La medicina popolare nell'alta valle Argentina" (Pro Triora Editore, 1997), p.133
404. ibid., p.132
405. Paola Giovetti, "I guaritori di Campagna: viaggio attraverso la medicina popolare in Italia" (Edizioni Mediterranee, 2016), p.55
406. Zanetti , "La Medicina della nostre donne", (Citta' di Castello: Lapi,1892), p.177
407. Oddo "La medicina popolare nell'alta valle Argentina" (Pro Triora Editore, 1997), p.43]
408. Mario Polia "Tematiche del pensiero religioso e magico (Editrice Centro Italia, 2009), p.671
409. Zanazzo, "Tradizioni popolari Romane." (Bologna: Forni,1892), p.67)
410. Chavez Hualpa, "Le donne nel mondo rurale della Valnerina" (Tipolito Federici, 2012), p.490
411. ibid.
412. ibid, pps.489, 490
413. ibid.
414. Giagnoni "Majarzas e sanadoras: tradizioni, racconti e usanza popolari in Sardegna (Editrice Democratica Sarda ,2009), p.46, 47
415. Oddo "La medicina popolare nell'alta valle Argentina" (Pro Triora Editore, 1997) p.149
416. ibid., p. 150
417. Oddo "La medicina popolare nell'alta valle Argentina" (Pro Triora Editore, 1997) p.117
418. ibid.
419. ibid., p. 149
420. ibid.
421. Giagnoni "Majarzas e sanadoras: tradizioni, racconti e usanza popolari in Sardegna (Editrice Democratica Sarda ,2009), p.47
422. Chavez Hualpa, "Le donne nel mondo rurale della Valnerina" (Tipolitografia Federici, 2012), p.493
423. Oddo "La medicina popolare nell'alta valle Argentina" (Pro Triora Editore, 1997) p.142
424. ibid., p.141
425. ibid.
426. ibid.
427. ibid.
428. Antonella Bartolucci "Le Streghe Buone : I simboli, i gesti, la parole, Come muta la medicina tradizionale nell'era di Internet"
Compagnia editoriale Aliberti , 2016), p. 47

429. https://superstizioni.blogspot.com/2012/02/la-nascita.html
430. ibid.
431. ibid.
432. Oddo "La medicina popolare nell'alta valle Argentina" (Pro Triora Editore, 1997) p.117
433. ibid.
434. ibid.
435. Polia "Tematiche del pensiero religioso e magico (Editrice Centro Italia, 2009), p.667
436. ibid., p.668
437. Giagnoni "Majarzas e sanadoras: tradizioni, racconti e usanza popolari in Sardegna (Editrice Democratica Sarda ,2009), p.52
438. https://ilterzoorecchio.wordpress.com/2016/02/18/i-guarito
439. htto://lovehonourandrespect.org/emotional-health/louise-hay-affirmations-for-illnesses/
440. Chavez Hualpa, "Le donne nel mondo rurale della Valnerina" (Tipolito Federici, 2012), p.491
441. Giovetti, "I guaritori di Campagna: viaggio attraverso la medicina popolare in Italia" (Edizioni Mediterranee, 2016), p.72
442. Manganelli, Tomei, "Indagini farmaco-botaniche in Garfagnana" (1996, 1997, Atti della Societa' Toscana)
443. Camangi, Tomei, "Curing animals with plants: traditional usage in Tuscany Italy (1997)
444. Giovetti, "I guaritori di Campagna: viaggio attraverso la medicina popolare in Italia" (Edizioni Mediterranee, 2016)
445. ibid., p.17,18
446. Polia "Tematiche del pensiero religioso e magico (Editrice Centro Italia, 2009), p.668
447. Giovetti, "I guaritori di Campagna: viaggio attraverso la medicina popolare in Italia" (Edizioni Mediterranee, 2016), p.82, 83
448. Giagnoni "Majarzas e sanadoras: tradizioni, racconti e usanza popolari in Sardegna (Editrice Democratica Sarda ,2009), p.52,53
449. "ATTI Terzo Convegno sulla Stregoneria-Le Streghe" (Pro Triora Editore, 2000), p.164
450. ibid.
451. translated and paraphrased from "I Guaritori di Campagna" Paolo Giovetti, (Edizioni Mediterranee, 2016), p.75
452. Chavez Hualpa, "Le donne nel mondo rurale della Valnerina" (Tipolitografia Federici, 2012), p.493
453. ibid.
454. Dessy "Sa mexina: Is ominis de mexina la medicina- I guaritori." (Alfa Editrice, 1989) p.17
455. Giovetti, "I guaritori di Campagna: viaggio attraverso la medicina poplare in Italia" (Edizioni Mediterranee, 2016), p.37
456. https://ilterzoorecchio.wordpress.com/2016/02/18/i-guaritori-di-campagna/
457. Giovetti, "I guaritori di Campagna: viaggio attraverso la medicina poplare in Italia" (Edizioni Mediterranee, 2016), p.93, 94
458. Chavez Hualpa, "Le donne nel mondo rurale della Valnerina" (Tipolitografia Federici, 2012), p.497
459. Giagnoni "Majarzas e sanadoras: tradizioni, racconti e usanza popolari in Sardegna (Editrice Democratica Sarda ,2009), p.52
460. Giovetti, "I guaritori di Campagna: viaggio attraverso la medicina poplare in Italia" (Edizioni Mediterranee, 2016), p. 74
461. Giagnoni "Majarzas e sanadoras: tradizioni, racconti e usanza popolari in Sardegna (Editrice Democratica Sarda ,2009), p.53
462. ibid., p.55
463. Gianfranco Mele, https://www.lavocedimanduria.it/rubriche/18134/il-tarantismo-in-manduria-e-dintorni-parte-5
464. Dessy "Sa mexina: Is ominis de mexina la medicina- I guaritori." (Alfa Editrice, 1989), p.4

465. Gianfranco Mele, https://www.lavocedimanduria.it/rubriche/16184/il-tarantismo-in-manduria-e-dintorni-parte-2?fbclid=IwAR37UnBiNBDxAq-e8uEhOmJ3fw9vt-vWrPmIESrCp9wp6WsPqXf9e2aECG0
466. Dessy "Sa mexina: Is ominis de mexina la medicina- I guaritori." (Alfa Editrice, 1989), p. 38
467. https://www.lavocedimanduria.it/rubriche/18134/il-tarantismo-in-manduria-e-dintorni-parte-5
468. Dessy "Sa mexina: Is ominis de mexina la medicina- I guaritori." (Alfa Editrice, 1989), p.39
469. ibid., p.38
470. ibid., p.39
471. ibid., p.41
472. ibid., p.40
473. ibid.
474. ibid., p.42
475. ibid., p.43
476. ibid.
477. ibid., p.42
478 https://www.lavocedimanduria.it/rubriche/18134/il-tarantismo-in-manduria-e-dintorni-parte-5
479. Eliade, "Shamanism: Archaic Techniques of Ecstasy (Princeton/Bollingen Paperback Printing, 1974), p.331
480. Paola Giovetti, "I guaritori di Campagna: viaggio attraverso la medicina poplare in Italia" (Edizioni Mediterranee, 2016), p.77
481. ibid.
482. Chavez Hualpa, "Le donne nel mondo rurale della Valnerina" (Tipolito Federici, 2012). p.207
483. Napoli, "The plants, rituals, and spells that 'cured' helminthiasis in Sicily," (Journal of Ethnobiology and Ethnomedicine, 2008) p.10
484. testimonizanza di una Legatura Amarosa con dei nodi ad una Corda in un Autodafe' del 1603 dell'Inquisizione spagnola in Sicilia. via Benedicaria facebook
485. Polia, "Il ciclo dei mesi" (Editrice Centro Italia, 2009), p.78
486. Chavez Hualpa, "Le donne nel mondo rurale della Valnerina" (Tipolito Federici, 2012), p.486
487. http://www.rimedinonna.com/7378-rimedi-contro-il-malocchio/] malocchio collection
488. ibid.
489. Napoli, "The plants, rituals, and spells that 'cured' helminthiasis in Sicily," (Journal of Ethnobiology and Ethnomedicine, 2008) pgs.11,12
490. Zanetti, "La medicina dell nostre donne" (Citta' di Castello, S. Lapi Tiografo Editore, 1892), p. 159
491. Mario Polia "Tematiche del pensiero religioso e magico" (Editrice Centro Italia, 2009), p.563
492. Dessy "Sa mexina: Is ominis de mexina la medicina- I guaritori." (Alfa Editrice, 1989), p.16
493. https://forum.termometropolitico.it/192921-malocchio-e-jettatura.html
494. http://microbemagic.ucc.ie/about_microbes/viruses_work.html
495. https://www.ncbi.nlm.nih.gov/pmc/articles/PMC4788752/
496. De Martino, "Sud e magia " (Milano, Feltrinelli, 1959)
497. Polia "Tematiche del pensiero religioso e magico" (Editrice Centro Italia, 2009), p.580
498. ibid., p.582
499. Polia "Tematiche del pensiero religioso e magico" (Editrice Centro Italia, 2009), p.581
500. Giagnoni "Majarzas e sanadoras: tradizioni, racconti e usanza popolari in Sardegna (Editrice Democratica Sarda ,2009), p.57
501. ibid., p.57
502. Polia "Tematiche del pensiero religioso e magico (Editrice Centro Italia, 2009), p.582
503. Giovetti, "I guaritori di Campagna: viaggio attraverso la medicina poplare in Italia" (Edizioni Mediterranee, 2016),p.165-172
504. "ATTI: Terzo Convegno sulla Stregoneria Le Streghe" (Comune di Triora, 2000) p.161

505. Giovetti, "I guaritori di Campagna: viaggio attraverso la medicina poplare in Italia" (Edizioni Mediterranee, 2016),p.165-172
506. ibid.
507. Chavez Hualpa, "Le donne nel mondo rurale della Valnerina" (Tipolito Federici, 2012), p. 304
508. ibid.
509. Polia "Tematiche del pensiero religioso e magico" (Editrice Centro Italia, 2009), p.656
510. ibid., p.656
511. Polia-Chávez, "Mio padre mi disse" (Rimini: Il Cerchio, 2002) p.159
512. Polia "Tematiche del pensiero religioso e magico" (Editrice Centro Italia, 2009), p.658
513. ibid., p.658
514. Giagnoni "Majarzas e sanadoras: tradizioni, racconti e usanza popolari in Sardegna (Editrice Democratica Sarda ,2009), p.34
515. ibid.
516. Mario Polia "Tematiche del pensiero religioso e magico" (Editrice Centro Italia, 2009), pgs.395,6
517. Chavez Hualpa, "Le donne nel mondo rurale della Valnerina" (Tipolitografia Federici, 2012), p.238
518. ibid.
519. Mario Polia "Tematiche del pensiero religioso e magico" (Editrice Centro Italia, 2009), pgs.397, 8
520. Chavez Hualpa, "Le donne nel mondo rurale della Valnerina" (Tipolito Federici, 2012), p.214
521. ibid.
522. ibid., p.304
533. ibid., p.305
524. ibid., p. 481
525. ibid., p.480
526. ibid.
527. ibid. p.479
528. Crisis, "Italy's Witches and Medicine Women Vol 1" (Golden Bough Books, 2017), p.221
529. ibid.
530. https://ricerca.repubblica.it/repubblica/archivio/repubblica/2004/06/30/patruneddi-nemici-dei-bambini.html
531. ibid.
532. ibid.
533. ibid.
534. ibid.
535. Chavez Hualpa, "Le donne nel mondo rurale della Valnerina" (Tipolitografia Federici, 2012), p.47
536. Mario Polia "Tematiche del pensiero religioso e magico" (Editrice Centro Italia, 2009), p.657
537. ibid., p.661
538. ibid.
539. ibid.
540. ibid., p.553
541. ibid., p.657
542. Chavez Hualpa, "Le donne nel mondo rurale della Valnerina" (Tipolito Federici, 2012), p.307
543. ibid.
544. ibid., p.480
545. ibid., p.319
546. ibid., p.215
547. Polia, "Le piante e il sacro: Le percezione della natural nel mondo rurale della Valnerina" (Quater, 2010), p.45
548. ibid.

549. Giovetti, "I guaritori di Campagna: viaggio attraverso la medicina poplare in Italia" (Edizioni Mediterranee, 2016), p.73

550. Polia, "Le piante e il sacrro" (Quater, 2010), paraphrased and translated from p. 45

551. Polia, "Il ciclo dei mesi" (Editrice Centro Italia, 2009), p.636

552. *compiled from testimonies in "Il ciclo dei mesi" by Mario Polia, p 636 and "Le donne nel mondo rurale della Valnerina" by Fabiola Chavez Hualpa pps. 209-212

553. Dessy "Sa mexina: Is ominis de mexina la medicina- I guaritori." (Alfa Editrice, 1989) p.77

554. paraphrased and translated by Karyn Crisis from Sa mexina Ugo Dessy, ibid.

555. Dessy "Sa mexina: Is ominis de mexina la medicina- I guaritori." (Alfa Editrice, 1989), ibid.

556. Finamore, "Tradizioni popolari Abruzzesi" (Aquila: Polia, 1997), p.107

557. Antonio De Nino, "Usi abruzzesi. 2 voll. (Auila: Polia, 1988), II p. 143

558. Luigi Mannocchi, "Feste, costumanze, superstizioni popolari nel circondario di Fermo e nel Piceno" (Fermo: Tipografia Economica,1920), p.129

559. Chavez Hualpa, "Le donne nel mondo rurale della Valnerina" (Tipolito Federici, 2012), p.209

560. Polia, "Le piante e il sacro: Le percezione della natural nel mondo rurale della Valnerina" (Quater, 2010), p.203

561. Giagnoni "Majarzas e sanadoras: tradizioni, racconti e usanza popolari in Sardegna (Editrice Democratica Sarda, 2009), p.82

562. ibid., p.82

563. Eliade, "Shamanism: Archaic Techniques of Ecstasy (Princeton/Bollingen Paperback Printing, 1974), p.164

564. ibid., p.116

565. Giagnoni "Majarzas e sanadoras: tradizioni, racconti e usanza popolari in Sardegna (Editrice Democratica Sarda, 2009), p.82

566. Turchi, "Lo sciamanesimo in Sardegna: credenze, rituali, pratiche e aneddoti alla scoperta di uni isola piena di mistero." (Newton Compton Editori, 2017), p.181

567. ibid., p.182

568 sham162.

569. Albert Gruenwedel, "Die Teufel des Avesta und ihre Beziehungen zur Ikonographie des Buddhisms Zentral-Asiens" (Berlin, 1924), p.68-69

570. Turchi, "Lo sciamanesimo in Sardegna: credenze, rituali, pratiche e aneddoti alla scoperta di uni isola piena di mistero." (Newton Compton Editori, 2017), p.184

571. Turchi, "Lo sciamanesimo in Sardegna: credenze, rituali, pratiche e aneddoti alla scoperta di uni isola piena di mistero." (Newton Compton Editori, 2017), p.182

572. Eliade, "Shamanism: Archaic Techniques of Ecstasy (Princeton/Bollingen Paperback Printing, 1974), p.161.

573. ibid., p.159

574. Turchi, "Lo sciamanesimo in Sardegna: credenze, rituali, pratiche e aneddoti alla scoperta di uni isola piena di mistero." (Newton Compton Editori, 2017), p.186

575. Ginzburg, "Ecstasies: Deciphering the Witches' Sabbath" (Random House, Inc., 1991), p.94

576. ibid., p.96

577. Lisa Muraro, "La Signora del gioco: La caccia alle streghe interpretata dalle sue vittime" (La Tartaruga edizioni, 2006), p.63

578. Ginzburg, "Ecstasies: Deciphering the Witches' Sabbath" (Random House, Inc., 1991), pgs.92,93

579. ibid., p.94

580. ibid., p.93

581. http://gds.it/2015/11/27/un-po-streghe-un-po-fate-ecco-chi-sono-le-donne-di-fuora_442390/

582. http://www.milanoplatinum.com/sibilla-pierina-la-signora-del-gioco.html

583. http://giacomodoc.blogspot.com/2013/10/le-donne-di-fora-o-donne-di-casa-donne.html

584. https://tradizioneitaliana.wordpress.com/2013/07/22/le-donne-di-fuora-e-le-animulari/

585. http://giacomodoc.blogspot. com/2013/10/le-donne-di-fora-o-donne-di-casa-donne.html

586. Ginzburg, "Ecstasies: Deciphering the Witches' Sabbath" (Random House, Inc., 1991, p .132

587. ibid.
588. ibid.
589. ibid., p.131
590. ibid., pgs.130-131
591. Muraro, "La Signora del gioco: La caccia alle streghe inerpretata dalle sue vittime" (La Tartaruga edizioni, 2006), p.63
592. Turchi, "Lo sciamanesimo in Sardegna: credenze, rituali, pratiche e aneddoti alla scoperta di uni isola piena di mistero." (Newton Compton Editori, 2017), p.131
593. https://tradizioneitaliana.wordpress.com/2013/07/22/le-donne-di-fuora-e-le-animulari/
594. http://guide.supereva.it/antropologia/interventi/2009/10/le-donne-di-fuora
595. https://www.facebook.com/benedicaria/posts/1855114764527738/
596. http://gds.it/2015/11/27/un-po-streghe-un-po-fate-ecco-chi-sono-le-donne-di-fuora_442390/
597. Ginzburg, "Ecstasies: Deciphering the Witches' Sabbath" (Random House, Inc., 1991), p.90
598. ibid.
599. Ginzburg, "The Night Battles" (Johns Hopkins Paperbacks edition, 1992), p.16
600. https://www.facebook.com/benedicaria/posts/1855114764527738/
601. Ginzburg, "Ecstasies: Deciphering the Witches' Sabbath" (Random House, Inc., 1991), p. 101
602. Muraro, "La Signora del gioco: La caccia alle streghe interpretata dalle sue vittime" (La Tartaruga edizioni, 2006) p.203
603. ibid., p.205
604. ibid. p.204
605. Ginzburg, "Ecstasies: Deciphering the Witches' Sabbath" (Random House, Inc., 1991), p.89.
606. ibid. p.93
607. Ginzburg, "Ecstasies: Deciphering the Witches' Sabbath" (Random House, Inc., 1991), p.130
608. Lisa Muraro, "La Signora del gioco: La caccia alle streghe inerpretata dalle sue vittime" (La Tartaruga edizioni, 2006), p.201
609. ibid., p.201
610. http://giacomodoc.blogspot.com/2013/10/le-donne-di-fora-o-donne-di-casa-donne.html
611. Ginzburg, "Ecstasies: Deciphering the Witches' Sabbath" (Random House, Inc., 1991), p.101
612. Muraro, "La Signora del gioco: La caccia alle streghe inerpretata dalle sue vittime" (La Tartaruga edizioni, 2006), p.203
613. ibid., p.204
614. http://giacomodoc.blogspot.com/2013/10/le-donne-di-fora-o-donne-di-casa-donne.html
615. Muraro, "La Signora del gioco: La caccia alle streghe inerpretata dalle sue vittime" (La Tartaruga edizioni, 2006), .p201
616. Ginzburg, "Ecstasies: Deciphering the Witches' Sabbath" (Random House, Inc., 1991), p93
617. https://tradizioneitaliana.wordpress.com/2013/07/22/le-donne-di-fuora-e-le-animulari/
618. ibid.
619. Lisa Muraro, "La Signora del gioco: La caccia alle streghe inerpretata dalle sue vittime" (La Tartaruga edizioni, 2006), p.203
620. Chavez Hualpa, "Le donne nel mondo rurale della Valnerina" (Tipolito Federici, 2012), p.354
621. ibid., p.385
622. ibid.
623. ibid.
624. ibid., p.523
625. ibid., p.525
626. Polia, "Le Piante e il Sacro" (Quater, 2010), p.16
627. ibid., p.22
628. Polia "Tematiche del pensiero religioso e magico" (Editrice Centro Italia, 2009), p.645
629. Finamore, "Tesori nascosti e stregherie nelle credenze popolari abruzzesi" (Aquila: A Polla, 1992), p.109
630. Polia, "Il ciclo dei mesi", (Editrice Centro Italia, 2004), p. 271

631. Crocioni, "La gente marchigiana nelle sue tradizioni" (Milano: Corticelli, 1951), p.130
632. ibid., p.131
633. Polia "Tematiche del pensiero religioso e magico (Editrice Centro Italia, 2009), p.647
634. ibid., p.647
635. ibid.
636. ibid., p.647
637. ibid., p.570
638. ibid.
639. G. Finamore, "Tradizioni popolari Abruzzesi" (Aquila: Polia, 1997), p. 98).
640. Polia "Tematiche del pensiero religioso e magico" (Editrice Centro Italia, 2009), p.570
641. ibid. p.566
642. ibid.
643. Dessy "Sa mexina: Is ominis de mexina la medicina- I guaritori." (Alfa Editrice, 1989) p.15
644. ibid. p.18
645. ibid.
646. Polia "Tematiche del pensiero religioso e magico" (Editrice Centro Italia, 2009), p.542
647. Chavez Hualpa, "Le donne nel mondo rurale della Valnerina" (Tipolitografia Federici, 2012), p.388
648. Coluzzi, Crescenzi, "La Nascita, Usi e riti in Campania e nel Salento" (Fridericiana Editrice Universitaria 2010), p.43
649. Chavez Hualpa, "Le donne nel mondo rurale della Valnerina" (Tipolitografia Federici, 2012), p.243
650. ibid., p.369
651. Polia "Tematiche del pensiero religioso e magico" (Editrice Centro Italia, 2009), p.566
652. Chavez Hualpa, "Le donne nel mondo rurale della Valnerina" (Tipolitografia Federici, 2012), p.388
653. ibid.
654. Coluzzi, Crescenzi, "La Nascita, Usi e riti in Campania e nel Salento" (Fridericiana Editrice Universitaria 2010), p.22
655. Mario Polia "Tematiche del pensiero religioso e magico" (Editrice Centro Italia, 2009), p.455
656. ibid.
657. ibid.
658. Giovanni Ginobili , "Folklore marchigiano" (Macerata: Tipo- Linotypia Maceratese,1963), p.103
659. Gimbutas, "The Language of the Goddess" (Harper & Row, 1989), p.200
660. Crisis, "Italy's Witches and Medicine Women Vol. 1" (Golden Bough Books, 2017), p..228
661. Eliade, "Shamanism: Archaic Techniques of Ecstasy (Princeton/Bollingen Paperback Printing, 1974), p.119
662. ibid., p.125
663. ibid., p.127
664. ibid., p.129
665. ibid., p.117, 118
666. Eliade, "Shamanism: Archaic Techniques of Ecstasy (Princeton/Bollingen Paperback Printing, 1974), p. 118
667. Oreste Grifoni, "Saggio di poesie e canti popolari religiosi di alcuni paesi umbri", (Bologna: Forni, 1191), p.42
668. Eliade, "Shamanism: Archaic Techniques of Ecstasy (Princeton/Bollingen Paperback Printing, 1974), p.259
669. ibid., p.119
670. ibid., p.137
671. Carlo Napolitano "Il Triangolo stregato: il mistero del noce di Benevento" (CSA Editrice, 2012), p.21

672. Fabio Garuti "Le Streghe di Benevento La Grande Bugia" (Anguana Edizioni, 2014), opening page
673. Silvio Falato, "Ce steva 'na vota ....Janare-lupi mannari- filastrocche-indovinelli" , p.38
674. Polia "Tematiche del pensiero religioso e magico" (Editrice Centro Italia, 2009), p.629
675. Chavez Hualpa, "Le donne nel mondo rurale della Valnerina" (Tipolito Federici, 2012), p.534
676. ibid.
677. www.villasinsicily.net/it/
678. Coluzzi, Crescenzi, "La Nascita, Usi e riti in Campania e nel Salento" (Fridericiana Editrice Universitaria 2010), p.35
679. unknown source
680. Polia, "Il ciclo dei mesi", (Editrice Centro Italia, 2004), p. 235-238
681. https://www.flipkey.com/blog/2011/08/16/the-valnerina-the-hidden-gem-of-umbria/
682. Polia, "Le piante e il sacro: Le percezione della natural nel mondo rurale della Valnerina" (Quater, 2010), p.185
683. Karyn Crisis's interview with Mauro Spadoni of Liquore di Genziana, 2016
684. Coluzzi, Crescenzi, "La Nascita, Usi e riti in Campania e nel Salento" (Fridericiana Editrice Universitaria 2010), p.61
685. Chavez Hualpa, "Le donne nel mondo rurale della Valnerina" (Tipolitografia Federici, 2012), p.483
686. ibid.
687. ibid.
688. Napoli, "The plants, rituals, and spells that 'cured' helminthiasis in Sicily," (Journal of Ethnobiology and Ethnomedicine, 2008) p.8
689. Polia, "Cosi pregavano i nostri padri: Preghiere popolari della Valnerina" (Editrice Centro Italia, 2009), p.845
690. ibid.
691. Benedicaria facebook via Fuochi nella nebbia facebook
692. Polia, "Le piante e il sacro: Le percezione della natural nel mondo rurale della Valnerina" (Quater, 2010), p. 107
693. ibid., p.108
694. https://lagrandemadre.wordpress.com
695. https://en.wikipedia.org/wiki/Flora_of_Italy
697. Polia, "Le piante e il sacro: Le percezione della natural nel mondo rurale della Valnerina" (Quater, 2010), p.17
698. ibid.,p.39
699. ibid.
700. ibid.,p.47
701. Polia, "Le piante e il sacro: Le percezione della natural nel mondo rurale della Valnerina" (Quater, 2010), p.57
702. Napoli, "The plants, rituals, and spells that 'cured' helminthiasis in Sicily," (Journal of Ethnobiology and Ethnomedicine, 2008) p.14
703. Polia, "Le piante e il sacro: Le percezione della natural nel mondo rurale della Valnerina" (Quater, 2010), p.191
704. Napoli, "The plants, rituals, and spells that 'cured' helminthiasis in Sicily," (Journal of Ethnobiology and Ethnomedicine, 2008) p.14
705. extracted from:Napoli, "The plants, rituals, and spells that 'cured' helminthiasis in Sicily," (Journal of Ethnobiology and Ethnomedicine, 2008)
706. Gianfranco Mele, Maurizion Nocera "La magia nel salento" (Spagine, 2018), p. 101
707. Gianluca Toro, "Sotto tutte le brume sopra tutti i rovi: stregoneria e farmacologia degli unguenti", (Nautilus, 2005) p.59
708. ibid., p.63
709. ibid., p.65

710. ibid., p.66
711. ibid., p.49
712. ibid., p.54
713. ibid., p.57
714. ibid., p.58
715. http://www.softrevolutionzine.org/2014/erba-del-diavolo-la-verita-sulle-stupefacenti-piante-delle-streghe/
716. Gianluca Toro, "Sotto tutte le brume sopra tutti i rovi: stregoneria e farmacologia degli unguenti", (Nautilus, 2005) p.134
717. ibid., p.90
718. Dessy "Sa mexina: Is ominis de mexina la medicina- I guaritori." (Alfa Editrice, 1989), p.18

CPSIA information can be obtained
at www.ICGtesting.com
Printed in the USA
FSHW021509131120
75761FS